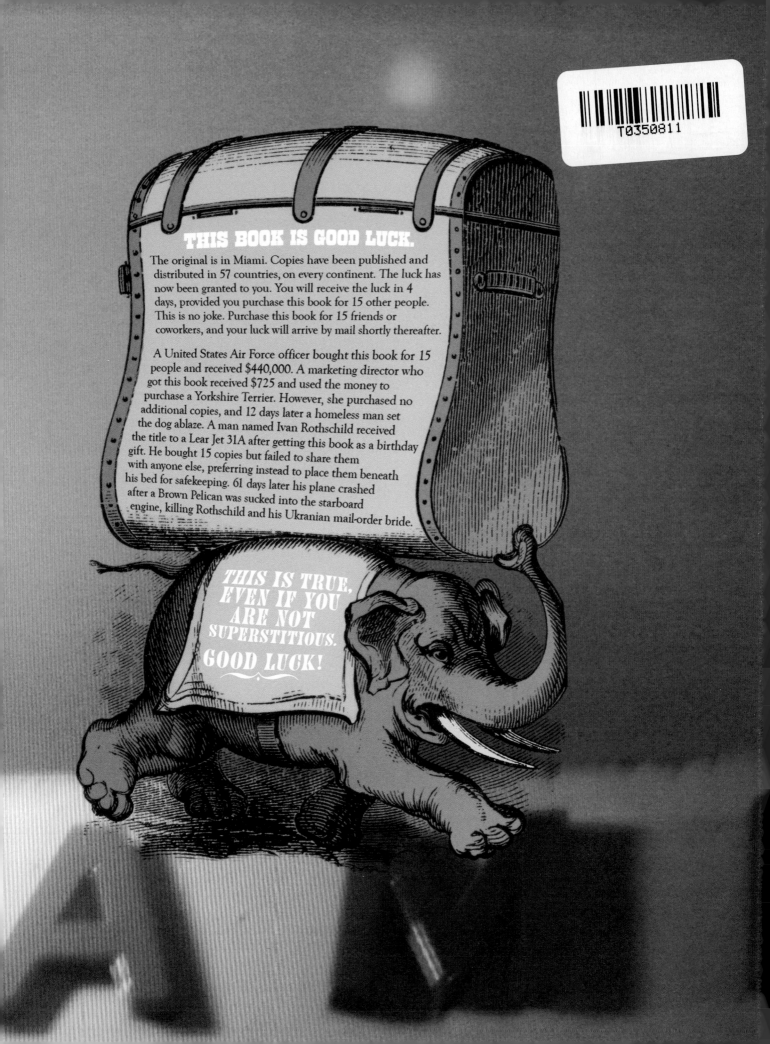

THIS BOOK IS GOOD LUCK.

The original is in Miami. Copies have been published and distributed in 57 countries, on every continent. The luck has now been granted to you. You will receive the luck in 4 days, provided you purchase this book for 15 other people. This is no joke. Purchase this book for 15 friends or coworkers, and your luck will arrive by mail shortly thereafter.

A United States Air Force officer bought this book for 15 people and received $440,000. A marketing director who got this book received $725 and used the money to purchase a Yorkshire Terrier. However, she purchased no additional copies, and 12 days later a homeless man set the dog ablaze. A man named Ivan Rothschild received the title to a Lear Jet 31A after getting this book as a birthday gift. He bought 15 copies but failed to share them with anyone else, preferring instead to place them beneath his bed for safekeeping. 61 days later his plane crashed after a Brown Pelican was sucked into the starboard engine, killing Rothschild and his Ukranian mail-order bride.

THIS IS TRUE, EVEN IF YOU ARE NOT SUPERSTITIOUS.

GOOD LUCK!

T0350811

PEOPLE

Sam Crispin Rosario Sotolongo Teresa Blanco Bill Adams Peter Barton Judy Bowen Edward Kanner Lou Massiavechio Geoff McGuire Bernie Schlossman Sharon Dowling Arnie Bloom Carlos Dominguez AJ Ackerman Connie Westfall Charles Crispin Alina Betancourt Delia Abascal Jodi Christianson Carlos Jiminez Tom Dwayne Mary Abreau Don Hicks Susan Kelley Rhonda Brodes-Siegel Teresa Bromagen Vincent Mennella Sarah Berry Laurel McIver Julie Ross Alan Torreano Cathy Williamson Eve Foster Karen Strolis-Lewe Chuck Porter Lilian Hernandez Phylicee Lubowsky Wai Tu Peter Pluymer Wesley Chaney Georgette Romeu Mary Douglas Patricia Sordo Gloria Schmall Cindy Goldsmith Susan Aussillou Sara Gennett Alex Bogusky Madeline Vallines Hope Bader Ida Thompson Jocarol Bines Marcia Jacobs Denise Thompson Isolina Penalver James Bryson Hilary Meyerson Sherwin Mena Donna Wadsworth Guillermo Zalamea John Penney Jay Swindell Lori Weiss Lourdes Delamata Nicole Zittman Daniel Weinbach Jill Devine Robert Geffert Nasreen Ahmad Alexis Paidas John Stofka Katherine Hernandez Aileen Lopez Carlos Perez Justine Bock David Swartz Barbara Spalten David Cappetta Peta Goldsmith Michael Bettendorf Ana Hernandez Beth Kaufman Nina Pandey Michelle Salom Hilary Lifter Amy Tomlinson Monica Moatz Ruth Ameil George Douglas April Patterson Michael Gentry Elizabeth Jackson Ed Leshansky Stephany Lobban John Nicholas Jeffrey Uncapher Darlene Haegele William Donnelly Steven Horowitz Alison Plummer Julie Courtright Brigett Bergmann Kristen Marcy Shelton Scott Amy Siegel Ana Maidique (Bogusky) Jeff Goldman James Dean Adam Stoik Markham Cronin Shawn Wood Juan Cardenal Penelope Petrosky Lisette Cendan Diane Durban Margaret Megee Sandy Gonzalez Virginia Carrillo Carol Viau Ricardo Rohaidy Martha Schwartz Yolanda Velarde Michael Tilis Kim Genkinger Scott Sussman Molly Reed Mary Trick Jim Houck Amie Miller Laura Kaplan-Lirman Sandra Pineres Dave Brokaw Bob Van Horn Laura Dacy Robin Polansky Jeff Steinhour Michelle Shankle Michelle Seiler Kristin Porter Pieter Blikslager Noah Bate Yolanda Leon Sharon Harms Paula Keiner Katherine Patterson Jenniffer Berkowitz Sebastian Gray Scott Linnen Grant Provost Wesley Morgan Richard Bloom Annie Porter Tony Calcao Patrick Harris David Wachs Jack Nitowitz Marc Ruggiero Amy Zambrano Stephen Mapp Patricia Morrell-Ruiz Amanda McConnell Meg Gerrish Martha Fernandez Corey Weiner Christine Sullivan John Castro Manuel Perez Cathy Dickinson Angela Attento John Trinanes Sally Field Doug Kellner John Herman Bill Wright Amy Correll-Crosby Tricia Chang Erin Armstrong Charlotte Althin Gail Barker Mark Hayden Christopher Colbert Barbara Suarez Jennifer Davidson Becky Sloneker Dawn Astley Susanne Saglio Raif Fluker Katie Kempner Tania Mecias Chris Schifando Alvaro Callejas Ellen Friedman Chris Breen Lisa James Alexandra Peralta Lisa Gordon Jennifer Weisberg Terry Stavoe Laura Bowles Barbara Karalis Tim Roper Erin Schumacher Susana Nudelman-Perczek T Grand Jenny Nolan Jeff Hicks Shelly Neill Amy Yatkeman Holly Allen Raphael Vera Jason Hall Tom Adams Michelle Bracken Lorenzo Lamadrid Rachel Parker Melissa DeLisle Nathan Swenberg Heidi Muelhaupt David Etz Stefani Zellmer Rich Rivera Rupert Samuel Andrea Hughes Andrew Speyer Paul Keister Jean-Paul Picard Linos Ermogenides Ruth Gonzalez Richard Mayora Marina Monsante Alex "Burnie" Burnard Francisco Cornelio Reed Carlson Scott MacMaster Renato Floresca Elizabeth Dowling Carlos Gutierrez Kelly Josephs Carolyn Washington Steve Barry Louisa Misrahi Janet Onate Susan Deverell Haley Patton Janet Cabrera Nichola Stewart Jennifer Urich Jay Kline Tom Bevan Steve Hulnick Andrew Keller Kala Horvitz Haydee Justo Danica Vorkapich Jason Friedman Tanja Cannon Claudia Contreras Lisa Lamb Ari Merkin Shawn Cloninger Risa Kahane Mike Howard Erica Mack Neil Riddell David Taylor Kim Eisnor Eduardo Garnica Janette Gonzalez Randi Wardlow Mark Rukman Natalia Martinez Silvana Widuczynski Stephanie Genovese Michelle Aristondo Andrea Catsicas Parde Bridgett Steve O'Connell Caryn Botknecht Rob Strasberg Mariella Avenarius Ryan O'Rourke Lisa Armand Jessica Stubbs Tameka Rolle Lynn Bianchi Mike Del Marmol Jose Barreiros Jeff Stevens Carter Nance David Rolfe Bryan Stone Bethany Diddle Patricia Ferrucho Aymara Beltramo Maribel San Juan Elizabeth Ayoub Eric Lear Michelle Maldonado Steve Sapka Jennifer Gallagher Kristen Phass Daniel Greenhouse Jennifer Albo Laura Glaser Joshua Miller Michelle Fernandez Jeff Costantino Claudia Machado Angela Ruben Tom Zukoski Josephine Blanco Colin Drummond Mary Duncan Steve Erich Karen Hodges Monica Pino Oscar Rivas Jen Erickson Karina Schmid Vanessa Hertz Kevin Koller John Reed Danielle Whalen Jason Grosz Sarah Pallett Katie Porter Carah Von Funk David Lawlor Chris Culpepper Ryan Haskins Marci Miller Jonathon Carlaw Jackie Hathiramani Adam Heathcott Swap Patel David Povill Erika Chassner Cindy Perez Chris Renz Stephen Williams Corey Bartha Haley Brothers Tricia Ting Mark Lewis Rob Rolfe Meghan Schlicher Rob Tripas Seema Patel Sue Ryan Elaine Phuong Isabelinda Miguel Jessica Dierauer Nick Munoz Ana Perez Julie Erich Helen Almeida Patricia Bentin Rebekah Mateu Josie Zimmermann Rebecca Williams Chauncey Zalkin Elizabeth Childs Nikki Girion Donna Carroll Annie Malenfant Karina Decoteau Olivia Heeren Ben James Michael Lee Nancy Lee Krystle Loyland Erin Swenson Sheri Flynn Liz Harper James Dawson-Hollis Natalie Fuentes Kimberly Goldsworth Katie Wilbur Ana Martinez Priscilla Arthur Caroline Johnston Kacine Kromrey Wojtek Szumowski Joe Miranda Sara Padgett Michael Ferrare Paul Sutton Norberto Acevedo Del Bracht Emily Greenberg Sheri Radel Ryan Kutscher Linda Desilets Steffon Ceruti Rahul Panchal Robyn Peal Jennifer Colina Bryant King Shawna Lopez Bertha Deshon Vivian Zaldivar Beth Pennekamp Michelle Gaitan David Niblick Juan Tapia Jessica Reznick Dan Sutton Jeffrey Hecht Stefanie Segar Matthew Bonin Andrea Quagliato Alejandra Guerrero Amy Bonin Natalie Gora Scott Brown Mandy Dempsey Vivian Cepero Carly Tietzer Melissa Goodis Maria Salazar John Castillo Miguel Leon Carmen Hirst Tammy Hockenstein Keith Scott Cullen Rainey Denisse Exposito Courtney Lord Jolly Banerjee Lindsey Allison Darren Himebrook Malsert Chapman Kevin Lavan Maureen Bongiovanni Neil D'Amico Margarita Quijano Janelle Guzman Vanessa Clavijo Andrew Crocco Emily Einheit Jason Leiva Mauricio Duarte Alvaro Ilizarbe Gary Gonya Todd Widell Stacy Kimball DJ Neff Ron Vazquez Wayne Bishop Elaine Hernandez Rebecca O'Neil Unai Ortega Anisia Rodriguez del Rey Sofia Guerrero Surf Melendez David Norris Joanna Lee Amy Levine Barbara Tejada Sylvia Shegota Marcelino Alvarez Jamie Edyvean Vickie Segar Kaitlyn Swedlow Roland Cayubit Crystal Downs Chean Wei Law William Mahoney Paul Ramirez Lilijean Adia Carl Corbitt Ryan Eckert Lauren Wolk Adam Paul Hazell Serrano Angelita Soriano Carlos Lange Thomas Martin Harrison Winter Jessica Beavers Donnell Johnson Dawn Yemma Antonio Shelton Juan Nunez Martin Galvez Geannella Gnocchi Allison Ritter Ailed Feijoo Guy Rooke Michael Gersten Megan Mensinga Shasta Crawford Aileen Echenique Anja Duering Joy Gloede Catherine Nikolic Gillian Perazzo Milagros Herrera Michelle Caston John Paul Travaillot Vivienne Wan Radha Agrawal Julie Carney Carl St. Philip Joakim Wijkstrom Sue Baile Annalisa Cariveau Winsy Dumwody Susanna Gates-Rose Keith Rose Margaret Chow Esteban Chinchilla Brian Rekasis Yajaira Fierro Courtney Medley Darryl Tait Yutaka Tsujino Brenda Aguilar Meghan DeBruler John Feijoo Luis Santi Hannah Kim Zach Whalen Asa Reed Sam Weekley Jennifer Bowser Allison Choban Jason Gagnon Johanna Prats Courtney Sadler David Clemans Jessica Bertematti Tammie DeGrasse-Cabrera Katherine Graham-Smith Scott Wild Conor McCann Melissa Melendez Rob Thompson Amanda Schultz Katrina Hofmann Jose Incer Brett Connor Nicolette Guidotti Chris Kyriakos Conrad Lisco Sonja Ebanks Jessica Christie Maria Salinas Amy Largaespada Doug Pedersen Daniel Shapiro Nicole Martinez Leslie Repetto Christina Carter Sebastian Eldridge Chris Leiva Sumer Ravey Daniel Buckley Irene Corke Da Young Ewart Paula Lewis-Warner James Martis Rick Valdez Winston Binch Debbie Casey Diane Garab Julia Giordano Mel Kreilein Anna Matuszewska Richard Coughlin Shaheen Salimi Richard Hamm Peter Grumbine Natalie Anzardo Nancy Espinal Sarah Holbrook Jessica Jones Vivienne Pestana Maribel Prieto Thomas Rodgers Anna Sarabia Zarina Zamora Rockland Bazemore John Broe Scott Frindel Jill Garrison Renee Lavecchia Katie Nance Elizabeth Nixon Jenna Sandoval Indira Zamor Joseph Rossman Amira Samara Bethany Abel Christian Isaias Matt Walsh Bret Faszholz Christopher Moore Michelle Thompson Sylvanna Perez Francisco Amoros Paula Guerrero Jennifer Higgs Anh Truong Gary McElhatton Amanda Rackley Julie Jalbert Miranda Parker Matt Payson Tania Ventolini Lais Matos Scott Prindle Ana Beatriz Salles Lori Epstein Yvette Guzman Cassandra Hamilton Meaghan Hinke Martin Soendergaard Wendy Gomez Keith Jackson Scott Reese Martin Steinberg Matthew Anderson Emily Moore Jenny Rivera Chuka Schneider Jozette Torres Albert Nance Spencer Holmes Jacqueline Brito Laura Hauseman (We know we're missing a lot of people who worked for Crispin in the early days and we'd just like to say either "we apologize" or "congratulations," depending on your point of view.)

Originally published in the USA by powerHouse Books, 37 Main Street, Brooklyn NY 11201, tel 212 604 9074, fax 212 366 5247, email hoopla@powerHouseBooks.com, www.powerHouseBooks.com.

Published in Europe, Asia, and Australia by BIS Publishers, Herengracht 370-372, 1016 CH Amsterdam, P.O. Box 323, 1000 AH Amsterdam, The Netherlands, telephone +31 (0)20 5247560, fax +31 (0)20 5247557 bis@bispublishers.nl, www.bispublishers.nl.

ISBN 90-6369-152-1

Separations, printing, and binding by Pimlico Book International, Hong Kong. Book design by Crispin Porter + Bogusky with GH avisualagency ™ Printed in China.

HOOPLA

CRISPIN PORTER + BOGUSKY

PEOPLE WHO CAN FIRE PEOPLE
Chuck Porter
Alex Bogusky
Jeff Hicks
Jeff Steinhour

FREELANCE WRITER WHO CAN'T REALLY BE FIRED
Warren Berger

CREATIVES WHO COULD HAVE BEEN FIRED BUT WEREN'T
Alex Burnard
Dave Schiff

PEOPLE WHO THE PEOPLE WHO CAN FIRE PEOPLE WISH TO THANK
Everybody

PEOPLE WHO ASPIRE TO BE PEOPLE WHO CAN BE FIRED
jobs@cpbgroup.com
internships@cpbgroup.com

TROPICAL OFFICE
3390 Mary Street Suite 300
Miami, FL 33133

ALPINE OFFICE
6450 Gunpark Drive
Boulder, Colorado 80301

SHADOWY HOLDING COMPANY
MDC Partners Inc.
45 Hazelton Avenue
Toronto, ON M5R 2E3

SENDING US STUFF
CP+B does not accept unsolicited
ideas of any kind and assumes no
responsibility for their return.

MADE IN DADE

BISPUBLISHERS

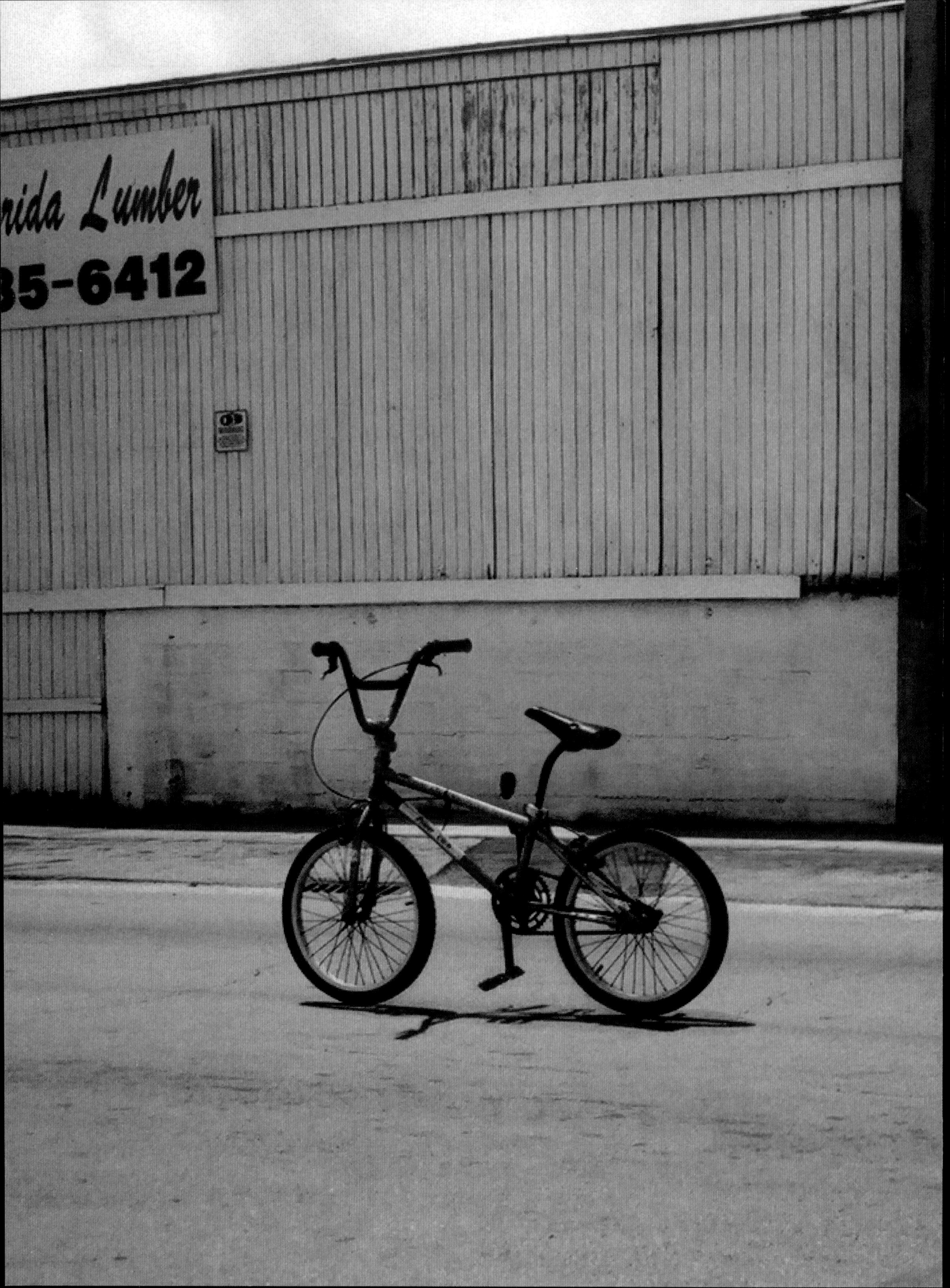
rida Lumber
35-6412

THERE IS NO ASSEMBLY LINE

This book contains Hoopla.

Whenever you open it, hoopla rays shoot out in all directions.
Don't even try to see them, because you can't. They're invisible.
Luckily, the stuff they emanate from is clearly visible.
~~Have a look.~~

CONTENTS

AUTHOR'S NOTE

About fifteen years ago, the magazine *Advertising Age* asked me to write one of those regional roundup stories that trade magazines often do (with headlines like "The Detroit market is revving up" or "What's brewing in Seattle these days," etc.). In this case, my assignment dealt with "advertising in Miami." But there didn't seem to be anything to report. There were no well-known ad agencies in Miami at the time. Companies simply didn't go there to get their ads made. Still, the magazine wanted me to come up with something, maybe because they already had a headline in mind ("The Miami market is heating up!"). I made a few phone calls, including one to a guy who ran a local advertising-awards show down there. He said, almost reluctantly, "Well, there is this one little agency named Crispin & Porter..."

Apparently, over the past couple of years, this little agency had been pissing people off by winning all the Miami ad trophies. And on top of that, they were kind of rowdy. All of which sounded promising to me.

I think I got the company's number from information, then called and spoke to a guy named Chuck Porter, who ran the agency and wrote the ad copy. Not long into the conversation, he admitted that he had come to Miami really because he liked to windsurf. And I learned that he had an art director working with him, Alex Bogusky, who had a passion for racing dirt bikes. I heard this and thought, "Interesting: So this is what passes for ad people in Miami." We had a nice chat, and I asked them to mail in samples of the agency's work. I figured that would be the end of it.

Then the package arrived in the mail, and I saw their ads. They were mostly for local banks, restaurants, clothing stores, and such. I think there might have been one for pineapples. But the thing is, all of them either made me laugh or made me think. Which is what ads are supposed to do but usually don't. As someone who specialized in writing about advertising, I was used to seeing the best of what Madison Avenue could produce. And damn if this stuff that arrived in the mail from Miami wasn't... a lot better. Seeing how good the work was, I was quite pleased with myself–I felt the way you feel when you stumble upon some little hole-in-the-wall eatery and discover that it makes the best food in town.

The little story I wrote for *Ad Age* was noticed by another magazine, *Communication Arts*, which actually flew me down to meet these guys. My main memory of the meeting is that Porter had some kind of gag item, a little mechanized stuffed animal that popped out of a paper bag, and he was endlessly amused by it. Bogusky, meanwhile, had the manner of a young surfer dude with not a care in the world. They worked in a cramped, frenetic place where everyone seemed to be having a hell of a lot of fun. But I figured that–their obvious talent notwithstanding–they were probably destined to remain a local treasure.

Over the next decade or so, I kept writing about Crispin Porter+Bogusky because they kept doing ads worth writing about. When I wrote a book called *Advertising Today*, the agency's work figured prominently as I tried to amass the best ads of modern times. But still, up until just a few years ago, I assumed the agency's prospects were limited–by their location foremost, but also by their freewheeling attitude and their unwillingness to adapt to the established Madison Avenue model for big-time success in advertising.

What I never anticipated was that Madison Avenue would someday be trying to adapt to the CP+B model–which is what's happening today. Because it turned out that CP+B wasn't just making better ads down there in Miami. They were on the road to making something new and different, something that seems to transcend advertising. And they were doing it largely off the radar. The lessons to be learned from this–about the surprising effects of isolation, mutation, reinvention, and other dynamic forces–are contained in this book. But the personal lesson for me is that there are great stories and wondrous experiments going on in places where one might not expect it. As it turned out, things really were "heating up in Miami." Who knew?

TO US, FROM US

You can tell a lot about a company by its internal e-mails. That's why a company thinks twice before firing its head IT guy. Anyway, have a peek over the firewall. Feast your eyes on a few e-mails you were never supposed to see.

Subject: the email Miranda
Date: Monday, April 26, 2004 8:49 PM
From: Charles Porter <chuckporter@cpbgroup.com>
To: All Agency <allagency@cpbmiami.com>

Periodically I have to write this and probably you should read it.

Please keep in mind that emails are not totally private. They can get copied, forwarded, and read by people you never intended to have read them.

Even after you delete them, they still exist on servers all over the place. So - whenever you're sending an email on behalf of the agency - please don't write anything that you don't want to be seen by a client or the New York Times or the U.S. Department of Justice.

Thanks
Chuck

Subject: scripts
Date: Wednesday, March 20, 2002 2:00 PM
From: Dave Schiff <daveschiff@oasisadvertising.com>
To: Bill Wright <billwright@cpbmiami.com>

My girlfriend just read me your feedback over the phone. I pack tonight and drive tomorrow AM, but I will find time to tweak the scripts per your instructions. I can't touch them until tonight, and then it'll be between box-loading sessions. I'll send revisions tomorrow AM. If they find me bound with packing tape and scissors sticking out of my neck, the bitch killed me.

Subject: Re: Good Day
Date: Tuesday, April 20, 2004 9:58 AM
From: Evan Fry <evanfry@cpbgroup.com>
To: Ben James <benjames@cpbgroup.com>

Good morning to you, Sir.

On 4/19/04 7:48 PM, "Ben James" <benjames@cpbgroup.com> wrote:

Good day to you sir.
What has been happening on the East Coast?

> Subject: Re: Good Day
> Date: Tuesday, April 20, 2004 9:58 AM
> From: Evan Fry <evanfry@cpbgroup.com>
> To: Ben James <benjames@cpbgroup.com>
>
> OODLES AND SCADS. Thanks for writing. BK is a monsteroid
> and I'm running the entire creative department. I have some new

> bitches. And some new hos as well. Bitches and hos. That's how
> I roll now.
>
> We also have a MotoCross track inside the agency now.
> And clowns come daily to bolster our moods with balloon
> animals and zany antics.
> Honey Bunny is now a total grump.
> Sam Crispin is back running the show.
> Rob Reilly still hasn't shaved his head.
> I bought a gun.
>
> Three of these things are true. Guess which three.
>
> Now what's up out on the left/best coast?

Subject: <no subject9>
Date: Thursday, November 02, 2000, 10:09 AM
From: Charles Porter <chuckporter@cpbmiami.com>
To: All Agency <allagency@cpbmiami.com>

If someone was sitting in a stall in the men's room on nine, and then if someone turned off the lights and shot a fire extinguisher under the door of the stall, that would be funny but it could be dangerous also.

Subject: wow
Date: Tuesday, March 04, 2003 8:15 AM
From: Paul Stechschulte <paulstechschulte@cpbgroup.com>
To: Tom Adams <tomadams@cpbgroup.com>

Last nights chat was great. We should tell people.

> Subject: Re: wow
> Date: Tuesday, March 04, 2003 8:22 AM
> From: Tom Adams <tomadams@cpbgroup.com>
> To: Paul Stechschulte <paulstechschulte@cpbgroup.com>
>
> So fuck me if that thing didn't work, where you IM each other
> instead of talking. Last night we tried it and the ideas flowed. It
> was fucked because me and Steck were just sitting there, right in
> view of each other, but not a word was said. You just heard the
> sound of both of us banging away on our keyboards.
>
> We were 10-feet away from each other in real life, but in our minds
> we were fucking INTERTWINED, like those snakes on a doctor
> sign.
>
>> Subject: Fw: Re: wow
>> Date: Tuesday, March 4, 2003 11:55 AM
>> From: Dave Schiff <daveschiff@cpbgroup.com>
>> To: All Agency <allagency@cpbmiami.com>

>>> Subject: i owe tom and steck an apology
>>> Date: Tuesday, March 4, 2003 12:52 PM
>>> From: Dave Schiff <daveschiff@yahoo.com>
>>> To: All Agency <allagency@cpbmiami.com>
>>>
>>> To everyone at Crispin, Porter + Bogusky,
>>>
>>> The email that earlier depicted Tom and Steck instant
>>> messaging each other was false. At no time were they
>>> intertwined like snakes or any other reptile.
>>>
>>> I was the person who fabricated the email and
>>> forwarded it to everyone. I don't know why I did it.
>>> Maybe it's because my mother didn't hold me enough as
>>> a child. Or maybe it's because I'm not getting enough
>>> out of my weightlifting regiment and I have to express
>>> myself in other ways.
>>>
>>> The reasons I did it are irrelevant to you all because
>>> that's something I have to deal with internally.
>>> What's more important is that Tom and Steck can
>>> forgive me and that we can all grow from this and
>>> still be friends.
>>>
>>> Sincerely,
>>> David Schiff

Subject: Agent Nance
Date: Wednesday, July 13, 2004 1:10 PM
From: Jimmy Carter
To: Carter Nance <carternance@cpbgroup.com>

A CONFIDENTIAL MESSAGE FROM THE WHITE HOUSE

Mr. Nance,
I will be attending your agency's party on the 23rd. Would you have any
interest in joining my Secret Service team? The Bureau tells me you would
be an excellent candidate. We would expect appropriate attire, including a
suit and dark glasses.

Jimmy Carter
Commander in Chief

END OF CORRESPONDENCE

Subject: MINI OR BUST
Date: Tuesday, February 6, 2001 12:45 AM
From: Alex Bogusky <alexbogusky@cpbmiami.com>
To: All Agency <allagency@cpbmiami.com>

we are on our way to the mini pitch and i just wanted to say how fun this
pitch has been. everybody has worked so well together and although the
hours were long and the stress high i never felt like we were anything other
than a team. pitches are when an agency gets to work together in maybe
it's purest fashion. and our ideas on this one are abundant and inspired. i
can honestly say that this is the best presentation we have ever put together. this week we were the best agency in the country doing the best work
we have ever done. that means we got some good shit. we're going up
there to bring this one back to miami. home of the best damn agency in
america. let's motor.
alex

> Subject: MINI
> Date: Thursday, February 8, 2001 5:12 PM
> From: Jeff Hicks <jeffhicks@cpbmiami.com>
> To: All Agency <allagency@cpbmiami.com>

> Still no word from MINI, but I wanted to again say thanks to all of
> CP+B. With or without their confirmation, you need to know that
> yesterday's presentation was out of control. As a group of 102 we
> have never looked better. Everything came together. Another cool
> part of the MINI review is the fact that we again broke new ground.
> CP+B presented a plan to develop and distribute branded creative
> that has the potential to make MINI famous. Famous in a way that
> few brands have ever enjoyed. More than ever before, the ideas
> covered the spectrum and looked very little like what most folks call
> advertising. This is the future and few, if any, companies (much
> less agencies) are approaching marketing in this way. Marketers
> didn't invent the :30 ad or the spread position in a magazine. These
> are conventions that have been jammed down our throats and they
> are not always the best alternative. Thinking about CP+B as a place
> that makes brands famous will be a great calling card for the future
> and needs to infest everything we do. That's it. Enough rambling. If
> anyone needs me I'm here in the hotel sitting by the phone with all
> my fingers crossed.

>> Subject: FW: Mini
>> Date: Thursday, February 15, 2001 10:44 AM
>> From: Alex Bogusky <alexbogusky@cpbmiami.com>
>> To: Creative Department <creativedepartment@cpbmiami.com>
>>
>> how about this shit. sorry about the jeans thing. who knew?
>>
>>> Subject: Mini
>>> Date: Wednesday, February 14, 2001 9:20 AM
>>> From: xxxx xxxxx <xxxxxx@xxxxxxx.com>
>>> To: Alex Bogusky <alexbogusky@cpbmiami.com>
>>>
>>> Hey, Alex.
>>> We've never met but I love your stuff. The GT work is killer. I always
>>> thought it was better than my Bell Helmet stuff. Congratulations on the
>>> Mini win. That's awesome. I've heard stories about how your work was
>>> better than xxxx's during the Land Rover pitch but that the dumbass
>>> clients were offended by the fact that you were wearing jeans.
>>> Unbelievable. Actually, at my first meeting I wore shorts and Tevas. That
>>> didn't go over too well. Talk about a brand with its head up its ass. In 10
>>> months of running this account I've sold one cool long-copy historical
>>> newspaper campaign but that's it. No real tube - no mag print. Just a
>>> whole lot of retail. (Uh, no, I had nothing to do with those crappy Dog and
>>> Pregnant woman tv spots.) So, you're better off without Land Rover. Trust
>>> me. Anyhow, good luck with Mini.
>>> My wife grew up in Miami so if we're there anytime soon, I'd love to
>>> meet you.
>>>
>>> Respectfully,
>>> xxxxx xxxxxx
>>>
>>>
>>>

Subject: Don't eat the red jello...
Date: Monday, May 12, 2003 5:05 PM
From: Sebastian Grey <sebastiangray@cpbgroup.com>
To: All Agency <allagency@cpbgroup.com>

That's not powdered sugar.

Subject: thanks for the cake but...
Date: Wednesday, November 20, 2002 3:16 PM
From: Aramis Israel <aramisisrael@cpbla.com>
To: All Agency <allagency@cpbmiami.com>

does anybody know where my birthday card is?
I never saw it but I heard it exists.

-Aramis

Subject: here we go again
Date: Wednesday, January 23, 2002 7:20 PM
From: Alex Bogusky <alexbogusky@cpbmiami.com>
To: Creative Department <creativedepartment@cpbmiami.com>, Jeff Hicks
<jeffhicks@cpbmiami.com>, Jeff Steinhour <jeffsteinhour@cpbmiami.com>,
Tom Birk <tombirk@cpbmiami.com>, Charles Porter <chuckporter@cpbmia-
mi.com>, Martina Mendieta <martinamendieta@cpbmiami.com>, Dave
Batista <davebatista@circle.com>

i took a big ikea brain dump while i was waiting in the jury duty pool.
there may be more. i welcome comments and additions. and yes i know i
constantly contradict myself. back off, it's part of the process.
if you are not in the creative department ignore the chastising tone of
the first graph of the brain dump. it is not meant for you. or maybe it is.

Subject: <no subject>
Date: Tuesday, August 10, 2004 12:32 PM
From: Alex Burnard <alexburnard@cpbgroup.com>
To: Jeff Benjamin <jeffbenjamin@cpbgroup.com>
Cc: All Agency <allagency@cpbgroup.com>

You think you can just hide in cyberspace?

Subject: Dallas Cowboys Cheerleaders
Date: Wednesday, January 12, 2005 10:39 AM
From: Jessica Reznick <jessicareznick@cpbgroup.com>
To: Alex Bogusky <alexbogusky@cpbgroup.com>
Cc: Andrew Keller <andrewkeller@cpbgroup.com>, Rob Reilly
<robreilly@cpbgroup.com>, Evan Fry <evanfry@cpbgroup.com>,
John Parker <johnparker@cpbgroup.com>, Brian Tierney
<briantierney@cpbgroup.com>, Ben James <benjames@cpbgroup.com>

Alex,
As we are getting closer to finalizing our deal with the Dallas
Cowboy's Cheerleaders, we need to decide which three girls we
would like to appear in our BK "Fantasy Ranch" spots.

Attached please find headshots of the cheerleaders that were recommended to us by their manager. Please keep in mind, you do not
have to use the recommended girls and the remainder of the squad
can be viewed by going to the below website site.

www.dallascowboys.com/cheerleaders/home.cfm

If you could please provide me with the names of not only your top
three choices, but also a few backups in case of unforeseen
scheduling conflicts.

Thanks, and please let me know if you have any further questions.
Jessica

Subject: Creativity
Date: Wednesday, April 10, 2002 5:44 AM
From: Alex Bogusky <alexbogusky@cpbmiami.com>
To: All Agency <allagency@cpbgroup.com>

In the second paragraph of the Creativity magazine article begins,
"Right now the agency (Crispin Porter + Bogusky) is probably the
hottest in the United States." It is amazing for me to read those words
being written about us. In a lot of ways it is the culmination of a dream
that seemed silly to everyone I know except my wife. She really did
see it happening all those years ago and has never been surprised by
our successes. Even when I wanted her to be surprised.
But dreams need to last a lifetime and we're not dead yet. Some of
you just arrived and I imagine you are hoping that you haven't gotten
here right after all the excitement either. So we need some new lofty
goals. I have a few that always get my blood going.
Being "hot" as they put it in the Creativity article feels pretty fickle. And
how "hot" something got usually is a pretty poor indicator of how
much impact it had on the world. Case in point: The Razor scooter. I
don't want to be a Razor scooter. I want to change the world. At least
a few little bits of it.

I want people to say "then cp+b came along and changed things and
now nobody does it that old way anymore."
I want to be the agency that ruined it for every other agency in the
world.
I want old fashioned agencies to look at us and see their own demise
because they know they won't be able to do what we do.
I want to continue to evolve and morph into what all the smart people
we hire want us to become.
I want to be a great place for clients to keep their brands and I want
to be an even greater place to work.
I want to become known as the best place to work in south florida.

I want us all to look for more ways to help out in our community.
I want to run our company the way every 12 year old dreams of running
a company because the 12 year olds are right.
I want to be the agency that ruined it for every other agency in the world.
We make our clients famous by any means at our disposal. We need to
be what ad agencies will become. When Steve Breen from Molson
spoke today you could see how excited he was about our bizarre and
fresh way of looking at brand building. And Molson hasn't even begun to
tap into that yet. They're still just using us as a typical agency and all he
can think about is what we will build that twists his product and his
marketing and his PR into one big Molson famous makin' machine.
Here's the tricky part. I want us to do all of this while keeping the
qualities that make us decent folks to hang out with.
I want us to remain humble. Past success is no measure of what we will
do so best to be humble. After all it's just advertising anyhow.
I want us to hold onto our ability to accomplish a lot with a lot less than
most agencies. The huge amounts of money that we are put in charge
with should always be looked at in terms of what it can accomplish
outside of what we are doing with it. $100,000 might seem like less
money than you might want to produce a national tv spot but remember
you can build a freaking house with it. Always keep perspective on the
money you are allocating.
And finally, I want us to keep having fun and being good to one another.
Because otherwise, why bother with all the rest.
A good friend of mine wrote me recently because he was frustrated with
the advertising business and frustrated by so many of the people he
works for and with. He wrote, "It astounds me how people are afraid of
so many things but mediocrity never seems to be one of them."
I'm afraid to be mediocre. I'm afraid to stop getting better. I hope you
are, too. Because to the rest of the world that looks like courage. Just
look at Creativity magazine.

Love,
Alex

Subject: FW: Integrity
Date: Tuesday, July 18, 2000 1:59 PM
From: Jeff Hicks <jeffhicks@cpbmiami.com>
To: All Agency <allagency@cpbmiami.com>

What's wrong with a little extra traffic.

-----Original Message-----
> Subject: Integrity
> Date: Tuesday, July 18, 2000 2:59 PM
> From: The Buma Family <buma@bumafuneralhome.com>
> To: Charles Porter <chuckporter@cpbmiami.com>
>
> Dear Mr. Porter,
>
> It is kindly asked that your firm remove a hyperlink to our funeral
> home from your website. When one exits your site, they are sent to
> ours. Whatever the intention, we wish for you to remove the link
> immediately.
> Thank you in advance.
> Respectfully,
> James R. Buma
> 508.473.5511

Subject: Keep cell phones with ya
Date: Thursday, April 14, 2005 9:23 AM
From: David Rolfe <davidrolfe@cpbgroup.com>
To: Integrated Department <integrateddepartment@cpbgroup.com>

Many of us have some pretty dope phones that Rup and I have pushed
for us to have because we are an almighty department and we all need
and deserve them. So, if you have a dope ride and even if you don't,
make sure it's on and you're using it, because it is a great form of
communication whether during work hours or outside of work hours.

Subject: Music
Date: Monday, July 18, 2005 4:47 PM
From: Eric Rasco <ericrasco@cpbgroup.com>
To: Integrated Department <integrateddepartment@cpbgroup.com>

Hello everyone,
I've gotten a couple of complaints about the musical selections that I've
been bumping today. I'm aware that my small (but powerful) speakers
can hit everybody in the department, so please let me know if you need
me to change what I'm playing because we're all in this
together and I want you to be happy. Although everything that I'm
playing is top gear 5th percentile shit, I can understand that you
might not like all of it.
Thank you for the collaboration,
Eric

Subject: Fred Cuts
Date: Monday, October 31, 9:09 PM
From: Alex Burnard <alexburnard@cpbmiami.com>
To: Alex Bogusky <alexbogusky@cpbmiami.com>

Headed to a party with eric carr (aka the fox) he's got some mad cool shit going down at butter. Anyway we'll have to get to the pipe guy removal in the am. Happy halloween.

> Subject: RE: Fred Cuts
> Date: Monday, October 31, 2005 9:11 PM
> From: Alex Bogusky <alexbogusky@cpbgroup.com>
> To: Alex Burnard <alexburnard@cpbgroup.com>
>
> I'm at gene simmons house.

Subject: Troubled youth
Date: Monday, January 20, 6:58 PM
From: Tiffany Kosel <tiffanykosel@cpbmiami.com>
To: Creative Department <creativedepartment@cpbmiami.com>

If you are reading this you are young, hot, and eager. Perfect for this assignment. Young Guns is an international award show for creatives under 30. Last year they did a campaign that included camel toes, drive-bys, No. 2, third nipples, homos, orthodox jews, cocks and pussy. We can do better.

We don't have much time. So no jerking off. We have less than two weeks to come up with a killer campaign. Meet in the WAR room tomorrow at 11 AM if you have the balls.

First round of work: this MONDAY the 24th
Second round: THURSDAY the 27th
Pencils down and comps done and approved: MONDAY the 31st.

Check out: www.ygaward.com
See you.
Tif

> Subject: Troubled youth
> Date: Monday, January 20, 7:27 PM
> From: Larry Corwin <larrycorwin@cpbmiami.com>
> To: Tiffany Kosel <tiffanykosel@cpbmiami.com>
>
> what if jerking off is part of the concept?
>
>> Subject: Re: Troubled youth
>> Date: Thursday, January 20, 2005 7:35 PM
>> From: Tiffany Kosel <tiffanykosel@cpbmiami.com>
>> To: Larry Corwin <larrycorwin@cpbmiami.com>, Creative
>> Department <creativedepartment@cpbmiami.com>
>>
>> I must clarify to everyone: You can spend time jerking off if it is part
>> of your concept. Sorry for the confusion. Thanks for helping out
>> Larry. We know you're the pro.
>>
>>> Subject: FW: Troubled youth
>>> Date: Monday, April 25, 2005 8:17 AM
>>> From: Larry Corwin <larrycorwin@cpbmiami.com>
>>> To: Tiffany Kosel <tiffanykosel@cpbmiami.com>
>>> Cc: Kevin Koller <kevinkoller@cpbmiami.com>, Jed Grossman
>>> <jedgrossman@cpbmiami.com>
>>>
>>> We actually weren't that far off...
>>>
>>>> Subject: RE: FW: Troubled youth
>>>> Date: Monday, April 25, 2005 8:36 AM
>>>> From: Tiffany Kosel <TKosel@cpbmiami.com>
>>>> To: Larry Corwin <lcorwin@cpbmiami.com>
>>>> Cc: Kevin Koller <KKoller@cpbmiami.com>, Jed Grossman
>>>> <JGrossman@cpbmiami.com>
>>>>
>>>> Wow. You're right. I just didn't expect that the concept would be
>>>> jerking off to pictures of me.
>>>>

Subject: *******WARNING*********
Date: Monday, March 21, 2005 10:04 AM
From: Carter Nance <carternance@cpbgroup.com>
To: Ryan Skubic <ryanskubic@cpbgroup.com>, Jeff Steinhour <jeff-steinhour@cpbgroup.com>, Eric Lear <ericlear@cpbgroup.com>, Charles Baumberger <charlesbaumberger@cpbgroup.com>, Mason Reed <masonreed@cpbgroup.com>, Ryan Moreno <ryanmoreno@cpbgroup.com>, Jim Poh <jimpoh@cpbgroup.com>,

Bill Wright <billwright@cpbgroup.com>

The bathroom is a complete disaster.

As I was walking in, I almost ran over Geraldo Rivera, who was reporting on the carnage live via satellite (in a flak jacket).

All three holes are stopped up.

Head for the hills.

 Subject: Re: *******WARNING*********
> Date: Monday, March 21, 2005 10:11 AM
> From: Jeff Steinhour <jeffsteinhour@cpbgroup.com>
> To: Carter Nance <carternance@cpbgroup.com>, Ryan Skubic
> <ryanskubic@cpbgroup.com>, Eric Lear <ericlear@cpbgroup.com>, Charles
> Baumberger <charlesbaumberger@cpbgroup.com>, Mason Reed
> <masonreed@cpbgroup.com>, Ryan Moreno <ryanmoreno@cpbgroup.com>,
> Jim Poh <jimpoh@cpbgroup.com>, Bill Wright <billwright@cpbgroup.com>
>
>This is not good. Yo E - Sound the alarm. Put Marlene on the case and
>attack. Full-court Funk Patrol.
>
>> Subject: RE: *******WARNING*********
>> Date: Monday, March 21, 2005 10:14 AM
>> From: Eric Lear <ericlear@cpbgroup.com>
>> To: Jeff Steinhour <jeffsteinhour@cpbgroup.com>, Carter Nance
>> <carternance@cpbgroup.com>, Ryan Skubic <ryanskubic@cpbgroup.com>,
>> Charles Baumberger <charlesbaumberger@cpbgroup.com>, Mason Reed
>> <masonreed@cpbgroup.com>, Ryan Moreno
>> <ryanmoreno@cpbgroup.com>, Jim Poh <jimpoh@cpbgroup.com>, Bill
>> Wright <billwright@cpbgroup.com>
>>
>> Saw it first thing this morning and Joey is getting on it.
>>

Subject: It's not our rule, but...
Date: Friday, February 14, 2003 11:11 AM
From: Eric Lear <ericlear@cpbla.com>
To: All Agency <allagency@cpbgroup.com>

We really shouldn't bring dogs to work. Especially if they are not trained. We've had a number of instances recently with dogs, doing what they do, on the carpet. Even if you clean it up, it creates an uncomfortable work situation for your peers.

Unless you have an emergency, please refrain from bringing your dog to work.

Thanks for your understanding and help.

Eric

> Subject: Re: It's not our rule, but...
> Date: Friday, February 15, 2003 12:08 AM
> From: Alex Bogusky <alexbogusky@cpbla.com>
> To: Eric Lear <ericlear@cpbla.com>, All Agency <allagency@cpbgroup.com>
>
> The doggy e-mail. Could this be the beginning of the end?
>
> I had a big problem with this idea of no dogs. Because obviously this would
> have to include chuck's dog too. And I used to have three dogs that
> occasionally dropped by.
>
> But the point that don't bring dogs that poop is a good one. If your dog can
> hold it 99 percent of the time and for some reason you need to bring it in then
> do it. Just use your head and as always be extra respectful of those around
> you.
>
> Alex
>

Subject: Mix up
Date: Friday, July 22, 2005 6:45 PM
From: Alex Bogusky <alexbogusky@cpbmiami.com>
To: Creative Department <creativedepartment@cpbmiami.com>

I asked Veronica to find out if we could buy megacpb.com.
I was joking but she sent out an e-mail to see what people thought.
The bad news is there were some of you that liked the idea.
And now you're all on double secret probation.

Subject: Your Hair
Date: Wednesday, January 26, 2005 3:19 PM
From: Eric Rasco <ericrasco@cpbgroup.com>

From: Sebastian Gray
Subject: <no subject>
To: artdept@cpbgroup.com

Who's got the digital elphs?

Schedule "Send &

ute

From: Dave Swartz
Subject: Re: <no subject>
▼**Attachments: elphjpg**
To: Sebastian G

Here's one

Schedule "Sen

From: Mike Delmarmol
Subject: Re: <no subject>
▼**Attachments: elf3x.jpg**
To: Dave

here's the other one.

Schedule "Se

From: Alex Burnard
Subject: Re: <no subject>
▼**Attachements: half-elf-ears.jpg**
To: Mike DelM

I had one too. Sorry about that.

Schedul

From: :-)Katm@cpbgroup.com>
To: Scott Linnen, Sebastian Gray, ...
Subject: Re: <no subject>
▼ **Attachments: IMG_1975.JPG**

I have a gnome....

Schedule "Send & Receive All" will run in 4 minutes

From: Scott Linnen
To: Sebastian Gray, ...
Subject: Re: <no subject>
▼**Attachments: digitalfaeries.jpg**

All I got's digital fairies,

Schedule "Send & Receive All" will run in 4 minutes

From: alex bogusky
To: Scott Linnen, Sebastian Gray, ...
Subject: Re: <no subject>

Who's got my bullets?
>
>

Schedule "Send & Receive All" will run in 4 minutes

Dan wants to cut his hair today and he was wondering what kind of hair cut you think he should get.

> Subject: RE: Your Hair
> Date: Wednesday, January 26, 2005 3:40 PM
> From: David Rolfe <davidrolfe@cpbgroup.com>
> To: Eric Rasco <ericrasco@cpbgroup.com>
> Cc: Daniel Ruth <danruth@cpbgroup.com>, Aramis Israel
> <aramisisrael@cpbgroup.com>
>
> Please cut it like Rob Strasberg's. He is very attractive.
>
> Thanks for checking in,
> Dave Rolfe

Subject: fashion luncheon
Date: Monday, January 31, 2000 1:15 PM
From: Charles Porter <chuckporter@cpbmiami.com>
To: All Agency <allagency@cpbmiami.com>

The agency will be hosting a gala fashion luncheon today from 2:00 to 4:00 at mezzanote in the Grove. We'll be introducing our new Spring Line - a dazzling collection of soft pastels, shimmering evening wear, and some sporty new looks for those "casual fridays" at the office. Tickets are $350 per person, however agency people (with valid and current agency id's will be admitted free). thanks.

> Subject: The Revolution will not be reinvited
> Date: Wednesday, February 2, 2000 1:20 AM
> From: David Clemans <daveclemans@cpbmiami.com>
> To: All Agency <allagency@cpbmiami.com>
>
> Someday, I will look back with a tear of pride in my eye as i bounce
> my young nephew on my knee and unwind the tale of that fateful day.
> I will beam as I say, "I was there. I remember when that initial shot
> rung out, over the heads of the First Bogusky Volunteers who stood
> diligently holding their ground along the ridge of Little Six Top. I was
> right there during the attempted assasination of President Hicks with
> a pat of butter. I saw Tony Calcao drop from a wound to the foot, not
> giving up but, rather screaming, "remember Rocky Blier! I'll be back!"
> I myself took heavy tiramisu at The Wine Stand and I remember sadly,
> watching Dave Taylor go down, ambushed in the Skirmish of The Grove
> Sidewalk. My little nephew may never understand the emotions we
> felt during the Crispin Revolution, but you can bet that he will hear about
> our exploits. For I petition that from this day forward, every January
> 31st, we shall all set aside our tasks for a few minutes, lift a glass of
> tequila and shout, "Viva la Crispin! Viva la Crispin! Viva la Crispin!"
>
> DC
>
> p.s. In the words of the great Chuck Porter, "When war breaks out, it's
> best to hold the position of Supplier of Munitions."

>> Subject: Mezanote Post Mortem
>> Date: Monday, January 31, 2000 5:06 PM
>> From: Jeff Hicks <jeffhicks@cpbmiami.com>
>> To: All Agency <allagency@cpbmiami.com>
>>
>> So i'm sitting here in my office with cake in my hair and a dried
>> chunk of butter on the sleeve of my shirt. truth is, I couldn't be
>> happier. This place is better than any job i ever imagined and you
>> guys (Clemans included) are an amazing collection of passionate
>> people that made our getting Agency of The Year a reality. thanks to
>> everyone. the credit for this and all of our accomplishments is yours.
>>
>> jeff
>>
>>> Subject: Re: Mezzanote Post Mortem
>>> Date: Wednesday, February 1, 2000 2:20 AM
>>> From: "Alex Bogusky" <alexbogusky@cpbmiami.com>
>>> To: Jeff Hicks <jeffhicks@cpbmiami.com>,
>>> All Agency <allagency@cpbmiami.com>
>>>
>>> Jeff,
>>> got your e-mail a little late. i had already terminated Dave
>>> Clemans. I'm sorry. I thought that is what you wanted.
>>>
>>> alex
>>>
>>>

Subject: email from Nadia
Date: Tuesday, June 7, 2005 3:51 PM
From: xxxxxx@aol.com <xxxxxx@aol.com>

To: Alex Bogusky <alexbogusky@cpbgroup.com>

Hi Dad
I love you and I will love you forever. You are always in my heart. I will be in great harmony. You will be in great harmony. Flowers make me think of you. Love, Nadia
----
Subject: BIG GUY DUEL
Date: Tuesday, September 28, 2004 7:23 PM
From: Alex Burnard <alexburnard@cpbgroup.com>
To: All Agency <allagency@cpbgroup.com>

LIVE   LIVE   LIVE   LIVE   LIVE
LIVE   LIVE   LIVE   LIVE   LIVE
LIVE   LIVE   LIVE   LIVE   LIVE

Arm wrestling duel

BIG SCHIFF (dave)
Vs.
LITTLE SCHIFF (ryan)

Wednesday 11am - agora

LIVE   LIVE   LIVE   LIVE   LIVE
LIVE   LIVE   LIVE   LIVE   LIVE
LIVE   LIVE   LIVE   LIVE   LIVE

Subject: Agency Status
Date: Thursday, August 25, 2005 7:43 AM
From: Marlene Root <marleneroot@cpbgroup.com>
To: All Agency <allagency@cpbgroup.com>

In response to the hurricane warning issued for dade and broward county, the agency will be closed. However, you may still access the agency up until 10:30 today at which time the elevators will be shut down. Once the elevators are shut down you will be unable to get into the agency.

We anticipate being open tomorrow by mid day. If that changes, we will send out another voicemail as early as 8:30AM so please plan to check in before coming in.

That's all for now. Be safe.

> Subject: RE: Agency Status
> From: Charles Porter
> Date: Thursday, August 25, 2005 8:43 AM
> To: Marlene Root <marleneroot@cpbgroup.com>,
> All Agency <allagency@cpbgroup.com>
>
> New news.
>
> By invoking the little-known Burnie clause in our lease, we've gotten
> the building to keep the elevators open until 11:30 or so. If you
> need stuff from the agency, stop by before then. Thanks.
>
>
>> Subject: RE: Agency Status
>> Date: Thu, 25 Aug 2005 09:37:20 -0400
>> From: Alex Burnard <alexburnard@cpbgroup.com>
>> To: Charles Porter <chuckporter@cpbgroup.com>, Marlene Root
>> <marleneroot@cpbgroup.com>,
>> All Agency <allagency@cpbgroup.com>
>> Conversation: Agency Status
>>
>> I believe that is the oldburnie clause. The newburnie addendum
>> got his stuff last night and is now hanging out with his buddies at
>> dennys laughing and stuff.
>>
>>> Subject: Katrina
>>> Date: Thursday, August 25, 2005 9:40 AM
>>> From: Dave Schiff <daveschiff@cpbgroup.com>
>>> To: Geordie Stephens <geordiestephens@cpbgroup.com>,
>>> All Agency <allagency@cpbgroup.com>
>>>
>>> We're all gonna die.
>>>
>>>> Subject: Re: Katrina
>>>> Date: Thursday, August 25, 2005 9:44 AM
>>>> From: Geordie Stephens <geordiestephens@cpbgroup.com>
>>>> To: Dave Schiff <daveschiff@cpbgroup.com>,
>>>> All Agency <allagency@cpbgroup.com>
>>>>

>>>> I just moved here recently, and am terrified. Could I stay with
>>>> you... Under the covers?
>>>>
>>>>
>>>>> Subject: Re: Katrina
>>>>> Date: Thursday, August 25, 2005 9:52 AM
>>>>> From: Dave Schiff <daveschiff@cpbgroup.com>
>>>>> To: Geordie Stephens <geordiestephens@cpbgroup.com>,
>>>>> All Agency <allagency@cpbgroup.com>
>>>>>
>>>>> Look, I'm gonna tell you what HR is scared to say. The
>>>>> second this thing makes landfall, you're dead. We all are.
>>>>> Everything else they tell you at work is just to cover
>>>>> themselves for insurance.
>>>>>
>>>>>> Subject: Re: Katrina
>>>>>> Date: Thursday, August 25, 2005 9:57 AM
>>>>>> From: Jeffrey Hecht <jeffhecht@cpbgroup.com>
>>>>>> To: Dave Schiff <daveschiff@cpbgroup.com>, Geordie
>>>>>> Stephens <geordiestephens@cpbgroup.com>, All Agency
>>>>>> <allagency@cpbgroup.com>
>>>>>>
>>>>>> Sounds like the final episode of six feet under
>>>>>>
>>>>>>> Subject: Re: Katrina
>>>>>>> Date: Thursday, August 25, 2005 10:01 AM
>>>>>>> From: Barrie Bamberg <barriebamberg@cpbgroup.com>
>>>>>>> To: Jeffrey Hecht <jeffhecht@cpbgroup.com>, Dave Schiff
>>>>>>> <daveschiff@cpbgroup.com>, Geordie Stephens
>>>>>>> <geordiestephens@cpbgroup.com>, All Agency
>>>>>>> <allagency@cpbgroup.com>
>>>>>>>
>>>>>>> I can't believe I ever got personally bitched out by Alex
>>>>>>> Bogusky for sending all CP+B emails

Subject: Coffee
Date: Tuesday, March 2, 2004 12:07 PM
From: Alex Bogusky <alexbogusky@cpbgroup.com>
To: Creative Department <creativedepartment@cpbmiami.com>

What happened to the full and steaming hot cup of coffee that was left
on my desk for me by Veronica last night? There have been some
comments made that is probably the cleaning crew. This does
not stand up to scrutiny as they don't even throw away empty Coke
cans covered in ants.

So we wait.

Subject: Style question
Date: Thursday, September 1, 2005 12:31 PM
From: Alex Burnard <aburnard@cpbgroup.com>
To: All Agency <allagency@cpbgroup.com>

We are having a serious discussion among a lot of us and we need
backup on this consensus. Does keister have the worst style of
anyone in the building? Thanks in advance for any input on this
serious manner.

Subject: tower of terror!!!
Date: Monday, November 06, 2000 02:09 PM
From: Ana Hernandez <hunnybunny@cpbmiami.com>
To: All Agency <allagency@cpbmiami.com>

have you been on the mgm ride at disney where the elevator drops
like 100 feet and you feel like you are just going to die, well there is
an elevator in our building that gives the SAME FEELING. it is the
freight elevator. the one that is by itself to the left. so stay off it for
today till it gets fixed.

love you

Subject: Thank you...
Date: Friday, November 8, 2002 2:28 PM
From: Veronica Padilla <veronicapadilla@cpbla.com>
To: Creative Group <creativegroup@cpbgroup.com>

Peanut Fairy!

Subject: New People
From: Charles Porter <chuckporter@cpbmiami.com>
Date: Tuesday, August 8, 2000 1:30 PM
To: All Agency <allagency@cpbmiami.com>

Okay, there are a bunch of new people here that I have to meet and

I'd like to do it by height. If you've joined the agency in the past week or two,
please email your height to Angela and we'll set up times to get together either
today or tomorrow. Thanks.

Chuck

Subject: The Party
Date: Thursday, December 8, 2005 5:25 PM
From: Charles Porter <chuckporter@cpbgroup.com>
To: All Agency <allagency@cpbgroup.com>

HERE ARE SOME ANSWERS TO THE MOST COMMONLY ASKED
QUESTIONS ABOUT THE PARTY TOMORROW

Q. Is there valet parking like there is at fancy hotels?
A. Yes. Turn from Mary Street onto Grand Avenue (where Borders used to be)
and uniformed attendants will be there to park your car for free and then
rummage through the glove compartment.

Q. The invitation says dress like a star from the Golden Age of Hollywood.
When was the Golden Age?
A. March through October, 1939.

Q. What if at the end of the party, due to all the excitement, I have to lie down?
A. Our travel department has gotten great hotel rates at all the places around
here. Also, there will be blankets in both the passenger and freight elevators.

Q. Are costumes okay?
A. Yes. The agency loves costumes.

Q. Was that really the Golden Age?
A. No. The Golden Age is whatever you believe it is. Look inside yourself,
follow your dream and listen to your heart. Unless your heart says "Battlefield
Earth".

Q. Can I bring my my dog?
A. Yes, if your dog is Lassie, Benji or Rin Tin Tin.

Q. Are real estate prices unrealistically inflated and will the bubble burst?
A. No, the US economy is extraordinarily robust and signs for growth remain
positive. On the other hand, if you've got one of those super-low-rate,
short-term, interest-only mortgages coming due, you might want to start
getting used to peanut butter.

Q. Will the band take requests?
A. Yes, but they won't actually play the songs you've requested.

Q. Can I bring anything? A salad? My homemade muffins?
A. No, there will be a lot of food including a spectacular dessert bar set up
where no one can find it. Again.

Q. Will people who stay past midnight be escorted out of the building by
uniformed security personnel?
A. That's okay with the agency as long as the security personnel are finished
for the night.

Subject: Re: fuck
Date: Thursday, February 19, 2004 10:40 AM
From: Dave Schiff <daveschiff@cpbgroup.com>
To: Jackie Guerra <jackieguerra@cpbgroup.com>

I am going to fucking kill Aramis.

> Subject: please help
> Date: Thursday, February 19, 2004 11:43 AM
> From: Aramis Israel <aramisisrael@cpbgroup.com>
> To: Eric Lear <ericlear@cpbgroup.com>
> Cc: Dave Schiff <daveschiff@cpbgroup.com>
>
> We all know this guy can fly off the handle. I'm scared.
> What should I do?
> -Aramis
>
>> Subject: RE: please help
>> Date: Thursday, February 19, 2002 11:54 AM
>> From: Eric Lear <ericlear@cpbgroup.com>
>> To: Dave Schiff <daveschiff@cpbgroup.com>
>>
>> Dave,
>> Physical or verbal abuse of a fellow employee will not be tolerated at CP+B.
>> Please refrain from hurting Aramis. At least during company hours.
>>
>> Thank you,
>> Eric

Bigfoot Feet. An A·nec·dote

One day me and my partner were trying to come up with concepts for Telluride, and one of the things we were tossing around was this big, furry fiberglass foot. The idea was that there would be this secret society of people bent on keeping Telluride friendly and uncrowded. So they would go around making footprints with this giant fiberglass Bigfoot foot, causing pretentious out-of-towners to get scared and never come back. Anyway, it wasn't the best idea—it never even made it out of the building—but it helped us realize that our job wasn't really about making ads. It was more about making Bigfoot feet. Since that day we call anything that's an ad, but not really an ad, a Bigfoot Foot. It gives us a little perspective on what we're supposed to be doing, and it's easier to say than "Things that are ads but are not ads."

People who have trouble describing something generally fall back on the same linguistic excuse: "Words cannot describe it." But if these people would simply take the time to invent words, instead of just complaining about the ones that are currently available, their little anecdote would be a lot more interesting for you, the listener. To that end, here are a few words we came up with over the years:

Non·tra·gue·ril·la *adj.* When you're describing some weird idea that the client will never comprehend, "nontraditional" or "guerilla" are simply not enough. But a cumbersome adjective that combines the two, and is nearly impossible to pronounce, well, who doesn't want that?

Whip·tas·tic *adj.* "Nimble" is lame. "Corners like it's on rails" is played-out. "Turns so fast your face will get pulled to one side and probably stay that way forever" is a bit cumbersome. So we called the MINI's handling characteristics Whiptastic, a snappy new adjective that said it all.

Man·tro·py *adj.* A killer was advancing stealthily across the American landscape, turning men into fragrant, impeccably groomed husks of their former selves. MAXIM was the first to identify this debilitating disease and give it a name: Mantropy. But soon, the *New York Post* was using it to describe male celebs that had gone soft.

Un·bör·ing *adj.* You're supposed to keep furniture forever. But that's boring. So IKEA proposed that the world of furniture should be more like the world of fashion, which led to the creation of Unböring, the first ever made-up word to work in both English and Swedish.

Bag·gler *n.* You know when you go through a drive through, and you order fries, and the fries come in a box, but a few of the fries fall out of the box and end up in the bottom of the bag, and you dig for them, because you know they're down there, and when you finally get hold of them they're the best fries ever? Well, we thought it was high time someone named those damned things, so we called 'em Bagglers, and printed a little tribute to them right there on the side of the BURGER KING® bag.

Je·tro·sex·ual *adj.* There's a certain kind of person out there who understands that air travel can be more than traveling in the air. People unafraid to get it on in the lavatory, or rock a briefcase made from some endangered reptile. They're neither metrosexuals, nor jetsetters, but a stylish and formidable amalgam of the two.

Egg·nor·mous *n.* When BURGER KING® introduced the Enormous Omelete Sandwich, scientific analysis showed that each sandwich contained between 60 and 70 eggs! Actually, that's a lie. But it doesn't change the fact that we needed a word to say this sandwich was loaded with eggs. *See also: Meatnormous, Cheesenormous.*

Bag·gler *n.* You know when you go through a drive through, and you order fries, and the fries come in a box, but a few of the fries fall out of the box and end up in the bottom of the bag, and you dig for them, because you know they're down there, and when you finally hold of them they're the best fries ever? W we thought it was high time someone na those damned things, so we called 'em glers, and printed a little tribute to them the side of the BURGER KING® b

SPECIAL LIMITED-TIME OFFER!
WILL <u>NOT</u> BE SOLD IN STORES!

<u>INCLUDES</u>: *EL BAILE DEL TIGRE • THE KINGS OF POP • AIR-GUITAR SERENADE • LOVERS TANGO • SURPRISE ATTACK ON WEDNESDAY AFTERNOON • AND MANY MANY MORE*

$7⁵⁰ | MORE THAN 30 MINUTES OF UNINTERRUPTED MANDANCE HYSTERIA
DON'T DELAY, ORDER YOUR COPY TODAY AT CPBSTUFF4SALE.COM

∞ *"AN EXPRESSION OF BEINGNESS"*

Mandancing originated in 2002 in the old CP+B offices off of 27th Avenue. The artform was pioneered by two restless CP+B employees of that era, Turi and Schiff. Originally conceived as a means to relieve pent-up stress at 3 AM, the Mandance soon developed into an exotic artform, not unlike the Middle Eastern belly dance or the New York City break dance.

BOOKS AS A MEDIUM

Right before his show arrived in a new city, P.T. Barnum would distribute 500,000 copies of The Advance Courier, a 24-page illustrated newspaper with most of the articles written by Barnum himself. Nothing could whip an otherwise sleepy metropolis into a frothy tornado of desire quite like the Courier. So we took a page from the book of Barnum and did a little homegrown publishing of our own. These little volumes did not contain drawings of elephants or midgets or women who looked like the guitarist from ZZ Top, but they help our clients go from mere brands to some of the greatest shows on earth.

What is CP+B? What constitutes Hoopla? And why should you care?

publicity—all of which is the desired effect sought by CP+B. The French origin of the word (*Houp-là!*) is a simple command: *Move! Take a step!* Which is what CP+B's version of hoopla is designed to do: to get people to react, respond, join in, do *something*. The idea being that if you can inspire enough people to do something in particular, *to take a step* together in the same direction, you can create a cultural phenomenon—something CP+B has achieved repeatedly in the past few years.

The agency may be best known for spearheading the immensely successful launch of the MINI Cooper car in America. Regarded as one of the more innovative marketing campaigns in recent years, the MINI burst into the public consciousness with all manner of fun and ballyhoo. CP+B created games, paper cutouts, billboards that seemed to come alive, and cartoon books.

The agency made up wild stories about robots and counterfeit cars and spread them around via elaborate hoaxes. It turned heads by using the MINI car as a prop in various live stunts, such as attaching a MINI to the roof rack of an SUV (with a sign reading, "What are you doing for fun this weekend?") and driving it around town, and replacing some of those quarter-a-ride mechanical ponies for kids with miniature MINIs. The MINI campaign had a kind of carnival effect, in that it seemed to be going on all around you as a living event, and you never knew what was coming around the next corner. So successful was the entire effort that it became almost impossible to get your hands on a MINI that first year.

But CP+B has also shown that Hoopla can do more than move cars out of a showroom or chicken sandwiches off the shelf. The agency honed its method while working on a social-awareness campaign on behalf of its home state of Florida back in the late 1990s. Florida was on a mission to stem the rising rate of smoking among teenagers and turned to then-tiny CP+B for help. The goal here was not to sell something but to try to change attitudes, behaviors, and a way of life. CP+B's creative team could have trotted out the predictable advertising solution: scare-tactic commercials, perhaps with images of blackened lungs—which almost certainly would have been tuned out by teens who think they've seen it all and don't scare easily.

Instead, CP+B created a cultural movement, with a bandwagon teens could hop on and a brand—the word *truth*—they could embrace as their own. The movement was fueled by hats, buttons, stickers, posters, T-shirts, and by staged events and publicity stunts; it became a traveling show that crossed the state on trains and in trucks, building a grass-roots-level movement that rallied teenagers against a common enemy, Big Tobacco. It all came together, and it all worked: Teen smoking levels throughout Florida began to drop almost immediately and continued to go down in the years that followed. The *truth* campaign was subsequently adopted by several states, eventually becoming a national movement that is still going strong and demonstrating that Hoopla can do almost anything, up to and including saving lives.

As CP+B achieved success with the *truth* and MINI campaigns, becoming "the ad world's most talked-about agency," according to *USA Today*, it began to attract clients from across the business spectrum and beyond the US borders. The Swedish home-furnishings company IKEA, the Canadian brewer Molson, the British-based Virgin Atlantic Airways, the German automaker Volkswagen, along with mammoth American brands such as BURGER KING, Google, GAP, Miller Brewing Co., and Coca-Cola, all came to this off-the-beaten-path Miami agency asking, essentially, for the same thing: Hoopla. Meaning, these companies wanted to find a new and far-reaching approach to getting on the cultural radar, being talked about, and connecting with people. They wanted fame and buzz, and they wanted it preferably at a reasonable price.

Who wouldn't want that? CP+B soon also found itself being approached by Hollywood producers, looking to tap into some of that Hoopla magic. Students of advertising, marketing, and culture began to analyze and debate the agency's work. And of course, competitors increasingly examined what CP+B was doing and found themselves asking: How do they do that? And can it be emulated?

The answers to those questions are relevant to more than just ad junkies or marketing executives. If one accepts the premise that Hoopla is about generating interest and getting people to do something—and about creating some type of phenomenon—then it stands to reason that the principles of Hoopla can be useful to anyone with a mission, a message, a product, or an idea around which they would like to build some momentum. In fact, CP+B believes that the laws of Hoopla apply not just to business and career but to life in general. To that end, the agency has created the concept of "Hooplaness" (a distilled sample of which can be found in this book's accompanying workbook, with a full-length book to follow). Hooplaness is based on the idea that people "consume" you, just as they do brands and products. Whether you, as a person, are embraced or ignored by your desired "target audience" may depend on your understanding of how hype works and your ability to generate it.

In today's cluttered and cacophonous media landscape, it's not easy to command attention, generate momentum, and start a phenomenon. In fact, it is exceedingly difficult, and would seem to require some combination of the seven elements (mutation, invention, candor, mischief, connection, pragmatism, and momentum) that are outlined in the succeeding chapters. All that plus some talent doesn't hurt. And a lot of hard work. And no small amount of serendipity. And a willingness to do bicycle wheelies through the halls–which is the kind of thing that happens on any given day at CP+B's frenetic headquarters.

Creating Hoopla may require all of the above, but what it *doesn't* necessarily require is huge amounts of money. Or Big Media connections. Or a fancy B-school pedigree. Or a window-office on Madison Avenue. Bogusky, Porter and their rough-hewn gang at CP+B, whom you will meet in the pages to come, generally haven't had any of these advantages. Yet they created serious amounts of exuberant noise in spite of that.

Or, more likely, they've been able to do it *because* they've lacked these things. Without the quick, easy fix of Big Money and Big Media, the agency was forced to do as Barnum once did, making up the rules of Hoopla as he went along. The fact is, the less money, status, and power you have as a promoter of any kind, the more you're forced to create your own unique brand of showmanship; in this regard, Hoopla is a very democratic way to think about fame-making and brand-building. The basic tools of mutation, invention, candor, mischief, connection, pragmatism, and momentum are available to just about anyone. Mix them together–and throw in a few sly hoaxes and a submissive chicken or two–and *voila!* You have *Houp-la!*

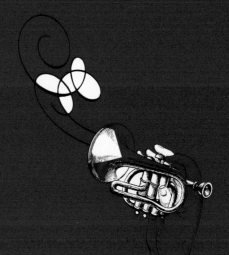

sandwich. stand. wait. stay. default. inactive. bow. congratulations. thanks. nice job. awesome. congrats. honored. konichiwa. chicken. bueno. cool. wow. amazing. i like you. nice. you're nice.
ulations. chicken. coolbo. scratch head. noggin. forehead. hair. think. mop. brow. sweat. inactive. turing. why not. what do you think. think so. yeah. maybe. dunno. i don't know. if you say so.
. crotch. balls. nutsack. scratch. knee. leg. pull penis. yank. crank yankers. between your legs. look between your legs. marilyn manson. brand launch. hokie. hokey pokie. pokey. spin. scratch.
adonk. tush. kaboose. trunk. buttock. buttocks. ares. tushy. toosh. tooshy tail. behind. lay and egg. egg. squat. scratch. stomach. belly. stomack. stomuck. tummy. abs. waist. midsection. flex.
unky chicken. chicken dance. boogie. jive. strut. march. travolta. saturday night fever. hit. slap. smack. punch. bang. head. noggin. forhead. brain. salute. klink. colonel. lieutenant.admiral.
. hunt. peck. couch. wave. do the wave. cheer. sorcery. spell. magic. ready to rumble. hop. right leg.leg. foot. right foot. hop. left leg. leg. foot. left foot. kick left. yoga. zen. chill. peace. calm
dog. sun salutation. stretch. exercise. lick floor. respect. dog. pee. crawl. hydrant. woof. ruff. fido. snoopy. santas little helper. jumping jack. jumping jacks. exercise. warmup. fly. calistenics.
cha. opera. theater. sound of music. foxtrot. fandango. rhumba. cha cha. ballet. plie. pleya. arabesque. first position. changement. raise. roof. raise roof. dance. victory. celebrate. booya. blow
e roof. run. chest. breast. breasts. boobs. jugs. tatas. nips. burning man. mardis gras. spread. part legs. hero. spread em. spreadeagle. spades. hearts. fly. bridge. leap. geronimo. lets launch over
arm. wing. point right. lift. raise. wiggle. right arm. wing. spread wing. jump. lift both legs. hop. die. knife. heart. romeo. ouch. romeo and juliet. romeo & juliet. choke. shakespeare. shakespere.
sing. american idol. croon. talk. speech. opera. walk like an egyptian. walk like an egyption. dance. egyptian. bangles. hoffs. egypt. flex. show muscles. wwf. bodybuilder. bodybuild. squeeze.
catch a wave. race. speed. woosh. sit. couch. loveseat. sofa. rest. relax. converse. seat. have a seat. chill. chill out. sit. knees. kneel. sit. indian. lotus. meditate. march. stomp. soldier. army.
ce. military. capital. admiral. colonel. lieutenant. leftenant. nod. yes. uhhuh. huh. salute. agree. alan turing. ok. okay. aye aye. yes sir. yessir. colonel. lieutenant. captian. admiral. shake head.
bad. no. no. weapons of mass destruction. wmd. alan turing. mcdonalds. wendys. please. golden arches. wmds. shrug. turing. shoulders. do you. what do. think. please. know. can you. can i. why.
ulder. behind. turn. paranoid. behind. get down. knee. kneel. neal. marry. propose. pick nose. eat booger. dig. gold. clean. nostril. cover face. don't look. touch. toes. toe. floor. stretch. bend.
n rouge. dance. touch. pat. rub. shoulders. shoulder. fart. arm. sound. noise. armpit. moon. show. ass. too shy. tail. shake tailfeather. shake tail feather. behind. anus. rectum. arse. fanny.
. break dance. michael jackson. backwards. dribble. basketball. b-ball. hoops. breakdance. disco.shake. eat. french fries. french fry. frenchfries. bite. chew. nails. finger. fingers. stick. mouth.
fret. peck. bite. hunt. walk. bite yourself. wings. arms. body. chest. breast. breasts. lick. smell. armpit. body odor. orgasm. tatas. your rack. nice rack. ymca. y m c a dance. village people. slap.
beek. nose. shock. surprise. awe. disbelief. stand. over there. corner. wall. walk away. pee. urninate. penalty box. piss. floor. clean. carpet. ground. wings. strut. look. looking. find. search.
id. under. look. looking. find. search. locate. danger. will robinson. darth vader. darth. vampire. devil. evil. referee. molt. preen. prean. feathers. lick. groom. show off. display. chicken. cover.
rass. cover your eyes. show muscles. wwf. wwe. bodybuilder. bodybuild. fight. scare. threaten. w.c.f.o. stand. wait. stay. default. cover. eye. sweat. wipe brow. mop brow. its getting hot in here.
ock-out, air guitar. party. party on. smoke. smoking. cigarette. puff. take a drag. take a puff. drum. drums. rock. headbang. head bang. rock and roll. gorge. binge. stuff face. ramone. play horn.
ow up. purge. puke. spew. hurl. sick. you're sick. squat. get down. crouch. hunker down. crying. cry. sad. upset.miserable. laugh. lol. hilarious. laugh. lol. happy. funny. joke. hysterical. cheerful.
ck. toe. mouth. beak. foot. picj feet. bite toe. cover. mouth. beak. sway. lean. bored. boring. pump iron. exercise. lift. weightlift. weight lift. weights. biceps. strong. flex. scoop. invigorating.
lose. eye. fall apart. blind. poke. stumble. gouge eye. stab eye. ouch. swing. bat. baseball. homerun. home run. sport. sports. hit. ball. batter. red sox. sports. shoot. score. basket. swish. michael
. face. black eye. bad. chicken. boxing. punish. uppercut. discipline. smack yourself. whack. warm up. robot. breakdance. break dance. dance. dance. pop lock. strut. model. runway model.
rfold. pose. playboy. seduce. pose. foreplay. sexy. naughty. ring girls. blum. sexy. walk. sultry. model. gyrate. shake. seduce. playboy. porn. elvis. model. runway. walk. strut. silly walk. ring girls.
dance. danse. conan. obrien. run around. circle. circles. drunk. dizzy. chase yourself. stumble. racecar. run around in circles. act drunk. oi. punk. punk rock. slamdance. fsu helicopter. syd. slam.
e. camera. show. face. look. camera. eye. i want my chicken. my chicken. freak. here kitty. look closely. show body. costume. suit. wing. arm. skim. time. show leg. foot. feet. ankle. hop. bounce.
latley. flaty. lord of the dance. irish. russian dance. dance. point. whree. right. wingspan. lift. show wings. fish. big fish. wide. fat. exaggerate. how big. elbow. wing. arm. knee. muscle. flex.
flex. point. camera. uncle sam. wave. hi. hello. o. what's up. what up. hey. hey there. yo. star. mornin. good morning. good bye. bye. ta. hop. both. bunny. feet. legs. bounce. boing. strike a pose.
ot. your so hot. hott. hot. rub. head. pat. stomach. belly. stomack. stomuck. tummy. abs. waist. midsection. happy. coordinate. rollerblade. roller blade. iceskate. ice skate. bullfight. scrape feet.
ng man. dance. dance. spring. jog. escape. peace. hippy. hippie. piss off. two fingers. two. light fart. gas. hemmroid. burn ass. burn. hot. too much curry. light a fire under. watch tv. turn on
put in a tape. tape the tonight show. sign language. i love you. hang loose. love. rock. barbarian. nejamin. metal. rock. heavy. metal. headbang. awesome. fist. rawk. awesome. too cool. keep the
not worthy. wings. together. flap. fly. rodan. loser. your lying. liar. i dont believe you. stick out. thrust. chest. breast. tights. thighs. big butts. mixalot. i like big. shake. polaroid. picture. shake
break. lay down. sleep. fetal. baby. rest. kick nuts. groin. pain. nap. take a nap. brb. breakdance. worm. dolphin. dance floor. boogaloo. breakin. matador. bull fight. bullfight. toro. ole. give the
. fuck off. flip off. flip me. flip them off. follow the rules. italian. flipping. fuck off. hands. arms. wings. under. chin. flip. your mother. spit. fucker. yo momma. yomomma. your mother. your mom.
. cabage. cabbage. cabbagepatch. dance. love. make love. camera. kiss. slut. seduce. french kiss. jussi. tendercrisp. soldier. creep. rambo. hunt. sneak. crawl. landmine. war. roger rabbit. roger
bend over. forward. forwards. honored. konichwa. bow. drink. drinking bird. look. camera. close. eye. come here. say cheese. play dead. die. fall. pole vault. polevault. track and field. track fild.
way. running man. dance hip hop. jig. split. splits. spread. legs. pain. do the splits. do a split. train. waddle. duck. quwack. quack. hemroid. sore. achy. ache. piroutte. pirowette. pirowet. spin.
breast. laugh. lol. boob. roll.. side. fire. stop. drop. stop drop and roll. roll. sdie. back. ass. meditate. yoga. pilates. diomedes. artemis. lotus. indian. sit. chant. zen. spiritualized. think. tanquil.
dance. mexican. spanish. latin. touch yourself. divynls. rap. yo yo. emak. skip. skipping. trot. trotting. gallop. gallep. joy. glee. spring. happy. walk a dog. walk the dog. shuffle. baby steps. walk
sack. kickball. step in gum. hackeysack. electric slide. dance. soul train. disco. sisters. cheer. pom. pompom. cheerleader. dance. happy. chicken sandwich world championship. xeni. klein.
l. around. spin. dizzy. rotate. move to side. side to side. rock back and forth. sway. swaying. scuttle. crab. shuffle. hustle. swordfight. sword fight. fence. lance. saber. foil. skewer. zorro.
ean. depp. muskateer. zorro. box. boxing. rocky. tyson. fight. punch. brawl. step up. dukes. ali. backflip. trick. show off. leap. okay. ok. whistle. wistle. hoot. hand stand. head. walk. hands. show
tand. handstand. show mouth. eat. inside. throat .bite. bite me. eat me. swallow. tongue. teeth. tap. dance. jig. have it your way. forward. flip. roll. somersault. booya. bump. blow me. my throat
ike.throw. patriots. high five. hi five. show breasts. breasts. tits. titties. slut. tramp. seduce. tatas. jugs. nice. rack. your rack. blow. nose. sneeze. beak. nosebleed. bloody nose. spicy. pledge
ute. thanks. soldier. hang loose. radical. surf. excellent. bill and ted. tubular. bogus. gnarly. eat. wing. smoke. bite fingernails. think. smoke up. toke. toke up. your wing. monkey. ape. gorilla.
a. show ass. elephent. elephant. ollyfant. elefant. bowl. strike. candlepin. ten pin. lebowski. kingpin. bowling. pro bowling. golf. swing. putt. tee. caddy shack. tiger woods. no shit. ass. fuck.
e. suck. dyke. bitch. clit. cum. dildo. feces. felch. foreskin. whore. jizz. jism. masturbate. jerk. anal. bastard. blowjob. butt. suck. choad. erection. fellatio. incest. semen. tit. breakpull penis.
oop. poo. doody. fart. gas. anus. rectum. penthouse. oui magazine. barely legal. leg show. celebrity skin. high society. porn. foreplay. hump. whore. hooker. bulemia. bulimia. vomit. bulemic.
frustrate. math. angry. mad. spicy. clap. lights. light. blackout. darkness. dark. turn off lights. turn off the lights. twist. shake. twist and shout. sit down. armchair. arm chair. tv. rest. take five.
ve. go away. room. get out. depart. scram. like a tree. be free. begone. buhbye. adios. vamoose. go away. pissoff. beat it. get lost. get out. go on. fly. tip. over. launch. over it. do the couch.fish.
. bookcase. read. drink. water. pitcher. liquor. drunk. charles shaw. two buck. chuck. whiskeye. rubenstein. lizstless. rich and mike. booze. gin. vodka. rye. jack and coke. tonic. tipple. warm up.
unce. walk. throw. pickup. pick up. pillows. pillow. cuhion. cushions. rage. mad. destroy. wreck. tantrum. temper. angry. crack knuckles. choke yourself. dust. fingerprint. clean. tidy. tidey. straighten.
t. prepare for match. idea. thought. think. ponder. wonder. pray. prayer. prayers. religion. god.. hope. wwjd. jesus. christ. holy. witness. savior. saved. salvation. epiphany. muy descardo. equity.
ou doing. hows it going. how ya doin. hows it goin. es. yeah. burger king. burger. chicken sandwich. dinner. sandwich. barbarian. rubenstein. tom waits. word up. word. jay leno. leno. thumbs.
tang. rock. paper. scissor. scissors. roshambo. why not. not worthy. beg. grovel. worship. homage. pray tribute. jesus. christ. savior. epiphany. save. bible. god. waynes world. wayne. garth. propose.
o. bawk. cluck. spit. loogie. hurl one. karate kid. crane. kick. kung fu. kung-fu. morita. stroll. walk. around. pace. look. explore. wander. bored. play with yourself. jerk off. take off mask. take off
. naked. nude. take it off. fet naked. take it all off. nekkid. get nekkid. whip em out. show your tits. show yer tits. take off your clothes. off like a prom dress. prom dress. do me. blow me. teke
cow. bse. run. circles. circle. hysterical. excited. freak. madness. manos de clavos. november d. w.c.f.o. run way. excited. freak. leave like a tree. tai-chi. tai. chi. taichi. meditate. kungfu. fight.
et li. lightening bolt. bogus. real. ultimate power. congratulations. thanks. nice job. awesome. omg. amazing. cool. neat. neato. rad. bogus. this is cool. la bomba. kick. couch. sofa. loveseat.
itch. chuck. toss. shot put. garter. sexy. panties. knickers. get yer kit off. plumas picante. bong. hit. get high. you're stoned. weed. chug. funnel. beer. hit. headbutt. sad. hate. disappoint..
ak-a-boo. peakaboo. peek a boo. peek. faceoff. face-off. cotton. look. under. cushions. couch. sparechange. lost. down there. no there. swim. fish. beach. beach party. surfs up. go go. back
sexy leg. seduce. hooker. sex. don the dragon wilson. sexy. sensual. naughty. dance. seduce. build. fort. cushions. pillow. lizstless. hide. bomb shelter. cowboy, lasso. laso. rope. rodeo. shock.
football. 3. point. three. stance. blitz. stance. run. block. camera. espn. superbowl. super bowl. ref. paint. picture. painting. create. creative artist. brush. teeth. beak. get ready. sick. your sick.
. urinate. bathroom. couch. throw pillow. flagellate. masochist. trash. temper. tantrum. wreck. destroy. tokyo. stomp. jonny rotten. punk rock. fsu. fuck shit up. make out. makeout. make-out.
. hug. love. caress. hold. kiss me. love me. hold me. put. place. hawaiin. hawain. hawaii. hawayan. rockaby baby. crispin. show ankle. tag. bracelet. anklet. ankle. ome alone. scared. culkin.
ith girl. random. something different. taco. exercise. side leg lift. thighmaster. statue. dictator. show beak. mouth. pecker teeth. pun. floor. pile. tetris. cluck. walk. question. abs. waist. midsection.
ame. pickle. onion. bun. beef. chicken. sauce. patty. pattie. yum. burger. fish. muy orgelloso. noble y inteligente. show breast. thigh. lift. raise. sit. rest. relax. sake. ass. booty. show me. money.
-up. push. exercise. work out. workout. strength. strong. favorite fighter. inactive. gay. homosexual. homo. gay. osama. saddam. suicide. kill myself. depressed. depression. cartwheel. acrobat.

SUBMIT

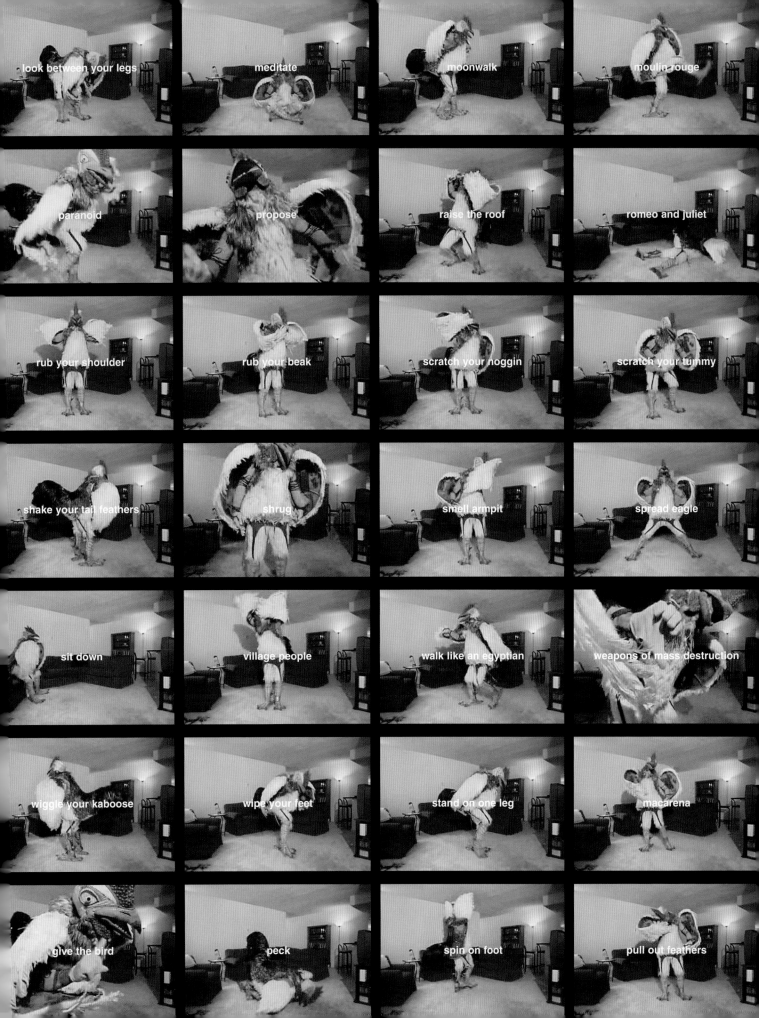

LIVE

2 JAPANESE CIVILIANS HAVE BEEN RELEASED IN IR

...there have been about half a billion hits to the Subservient Chicken website. And in each case the hits have come from people who've decided to go to the site because they'd heard it might be fun. Not a single one of these people had the site forced into their home. They went to be entertained. On average they spent seven minutes getting the Chicken to do all the things they doubted it would really do. On average that's fourteen times the length of time they spend with a 30-second spot. Oh, and the site cost about $50K to create.

Subservient Chicken has become the shorthand in marketing circles for a viral phenomenon. "We want our Subservient Chicken" has been heard on the lips of lots of clients. But a phenomenon is different from a success. We have lots of successes online. But this was different.

People think they are like snowflakes. In fact, we're taught in school that we're all different so that we feel special. We are special. But there is a lot of evidence that we are be more similar than we actually feel. This website is part of the evidence. To create the site, we sent out a picture of the Chicken in a room and asked each person in the agency to fill in the box below with all the crazy requests they could think of. How many things can you ask a chicken in a room to do? You might think that the list would be infinite, but after about 500 responses all we got were the same requests over and over. We kept asking, but we just didn't get any new ones. Now some were perverted, and since this was marketing we had to eliminate those. For instance, if you asked him to "fuck himself," he would just wave his finger at you like, "Shame on you." But if you asked just about anything else, we were ready. So when people thought they were being so clever and asked the chicken to "make a sandwich," he would do it. At which point, people would freak out and wonder if there really was somebody in a room doing what was requested of him. And so they sent the link to friends and they sent to friends millions and millions of times over.

Bottom line: You are not a freaking snowflake. Sorry...

DIRECTIONS:

1. Tear along perfed line
2. Attach tab A to tab B
3. Insert band into mask
4. Put on mask
5. Be subservient

Be the chicken this Halloween. SUBMIT

BURGER KING

HAVE IT YOUR WAY

rock1053.com/pages/virtualstripper/index384.html

subservientblair.com

virtualbartender.beer.com/tammy.swf

oneofthelads.com/carwash.php

subservientdonald.com

Love it or hate it, porn is usually the vanguard of Internet promotional thinking. But Subservient Chicken was something even they hadn't thought of. Not that it stopped them from knocking it off...

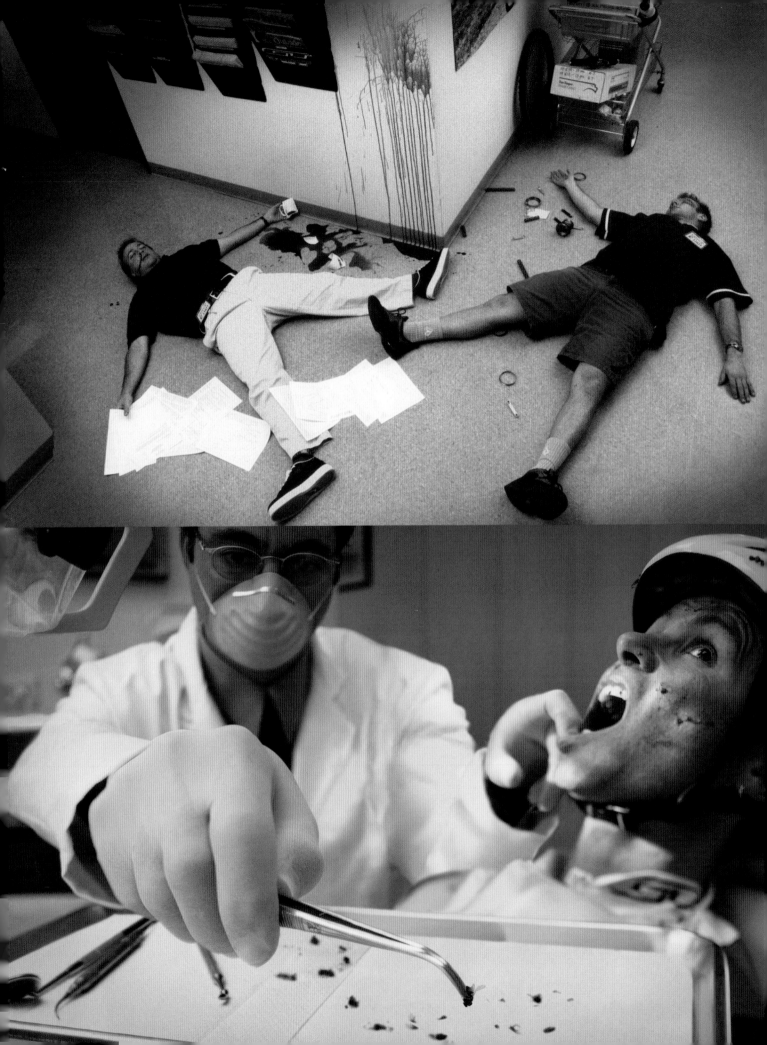

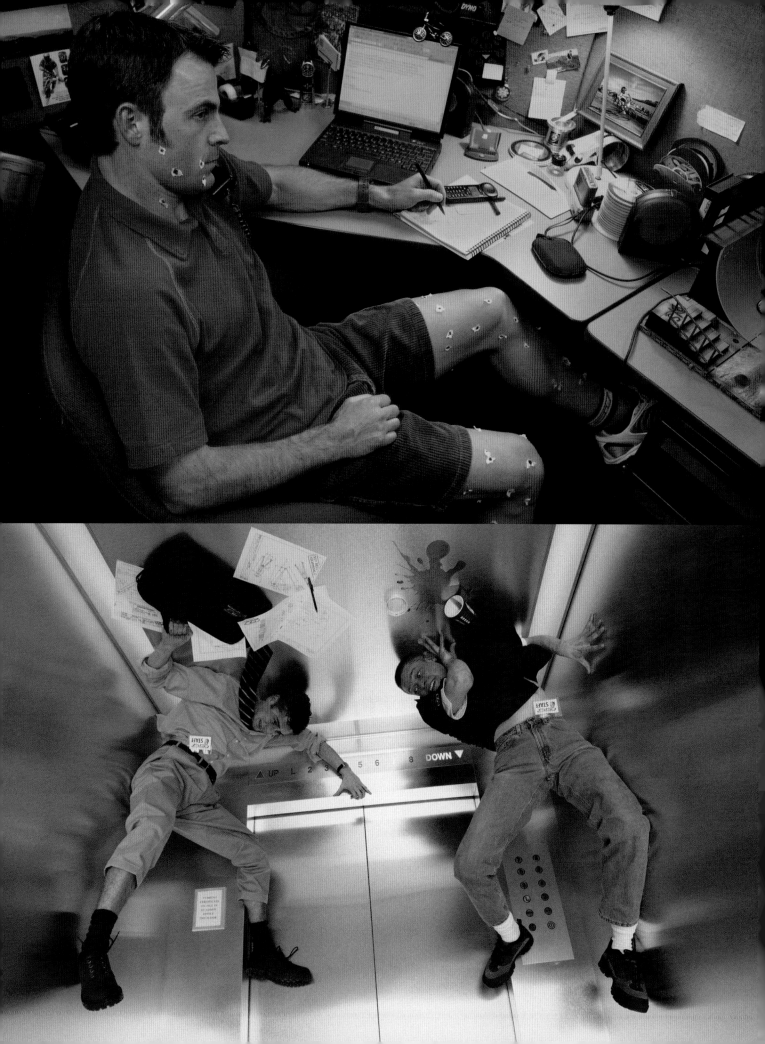

AM 10:00:14

AM 10:00:15

AM 10:00:18

AM 10:00:19

AM 10:00:22

AM 10:00:23

FAST. IT'S CORPORATE POLICY.

QUARANTINE
The delightfully violent driving game.

YVES BEHAR vs CP+B

Hey man, how's it going? Yves: Hey buddy, how are you? Pretty good, its been a while, what's up? Yves: Yeah it's been a while. I saw the Volkswagen stuff a few nights ago. Oh cool, what did you think? Yves: I was like, there you go, once again, you guys did something that I would never have thought of, and that's really good, so I thought the stuff was great. Yeah, we're excited about it, there's so much of it, its going to be pretty fun. So I think I talked to you a little bit a while back about this book that we are making. Yves: Uh…yeah…tell me again what it is you guys are doing? It's a book about the agency, it's called Hoopla. Yves: Oh yeah yeah yeah, of course, I sent you some images and stuff right? Yeah, I don't know if I recieved them yet, but I know we talked about it. Yves: Ok We'll sort that out though. But what we have is, inside the book we are conducting a handful of interviews with people that we work with or that we respect Yves: Ok, fantastic! And this is it, this is the interview. I am at this very moment doing some sort of crazy Charlie Rose shit to you. Yves: Ok So, the first thing I wanted to talk to you about was when the two of us worked together. I think we could start with that first experience. We were first introduced to each other through the MINI Motion Gear project. Yves: Yeah, we were invited by MINI to work on the gear and in parallel you guys were just starting to work on the campaign, so the fun thing was we were thrown together, before we really knew much about one another. I remember there were lots of shared ideas that went outside of what you would typically expect a brand to do. Everybody was really excited in the room because we were all talking about other vehicles to communicate. Whether it was the actual owner's manual, a product, or something you do purely for fun, or something you do for credibility, it seemed like we were reaching out past our respective mediums. That made it exciting for me. Yeah, we sort of got thrown together in this conference room, and it was like, "OK, you guys need to make a bunch of cool stuff that's unique to the Motoring lifestyle, and here are some finger sandwiches and some Diet Coke, we'll check back with you in a few hours." But what I remember, other than being thrown together with very little introduction and some tiny triangular sandwiches, was that we were super stoked to have access to you. To your thinking and your ability to turn ideas into real shit. I have to tell you, with most gear projects, we would never have access to someone with your talent or skill set. The way it normally goes is some shady vendor pulls out a bag of tchotchkies, or we end up trying to cobble together a prototype with whatever is laying around the office. Yves: (laughs) Well, we definitely all agreed very quickly that there would be no tchotchkies. Was it weird being a pure design guy and developing a creative relationship with an advertising agency? Normally agencies and product design guys kind of work in isolation. Hopefully it didn't feel like a total bastardization of what you normally do. Hopefully it was more like a welcome departure or whatever. Yves: I don't look at it as a relationship with an ad agency. Creative relationships are creative relationships no matter what medium you work in. Collaboration is what pushes you forward. You have to believe in it. You can't live in a cave, doing work in isolation. What about chemistry? I know, for us, the chemistry is sacrosanct. It is at least as important, maybe even more so, than pure talent. So how do you feel about teaming up in general? Yves: I think creative relationships/collaborations are tricky and it's rare to find the people you can actually share them with. You should never partner with people for money. You should partner with people based on how far you can push it, and how stimulated you can be with the other creative people in the room. Yeah, I know for us, working with you means we can go farther. The partnership allows us to effect change in the product, and in essence, make pop culture. Yves: Yes, for me, the product is very much at the center of the experience. It's very much at the center of what you want to communicate or what you're about. I think no matter what business you're in, the right way to do it is to conceive your message, the idea of what you're about, at the same time as you are making the actual product. I always find myself pushing for an earlier involvement in the process from agencies. Am I putting the chicken before the egg? The truth is I think they all have to happen at the same time. Yeah, we kinda think the advertising surrounding a product is never going to be as cool as the actual product itself. Yves: You guys actually say that? Yeah, I guess it sounds a little weird coming from the people who are charged with making advertising, but it's the truth. I mean, the advertising for MINI is not as cool as the actual MINI. There's no way it ever could be. It would be a shame if it was. Yves: Right. Right. How do you feel about the ability to invent things from scratch that people can actually use? That they touch and integrate into their lives. It seems like a pretty cool thing to do on a daily basis. What is it like to wield that kind of power? Yves: It's really about participating in culture. I think companies putting products out there intended only for the continuation of the business are dismissing the fact that they participate in culture. Yes, it's a power; but it's a responsibility as well. It goes beyond business. What gets us to do what we all do? What happens when we push business closer toward our personal beliefs? Nothing is more exciting than participating in culture. Business is just a result of proper use of that power. I teach kids at the Miami Ad School a similar thing: that done properly, advertising can be a sort of a wierd voodoo power. Ok, so we are winding down on this interview. I have kind of a silly question: Is it hard to live in your head? You know, to be walking around and go to like an Outback Steakhouse and look at the bathroom and just go, "Ugh."? I always thought it would be kind of a burden to be so visually attuned to the world around you, you know? Yves: No, I don't have that kind of professional defect. You know, moving about the world and bitching about everything that I see. That would be a horrible life. I think I get really passionate when I'm able to intervene, when I'm asked a question about something, when I can give feedback on something. But the rest of the time I'm not particularly tortured about how I want to design everything and how everything should be redone. I think you need to have a positive outlook on things, whether they're yours or not. You can't walk around with a negative outlook.

"Big Meanie"

Frustrated with its hyperactive disposition, Alex Bogusky captured a coworker's labrador retriever and drew thick, scared eyebrows on it with a Sharpie.

○ Fake
○ True

x

HOOPLA COUTURE

If we didn't call ourselves an "advertising agency," we'd go out of business. After all, brands aren't exactly lining up to hire a modular plastic chicken doll agency. But the truth is we make all kinds of things that aren't ads. They're little pieces of pop culture. And they go just as far as million-dollar TV commercials when it comes to making brands famous.

SUBSERVIENT CHICKEN TOY

When we realized, as all companies eventually do, that we needed to make a plastic chicken in garters and a Mexican wrestling mask, we partnered with Tristan Eaton for the design. A perfect injection-molded expression of the BURGER KING® "chicken your way" strategy.

MINI ROBOT TOY

If you want to turn a grown man with $21,500 of disposable income into an overgrown kid with a cool car, make a plastic toy robot. No, this logic isn't perfectly linear, but few aspects of Hoopla are. Hoopla seldom calls for a straight line from A to B. More often than not, it involves doing a bunch of cerebral donuts in between.

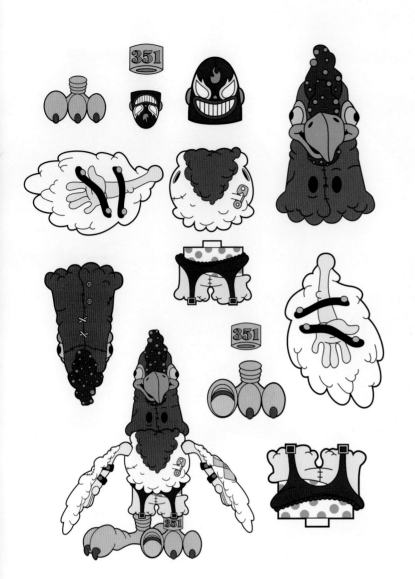

TRUTH T-SHIRTS

One way to participate in pop culture is to find people who are already established within it and seed your message through them. *truth* partnered with some of the most relevant graphic designers in the country to come up with these cool anti-tobacco T-shirts.

MINI MOTION WATCH

When your hands are on the wheel, it can be hard to read the face of a traditional watch. But when you're doing 80 mph through a left-hand sweeper, it's not always a good idea to take your hands off the wheel. Designer Yves Behar came up with a stylish solution to this chronometric conundrum. A MINI Motion watch with digital display that rotates 90 degrees for optimal viewing in even the sharpest of curves.

MINI MOTION JACKET

This jacket features an integrated map case/front pocket that comes with a set of MINI Motoring Maps already zipped inside. And instead of directing Motorers to cheap hotels or all-you-can-eat buffets, each map highlights the area's best curves. Another YB creation.

MINI MOTO-GO GRIP™

Most cars have "oh, shit" handles, those cleverly placed dealies that you grab to prevent ending up in the driver's lap when he takes a hard right. But a MINI Cooper pulls the kind of G's that make the handle inadequate–at least, that was the thinking behind the GRIP™, a cushioned sleeve that we sold on late-night infomercials to celebrate the MINI's renowned cornering ability.

MINI DRIVING BAG

It happens to the best of us. A whitetail deer jumps in front of our car, we stomp on the brakes, and then watch helplessly as whatever we had in the front seat is jettisoned into the dashboard at Mach 1. But hey, nothing to worry about, it was only a G4 laptop and $400 sunglasses. This bag offers Motorers a stylish solution to Front Seat Stuff Ejection Syndrome (pronounced "fsehs") by clipping right into the MINI's OEM safety restraint system. You guessed it, by Yves Behar.

PUMA DRIVING SHOE

Motoring is not driving. It's driving for the sheer pleasure of driving. And as any podiatrist can tell you, pleasure begins with the feet. So we combined forces with Puma and designed the MINI Motion shoe, a soft inner shoe designed for long road trips and a more protective outer shoe for the heavier clutch work of in-town trips. By Yves Behar.

BURGER KING

HAVE IT YOUR WAY*

EST. 1954

This cup makes a statement about you. It says,"Hey, look at me, I'm an ambitious yet responsible person." You could have gone larger, but you didn't. You could have gone smaller, but, again, you deferred. No, you know exactly what you want in life- nothing more, nothing less. It's good when you **HAVE IT YOUR WAY.***

BURGER KING® CUP

Writing copy for the side of a BURGER KING® cup isn't exactly the world's most high-profile project. Until you find out that a BURGER KING® cup gets the same number of media impressions as a Super Bowl TV spot. Then it pretty much IS the world's most high-profile project.

HALLOWEEN MASK
SUBSERVIENT CHICKEN

If you didn't want to trick-or-treat as the King, you could go as a giant, humanoid chicken. How do thousands of people walking around in chicken masks translate to a spike in chicken sandwich sales? Hell if we know.

HALLOWEEN IS OVER
BUT THE FUN HAS JUST BEGUN

HALLOWEEN MASK
BURGER KING®

Conventional wisdom dictates that the mascots and/or iconic characters should be infinitely likeable. But since Hoopla flies in the face of conventional wisdom, we made Burger King's icon kinda creepy. And we celebrated the creepiness by creating and distributing this Halloween mask.

CP+B BAG

Back in the old days, if you were some kind of gunslinger and your gun didn't come out of its holster very fast, then, well, that was not so good. Same thing when your job is firing off killer ideas on a moment's notice. With lightning-quick side access to your laptop, this bag gives the wearer a major drop on the competition.

TRUTH CLOTHING LINE

Turning the target into media is one of the most powerful things a brand can do. So *truth* spent time making some really cool clothes. Next thing you know, there are all these people walking around, taking the message places media giants like Viacom and Starcom and Humongocom could never really go.

If you are reading this book, there is a reasonably good chance you are a mutant.

The mere act of picking up a book as unconventional as this one would indicate you are seeking out things that are different, perhaps because you are aware of being a bit different yourself. Mutants tend to seek out one another.

If you are, in fact, a mutant, the good news is that according to the philosophy of Crispin Porter + Bogusky, we are currently living in an age in which a mutant is not a bad thing to be. In fact, the CP+B worldview holds that at this moment in time, mutants actually kind of *rule*.

Consider what's happening in the current business environment: In recent years, a newly evolved breed of entrepreneurial marketers–some emerging from the coastal surf/skateboard culture, others from Silicon high-tech, still others from the coffeehouse culture of Seattle, not to mention countless other off-the-radar spots–have crawled from the primordial muck to challenge the existing business establishment and its ossified ways. These mutant companies and brands have embraced unconventional business practices, fresh approaches, and novel ways of connecting with a new generation of consumers.

Meanwhile, that consumer audience–a.k.a. the public–has also begun to mutate in interesting ways. Mutation occurs when changing conditions force organisms to adapt; and in an age of information explosion, people *had* to mutate so they could manage to breathe in all that new information without drowning in it. With the rise of the Internet, the growth of digital personalized media, and the constantly multiplying array of entertainment and communications options, the only way to navigate and survive was for people to develop mutant multimedia, multitasking skills that simply did not exist among those in the previous generation. These new powers enabled people not only to consume information but also to absorb it, reshape it, and use it for their own individualized purposes.

All of this has major ramifications for anyone who would aspire to create Hoopla in the current day and age. In a nutshell, it means that *the old rules no longer apply when it comes to communicating effectively, building a brand, making something famous, or creating a cultural phenomenon of any type*. The trouble with the old rules, observes CP+B's Alex Bogusky, is quite simply that "they are freaking *old*." Most were created for another era, when there was less noise, less hype, less technology; a time when the people you might be trying to communicate with were easier to reach and influence–before they developed advanced mutant powers enabling them to sort, filter, manipulate, or just ignore information.

To have any hope of successfully adapting in this new and highly evolved communications landscape, it can help immensely if you happen to be a mutant yourself. And so, mutation is a good place to begin on the road to making Hoopla. The good news is, it's never too late to begin the mutation process or to accelerate it. Though it doesn't hurt if, from the very outset, you see yourself as an entirely different breed.

Such was the case with CP+B, whose own evolution is a good example of how mutation can and quite often does occur well outside the mainstream, in places where no one is even looking. The agency seems to have quietly risen from the surf of Miami Beach, whereupon it began to steadily grow and develop, largely off the radar of the Madison Avenue advertising establishment. Being far removed from big agencies and big media allowed CP+B to evolve as an independent species. "Those guys weren't breathing the same air as everybody else in advertising," observes Brian Collins, a top creative executive at the Ogilvy & Mather agency in New York. "Instead of being surrounded by ad people, they were surrounded by artists, music people, and the whole South Beach culture."

Alex Bogusky was a homegrown product of that culture, a Miami kid with an interest in graphic design and dirt-bike racing. He linked up with Chuck Porter, a longtime freelance copywriter who had come to Miami primarily to windsurf, then decided to join a small Miami ad agency as partner and creative director. Porter bought out agency founder Sam Crispin, hired Bogusky, and the two of them gradually took that small agency and began to turn it into something different and a little strange.

They didn't know all that much about how an established, professional ad agency was supposed to operate, which seemed to work in their favor. "Chuck and I were freelancers who wound up running an agency, so we were never taught what to do," says Bogusky. Being in an advertising backwater like Miami, the agency tended to hire others who were similarly lacking in big-agency experience–"mutts," to use Bogusky's term. Porter's own feeling was that experience was overrated anyway: "Experience matters only to the degree that the future's going to be like the past," he says. "From day one, our hiring priorities were brains, talent, and passion. Everything else you can teach." The partners weren't interested in being told the "right" way to do things; they wanted to figure it out for themselves. And Bogusky believes this might be an important first lesson for anyone looking to communicate in a way that truly stands out: You have to first separate yourself from the "mainstream" as much as possible.

The agency attracted and sought out people with eclectic backgrounds, often unrelated to advertising. Many of them brought skills and hobbies–', zine publishing, T-shirt making, music–that would later prove useful as the agency gradually began to create various forms of pop culture and "Hoopla Couture" for clients, instead of just ads. Another common denominator among those who gravitated to CP+B seemed to be a love of adventurous living: There were bikers, surfers, and skateboarders, known for playing as hard as they worked. One former employee noted that the agency "seemed to approach advertising as an extreme sport," relishing risks and challenge. "We benefited from a kind of forced inbreeding," Bogusky says. As for the downside of isolation—the problem of being too far removed from the power centers—Bogusky says the Web helped solve that issue, making it easier to "connect" from anywhere. ("The Web is responsible for the rabid takeover of the mutants," he says.)

Within the walls of the agency, everything seemed to happen rapidly; people were known to skateboard through the halls, meetings were held on the fly, and ideas flew around at the speed of light. Perhaps not surprisingly, a number of the early clients that gravitated to CP+B were, themselves, associated with "extreme" activities and mutant culture: biking companies, video gamers, makers of hiking shoes and surf gear. Like CP+B, these companies tended to be in a hurry. "These brands had neither the time nor the resources to adhere to the traditional slow-build model of brand-building," says CP+B's Paul Keister. "They had to quickly become relevant and then maintain momentum—or perish. For them, it was survival of the fastest."

Such companies were also willing to experiment to try and find new ways of connecting with a younger, more media-savvy audience. That helped provide CP+B with the freedom to begin to establish new rules as it went along. And if clients did *not* provide enough creative freedom to the agency, CP+B tended to part ways with those clients. Early on, Porter developed a reputation (rare in the ad industry) for being willing to walk away from lucrative accounts that did not allow the agency to do its best work. Herein lies another potential lesson for those who would aspire to mutate to a more creative form of communication: Being a mutant requires a certain amount of resolve because mainstream forces can easily suck you back into the muck of the established way of doing things.

From the outset, the agency's work bore the signs of mutation. It hadn't quite evolved to be full-blown Hoopla yet, but it was clearly a departure from conventional ads. "We had small clients with small budgets," says Porter, "so we had to use imagination instead of money." Many early ads favored understatement, which stood out in an ad world that typically overexplained and oversold. When CP+B was asked to promote a Gametek video game that involved car crashes, the agency's ad managed to stand out by dispensing with the trusted tools of a print ad—there was no headline, no copy—and opting for a purely visual message in the form of a stark, arresting illustration that suggested a blood-covered windshield. Another series of early ads by the agency, for the bicycle-components company Shimano, also did away with basic explanatory elements and presented an intriguing story of espionage, told primarily through pictures; it was up to the reader to connect the serial parts of the story and figure out what was going on. As CP+B was mutating and developing its own rules on how to reach people, one of the early rules seemed to be: Respect the intelligence of the people you're trying to influence—and play to their natural curiosity.

Gradually, the agency began to play with the basic format of advertising. Bogusky was taken with the radical idea that an advertisement didn't have to follow the forms everyone was used to. (i.e., a 30-second commercial or a print ad). Instead, it could mutate into other forms—basically anything that might command attention and thereby make a brand famous. CP+B began to think of what it was creating not just as "ads" but more along the lines of something that could be called "creative content"; such content could not only be designed and molded not just for traditional ad media, such as TV, print publications, and billboards, but could also be distributed on T-shirts and in online films, live events, books, or something that hadn't even been invented yet.

A good example of this was an early campaign the agency created to raise contributions for a local homeless shelter in Miami. The shelter didn't have enough money to pay for expensive TV commercials, so "we found ways to cheat a little and still get noticed," says Bogusky. They did so by transforming ordinary shopping carts, trash dumpsters, and park benches into ad vehicles, putting signs with the word "closet" on the shopping carts, "bed" on the benches, and "kitchen" on the dumpsters; these one-word headlines were explained by a line of copy underneath: "When you're homeless, the world looks different." "It wasn't just the coolest TV spot or the coolest billboard," explains Lee Clow, Executive Creative Director of TBWA/Chiat Day; "it was actually an idea, a media concept, and a way of delivering a message that was totally different from anything that'd been done in the business."

One of the most important ideas in those early years was for a tiny, cash-strapped athletic-shoe company named AND 1. The company was under pressure from retailers to promote itself Nike-style, by relying on superstar endorsers. Since AND 1 couldn't possibly afford to play in that league, CP+B devised a plan for the company to "create fame" for a previously unknown streetball player. At first, using found video footage of Rafer "Skip to my Lou" Alston in action, the agency produced a VHS tape called the AND 1 Mixtape, Vol 1. Set to unreleased music and featuring 17 minutes of dazzling playground basketball moves never seen in the NBA or anywhere else, the tape quickly became a pass-along, word-of-mouth phenomenon. On Internet chat rooms, basketball fans worldwide clamored for copies of the tapes, which were scarce and therefore sought-after. It was the agency's first brush with eBay, where boxes of tapes that were supposed to be given away for free were being sold for nearly $50 apiece. Soon, without any conventional media placements, the Mixtape had established AND 1 as a leader in the basketball category—second only to Nike.

The success of the first tape found Alex Burnard and agency producer Rupert Samuel on a two-week scouting trip in NYC, where they were given the task to "make more." They returned with the AND 1 Mixtape, Vol 2, and an entire roster of unknown streetball players for AND 1 to sign to contract. These players would become the nucleus of an eventual series of tapes that spawned an entire subcategory in the world of basketball. Volume 3 of the series had the players embarking on a summer tour that set the table for an ESPN television show, a world tour, and even a video game. A few years later, AND 1's low-budget streetball heroes were gracing the cover of *Sports Illustrated*—all confirming the agency's original thesis that it was possible to "create" fame without having to purchase it.

It was the first of a number of break-the-rules successes for the agency. In fact, according to CP+B's Burnard, the agency gradually became aware that "just about every major success we had came as a result of a conscious decision to reject a basic premise or fundamental principle of our industry or of our clients' category." Among the violated principles: the notion that advertising had to be expensive; that it had to take certain basic forms, as dictated by the existing media; and that ad messages had to be clearly spelled out and then repeated over and over to get through to people.

In successfully flouting these rules, the agency began to form some of the basic principles of creating Hoopla, an evolving form of communication that seemed to have inherent advantages over the old model, in that it could achieve more impact with less money, could seep more deeply into the culture, and could connect particularly well with younger consumers who'd mutated to the new media way of life. But it was in many ways harder to create this new kind of communication. It required constant inventiveness—not just in crafting a stream of original and compelling messages but also in coming up with diverse and unique ways to deliver those messages and enable them to connect.

The chapters ahead will examine how the agency fueled that inventiveness, and how it forged those connections, on major campaigns that would have a significant impact on the popular culture and on the world of marketing, branding, and communications. But it's worth noting that none of it would've been possible if the agency hadn't started with the basic recognition and belief that it was fundamentally different from other, existing organisms of its type and that therefore the rules, habits, and ways of those old organisms did not apply. The agency had to embrace its own mutant status, and revel in being an outsider.

Likewise, for others embarking on La Vida Hoopla, mutation is where it all begins, CP+B maintains. Whether you're a company building a brand, an ad agency, a publicist, a graphic designer, a blogger, or anyone looking to get a message out and create buzz, you have to start with a commitment to doing things your own original way. As CP+B's Wojtek Szumowksi advises, "Mutation is a license for interpretation." Even long-established, mainstream entities can begin to move in this direction—they can unlock their inner mutant—by starting with an attitude adjustment. If you simply resolve to be different—to look beyond established rules, to seek out unusual influences, to bring in outsiders, to experiment—then you'll have taken the first step on the road to what's next.

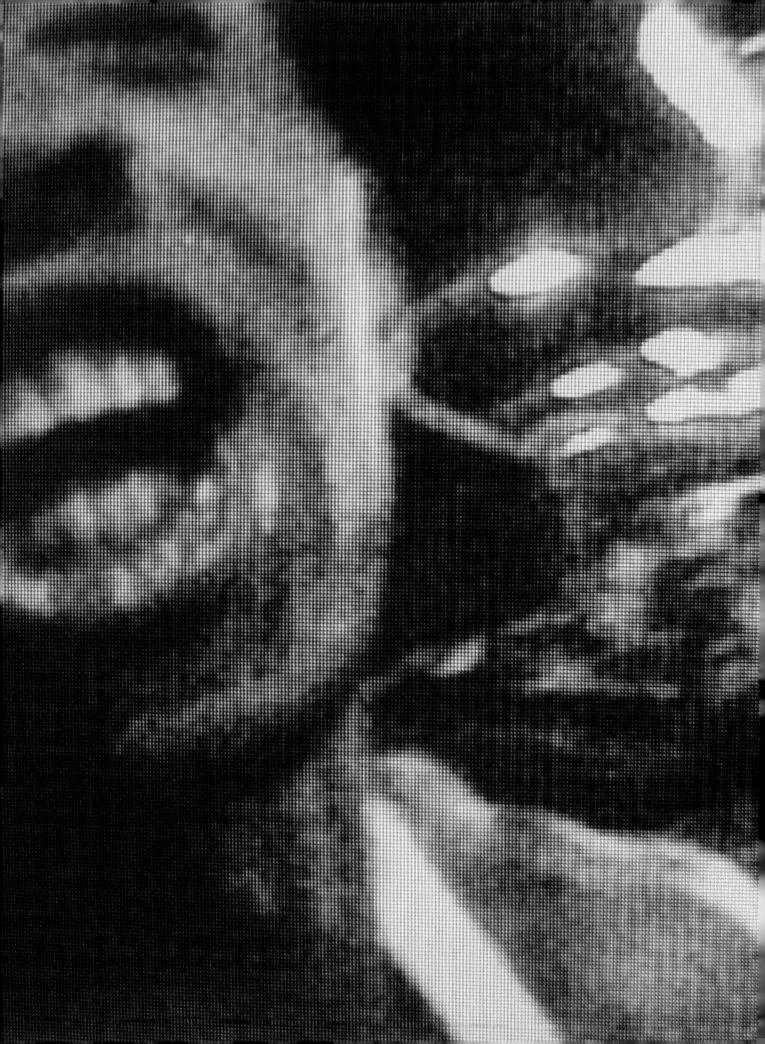

"... it was similar to the effect of the films WILD STYLE and BEAT STREET when they hit Europe in the mid '80s!!"

—BOUNCE Magazine

BOBBITO vs CP+B

Hello? Bobbito: Yeah, how you doing? Hey, man, how's it going? Bobbito: Good. So, last time we hung out was like a long long long time ago Bobbito: Uh-huh. George Stork introduced us. Bobbito: Yeah, George. That was when we had you come out for that first taping. Bobbito: Yeah, yeah. So long ago. Bobbito: I lived in New Jersey. I was just watching that shit last night Oh, really? Bobbito: Yeah, I'm like, yo, why did I go out there looking so ungroomed? (Laughs.) Cuz you didn't know it was going to be this big thing, maybe? Bobbito: Nah, I mean (laughs) I didn't know ten years later people would still be watching it. Yeah, right? Bobbito: My my facial hair looked, I mean 'cause I'm a barber so like whenever I make public appearances I try to look well groomed, you know. Yeah. Bobbito: Anyway. But uh, yeah cool. Nah I definitely remember that. Alright, let's start. So first off I'd like you to just kind of explain who you are and what you do for anyone that doesn't know. It's hard for me to kinda describe to people all of the hundreds things that you're into. Bobbito: Yeah, yeah I'm kinda a multi-media person. I'm a DJ, club DJ, former radio DJ here in New York for twelve years. I'm also a columnist with *Vibe* magazine, the editor-in-chief of *Bounce Magazine*, and the author of *Where'd You Get Those? New York City Sneaker Culture 1960 to 1987*. So how'd you get into *Bounce Magazine*? Bobbito: *Bounce* we started in 2003. It was after I completed the book and was kinda looking for other venues to write about basketball because I really enjoyed it. There were three of us originally and then it became four and we all just had the common goal of uncovering the underground of basketball. Which had just come to the attention of the masses, but there wasn't really a magazine that was completely dedicated to it. It was definitely getting coverage in *Slam*, and starting to get coverage in other magazines but we didn't really see a whole publication and you know every issue dedicated to playground. We arrived at the same kind of situation when we started working with AND 1. Bobbito: Mmhhm. We noticed that there really wasn't any kind of mention of playground basketball anywhere. The only stuff you could find, if you did your research, were some Nike ads that talked about a bunch of guys that were in their 60s. No disrespect to them. Bobbito: That's right though. That work was more about retelling legend and folklore versus telling like it actually was happening today. We figured that nearly all innovation in basketball history had come from outside the NBA. So, if we could nurture that innovation and figure out a way to tell everyone, things would work out. Bobbito: True. I like what you are doing though. You are really showcasing it. Bobbito: Yeah, well we've done six issues. We have a website called theplayground.com. We're about to drop our seventh issue in March. You know I'm really proud of what we done. Pre-Mixtapes, what do you think the atmosphere regarding basketball was like in terms of on the streets and even outside of New York? Bobbito: Yeah, well, there was definitely a culture of basketball outside of school and the pros. I mean for as long as the sport has existed, it's been there. But unfortunately it really wasn't a mainstream thing outside of little mentions in books. For example, *The City Game* by Pete Axthelm, that's kind of like the granddaddy of, you know, coverage of playground legends. You know they mention Earl Manigault and they talked about the Rucker and the 60s and the 70s and then from there you have Rick Telander's *Heaven is a Playground* where he stayed a whole summer in Brooklyn and followed Albert King and Fly Williams. And then, you had the *In Your Face Basketball Book* by Alex Wolf. That's like that's the bible right there. That was the first book that outlined like every single playground across the country that where you could play ball and rated each court. Yeah, I have that. Bobbito: So those are the beginnings. But those are all in printed form. As far as film footage, or radio coverage, it was kind of nonexistent. And so there was this whole world that existed of incredible basketball that basically went unnoticed to the rest of the world. Cuz you can't compete with the marketing budgets and the advertising dollars that's spent on promoting the NCAA and the NBA. Yeah. Bobbito: So everyone just thought, "Wow, the greatest basketball we can watch is going on in the NBA arenas." It's because that's what's been said to you all your life. Yeah, there was a sort of stylistic monopoly. Bobbito: Yeah. And meanwhile, there's this incredible amount of players, this incredible aesthetic, this incredible subculture, this incredible statement of being that exists from the playground and it's unfortunate because like you said, with all the older legends, there's really not much, if any video footage of them. No one knew about it. Yeah. Bobbito: So, when you guys and AND 1 put out Volume One of Skip and you saw raw footage of him playing and playground tournaments, I mean it flipped the world upside down. Cuz all of a sudden every kid that didn't live uptown or didn't know about that kind of basketball, it was brought straight to their homes. All of a sudden the fear of having to go into a rough neighborhood to watch a basketball game became alleviated. You didn't have to face that to see great street athleticism. You could just watch it from your home so that really flipped the whole door open. The accessibility. And then from there, Volume Two came out and now it's like an annual thing that kids look out for. And the style of play that's presented in in these tapes is very pervasive. That accessibility is what excited us. We wanted kids to spend hours practicing this stuff. To look at it from AND 1's point of view—a kid spent fifteen minutes with their brand watching it, a ton more minutes playing it back over and over and then hours practicing it. A company that size can't buy that kind of attention. Bobbito: Yeah, now you see a kid from any place in the world, who years ago you get identified as, "Oh he's not from New York." You know now, it's like you can't tell. There's guys in Cape Town and London that play like they're from uptown. Bobbito: Yeah, they dress the same, they have the same sort of gestures and the same style and same level of creativity and so now you know it's great. I think it's improved the game by expanding the game. It's expanded the horizons of creativity in the game of basketball and it's presented an alternative that lets people decide. I can enjoy organized ball or I can enjoy, just sort of, raw basketball. When we started doing this, it was all about blowing up AND 1.

So we had ideas to turn the Mixtape into a traveling tour, a videogame, a TV show. The works. One of the things we didn't think about was that we would be creating an alternative route of success for basketball players. There was a segment on the ESPN show that had Alimoe on it and he was talking about how he always wanted to play professionally. The Mixtapes and the tour have redefined what that means. He was like, "I don't have to be in the league, I can provide for my family other ways." Bobbito: Right. It kind of fucked me up. Bobbito: Sure, and he can play an enjoyable brand of basketball, too. I mean, you gotta understand if you're not playing in the NBA, you're playing in CBA or you're playing overseas. You're playing very structured basketball. And I'm not taking anything away from the AND 1 coaches, but essentially, they're not running plays out there. It's very similar to when you play in a park. When you go to a pickup game in a park you don't have a coach on the sides subbing you in and out when you're playing poorly. Yeah. Bobbito: You don't have a coach on the side you know telling you like, "Yo, make sure you set a pick for this dude," and, "Let's run an inbounds play." You're basically just going off the top of your head every single play on instinct. And to say, "Yo we want to stay on the court. This is how we're going to do it." That's a beautiful thing. I think that's a beautiful moment. Yeah. Bobbito: And it's a moment that I live for daily. There are obviously a lot of other people that enjoy doing it and watching it, too. I want to talk more about the money in the NBA and the NCAA and the influence that it has. When we first started working with AND 1, one of the things that we came across with them is that the more successful they became, the more the buyers and the distributors at the shoe stores kind of forced them into a different kind of marketing. They wanted them to emulate a kind of pro-endorser model that worked for Jordan. Bobbito: Mmhhm. And with the money that they had, they were trying to be in that thing. With the guys like Rex Chapman and Raef Lafrentz and so forth. Bobbito: Yeah. And so the tapes were really just like a thing I think that came out of an "OK, that's not gonna work for you, you're going to fail," let's figure out a new way. And we took a lot of influence from skate companies, trying to figure out how can we be aggressive and small and scrappy and get something out there and see what can happen. Bobbito: Yeah. When you saw the first tapes, would you ever have been able to predict this being as big as it's gotten? Bobbito: Um, I think the first tape is, like, that's classic. That's legendary. For me, it was gratifying because I was a teammate of Skip at one point out in Queens in a tournament called "Over the Rim." But you know, I never saw any video footage. And I definitely heard about his exploits at EBC, but I never got to go up there and watch him cuz I was always playing myself. Yeah. Bobbito: Am I surprised by how popular it became? Nah, not really. There was nothing ever really out there like that and it was strong. You know? Could I have predicted that they they would like be doing national tours, and big arenas from that? No, I couldn't have predicted that. But I definitely wasn't surprised by AND 1's popularity after Volume One and Volume Two. Could you talk a little bit about the first couple tapes? They were pretty authentic. For sure more authentic than the big arena tours it started turning into. There's a bunch of criticism about the guys being the modern-day Globe Trotters... Bobbito: Mmhhm ...and so forth. You mentioned earlier how you think it's good for basketball. But can you talk about what you think some of the people are getting at when they are saying it's detracting from basketball? Bobbito: There's definitely critics that say it detracts from basketball because it's, it's like I said, basketball in a very raw and unorganized sense and there is illegal dribbling, but to me it's entertainment. Yeah. Bobbito: And as long as kids are obviously flocking to go see it—to either watch the videos or to watch the live games then it obviously has a value. And just as I can watch the Harlem Globe Trotters take a rubber band and throw a basketball towards the rim and have it bounce back to them with the rubber band, and find that entertaining, I can also find entertaining somebody dribbling down the court and carrying the ball and dribbling out of bounds and coming back in without the referee blowing his whistle. That's entertaining to me, too. Just as I find it entertaining to watch a game with a whole bunch of X's and O's, and see a beautifully executed backdoor cut. I love basketball. I don't even have to watch a game I could just see a kid dribbling in front of a barber shop window looking at his reflection and I find the beauty in that. So that's where my head is at. I think any true basketball enthusiast would see a great, great value in all of it. That's cool. I know the first time, when we were out in Linden. We were like up there for what, a week and a half, I think. And George was just bringing us around to like two or three games all over the city pretty much a day. And we didn't think we had enough for the tape really, remember? So we talked to Wally Dixon (at Main Event). He helped us organize some guys together out in Linden. Bobbito: Yeah. And I remember just being freaked out. I was one of the camera guys and I was dropping the camera because I had never ever seen a half-court bounce pass ally-oop before. Bobbito: Right, right, right. It was like finding the pyramids for the first time or something. Bobbito: Ha. Yeah, I remember I was invited to play in that game. I remember I saw I'll Be Right Back make a move, where he was warming up, where he threw the ball behind his back and then did a hand change back to the same hand and I was just like "Holy shit." I felt like I had some tricks in my game, but I didn't feel like I was on that level. He was doing some extraterrestrial shit. You know? I got intimidated I was like, "Uh…maybe I'll just DJ." (Laughs.) Bobbito: Which I regret to this day because I kinda feel like if I'd gotten in that game and just gotten off one or two passes, I woulda had a highlight. And would have been immortalized. I mean, anyone in that Volume Two is immortalized at this point. Yeah. Bobbito: But it's all good. Well, I think that's pretty much everything. Bobbito: Cool. Well, good luck with the book and good luck with the agency and everything. No problem. Hey, we'll send you a copy and let you check it all out. Bobbito: Sweet, bro. Alright, man. Bobbito: Alright. Be good my brother. Take it easy, bye.

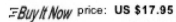
er or seller of this item? <u>Sign in</u> for your status

<u>Watch this item</u> in My eBay | <u>Email to a friend</u>

 *Buy It Now* price: **US $17.95**

(Buy It Now >)

Best Offer: **<u>Submit Best Offer</u>**

Time left: **2 hours 16 mins**
7-day listing, Ends Jul-18-05 09:40:56 PDT

Start time: Jul-11-05 09:40:56 PDT

Item location: Yeadon, PA
United States

Ships to: Worldwide

Shipping costs: Check item description and payment instructions or contact seller for details

 <u>Shipping, payment details and return policy</u>

Seller information

selrahs7315 (0)
  Feedback Score: 0 feedback reviews
  Member since Apr-30-04 in United States

<u>Read feedback comments</u>

<u>Add to Favorite Sellers</u>

<u>Ask seller a question</u>

<u>View seller's other items</u>

<u>Safe Buying Tips</u>

---

ription (revised)

Specifics - Movies: Other Formats

Format: --
Sub-Format: --

Genre: **Sports**
Condition: **New**

PAY CLOSE ATTENTION!!!

BEFORE HOT SAUCE, SIK WIT IT AO,THE PROFESSOR,THE MOUNTIAN DEW COMMERCIALS,AND THE BIG CONTRACTS

THERE WAS ONE MAN........

SKIP TO MY LOU

OFTEN IMITATED NEVER DUPLICATED

THIS IS THE FIRST AND 1 MIXTAPE,THIS VOLUME STARTED IN NEW YORK,then slowly but shortly started to spread out everywhere.This mixtape includes skip to my lou,with clips from 91' to 94'.And 1 never commercially released this tape,So the rarenest is high.Check out the young skip to my lou [around 17],the originator of th culture.And check out some of the ballers that play today on and one, back in the day,such as main event,alimoe,future,the dribblin machine.

YOU AND 1 FANATICS!!!

eBay: AND ONE MIXTAPE VOL.1!!!!!!!!!!!...4058 end time Jul-18-05 09:40:56 PDT)

http://cgi.ebay.com/ws/eBayISAPI.dll?ViewItem&ite Google

eBay: AND ONE MIXTAPE VOL.1!!!!!!!!!!!...4058 end time Jul-18-05 09:40:56 PDT)

http://cgi.ebay.com/ws/eBayISAPI.dll?ViewItem&ite Google

Name: Travis G. "BrickLayin"
Email: X▮▮▮▮▮▮▮▮▮▮▮.com
Location: Houston
Date: Monday, May 22, 19100 at 15:13:48
Comments:
The And1 Mix Tapes are off the Hook!!!! I will be visiiting New York soon and im gonna come see Bad Boy whip some Ass!!!!!

Name: DJ Blakk
Email: m▮▮▮▮▮_▮▮▮▮▮▮tboy@hotmail.com
Location: New Orleans, LA USA
Date: Sunday, May 7, 19100 at 01:04:08
Comments:
Wazup I just wanna give big ups to my man Future, man got mind-bogglin' handlez. And big ups to Skip, dat kid iz unbelievable. Somebody please hola at me here in da N.O. on where I can get dat and 1 mix tapes vol.2 and 3.
One

Name: Tim G. aka "Steady"
Email: t▮▮▮▮▮▮▮@hotmail.com
Location: Macon, GA US
Date: Wednesday, May 17, 19100 at 11:37:33
Comments:
Will someone send me a copy of the and1 videos? Ok who were they talking about in the commercials, Shaq or Stack, what's the story, who got dunked on and by who? Again, Run-N-Gun Basketball is the team that everyone loves to hate. If there are any more tournaments(especially pro-am tournaments) around and you want a quality team from the south, email me and I will bring the dirty south to your town. Fill free to e-mail me, and much love to the brothers that play at the rucker, one day I'll be there!!!!
Tim G. aka "Steady"

Name: Rusty H. "Special K"
Email: r▮▮▮▮▮▮▮▮▮▮il.com
Location: Nap-Town, Indiana US
Date: Wednesday, May 17, 19100 at 01:48:22
Comments:
Skip got some handles. I saw em on the AND1 commercial though. TIGHT HANDLES. Anyone know where i can get the AND1 vol tapes e-mail me. i will pay straight loot for em. SPECIAL K ebcause i leave the mutha f***** KRIPLED with my Krossover

----

Name: D. Martin
Email: D▮▮▮▮▮▮▮▮▮▮▮@hotmail.com
Location: Columbia, SC USA
Date: Sunday June 18 19100 at 12:29:18
Comments:
I am 14 years old and been ballen since I was about 4. I never seen no s***t like that the rucker. Main Event, Future, Biz, I'll be right back and Whole lot of game be rippin the court, I moveing to NYC and u will deffinetely see me playing for my age group because I be killing niggaz with my cross and be making the net pop with my jumper. Keep doing what u doing EBC and represent for Rucker. Pease!!!!

Name: Jermaine L. "MR TOON"
Email: n▮▮▮▮▮▮▮▮▮l.com
Location: Gardena, CA USA cuzz
Date: Thursday, May 18, 19100 at 04:13:36
Comments:
Yo this is a tight page and every hooper would enjoy the mix tapes, I wish cali had some crap like that but all we got is venice beach, any hoopers got street game in cali come to Venice Beach in cali ask who toon is... and why my nigga rafer didnt get no time on volume 2? ???

Name: Michael C. aka Streaker
Email: m▮▮▮▮▮▮▮▮▮▮▮▮.com
Location: columbus, oh US
Date: Sunday, May 14, 19100 at 02:16:44
Comments:
I THINK AND 1 MIXTAPES ARE THE TIGHTEST BASKETBALL TAPES I SEEN, ME AND MY DUDES (ILLEST IN THE LAND, SOMETIMES NASTY, SWEET TOUCH, AND RAW DAWG) CAN SEE THE PEOPLE AT RUCKER PARK. WE ONLY IN HIGH SCHOOL

Name: Benny 'Smoothie" K
Email: ▮▮▮▮▮▮▮▮▮▮▮▮▮
Location: the LOUIS, MO US of A
Date: Thursday, May 11, 19100 at 22:12:07
Comments:
The mixed tapes..... the SH*T

Name: Joshua Fears
Location: Valley, AL USA
Date: Monday, May 8, 19100 at 13:38:44
Comments:
i saw the and1 mixed tape volume 2 and it was tight. next summer i am planning on
visiting the rucker. I would liek to know how i can become part of one of the
teams and would like to get the and1 volumes 1,2,3,and4mixed tapes. currently i am
working on my game and i have improved greatly. i would like to learn more of the
moves that i can get the crowds hype.

Name: SHY
Email: k■■■■■■■■■■■■■■■.com
Location: Inglewood, CA USA
Date: Sunday, May 21 19100 at 15:48:34
Comments:
Future and Headache is tight. Half Man-Half Amazing is tight and so is Nappy.
I've seen both the And 1 mix tapes and they are real.

Name: Byron W. "Lockdown"
Email: l■■■■■■■■■■■■■■.com
Location: LV, NV
Date: Sunday, May 7, 19100 at 00:57:22
Comments:
Yo, Does anyone know how to get the And 1 Mix Tape volume 1? I got vol.2 already.

Slam mag
6-17-2000 4:54 PM
I can sell you "The Remix" if you'd like it will be copied onto a high quality VHS Tape. If interested email me at:
bba■■■■■■■■■■■■■.com
----

jflballer
6-17-2000 5:23 PM
Go to a Footaction store and the employees might sell u one or give you one if u ask them. Volume 1 was free, volume
2 I got w/the tochillin' lows and I'll buy a remix off of a footaction employee prolly this weekend.... lata ballas
----

thabombkid
6-05-2000 9:11PM
I got this move thats just too ill. My boys call it the "Ill Move." I think if they saw it, they'd put a pic of it
on the cover of AND1 mixtape Vol. 3. Yo, I think you and me are the Futures of the game of bball. Our games appear
to be so ill that I can't even show these cats cause they'll try to steal em. I'm in the middle of getting them
copywrited so it'll be OK for me to only show you my moves. Don't think you can steal them either because my boys
will be patrolling the nation for imposters that wanna be JUST like me. But dont' worry, and remember: If you pray
enough, you could be just(not quite though) like me (and maybe the kid above, my scouts coming to check you out).

HeAdAcHe2k
5-30-2000 9:12 AM
you obviously dont know about rafer alston. check out the and1 mix tape volume 1 to get a glimpse at skip in his
prime. i think the skip back then would whoop teh futures ass but now skip is like almos turning 30 and hes gotten
slower so teh Future would kill his slow ass today
----

calboogy
5-30-2000 11:57 AM
Got it backwards. AND Vol1.... Rafer was like 17-18. Those highlights go back to 94, son was just coming out. Future
is the one pushing 30. Molloy never was, is not and will never be the SugarHoneyIce.. Only the fans like him while
ballplayers see the real. Not saying he can't' go , but he's not all that. Even in his prime (late 80s - early 90s)
the younger cats who held it down were Karlton Hines, Jamal Mashburn, Speedy, Malik Sealy, Darrel Parsons, Mike
Boogie and Master Rob. Future wasn't seeing any of those guys.
----

wlightnin
5-30-2000 12:03
Rafer is like 24, the future is older, i think you got mixed up
----

jd_skillz
5-30-2000 3:48 PM
i'd putmy money on rafer

Name: JD aka "wink"
Email: p■■■■■■■■■■■■■■■
Location: lv, tx US
Date: Thursday, June 22, 19100 at 21:22:45
Comments:
all i got to say to yall is censored! saw mix tapes 1, 2, and da remix..... censored... future is da best1 out

there, headache is tight he tearin up everybody and u can't forget mainevent... mad hops.. boy's got mad hops..
ruck, yall keep on doin that censored.. west4th vs ruckerpark.. comin up.. peace

----
Name: Jason D. aka "sleepy"
Email: [redacted]
Location: auroura, IL USA
Date: Thursday, June 22, 19100 at 13:39:41
Comments:
I just want to thank yall niggas for givin me some real baller action. Im a city nigga born an raised got all my
ballin skills from chicagos south an west side. now im in teh suburbs surrounded by all these shiesty niggas wit
no game but they swear they the censored. I even got cut from teh danm team cause the coach said i was too
flashy. anyway thanks for representin real ballers. p.s. Im going to the EBC in august i want to see my nigga
Skip to my lou tear it up with blackhand. "ONE"

Name: RobDog
Email: [redacted]
Location: Auberry, CA United States
Date: Thursday, June 22, 19100 at 00:24:04
Comments:
All I half to say is that skip is one of the illest playground ballers ever. If anybody has any dunk pics of
MAIN EVENT send them to me. Peace

Name: Jason F.
Email: [redacted]
Location: Summerville SC USA
Date: Tuesday, June 20, 19100 at 22:36:08
Comments:
i love watching the mix tapes and i know more about y'all then most of my friends also i love to watch Skip to
my Lou on AND1 vol. 1 and how he shook up Future also can you try come down here more in SC not alot of people
know about us.

Name: Jason C.
Email: [redacted]com
Location: London, England
Date: Tuesday, June 20, 19100 at 02:38:18
Comments:
UNFORTUNATELY, THE ONLY RUCKER PARK FOOTAGE I HAVE SEEN IS AND1 VOL.1 AND CLIPS OF 2 AND THAT WAS HEAVY. PEOPLE
R TALKING ABOUT THIS KID "THE FUTURE". EVERYWHERE I GO PEOPLE R TALKING ABOUT HIM AND SKIP. IF NE1 COULD GIVE ME
SOME INFO ON WHERE TO FIND SOME OF THESE VIDEOS. PLEASE CONTACT ME. I AM FLYING OUT TO NY LATER 2DAY, SO WILL BE
MUCH OBLIGED IF I COULD HAVE SOME ADDRESSES OF STORES OF WHATEVA.

Name: D. Slasher
Email: [redacted]
Location: South Dakota USA
Date: Wednesday, May 24, 19100 at 10:25:12
Comments:
Can anybody get me the AND 1 Mix tapes? Will pay top dollar, for what your asking. email me and we'll figure
something out.... PEACE!

Name: Blazin Balla
Email: [redacted]net
Location: Palm bay, FL USA
Date: Wednesday,June 14, 19100 at 19:46:51
Comments:
Yo like captain nappy said " The NBA aint got nothin on us" He censored right yo. Yall are off tha heezy fa
seriously. I liked tha Rucker Park special and I like tha AND1 Mix Tapes. All tha players are off the chain in
there own unique ways. Keep up tha fab work to all. Streetballazgonerule tha basketball era and thats serious.
ONE LUV

Name: B/Kevin Garnett/6ft7in
Email: [redacted].com
Location: Columbia SC USA
Date: Tuesday, June 20, 19100 at 18:46:19
Comments:
On the real though, y'all nigga DO need to have Rucker Park video game. I'll "cop 10 of'em!" I'm sayin' I copped
the AND1 Mix Tape Vol. I & II and Vol. II The Remixes, and I taped that EBC speical on TNT, I'm sayin' thought!
Tha Rucker Park cats is off the chissain! And me bein from DC and all, Rucker played us! It was tied though, 53
to 53, they playin' again this Sunday, the 25TH, I wash more than anything that We(DC), will win, but them Rucker
boys still the shishnitz! I'm sayin' Future, Main Event, Hedace, (the ORIGINAL) Half Man, Half Amazing, Whole
Lotta Game, I'll Be Right Back, Mac Nasty, Skip to my Lou., Aircraft (Half Man) "2 yrs, 3yrs, from now we need
to have a NBA, Hood All-stars game" I'm sayin' who gone stop the Rucker? Like they said n the commerical,
(aircraft) "Shaq come down to Rucker, not Rucker, but Hunter College, and got cracked by Juni. Cracked! By Juni."

NBA FINALS: SAVVY SPURS vs. POWERFUL PISTONS

Sports Illustrated

THE OTHER GAME

HOW A TINY SHOE COMPANY (AND 1) HAPPENED TO START A BASKETBALL REVOLUTION

BY ALEXANDER WOLFF

The Reinvention of SAMMY SOSA
BY TOM VERDUCCI

CONGRATULATIONS AND THANKS BUCKIE! THIS IS ALL YOU MY FRIEND. YOU MADE EVERYONE A BELIEVER AND THEN YOU MADE IT HAPPEN. WITH MOTIVATION AND GRATITUDE, JAY

Before the Mixtape Tour became the sports entertainment juggernaut it is today, it was just a bunch of guys driving around in an Escalade, picking up ballers at Rucker Park.

$29.99 US
$40.50 CAN

Dr. Angus

Eating the
ANGUS DIET

In this, his latest book, Dr. Angus supplies the reader with a roadmap for living what he calls "The Good Life." An exciting and refreshing approach for a book mostly because it's not a real diet book or even a real diet, *Eating The Angus Diet* covers a wide range of seemingly unrelated topics. From "How to Eat Food That Tastes Good" to "Catching a Greased Pig." Dr. Angus illustrates his "lifestyle plan" via The Angus Steak Burger from BURGER KING.® *Eating The Angus Diet* is a must read for anyone with a whole lot of time to burn.

Eating the
ANGUS DIET

DR. ANGUS

RE-CAP:

1. The Angus is a new steak burger.

2. The Angus Diet is the newest diet.

3. Which makes it the best diet.

4. Even though it's not a real diet.

Acknowledgments

Dr. Angus would like to thank The Burger King – wi
whom this inspirational book, its philosophies and life-c
ing notions would not be possible. Long live The King

Does This Look Like a Fad?

As you now understand, The Angus Diet is not a real diet
you know what else it's not? It's also not a fad. How ca
so sure? Because I have eyes in my head and those eyes
I trust my eyes. With them I can spot a fad from a mile
And with this sort of incredible vision, I can tell you tha
Angus Steak Burger is no fad. Look at it for yourself. D
look like a pair of acid-washed jeans? Does it look like
rock? No. Tell me I'm wrong. You can't, can you? You c
tell me I'm wrong because I'm right. The Angus Steak B
is here to stay. Which effectively removes it from fad
Don't believe me? Go to a BURGER KING® restaur
about five years and order The Angus. I'll be the one
corner chowing down, still living the good life on The A
Diet and loving every second of it. Then maybe yo
saunter over and we can chat about welding. I was a w
once. I can talk TIG, ARC, OxyAcetylene, the whole ga

*Fadulity: I tried Fad-dom but didn't like the hyphen. So I made up Fadulity. I hope yo

新のダイエツトはいつも最高です。

初めてアンガスダイエツトを考え出した時、直ぐに
が素晴らしいアイデアだと確信しました。でもその
私の分析的な面が出てきてしまいました。それは多
フェンシングをやった後だったと思います。試合の
を愈そうと、お風呂にお湯を入れていた時、「他の
この良さを理解しくれるだろうか。」とふと疑問に
ました。この基盤と方向性は完璧なものだと十分理
ていたし、アンガス自体が世界中で最高の牛肉であ
とも十分承知していました。私は知っているが、皆
がそれを知っているだろうか。その時気づきました。
んがアンガスダイエツトに注目し、それが最高のダ
ツトであると思う理由はただ一つ。アンガスダイエ
は最新のダイエツトであるということです。考えて
ください。注意を惹き人気を得て、そして人の心を
惹きつけるダイエツトとは、ダイエツト業界の出血
あるダイエツトです。アンガスダイエツトが事実上、
のダイエツトであることを保証するために、私はこ
発表する前に最後のプログラムが出てしまうまで待
を決断しました。完璧な時机に合わせたと思います。
きり言って自分自身惊いています。

Wrestle a Supermodel

The great thing about supermodels, besides the fact tha
tend to be leggy, lovely and "on" in front of the cam
that they are often willing to do more than pose for
and act all pouty. I have found that if you ask nice
promise not to bite, most supermodels are willing to w
And this, friends, really gets the blood pumping. Her
are my tips for making your very own round of super
wrestling happen.

A diet is what you eat. This woman looks to be eating a lot of sausage. One could say she is on the Sausage Diet.

What Is The Angus Diet?

This Is Not a Real Diet

Now you're probably saying to yourself "Hang on, if The Angus Diet is not a real diet, then where does this quack get off calling this book *Eating The Angus Diet?*" Easy, Cheetah. Allow me to explain. I call it a "diet" because if you look in most any dictionary (under D) you'll find the following. Take it away, Mr. Definition:

Diet (diet) n. 1. a) What a person or animal usually eats and drinks; daily fare.

See that? Technically, a "diet" is what you eat. So if you eat The Angus Steak Burger, you're on The Angus Diet. But I

I put my hands in this position first. The Queen totally copied me.

In my 20's I used to read huge books near stained-glass windows.

Eat Like a Monkey

I've been fortunate enough to have lived in a lot of places and experienced an extraordinarily vast range of cultures. And in every one of those places I was taken by the diversity of animal species. I've sprint-paddled my canoe away from a charging hippo. I've smelled the breath of rhinoceros. I've unwittingly shared a sleeping bag with a seven-foot rattlesnake and I've been bombarded with puffin dung while camping under the cliffs of South Georgia Island. At no time while observing these different animal species did I ever stop and muse to myself or my traveling companion, "hey look at that emu, it appears to be hungry yet it is ignoring those extremely fulfilling seeds scattered right underneath its beak.

How extremely odd of that emu." Granted, it's easy to forget while driving around in our S.U.V.s and gabbing away on our cellphones that we humans are animals. But nevertheless it is the truth. We are animals just like cats, dogs, rats, pigs, sharks, fish, giraffes, crocodiles, cockroaches and butterflies are animals. The only thing that separates us from this distinguished group? We often turn our pursuit of food into a far more complex ordeal than it needs to be. That is another reason why The Angus Diet is more a way of living than a diet. It approaches eating in the way that other animals do – consuming good-tasting food that is easily accessible. For an example of what I'm driving at, think of it this way: If a squirrel were to come upon a drive-thru nut restaurant, I'll bet you dollars to doughnuts that squirrel would scurry in, order some nuts and eat them like they were going out of style. Well, BURGER KING® drive-thrus are just about everywhere. So do as the squirrel would: Scurry in and order The Angus.

So do as the squirrel would: Scurry in and order The Angus.

1. Find a Supermodel. For some, this will be the most difficult step. You might want to hang out in Paris, New York or Milan. Keep your eyes peeled. They're everywhere.

2. Start with a Camera. Remember, she is used to being in front of one. This will relax the supermodel. So have one on hand. You don't even have to have film in it.

3. Move in for Close-ups. This will get the supermodel used to you.

4. Powers of Suggestion. Supermodels are used to photographers asking them to do all sorts of stuff. But they're not used to people asking them to wrestle. So bring it up slowly. Try "hey, ever watch wrestling? I really like Greco-Roman. It looks so fun!"

5. Move to the Mat. Slowly move the "photo-shoot" to your wrestling mat that you've wisely laid down in your "studio" beforehand. Put the camera down at some point and pretend to re-load its film. Ask her to help you.

6. Full-Nelson Time. When she gets down on the mat to help you "re-load" the film, gently put her in a full-nelson. Now you're supermodel wrestling! And that's living!

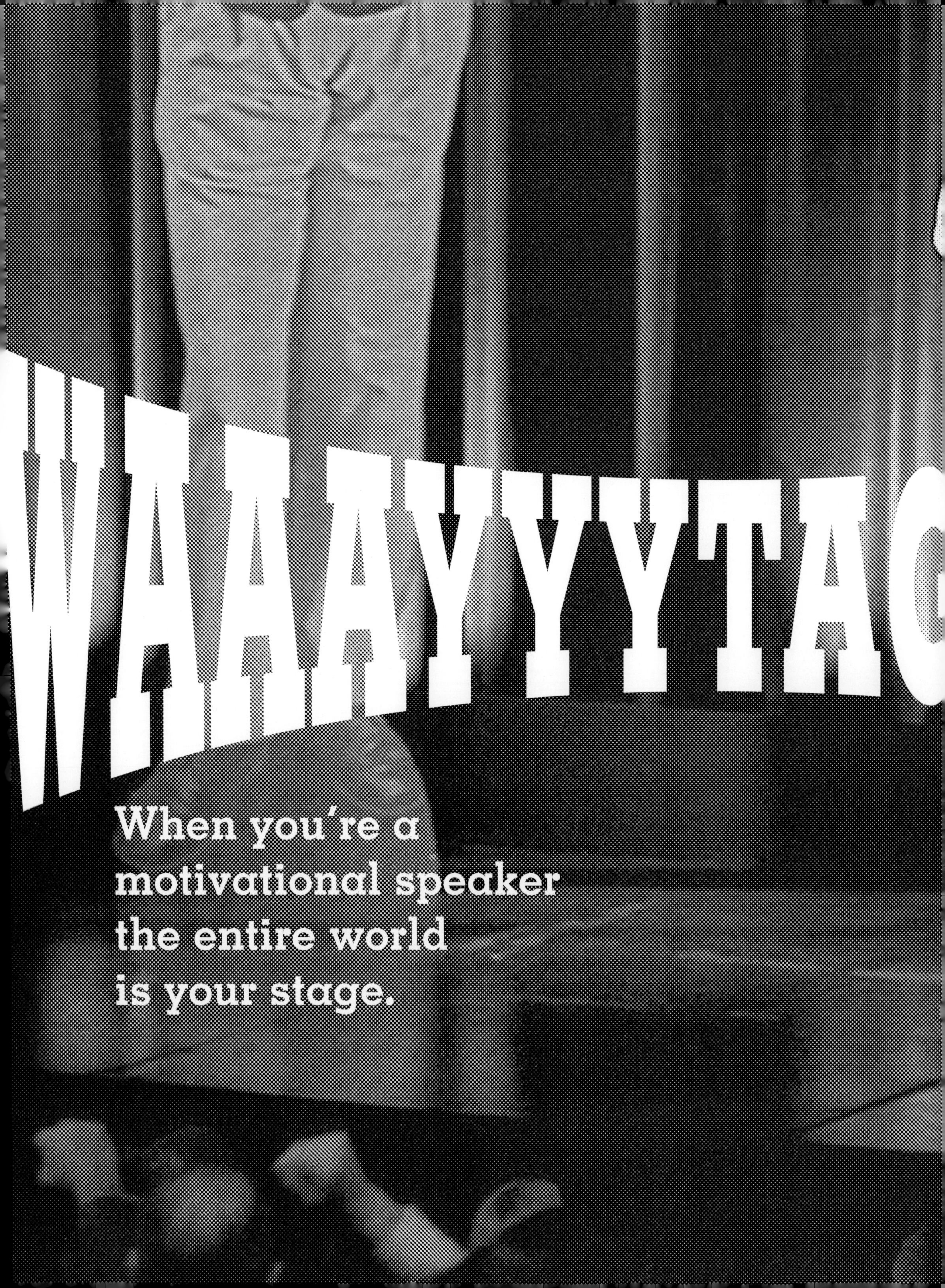

WAAAYYYTAG

When you're a
motivational speaker
the entire world
is your stage.

(continued from front flap)

Eating the
ANGUS DIET

Eating The Angus Diet is not:

- A real diet book.

- Grounded in a little thing called "reality."

- Intended to be taken seriously.

- Limited to The Angus Steak Burger from BURGER KING.®

- "Full of intellectual banter."

- "Streaking to the top of any best seller list."

- A critics' favorite.

- Worthy of over-analyzation.

- A brilliant work of art.

- "Full of misspellings and grammatical errors."

NOW FROM BURGER KING

All Major Credit
Cards Accepted

www.angusdie

 # 1-866-E

In 1975
WE MADE IT
SOCIALLY ACCEPTABLE
TO LAUGH AT
MOMENTS LIKE THESE

A well-constructed joke engages its audience, builds antic-ipation & always arrives at a most unexpected conclusion. A comic formula you're no doubt familiar with if you've ever seen someone fall off a bike while wearing a Bell helmet.

Bike crashes weren't always funny. There was a time when cyclists hit the road (sometimes quite literally) with their heads covered only by a flimsy leather cap held on by an even flimsier leather chin strap. And, perhaps, a prayer.

Then came Bell. A company that set out to make auto parts. Not helmets. A company dedicated to making things faster. Not safer. In fact, it wasn't until those record high speeds became something of a health risk that Bell founder Roy Richter decided to start manufacturing some dependable head gear.

In 1954, Roy, along with his team of mechanics and engineers, worked around the clock in a tiny garage behind the Bell Auto Parts shop to create the very first Bell helmet.

It didn't take long for Bell helmets to catch on. In fact, if there was a head to protect after 1954, you could be sure there was a Bell protecting it. They were worn by Indy car drivers, fighter pilots, hockey players, ski teams, riot police. Must we go on?

The original Bell Biker

By 1975, Bell began focusing its efforts on the noggins of pro cyclists. That's when they created Bell Biker. The first bike helmet to meet CPSC standards. The first bike helmet built with a fully expanded polystyrene (EPS) liner. And the first bike helmet actually built with the cyclist in mind.

Bell Biker certainly wasn't the last of the innovations to come from Bell. They continued to improve helmets with features like the GPS Fit System, the Blade Visor attachment, and of course, the Fusion In-Mold Microshell. A technology that made shells stronger and more durable.

Today, Bell isn't just changing the way their helmets are made. Thanks to Universal Fit, Bell is changing the way helmets are bought, stocked and sold.

The fact is, Universal Fit may be the first helmet actually designed to protect bike dealerships. It can help reduce your high volume SKUs by as much as 66%. And you won't have to deny customers the protection of America's most trusted helmet just because of size or color preference.

You see, ever since we began making helmets, our mission has always stayed the same. To keep people safe, and maybe have a few laughs along the way. Something we believe can only be accomplished when you take the business of helmets as seriously as we do.

IMPORTANT DISCLAIMER: Bell is constantly working to ensure survival. But please remember that Bell cannot guarantee safety in the event of a crash. After all, you could die laughing.

FOR INFORMATION, CALL (800) 776-5677 OR VISIT BELLBIKEHELMETS.COM

BELL

Est. 1954
Proven ever since.

FedEx

Personal Vehicles

A day hardly ever goes by at CP+B without someone rushing out to make a FedEx before it closes. Here is a profile of some of the reliable employee vehicles that help make it happen.

☐ **MAKE:** VOLKSWAGEN ☐ **MODEL:** JETTA
☐ **YEAR:** 1995 ☐ **OWNER:** Elizabeth Harper

NOTES: Nickname: Mean Green Machine. A trusty 10-year-old Volkswagen, she frequently makes manic runs to the Miami Airport FedEx. Record time door to door: 17 minutes. I've been known to run people off the road. But who's counting?

☐ **MAKE:** MITSUBISHI ☐ **MODEL:** MONTERO
☐ **YEAR:** 2002 ☐ **OWNER:** Geraldine Drpic

NOTES: In the fairytale version, I mount the Black Stallion at dusk and he gallops into the FedEx sunset. In actuality, Black Stallion isn't always the faithful steed and as I stand on the other side of the door at 8:01, there are no heroes. So once again, I mount Black Stallion and he takes me to the far, far away FedEx airport kingdom, where all the packages live happily ever after.

☐ **MAKE:** FORD ☐ **MODEL:** BRONCO II
☐ **YEAR:** 1990 ☐ **OWNER:** Soddi Schiff

NOTES: This car hasn't made too many treks to FedEx, to be quite honest. But it does have a stunning burgandy interior which has kept nicely over the past 15 years. The curved rear panel windows also add a nice touch. And the single-speaker system is tops.

☐ **MAKE:** VOLKSWAGEN ☐ **MODEL:** JETTA
☐ **YEAR:** 2002 ☐ **OWNER:** Shannon Bicknell

NOTES: I get my mojo workin' when I hit the Miami streets and drive like a bat out of hell to FedEx. Nearly missing both the 8:00 Gables and 9:00 airport drop-offs every time. Do I live on the edge? Most definitely. Even when that box is ready to go at 8:15, I'll wait the extra 20 minutes. Just for the adrenaline rush.

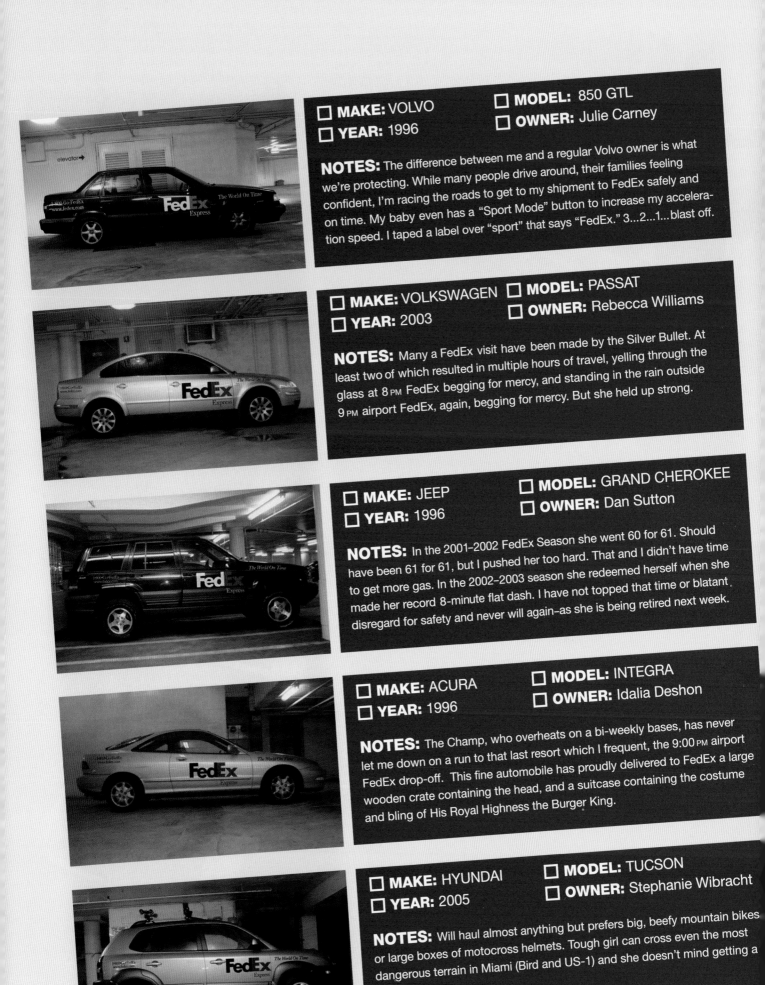

☐ **MAKE:** VOLVO ☐ **MODEL:** 850 GTL
☐ **YEAR:** 1996 ☐ **OWNER:** Julie Carney

NOTES: The difference between me and a regular Volvo owner is what we're protecting. While many people drive around, their families feeling confident, I'm racing the roads to get to my shipment to FedEx safely and on time. My baby even has a "Sport Mode" button to increase my acceleration speed. I taped a label over "sport" that says "FedEx." 3...2...1...blast off.

☐ **MAKE:** VOLKSWAGEN ☐ **MODEL:** PASSAT
☐ **YEAR:** 2003 ☐ **OWNER:** Rebecca Williams

NOTES: Many a FedEx visit have been made by the Silver Bullet. At least two of which resulted in multiple hours of travel, yelling through the glass at 8 PM FedEx begging for mercy, and standing in the rain outside 9 PM airport FedEx, again, begging for mercy. But she held up strong.

☐ **MAKE:** JEEP ☐ **MODEL:** GRAND CHEROKEE
☐ **YEAR:** 1996 ☐ **OWNER:** Dan Sutton

NOTES: In the 2001–2002 FedEx Season she went 60 for 61. Should have been 61 for 61, but I pushed her too hard. That and I didn't have time to get more gas. In the 2002–2003 season she redeemed herself when she made her record 8-minute flat dash. I have not topped that time or blatant disregard for safety and never will again–as she is being retired next week.

☐ **MAKE:** ACURA ☐ **MODEL:** INTEGRA
☐ **YEAR:** 1996 ☐ **OWNER:** Idalia Deshon

NOTES: The Champ, who overheats on a bi-weekly bases, has never let me down on a run to that last resort which I frequent, the 9:00 PM airport FedEx drop-off. This fine automobile has proudly delivered to FedEx a large wooden crate containing the head, and a suitcase containing the costume and bling of His Royal Highness the Burger King.

☐ **MAKE:** HYUNDAI ☐ **MODEL:** TUCSON
☐ **YEAR:** 2005 ☐ **OWNER:** Stephanie Wibracht

NOTES: Will haul almost anything but prefers big, beefy mountain bikes or large boxes of motocross helmets. Tough girl can cross even the most dangerous terrain in Miami (Bird and US-1) and she doesn't mind getting a little dirty...

[00014:42] **CHANNEL-FORGED CRANKSET** DEVICE SECURED. REPORTS INDICATE COMPONENT IS FORGED UNDER 200 TONS OF PRESSURE, YET HOLLOW. PROCESS: *unknown.* SPIDER-LESS CRANK DESIGNED TO DRIVE ALL CHAINRINGS DIRECTLY FROM THE SPINDLE. COMPATIBLE **BOTTOM BRACKET** HOUSES NEEDLE BEARINGS, NEW LARGER DIA. HOLLOW SPINDLE; TAPER-SPLINE AXLE ENDS FORM A SOLID INTERFACE WITH THE CRANK. GRAM SHAVING: APPROX. 200 (JUST UNDER ONE-HALF POUND). POWER TRANSFER: WAY ENHANCED. PRIME DIRECTIVE: HELP MOUNTAIN-BASED RADICALS MAXIMIZE POWER IN AN INCREASINGLY HOSTILE FAT TIRE WORLD. ADDITIONAL INFORMATION IS PROVIDED ON A NEED-TO-KNOW BASIS. IF YOU NEED TO KNOW, PUNCH IN 1-800-833-5540 EXT. 157M.

Before there were MINI robots, or a budget for it, the agency cut its episodic storytelling teeth on Shimano with a cool international espionage-inspired print campaign.

TECHNO-THRILLER

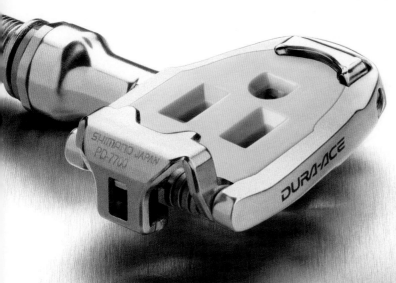

⚡ **POWER TO THE PEDAL**™ ⚡

Clicking your MegaPavemantis™ shoe into an SPD-R™ pedal could cause a surge of energy that would make the hair on your legs stand on end. If you haven't shaved. For a catalog, call 1-800-353-3817 ext. 820G.

Use with Dura-Ace® 7700 pedals.

SHIMANO®

Individual Racing Agreement

I,_____ ,do hereby agree to ride for Me™ and Me exclusively. Effective this date forward, I agree to represent Me to the best of my physical and mental abilities.

During any and all contact with the cycling media or the general public, I will represent Me, and uphold an image of professionalism and moral rectitude that are hallmarks of what it means to be associated with Me.

I also agree that any actions which might be construed as embarrassing to Me, or counter to the positive image created by Me, could lead to the immediate termination of all racing benefits and privileges provided to me by Me.

Date: _____

Signed:_____

Witnessed: _____

Shimano created this self-sponsorship kit for the large number of grassroots racers who used their products. Turns out a little recognition goes further than a team van.

For some reason, the corporate world tends to frown on employees who have cool side projects going. But people who produce one form of pop culture are probably pretty good at producing another. And when their stuff meets your stuff, the resulting combination of stuff is bound to be unique.

EXTRA CURRICULAR

Black Flamingo & Fingers le Roy'

Black Flamingo & Fingers le Roy make art devoid of intent but richly dripping with texture and romance. With the energy of 1000 rats turning 1000 rat-wheels, Flamingo & le Roy thrust pens to paper and mice to pixels, creating work as ancient as the Gizan Pyramids yet as modern as the Concorde Jet.

Critics have been known to chew their tongues into mush when attempting to praise (or even slander) their works of art. Pieter Jean Languist, the renowned astrophysicist, might have come closest to summing up their genius when he once stumbled into a showing of their works and, as legend has it, muttered these words: "I have studied every physical science known to man, and I have seen and experienced wonders that no other man living or dead has ever had the pleasure of even imagining, but it is not until this exact moment in time that I have witnessed powers capable of slowing the infinite expansion of our very universe." Later that night, Pieter was shot and killed mid-slice at a pizza parlour down the street. Oh, they also sell T-shirts!

BlackFlamingoandFingersleRoy.com

Freegums'

Searching for a way to make his artwork more accessible to the public, Alvaro began to print his designs on T-shirts. He eagerly set out for a trade show in Las Vegas with a bookbag full of shirts, not knowing what to expect. With the help of friends already established in the industry, he was able to infiltrate the garment industry's trade show Magic. Right off the bat, he was able to land accounts in Puerto Rico, Taiwan, and cities in the US. With that, Freegums was born. Slowly but surely, Freegums gained momentum and can now be found in major retail locations across the world.

Alvaro's favorite part of the whole Freegums process is meeting and working with many talented people, receiving random compliments from strangers, and seeing his artwork featured in various media outlets. He hopes Freegums inspires other people to pursue the fulfillment of their dreams. Thanks to Freegums, Alvaro is known as the originator of the Reversible T-shirt.

freegums.com

Feathers′

Little is ever published about this perplexing and inscrutable group responsible for some of the greatest records of the past 10 1/2 months. Despite an ever-increasing following from collectors since its inception, for the past 29 weeks Feathers has stubbornly resisted attempts to uncover the truth behind its mythology. Almost every aspect of the group seems to beg unanswered questions. To begin with, there is the name itself. Short and stupid, it seems designed to defy recollection and sink the hearts of label bosses. Was it an eight-letter manifesto of creative intent? Or simply a cynical attempt to climb aboard the stupid band-name bandwagon?

Then there are the song credits and band photos, according to which a certain Eddie Alonso is the band's driving force, a position seemingly confirmed by the appearance of his first "solo" LP: "A Portrait Etched in Lime." Yet, somewhat confusingly, on the back of that album's sleeve there appeared–for the first time since the band's debut on the Hometapes label–pictures of all three original members!!!! Last, and definitely not least, there are the songs themselves. Along the way the music encompasses almost every musical genre–inharmonic guitar pop, psychedelic rock, monster-mashy two-step, fake jazz, and "avant-garde dancehall."

home-tapes.com

LIES KILL

typestereo'

Excerpt from "A Line Art Shadowland," The Miami News, August 29, 2004

It wasn't until 1988 that the duo once again surfaced, creating a limited but explosive portfolio that would set the stage for later projects. By the summer of 1991, with the acquisition of expanded technological provisions, typeStereo went underground once again.

Returning in 1996, amid the tumultuous and ultimately directionless boom of the dot-com era, typeStereo maintained a low-radar signature and continued its experiments with mixed results.

At a conference in May 1999, six months prior to the projected "Y2K" meltdown, typeStereo officially rejected technology and in a statement cited "...the overwhelming and uncontrollable influence of 'Undoism' on contemporary culture" as a chief factor in its decision. Today, many experts believe that it was the duo's early and influential pre-Y2K statements that may have prevented a widespread digital catastrophe worldwide. To this day, typeStereo maintains only a limited presence on the Web.

typestereo.com

Lance. Defender of the human spirit.

Giro

passion

go jet set, go!™

Airline advertising always focuses on the destination. A sandy beach in the Caribbean. A cute kid running through the terminal toward a joyous mom. The reason this happens is that on most airlines, the travel experience itself really sucks. But flying on Virgin Atlantic is so cool travelers are often loathe to deplane. So instead of celebrating what happens after the plane lands, we decided to celebrate what was happening at 40,000 feet. We even went so far as to make each individual flight a sub-brand, based on what kind of vibe that flight was known for. The redeye is all about rock stars, while earlier flights might be more suited to the corporate raider planning his next hostile takeover. In either case, it's all about the flying. And touchdown is met with a twinge of sadness rather than a smattering of applause.

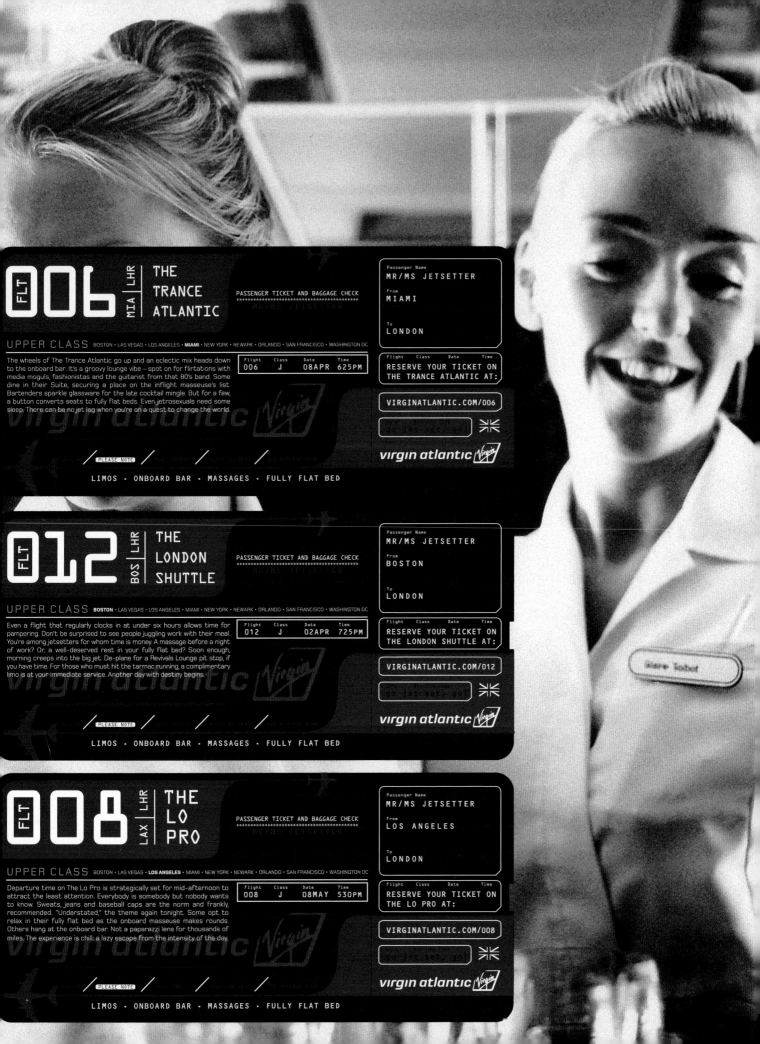

was eaten by a tiger in the middle of a park while sitting on a bench.   >>I dream I
plane flying into a metropolitan airport and we are flying along streets, underneath
asses, the wings are barely missing the buildings and I can see people in their apartments
y seat.   >>I'm falling off a cliff.   >>Donkeys were dancing around and one of them
ed doing backflips while he was going heee haaaw   >>My dog was sitting in my living room
she was talking to my daughter but she couldn't hear what my daughter was saying at all
I dream i'm at work all the time   >> i am taking a shower with everyone at work in the big
open community shower when some sort of federal police show up and start asking
questions. everyone else stops lathering and stare at the feds, but i keep showering. The
feds make their way to my area. when they get close i realize i've been haunched over under
the shower head so i stand up fully to talk to them. to my surprise and everyone elses i'm
about 8 and a half feet tall. the tops of the bathroom stalls are about shoulder high. then
everyone steps back rather disturbed and i wake up. this happened last night   >> My co-
workers and i were forced to evaculate due to an impending hurricane. Unfortunately, the house
were were taking shelter in, was haunted. I call these my "natural disaster-mares" because i
dream about tornados, hurricanes and other natural enemies all the time.   >> i was running
through a parking garage trying to find my bag, which i had put down. Then suddenly i
was on a raft, and the floor of the garage was water. There was a large panther
on the raft with me. Then i woke up.   >> I did something really mean, I don't
remember what, and this classmate in college who was so annoying kept trying
to get proof and get me in trouble. I remember feeling really panicked.   >> I was
in this mountainous surrounding, kind of like summer camp next to a lake. All my
friends and family were there, people from all different parts of my family. And I
was getting married to my boyfriend. But it wasn't a normal or formal
ceremony. It was sort of a wedding before a wedding. But the weird part was
that I was watching myself from afar, kind of like an out of body experience
commenting on how in love I looked. So weird.   >> I was climbing up a giant
microchip thing that had steam coming out of it. I wore something like a diaper made out
of dark feathers. In my hand was a porcelain dish and i was trying to catch little thing
were falling down as i climbed up. It was a really dark environment.   >> somebody i kr
again, because of something i did, would not give me a handshake, and this person was
in a brown paper grocery bag, in a grocery cart, being wheeled swiftly down a remote
were lots of trees on either side and nobody could hear me were i to scream.   >> I ki
>> go to work naked   >> I had a dream that I won the election for president of the ha
the police stopped me in a 20 mph college zone. I tried to explain that I had to speed up b
behind me but he wouldn't listen. The ticket was only $6 so it wasn't a big deal.   >> I
to work with clothes on and everyone else was naked so I took off all my I clothes a
breakfast >> i was falling   >> i was being chased   >> I was flying   >> i
went to buy Robbie Williams concert tickets for my
friend's birthday, (which was apparently
happening on a completely different day
from her actual birthday)

was the devil and he was turning America into hell. Wait a sec, i'm actually awake right now   >> I dreamt i

t really could not control it   >> walking into a giant party in a huge Roman style looking house.

marble floors, giant pool in the middle. I'm early. There are not too many people there yet. It's purple

ng to start pouring rain. Then I just walk around and marvel at how gorgeous it all is.   >> i was a

was being chased by someone i work with. he chased me through a forest and over a bridge. at one

joined by my former boss so I had to figure out how to divide and conquer. i lost my current co-

t was eventually caught by my old boss back in the forest. i woke up right as he caught me.   >> I

d a part in Love and Basketball (the movie)   >> I was driving along a canyon at night and the

kes in my car went out...I spent the rest of the dream trying to control my car from swerving off

road.   >> I get up early in the morning and realize that I have missed one of my college classes. I

de I need to start attending class and definitely want to take the final exam but I can't figure out

ere the class is located on campus and when the class starts. I have lost all my paperwork telling

me which course I was enrolled in.   >> train in tunnel   >> My cock fell off and chased me

around until it jumped in my mouth. I woke at this moment.   >> i have a baby in my arms, but

don't have a child in real life   >> I was running through a forest but I didn't know what I was

ning from. I did not hear footsteps behind me but I knew that I had to keep running. It was a

ter of life or death   >> colorful dancing bears suround my house and start urinating on it. I

ump from the window and the yellow one starts chasing me. We fall off a cliff and land on his

belly. I'm okay because he's made of gummy.   >> I dreamt about someone dressed in thick black

heavy shiny wings like a black bird that couldn't fly. They were standing there, face painted

black, looking down   >> I had a dream about my boss   >> I was married to Blair

Underwood   >> I had a dream that I saw one of my client's aging reports and they had

paid a significant amount of their outstanding payments. Then the next day we received

a huge check from them. The amounts were almost identical to those in my

dream. Seriously. This really happened.   >> i had to dress up like

Mighty Mouse for a ball. And then the girl I

went with to the ball dressed up like a shrimp

and turned out to be a

terrorist. She blew up

a staircase. It was

will never see

ery friendly   >> I was   unimpressive.   >>

some kidnappers. There   Playing in

Benjamin with a hammer   waterfall I

r men   >> I had a dream   had a dream in

n ambulance was   which I was

hat i came   losing my

                                              teeth one at a

                                                time. It started

                                                  with my molars

                                                    and then

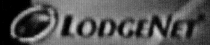

ACCESSING
Interactive Services

LODGENET

Movie Categories

1 Still in Theaters

2 Hollywood Hits

3 Adult Desires

1 Barely Legal   **2** Fluff and Fold   **3** Suite and Innocent

All Stars

AAAAA Rated

FREE MOVIE!

◄ **4** Browse   Screen 1 of 4   Browse **6** ►

FREE MOVIE!

SUITE AND INNOCENT

Watch the sexy saga of one woman's initiation into the mile-high world of business deals and Upper Class high jinks. Includes seven scenes and a finale you won't want to miss.

FREE! MA for strong sexual content

Choose ORDER to purchase this movie.
A charge will be added to your room.
Cost of this movie is $0.00 + TAX

◄ **4** Browse   Browse **6** ►

Go Jet Set, Go!
PRODUCTIONS

"Suite & Innocent"

...the world is not fair. And depending on how you look at it, that is either very bad news or very good news. It wasn't fair that British Airways had a big budget that allowed it to advertise its new flat bed on TV. It wasn't fair that Virgin's flat bed was just as good but nobody knew about it. So as usual, we had a choice. Play fair and come up with our own print advertising plan and deal with the fact that not that many people would see it, and those who did would not be people who would ever fly to London anyway. Or we could cheat. And this being CP+B, we of course decided to try to cheat the system.

So the mission became to find a new way to have a conversation with business travelers and only business travelers. It immediately became obvious that the best way to speak with business travelers with the least amount of waste was to reach them while they are traveling. Now we're fond of saying that "everything is media," but in general it is hard to see media as anything beyond the existing media that is already for sale. Even when it's staring you in the face on every business trip you take. For us, that media was LODGENET.® The in-room entertainment network. We wondered if anybody ever used the adult section of the service. We can't tell you the exact numbers here, but, oh yeah, they use it. Movies are second only to room charges in hotel revenues. More than food and drink. And the majority of those are of the adult variety.

Soon a plot was hatched. What if we had a short film that appeared to be an adult title in the adult section? And what if it was labeled as a free preview? One of the interesting facts we learned was that on average these movies were viewed for less than three minutes. A free preview might do just the trick. We title our little feature "Suite & Innocent," after the new flat bed UpperClass® suite. In three months it was viewed by almost one million people, and on average they watched almost seven minutes of a nine-minute film.

Awareness of the new flat bed among business travelers who fly to London is almost 100 percent now. Yet nobody will ever tell you how they found out about it...

go jet set, go!™

virgin atlantic

When your target is somewhere in the ionosphere, traditional media isn't always going to work. Who knows, maybe one day Viacom or Clear Channel will buy the rights to your roof.

012

Boston to London

virginatlantic.com

ALL SEATS MUST REMAIN ON AIRCRAFT
TODOS LOS ASIENTOS DEBEN PERMANECER EN LA AERONAVE

Complimentary in Premium Economy℠:
- Dedicated check-in
- Preflight champagne
- More personal space, with extended legroom
- Separate cabin
- Expedited baggage handling

Not Complimentary in Premium Economy:
- Seats: All seats must remain on aircraft.

De cortesía en Premium Economy:
- Check-in especial
- Champaña antes del vuelo
- Más espacio para extender sus piernas
- Cabina aparte
- Manejo rápido del equipaje

No son de cortesía en Premium Economy:
- Los asientos: Todos los asientos deben permanecer en la aeronave.

go jet set, go!™ **virgin atlantic**

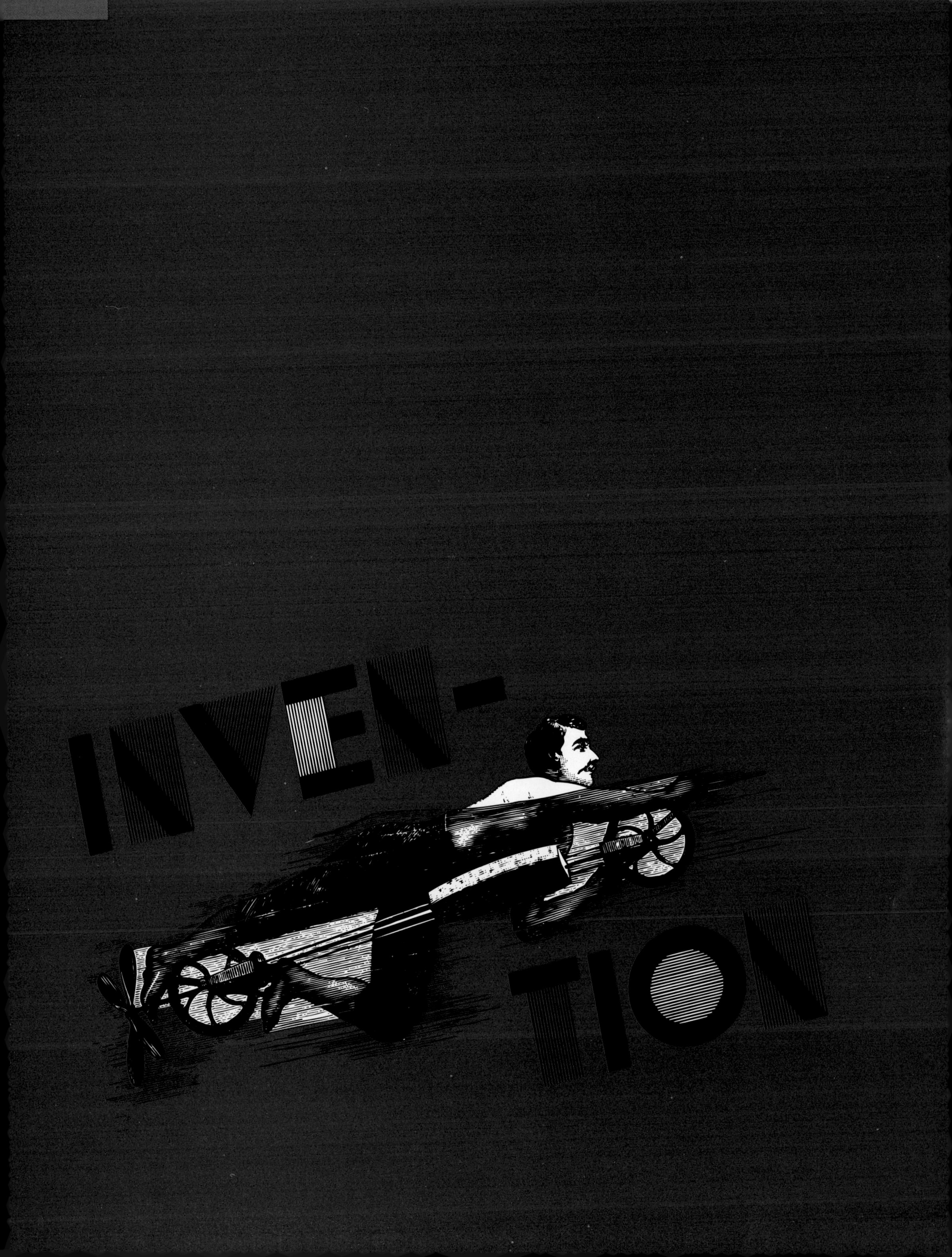
INVEN-
TION

When the airline of the British entrepreneur Richard Branson went looking for a new ad agency a few years ago, a fairly typical process ensued: A handful of well-regarded agencies were approached and asked to present ideas about how best to promote the brand in question, Virgin Atlantic Airways. Such competitive "pitches" are a time-honored tradition in advertising, with each contender taking its turn at trying to impress the potential client with a clever slogan or a funny script for a commercial. As it happened, Virgin Atlantic was only partway through the process of meeting with agencies when it paid a visit to Crispin Porter + Bogusky in Miami. What transpired at that meeting brought the airline's search to an abrupt and unexpected end. In a highly unusual turn of events, Virgin Atlantic cancelled its meetings with other agencies and hired CP+B on the spot. The client seemed to recognize almost immediately that it had stumbled upon not just a good idea but a factory full of them.

In subsequent weeks, as the client continued to meet with its new agency, the ideas just kept coming from CP+B—about 165 of them by one count, encompassing almost every aspect of Virgin's business. There was a tagline—"*go, jet set, go!*"—designed to bring back the glamour of jet-setting. There were ads designed to look like flight safety cards found in the pocket of an airplane seatback. There was an original comic strip created by the agency, called *The Jet Set*, as well as a glossy newsstand magazine for Virgin, called *Jetrosexual*. There was even an illustrated bedtime storybook, intended to lull passengers to sleep on the overnight flights. Beyond that, the agency had ideas about how to change the uniforms of the flight attendants and thought it might be interesting to hire celebrities to work as "guest flight attendants," and also to stage occasional "concert flights." CP+B even concocted a plan to have Virgin's pilots fly at a higher altitude—so the airline could claim that it soars above the competition (which, it turned out, wasn't feasible, but it was interesting nonetheless). As Virgin's advertising manager, Chris Rossi, commented at the time, "Most agencies hit you with one TV or print campaign, but these guys come at you from every direction."

A hundred ideas may seem like overkill, but in the realm of Hoopla there's no such thing as too much invention. P.T. Barnum, a master of invention in his time, understood that people never tire of surprises and invariably respond to novelty. (Barnum even invented original words, like "Jumbo," because the existing language couldn't do justice to all of his new creations; CP+B invents words too, such as "baggler," which describes a lonely French fry found in the bottom of your BURGER KING® bag.)

Today's wired world may offer more amusements and diversions than Barnum ever could've imagined, yet people still perpetually crave something fresh and original. For that reason, invention is at the heart of Hoopla. And it seems to be a way of life at CP+B, where, as the magazine *Fast Company* observed in a recent profile of the agency, "ideas are an almost unhealthy obsession."

The agency devotes many of its waking hours (and a fair number of its sleeping ones) to searching for and grappling with ideas. The process often involves starting with something raw and building upon it, often rejecting it along the way or else refining it until it's smooth, finished, and ready for rollout. If that sounds like an industrial process, to some extent it is: CP+B has embraced a "factory" model when it comes to inventing and producing ideas (though, as Bogusky notes, Hoopla can never be an assembly-line product, per se, because it must always be custom-made).

CP+B's idea-factory approach is, in itself, a mutation of the traditional way of thinking in advertising. Most ad agencies view themselves as service providers, not producers. But Bogusky maintains that if an ad agency is focused primarily on service (aiming only to please the client, always ready to acquiesce), that's probably a means of covering for a weak product in the form of mediocre, unoriginal ideas.

One of the credos that CP+B lives by is "*Ideas are currency.*" Which, again, is a shift in the old advertising formula that valued everything by levels of media expenditure. In the long-ago days of three television channels, advertisers could somewhat predict how much share of mind they'd command based on how much they were investing in TV airtime. The audience had not yet built up the filters that today's viewers have, and there were fewer media options and escape hatches. Hence it was assumed that if a marketer spent enough money hammering away at that captive audience, the message was bound to sink in eventually.

But once the audience mutated and the media landscape exploded with new options, that formula began to unravel. In the new value-equation that has taken its place, "surprise" has become more important than repetition. To purchase awareness now, it's not enough to just buy more airtime. It's increasingly critical to invest in ideas. And the return on that investment will likely depend on the inventiveness of those ideas—their ability to surprise, intrigue, engage, and stir conversation.

The beauty of invention is that it's within reach of almost anyone—the modest entrepreneur, the small agency, the solo communications artist or designer (or an innovative person who happens to be working within a larger establishment). Invention, and particularly the invention of Hoopla, does *not* require huge capital expenditures. "A small budget is the mother of invention," says Andrew Keller. This has resulted in a leveling of the playing field: Small brands with modest media budgets can end up having greater cultural impact than the big spenders—*if* they're willing and able to come at the audience with something that has never been seen before.

CP+B learned that lesson firsthand through several of its early marketing experiences, including an influential campaign for the Internet startup site PlanetOutdoors.com, which sold outdoor adventure gear. While most dot coms at the time were pouring their venture-capital money into lookalike 30-second commercials, CP+B felt that PlanetOutdoors could garner more attention, for less money, by venturing into new, unexplored territory. Thus was born "The Lost Tribe Mission," a journey deep into the dark heart of…the island of Manhattan.

The agency set up a three-day filmed expedition–in effect, a 72-hour nonstop live advertisement– in which a team of adventurers, bearing the PlanetOutdoors brand's flag and a bunch of the company's products, invaded New York City like explorers coming to the New World. The team arrived by boat, rope-scaled the sides of skyscrapers, camped on rooftops, and along the way tried to communicate and barter with the city's local natives–who, according to the tongue-in-cheek premise of the documentary being filmed, represented a lost tribe, cut off from outdoor life and cooped up in Manhattan offices and apartments. While the film was being shot, a live website tracked the expedition as it was happening, complete with journal entries from the missionaries; simultaneously, film clips of the journey ran as "live" TV commercials–and people also followed the ongoing event through the press (including a front-page story in *USA Today*), as part of a well-coordinated PR effort. The net effect came across as a compelling, real-life happening–as opposed to an advertisement. At the time, one Madison Avenue executive commented to *USA Today* that the PlanetOutdoors effort had the potential to "rewrite the rules for creating an ad campaign."

Within a few years, a growing number of advertisers were creating live events or "advertising-as-theater" experiences, blurring the lines of reality and using the Web to tie multimedia elements together –just as the PlanetOutdoors campaign had done. But back when CP+B first did it, sending a group of people rappelling through New York and acting like missionaries…it just didn't seem like an ad.

Nor, for that matter, did a later CP+B campaign involving a petition to have "man" declared an endangered species, as part of an offbeat effort on behalf of the client MAXIM magazine. Of all the forms ads have taken through the years, it's safe to say this was the first ad to take the form of an exhaustively detailed government document, submitted to the US Secretary of the Interior, endeavoring to show why modern man should be protected under the Endangered Species Act due to a debilitating disease (dreamed up by CP+B) known as "Mantropy"–whose symptoms involved using too much hair product, eating tofu, and riding on rollerblades. In reality, the petition was a way for MAXIM, a "guy's guy" kind of magazine, to take a humorous stand against the gender-blending social phenomenon known as "metrosexuality." By inventing a disease, then inventing a social movement on behalf of that disease, CP+B gave MAXIM a cause around which to rally its own readers while attracting new ones. That original government petition (which was also posted online and allowed visitors to electronically sign onto the cause) became the linchpin of a multimedia campaign in which the agency created short video vignettes that looked like public-safety films, as well as educational flyers, brochures, and other materials, all designed to help men ward off the growing Mantropy threat.

It takes quite a leap to get from making an ad to organizing a make-believe expedition or dreaming up a new endangered species. For CP+B, that leap often seems to happen within the lively imaginations of the agency's creative teams. "What we really do is *pretend*," Bogusky says. "That's such a kid's word, and it's not taken seriously by people. But it's the key to inventing."

But that doesn't mean the process is child's play. In fact, it often begins with painstaking research, in which a product or service is looked at from every possible angle, in an attempt to distill some fundamental insights and truths. The idea is to learn everything there is to know–and then forget all that and just venture into the unknown.

There is a certain mindset that allows a person to be inventive, Bogusky says. "I think you have to come to the realization that it's okay to make things up. That is how you start to invent. I don't know why it is so hard to get to that point, but it is." One of the ways Bogusky stimulates invention is by encouraging people to "do the opposite of what everybody else is doing–that will almost always get you halfway to success. Then all you need is to figure out why you're doing the opposite." Pushing in radical new directions is more effective than just trying to "innovate," he says. "The trouble with looking for innovation is that it can lead you toward small adjustments that go totally unnoticed. Even most revolutionary ideas go unnoticed."

The agency studies and compiles lists of the conventions that are used in any given product category so that it can then deliberately try to overturn those conventions. Making Hoopla can be a bit like jujitsu, in that one is always trying to flip reality on its head; as CP+B creative director Andrew Keller notes, "You have to be able to step outside your own culture. You have to know it's not permanent and it wants to change. And then you change it. We are always fucking with culture because once you start, once it works—you never want to stop."

The industrial-style headquarters of CP+B—mostly metal and concrete, with a cavernous open space in the middle of the facility—was designed to encourage invention. Porter says of the open space: "It facilitates a scientifically proven group dynamic which we call 'bumping into each other all day.'" That openness carries over to brainstorming sessions, which are often held in common spaces and which are also open to input from any person in any department; this differs from the inventive process at most ad agencies, which tend to wall off creative people from everyone else. Bogusky tries to avoid that kind of territorial separation, believing that "a good idea can come from anyone, anywhere."

There are scattered pillows on benches in the agency's main area, which is appropriate because the people at CP+B tend to work to the point of exhaustion. The agency has embraced the philosophy that when it comes to ideas, more is better, and that there's always room for improvement. Even an idea that has proven to be successful is subject to rapid replacement (another departure from conventional advertising, which generally holds that a successful idea should be extended and milked for all it is worth). CP+B's internal rule is to *"preach and practice obsolescence."* In effect, the agency is always trying to make a current idea obsolete by inventing a new and better one.

This approach can be seen in a number of the agency's efforts, particularly with the current BURGER KING® campaign. After reintroducing the classic BURGER KING® line—"HAVE IT YOUR WAY®"—by way of a series of well-received commercials involving office workers, the campaign immediately began to take various other, completely different directions, introducing a fictional character named "Dr. Angus" (a parody of self-help/diet gurus), as well as another fictional character, "Ugoff" (a take off on the pretentious world of fashion); the campaign also included a sensational "Chicken Fight" event between two men in chicken costumes, presented with all the hype and ferocity of a real championship boxing match. Eventually, the campaign rolled out the Burger King himself, who came to life in a slightly creepy mask.

According to Bogusky, these constant reinventions and new iterations are all part of creating successful Hoopla, which requires infinite variety in order to keep people surprised and interested. "One of our philosophies," Bogusky says, "is to think of a campaign as a continuing conversation or correspondence. It should always be bringing you something new, something you didn't know already. Whereas most advertising is like the same Xeroxed letter that gets sent to you over and over again."

The creation of Hoopla necessitates not only constant invention and occasional sleep deprivation but also death on a daily basis. Because the only way to produce consistently good ideas is to be ruthless about weeding out the mediocre ones. "Ideas do die here, all the time," Bogusky says. "Emotionally, the way to get through that is to keep going. You have to have the passion, confidence, and work ethic to believe you can continue to come up with more good ideas, if and when your original 'good' idea gets bludgeoned to death."

EXPEDITION TO THE
Island of Man·Hat·Tan

1999 Mission
Becomes Multi-Media Milestone

For 5 Days, World Watches Live Via Web Cam

Team Carries No Money
Only Shiny Gear Trinkets to Barter for Survival Basics

"Blair Witch" Filmmakers Give Code Word
"Bulldozer" if Things Get Hairy

Ad Content Mixes With Real-Life Expedition,
Social Commentary—Becomes Cultural Phenomenon

MISSION CONTROL ▶ EXPLORER BIOS PAST MISS

WEB CAM

DATE/TIME

10/10/99
5:30 PM

LIVE

DAY ONE—11.2.99 6 a.m. E.S.T.
The team makes landfall on the island of Man•Hat•Tan. Their mission: Make
contact with the Lost Tribe—a people who live cut off from the outside world.
And introduce them to the tools they'll need to escape the concrete jungle.
Mini-cameras mounted on the team's helmets stream live video to the
PlanetOutdoors.com website.

CONVERSING WITH THE LOST TRIBE OF CIVILIZATION

THE ISLAND OF MAN·HAT·T0

LOWER BROADWAY CANYON

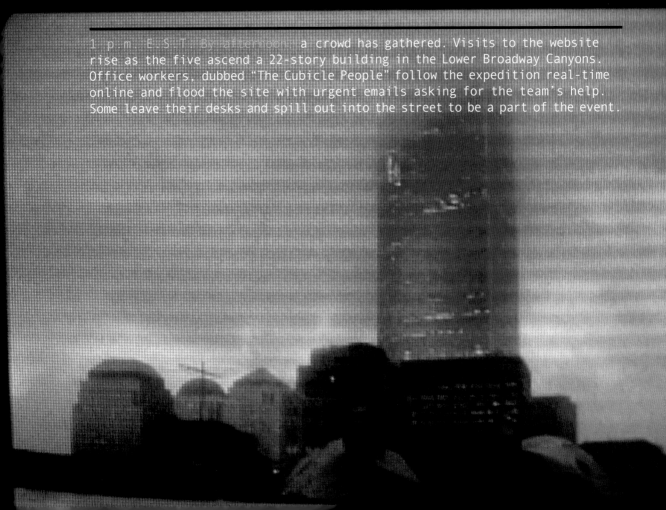

1 p.m. E.S.T. By afternoon, a crowd has gathered. Visits to the website rise as the five ascend a 22-story building in the Lower Broadway Canyons. Office workers, dubbed "The Cubicle People" follow the expedition real-time online and flood the site with urgent emails asking for the team's help. Some leave their desks and spill out into the street to be a part of the event.

LOST TRIBE MISSION
NOVEMBER 1999

1. Landfall. Cape of Man•Hat•Tan [DAY ONE– 11/2/99, 6 a.m. EST]: Dawn's light. Team navigates the treacherous coastal waters where the mighty Hudson and East Rivers converge. Currents and adrenaline levels run high in the inflatable Zodiac. No one knows how the natives will react to the presence of suntanned people from the outside world bearing gear. Team begins hike/bike trek into Wall Street Canyons.

2. Plight of the Cubicle People/ 400' Vertical Ascent to Camp One [DAY ONE– 11/2/99, 1 p.m. EST–SUNRISE 11/3]: Wall Street Canyons, Lower Broadway Range. Outfitted with latest climbing shoes/gear, the team mounts a 400-foot vertical ascent of a ("22-story") concrete/steel peak. Objective: Make contact with palest of Lost Tribe clan, the Cubicle People. Teach them how to be self-sufficient in outside world – get online and gear up. Help compose convincing Sick Day email to send to corporate chieftain. Ascend to summit, set up tents, pray light pollution doesn't spoil Milky Way visibility.

3. Underground with the Nomadic "Sardine" People [DAY TWO– 11/3/99, 8:00 a.m. EST]: Explore cave entrances in urban jungle floor. Sporting the latest spelunking garb, the team plans a descent into the subterranean labyrinth of tunnels. Objective: Introduce

hiking/biking gear to a people who pack themselves into tin cans on rails to get from point A to point B, instead of enjoying sunshine/fresh air and adrenaline rush of human-powered transit.

4. East Village Counter-Culture People [DAY TWO– 1/3/99, Afternoon]: Macro study of East Village LandSat imagery reveals habitat of artisans in mostly monochromatic black ceremonial garb. Small concentration of tie-died people. Tribal tattoos, nose rings, body piercings, adornments, all elevated to new art form, and appear to cross boundaries of race, creed, age, and socio-economic caste.

5. Chinatown. Day of Thunder. Night of Neon [DAY TWO– 11/3/99, Sunset-Dawn]: The team claims a traffic island deep in the heart of the Chinatown territories to camp for the night. The low-lying paved regions surrounding the campsite are believed to be the nocturnal migratory route for thundering herds of 18-wheeled behemoths. The night sky burns with the glow of the locals' neon fire. The team calls upon their urban sleep deprivation training to pull through.

6. Times Square Cookout Jamboree [DAY THREE– 11/4/99, 10 a.m. EST]: Objective: Team prepares a hearty camp brunch in the hopes of attracting curious alpha males and females to explain the feature/benefits of their ultralight camp stove and 7-piece aluminum cookware set.

7. Monolithic Lion Deities [DAY THREE– 11/4/99, 1 p.m. EST]: Objective: Research what on sat. photos appears to be N.Y. Public Temple of Written Knowledge, guarded by two heroic stone felines (Panthera leo)– icons from a time when humans worshiped the outside world.

8. Empire State Ziggurat [DAY THREE– 11/4/99, 2 p.m.]: Team researches unconfirmed urban legends of others from outside world who mysteriously disappear after climbing or base jumping from monolithic stepped structure– rumored tales of capture by village chieftain.

9. Central Park Green Zone [DAY THREE– 11/4/99, 4 p.m.]: Investigate encouraging signs that the outside world is encroaching on the urban landscape.

10. Boiled in Hot Water [DAY THREE– 11/4/99, 5 p.m.]: The team forgoes cooking their last meal of the expedition and attempts to barter gear to sample a few of the local island delicacies like chestnuts roasted on open spit and boiled hotdogs from a street cart vendor.

11. Cul de Sac People of Outer Suburbia Brooklyn Bridge Crossing [11/4/99, p.m. rush hour, EST.]: Team investigates mass exodus from urban environment with hopes of attracting followers. Objective: Use latest shiny gear to woo Urbanites, convert as many as possible into devout outdoor enthusiasts. Sacrifice cell phones to river god. Continue trek out of urban territories to asphalt tar pits and malls of Outer Suburbia.

ROBIN COWIE vs CP+B

OK. Tell the readers a little bit about what you do. Robin: I am a producer, a director, an Internet entrepreneur. I've owned an Internet company and have been running it for the last three years. I continue to produce movies. At one point, I produced a tremendous amount of television commercials. And you were one of the, "Blair Witch Guys"? Robin: (Laughs.) Yeah. So did you ever have any sort of formal advertising training or anything like that? Robin: No, I got a degree in film production and also creative writing. So I just have a creative writing background and a film background. So, I read that when you were doing *Blair Witch* you started the websites after people began reacting to some early exposure. Robin: Yeah, a guy named John Piercen had a television show on the independent film channel called *Split Screen*. It showcased independent filmmakers in different stages of production. We had met John through the Florida Film Festival and had given him a tape. This was before we had actually shot the film. He had so much demand that it shut down the servers on *Split Screen's* website. This was way before we ever shot the film. So we decided to start our own website, and that became the very early days of blairwitch.com. The movie originally had two components: One was the footage, and the other was kind of a documentary about the movie. Well, we ended up taking a lot of that material and putting it on the website because we really believed in the mythology behind the movie. And we thought a content-rich website would really engage people from all over the world. We invested a lot of content at a time most sites had very little. Adding that sort of web component turned the whole thing into a big, scary play. Nobody knew whether it was real or not. Robin: Yeah, and you gotta remember that this is before reality TV. Now you think of reality TV as part of life, but it wasn't then. We loved that idea of exploring a witch story as realistically as we possibly could. And it was certainly creativity that was born out of the restrictions of budget. A lot of people think small budgets restrict creativity, but I know for us it has enabled us more than it's ever really held us back. When there's no money, you have to fight to get noticed. And when you are really, truly fighting – there are no rules. Robin: With commercials, not only are you restricted in the amount of money, but you're restricted in the amount of time. You've only got thirty seconds, or on a website, the average person spends like five seconds deciding if they're gonna stay. So could you talk a little bit about the whole concept of the PlanetOutdoors campaign? Robin: The concept for PlanetOutdoors was to communicate the idea of getting out there and having fun. You guys developed an idea of literally pulling people out of their office cubicles and getting them to explore the outdoor world. So we adopted some of the first person perspective that we had used in *Blair Witch*. This so-called advertisement turned into what really was an exploration, kind of an assault on Manhattan. So we actually did it, as opposed to creating a story about it. We literally scaled a building and pulled people out of the office windows. The team really went spelunking in the subways and then emerged to bring a message to people in Manhattan. And we documented all of it. We silmulcasted on the web, and archived the experience for people on the web so they could go watch the event. And nothing like this was really being done at the time. Robin: Yeah. Today, we all think of watching short films on websites as just kind of a thing that happens, but at the time there weren't those kinds of advertising tools yet. To me, the crazy nutso thing is, that doing it this way meant you had to direct a three-day-long live advertisement. Robin: Right. And it's funny, especially from the advertising perspective. You would think everyone there would be obsessed with every frame being shown, but really we were doing the complete opposite. Thankfully we live in a digital age where you've got digital editing and you can pour all of that footage onto drives and then get those slices of life that you captured. At CP+B we learned a lot from the PlanetOutdoors campaign and we started applying it to other projects. Instead of just doing a TV campaign, we started producing entire plays within pop culture, using the Internet, live events, or whatever. We found that in a short amount of time you can build an insane amount of momentum. But it doesn't only work in the short term for individual campaigns. By applying that same philosophy to overall brand strategies, we've been successful at creating long-term momentum, too. Robin: That project was so much bigger than just creating the advertising. It was so much bigger than just doing a 30-second spot. The footage was not only used in the 30-second spot, but it was also used in the corporate imaging, on the website, and beyond that, the fact that we were making an assault on Manhattan became a story in the press. Yeah, and it seems like the press, or you know, making things that the press embraces, can be part of the equation when you are trying to make something famous. Robin: That is absolutely true. We even made up a dorky internal slogan type thing so we would always keep the power of the press in mind: Forget news in the pipeline, news IS the pipeline. Really, the press is just another avenue. You have to go at things from a million different angles. Robin: The key to concepts like PlanetOutdoors is to be nonlinear and creative in the way that you approach the message. You don't say, "Well I've gotta go from A to B trying to make a straight line." There's many different ways to get there. Another thing we took from it was search engine marketing or whatever people call it. You know, where you sort of seed stuff for people to find on the Internet or fill a Google search with content. I know you've continued doing a lot of stuff like that as well where you put little nuggets of content out there, and the cumulative effect happens when someone Googles it or whatever. Robin: 80 percent of all I do is in the online world. So I've learned a tremendous amount about search engine marketing, whether it's about optimization or marketing or affiliate marketing or blogs. The old adage of push advertising versus pull advertising–that's all really come true. On-demand content has come true. So now I make sure that I've got as many lines out there as I can possibly get out there that other people can use. Then I make sure my web content is as rich as it possibly can be. Then I push as much energy into that center and really trust and enable the users of that website and the promoters of that website to do their own thing. Seems to be working so far. We're still here. Yes. We are still here.

Commercial vérité

'Blair Witch' team plans island adventure for PlanetOutdoors.com

By Bruce Horovitz
USA TODAY

BOULDER, Colo. — Few people know this.

But moments before the actors in the hit movie *The Blair Witch Project* disappeared into the woods, they each were handed a code word that, in a crisis, would bring the filming to an immediate halt: bulldozer.

It never was uttered.

Good thing, too. The spooky film, about three filmmakers who go into the woods to document a story of witchcraft, went on to bulldoze Hollywood and rank among the most profitable films ever made. While it cost less than $50,000 to film, its box office

COVER STORY

recently passed $140 million. The film was made with ___ script. The actors each received

Who's going on the Big Apple expedition?

PlanetOutdoors.com hired a talent agency to help find five outdoors experts for the trek. Here's who made the final cut:

▶ **The anthropologist.** Allison Horovitz, 28, is a cultural anthropologist who helped research construction of a chimpanzee sanctuary in Tanzania. She will keep a daily journal on the Web site.
▶ **The climber.** Lisa Rust, 30, is a climbing instructor who is studying to be an emergency medical technician at 23,000 feet.
▶ **The cameraman.** Chris Davenport, 28, is the 1996 World Extreme Skiing Champion who also knows how to handle a video camera.
▶ **The psychologist.** Brad Buikema, 29, is a psychology major who recently led a two-week wilderness expedition for urban teens who committed adult crimes.
▶ **The CEO.** David Secunda, 36, founded PlanetOutdoors.com in February 1999. He is a rabid outdoorsman who several years ago took 12 Vietnam veterans on an emotional, month-long bicycle tour from Hanoi to Ho Chi Minh City.

By Patrick Kramer for USA TODAY

Team talk: Crew members from left, director Robin Cowie, cameraman Chris Davenport, psychologist Brad Buikema, anthropologist Allison Horovitz, CEO David Secunda and climbing expert Lisa Rust.

street ___ ___ ___ omoting PlanetOutdoor-
___ ___ Each member of the
___ ___ ___ PlanetOut-

taxi rides.
Is ___ op selling out — partic-

million budget is roughly 60
times the estimated $50,000 it
cost ___ ___ lm the *Blair Witch*

conventiona'
___

LOST TRIBE EXPEDITION
MANHATTAN ISLAND 1999

Planet
Outdoors
.com

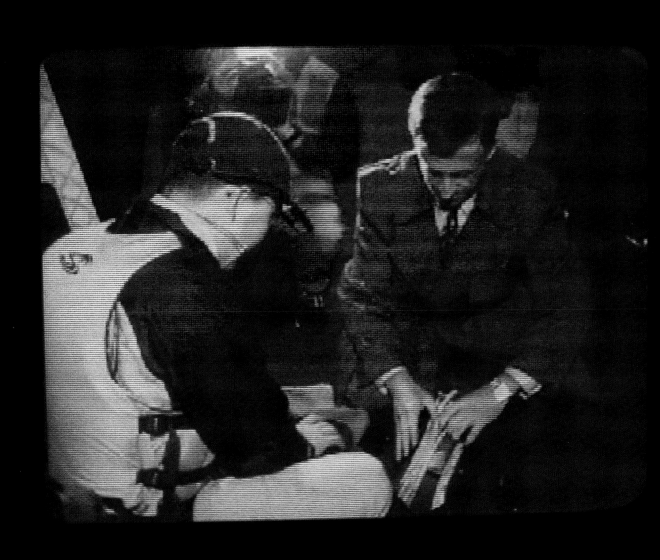

EPILOGUE: A Bond is Forged. In the three days that follow, the team woos the local and national news media and attracts record numbers of site visitors hungry for the latest outdoor gear. The team is also joined by hundreds of followers who trade their wingtips and primitive animal hide satchels for trail runners and lightweight daypacks. They follow the team on foot over the Brooklyn Bridge and out of the city

Two current employees maintain (separate) amateur pornographic websites.

○ Fake
○ True

Attn:
U.S. Fish and Wildlife Service
NOVEMBER 15, 2004

A Petition to List Man (*Homo sapiens masculus*) as an Endangered Species Pursuant to the U.S. Endangered Species Act of 1973

SPECIES INFORMATION

A. Classification and Nomenclature

1. Scientific Name: *Homo sapiens masculus*
2. Common Name: *Man*
3. Pertinent Synonyms: *Guy, Dude, Bro, Hombre*
4. Size of genus: *1 species*
5. Family Classification: *Hominidae*

✶✶✶

B. Description

An adult Man stands approximately 180 centimeters high and weighs about 80 kilograms, though these numbers can vary significantly. A coat of fur extends from above the eye line to the upper posterior portion of the neck. Skin color varies, and while generally uniform in texture and hue, it may feature distinctive markings such as pin-up girls, grim reapers, or old English lettering. During colder months, a winter coat may appear in the form of a handlebar moustache or mutton chops.

Healthy Men generate a mildly acrid scent comprised of sweat, gasoline, hardwood, scotch whiskey, and the hide of dead cattle. During a rutting period, this scent may be augmented with an alcohol-based aftershave.

fig 1. HOMO SAPIENS MASCULUS *IN HIS NATURAL ENVIRONMENT.*

C. Significance of the Taxon

Man is the cornerstone of life on earth, and his continued existence is vital to the health of the planet. To date, Man is the only species capable of driving a 1969 Dodge Charger, operating a Microsoft X-box game console, converting simple grains into courage-boosting Tennessee whiskey, making cowboy boots out of other animals, turning redwood trees into balustraded sundecks, converting dead stegosauruses into high-octane racing fuel, spinning direct-drive turntables the wrong direction on purpose for a percussive scratching effect, videotaping *(and distributing over the internet)* part of his own reproductive cycle,[1] helping pristine wilderness areas blossom into national caliber motocross tracks, and harvesting crystalline carbon from the earth's crust to produce 6-inch iced-out nameplates.

D. Geographical Distribution

The geographical range of North American Man extends from Yankee Stadium in the Bronx west to Laguna Seca International Raceway, and from Legends Gentlemen's Club in Minot, North Dakota to the South Laredo Rodeo Grounds in South Laredo, Texas. Within this immense range, Man has been sighted at virtually every elevation, frequenting the below-sea-level billiard halls of New Orleans, Louisiana and driving commercial dump trucks at the 11,300-foot-high molybdenum mine near Freemont Pass, Colorado.

fig 2. *MAN'S CONTRIBUTION TO LIFE ON EARTH IS UNASSAILABLE.*

E. Populations Known or Assumed Extirpated *(extinct)*

Throughout North America, once thriving populations of Men have all but disappeared. The melodious clang of the Pennsylvania Blacksmith's hammer and the soothing hum of the Oregon Lumberjack's chainsaw are largely inaudible. The St. Louis Riverboat Gambler died off near the end of the last century, followed closely into extinction by a symbiotic subpopulation, the St. Louis Riverboat Pilot. Gone are the Kansas City Cattle Baron, the San Francisco Railroad Baron, and the Albany Steel Magnate.

Even some of the more contemporary populations of Men have been decimated. The Barber has been uprooted by the Hair Stylist – an entirely different species than Man. The Vigilante has given way to the Whistleblower, and the Daredevil has been replaced with another non-Man species, the Sky Surfer.

F. Habitat Description

Man prefers a wide variety of natural surroundings. He may fraternize on the concrete slopes of an open-air sports coliseum, or he may retreat to the dark recesses of a local tavern for shelter from the elements.

No stranger to high elevation, Man terrifies majestic elk as he rips through alpine terrain on 145-horsepower, 4-stroke snowmobiles.

And he is equally at ease in the water, skimming across tropical wave tops at the helm of offshore racing boats,[2] relaxing in the turbulent shallows of inland hot tubs, or sinking deftly beneath the ocean's surface to spear beautiful, reef-dwelling fish.

Man may construct a home almost anywhere, but is often hesitant to venture inside of it, preferring the cedar expanses of his adjacent sundeck, or the cozy confines of his well-appointed garage.

G. Diet

Man kills and eats animals. He marches them into meat packing plants, submerges them in zesty marinade, cooks them over an open flame, and serves them on paper plates.[3] Stainless steel cutlery allows Man to hold delicious animal chunks in place while he goes to work on them with sharp, blade-like incisors specially adapted for shearing meat.

At one time or another, Man has eaten every animal on earth. In fact, Man's curiosity about the taste of animals has even led him to eat ones that were already extinct! In 1900, Man scientists who found a 40,000-year-old wooly mammoth frozen in Beresovka, Siberia celebrated the discovery with a hearty banquet of mammoth steak.[4]

fig 3. *THIS MAN TOTALLY WASTED THIS WILD HOG WITH A FREEDOM ARMS .454 CASULL SINGLE ACTION REVOLVER.*

H. Migration

In the spring, Man migrates to baseball stadiums, foraging on cold beer and heated, cylindrical helpings of slain pig. When the leaves begin to turn color, Man makes the arduous trek to nearby football stadiums, sipping from thermoses of heavily-spiked Irish coffee to compensate for the crisp fall weather. During the winter months, Man may retreat to a cabaret, where he is sustained almost entirely by lap dances. Then again, he may not retreat at all. If Man is in the mood, he will don special clothing filled with the feathers of dead geese and snowboard off a 30-foot cornice.[5]

fig 4. *RIVAL MALES CAN ACHIEVE SOCIAL ACCORD WITH A RITUALISTIC HAND CLASP.*

I. Herd Dynamics

Man is a social animal who tends to travel in pods. These pods, commonly referred to as "crews" or "posses," usually have a defined hierarchy, with an alpha male situated at the top. Intracrew communication happens in the form of various handshakes, or the running of two crew members toward each other, followed by a synchronized jump and symbolic coming-together of the chests.

II. EVIDENCE OF THREATS OF SURVIVAL
A. Destruction, Modification, or Curtailment of Habitat

1. Disappearance of the American Barbershop

Red and blue barber poles once swirled hypnotically across the North American landscape – marking sanctuaries where North American Man could discuss sports, second amendment rights, and sexual indiscretions. But these safe havens have been replaced with "hair salons," establishments that are lethal to Man. In 1997, the number of barbers in the U.S. was 70,900,

compared to 54,000 this year. Meanwhile the number of hairstylists has leapt from 638,000 in 1997 to 669,000 today.[6]

2. Decline of the American Gymnasium

Not to be confused with "health clubs," where patrons straddle fancy machines with pastel-colored upholstery and sip fruit smoothies between sets, the gymnasium contains only free weights, a heavy bag, and a water fountain. In these surroundings, Man became stronger and more able to fend off rivals for his territory or a mate. But American gyms have all but vanished, leaving Man in a weakened and vulnerable state.

fig 5. *YEARS AGO MEN ROAMED ALMOST ALL OF EARTH.*
☐ *PLACES THERE WERE MEN*
■ *MAN-FREE*

3. Destruction of Important Migratory Grounds

Las Vegas, Nevada – once an important migratory destination where Man could rejuvenate himself with free drinks, gambling, and legalized prostitution – has become a family destination. Equally disturbing is the decline of Route 66. This vital migratory route, which runs from Chicago to Los Angeles, afforded Man the opportunity to drive 18-wheelers, consume bowls of chili, and make suggestive comments to sassy waitresses. However commercialization of the route has turned it into a sad cavalcade of pasty, sandal-shod tourists.

fig 6. *A MAN HERD ROOSTS THE HELL OUT OF DELICATE FLORA IN THE GREAT BASIN DESERT.*

4. Curtailment of ATV Land Access

In order to thrive, Man must have the ability to ride something with an internal combustion engine through pristine wilderness, sending giant spouts of loamy earth skyward as he opens the throttle and emits guttural war cries into the replaceable dust filter of his full-faced helmet. But in 1992, the Bureau of Land Management closed over 60 million acres of wilderness to Man, unless he entered them on foot *(not an option, since nature walks are lethal to Man).*[7]

5. Modification of Workplace

Throughout the 1970s, Man's office was equipped with a dedicated bar. Fashioned from exotic hardwood and stocked with top shelf liquor, these bars sustained Man on the corporate battlefield and provided him with a valuable way to expedite interoffice courtships. Today, Man's workspace is bereft of nutritious alcohol. Even worse, since the U.S. courts began interpreting sexual harassment as a form of illegal sex discrimination in the mid-1970s, Man can no longer grab the ass of a female coworker with impunity.[8]

6. Loss of Rangeland to Chickens

Until recently, chickens destined for commercial use were properly confined to tiny steel cages. But with increased demand for "free range" chicken, many of these fat, flightless birds have been turned loose on open expanses of prairie, unspoiled rangeland that could be utilized by Man for paintball or some kind of Burning Man type thing.

B. Disease or Predation

In recent years, a new disease has advanced unseen across the American landscape. Mantropy. A cruel degenerative disease that sets in during the best years of a Man's life, causing the Man inside that Man to slowly wither and die until the victim is literally a husk of his former self. By attacking on a non-cellular, spiritual level, the disease often avoids detection until its victim is irreversibly hollowed out.

Mantropy knows no social or economic boundaries, attacking Men of all races and tax brackets without warning. Although most of its victims are between 18 and 34, severe cases of Mantropy have been documented in Men of every age. And while there are no physical symptoms, subtle warning signs common to many afflicted Men have been documented.

C. Inadequacy of Regulatory Measures

The fact is, there are too many regulatory measures. Emission controls that prevent Man from using high performance exhaust systems. Roughing the passer penalties that prevent one Man from rendering another Man unconscious well after the ball has been thrown. Speed governors that won't allow Man to do 110 in a 22-foot box van. Copyright laws that preclude Man from sharing mp3 files. Municipal

---

Common Mantropy Risk Indicators:

- *pretend car-racing shoes*
- *excessive smoothie consumption*
- *two-wheeled transportation under 500cc's*
- *pet less than 8.7 kilos*
- *hard lemonade*
- *wallet over 150 square centimeters (*"man purse"*)*
- *temporary tribal tattoo*
- *frequent seaweed wraps*
- *buffed fingernails*
- *lightly tinted glasses (*does not include ANSI-rated safety glasses*)*

---

noise ordinances that discourage Man from replacing the rear seat of his '59 Impala with giant subwoofers. Wildlife statutes that make it illegal for Man to fish with dynamite. Heavy fines that make it expensive for Man to go street racing. Why, Man is being regulated right out of existence! The whole damned situation is inadequate.

D. Other Evidence of Threat

Liquid-cooled Harleys, egg substitutes, roadside assistance, synchronized diving, sensitivity training, hybrid cars, decaffeinated coffee, scented candles, recumbent bicycles, NASCAR restrictor plates, explicit lyrics stickers, in-line skates, aerobic kickboxing classes, the word "carb," celebrity-endorsed grills, lightweight hiking boots, terry cloth wristbands *(in non-sporting environments),* and a whole bunch of other stuff that's too sickening to write down.

III. LISTING RECOMMENDATIONS

The North American Man should be listed as endangered by the USFWS. Without an ESA Endangered listing, Man will surely succumb to the ravages of an effeminate, Feng shui world-gone-mad. But if you, the Fish and Wildlife Service, will intervene on his behalf by protecting him with Endangered status, Man can bounce back. He can once again roam North America in large numbers, living life with gusto and making the world a better place.

Also, it is recommended that Man be granted unlimited access to MAXIM Magazine, and be allowed to freely pursue the lifestyle outlined in its pages. This will give Man a fighting chance in the critical post-recovery period.

Respectfully submitted this 15th day of November, 2004,

Ed Needham
Editor-In-Chief
MAXIM Magazine

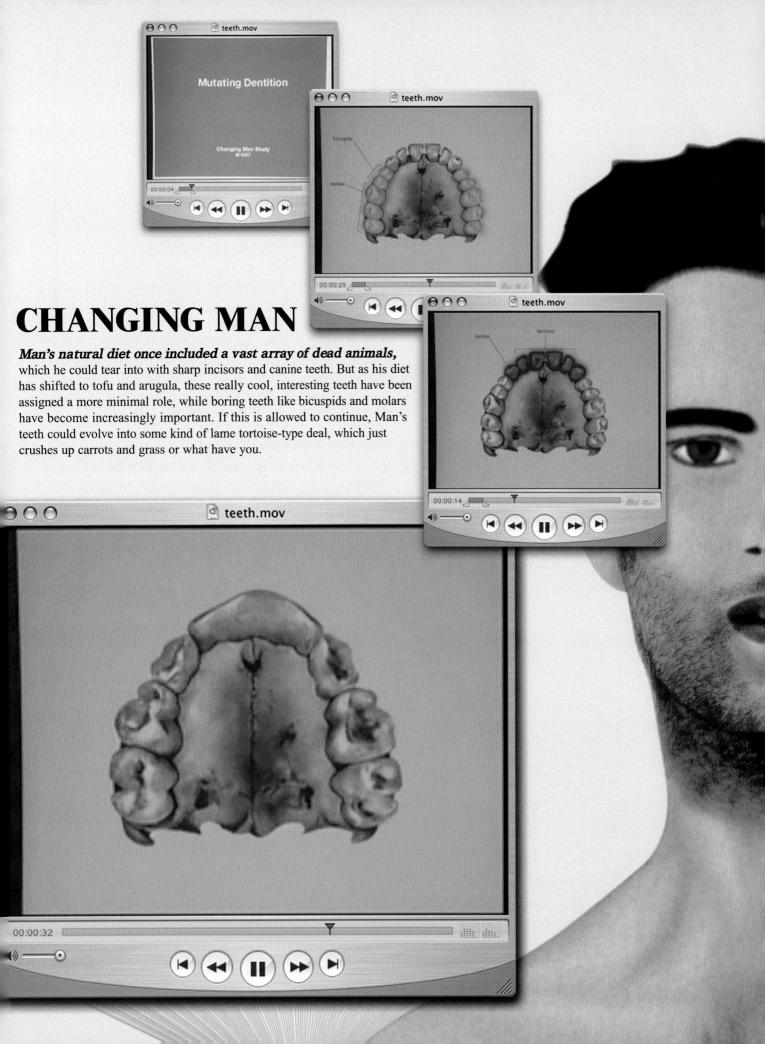

CHANGING MAN

Man's natural diet once included a vast array of dead animals, which he could tear into with sharp incisors and canine teeth. But as his diet has shifted to tofu and arugula, these really cool, interesting teeth have been assigned a more minimal role, while boring teeth like bicuspids and molars have become increasingly important. If this is allowed to continue, Man's teeth could evolve into some kind of lame tortoise-type deal, which just crushes up carrots and grass or what have you.

Dermal Transition

M 0413

You know how when you see a supermodel in a macramé bikini, you think, "wow, her skin looks buttery." Well, that. Except now the model has a mustache.

Mutating Dentition

M 0227

Man's teeth are being used in ways nature never intended, and the consequences won't be pretty.

Cranial Flux

M 0305

Hopefully you are sitting down when you activate this animation deal, because you're not going to like it at all.

Trans Hands

M 0411

Man's hands aren't really the hands of a man anymore. Now they are the hands a Man likes to hold. But they are already attached to him, so it's weird.

In the days of Abe Lincoln, Men wrestled and made houses out of logs and fashioned hats out of unsuspecting woodland creatures. This resulted in a certain set of shared physical characteristics. But as Man's way of life has been curtailed, so has he been reduced to a sleek, seductive shadow of his former masculine self.

SIGNS OF INFECTION
Frosted Tips
Noticable "Plucking"
Colored Contacts
Artifical Tan
Removed Body Hair

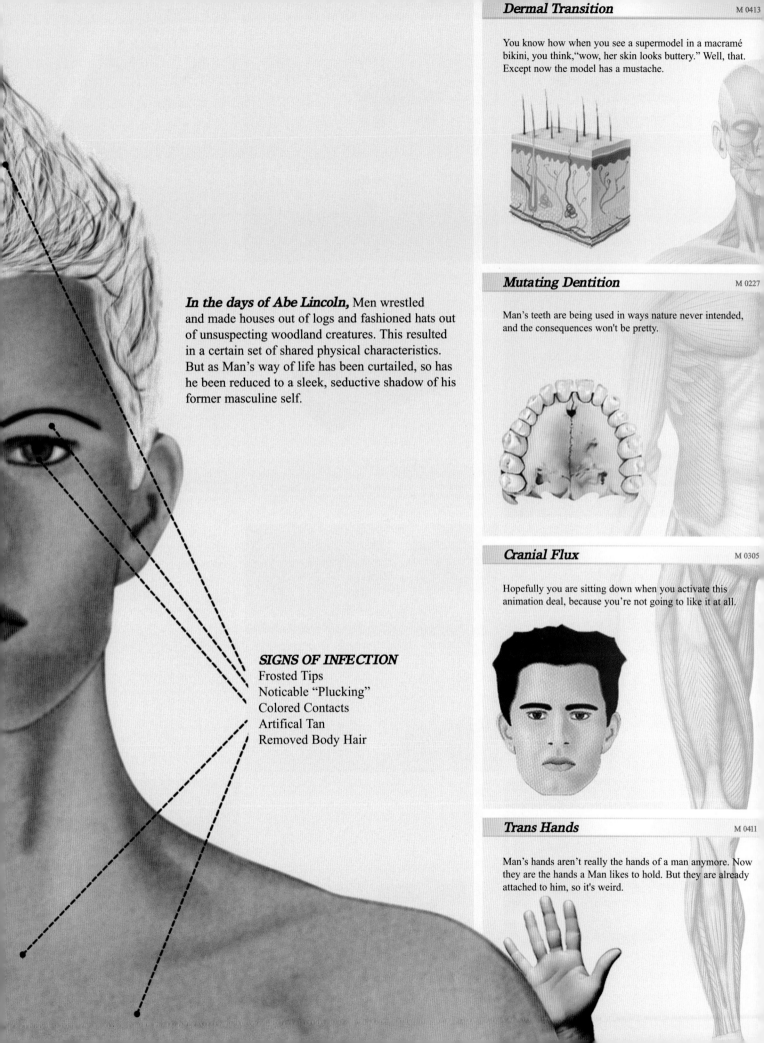

Legal Rampage Control Unit

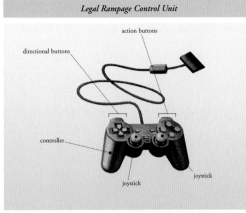

- action buttons
- directional buttons
- controller
- joystick
- joystick

Allows Man to legally punch people, shoot people, drive over people, hit people with golf clubs, or back over people who have just been driven over.

Pro-Bono Dentistry Kit

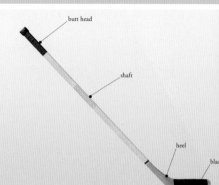

- butt head
- shaft
- heel
- blade

This handy item makes it simple for one Man to remove the incisors and canines of another Man, entirely free of charge.

Territory Indicator

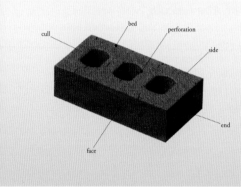

- cull
- bed
- perforation
- side
- end
- face

Allows Man to mark his territory, preferably with a 4-bedroom, 3-bathroom Tudor mansion that includes a detached 3-car garage.

NUNCHAKU
A Ninja will move these all around their body until the enemy is afraid and mesmerized, at which point he will immediately club the person to death.

KATANA
Ninjas prefer to kill people with exotic weapons, but every once in awhile they roll with something traditional.

TANTO
If a Ninja has an off day, he will reflect on what went wrong while cutting himself in half with this.

TONFA
Cops aren't stupid. That's why they adopted this weapon from the Ninja arsenal. Anyone who's ever resisted arrest knows this thing is bad news.

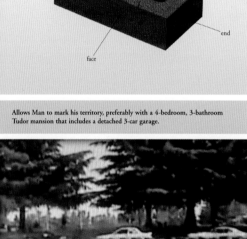

CROSSBOW
A Ninja won't kill people with this. He'll use it to shoot an arrow attched to a rope, then climb to where the people are, then kill them.

GRAPPLING HOOK
All of a sudden, your impenetrable fortress isn't so impenetrable.

KUSARIFUNDO
Forget even trying to figure out what this does, or how it works. Let's just say they'll be needing dental records to even figure out who you are.

HAND CLAWS
At some point in their life, every single Ninja will fly up the trunk of some conifer tree and fire an arrow into another man's eye. These are for that.

Reading Machine

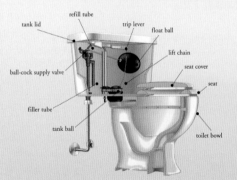

- tank lid
- refill tube
- trip lever
- float ball
- lift chain
- ball-cock supply valve
- seat cover
- seat
- filler tube
- tank ball
- toilet bowl

Causes Man to grab the nearest publication and pour over its contents with real intellectual thirst. Induces moments of quiet reflection between articles.

Meaning of Life

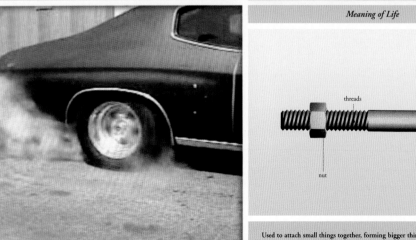

- threads
- nut
- head

Used to attach small things together, forming bigger things, which are then attached together to make even bigger things to infinity...

ARE YOU DYING INSIDE?

Mantropy Disease
A silent killer that strikes men in the prime of life.

----
mantropycontrol.com

-------- End of Forwarded Message

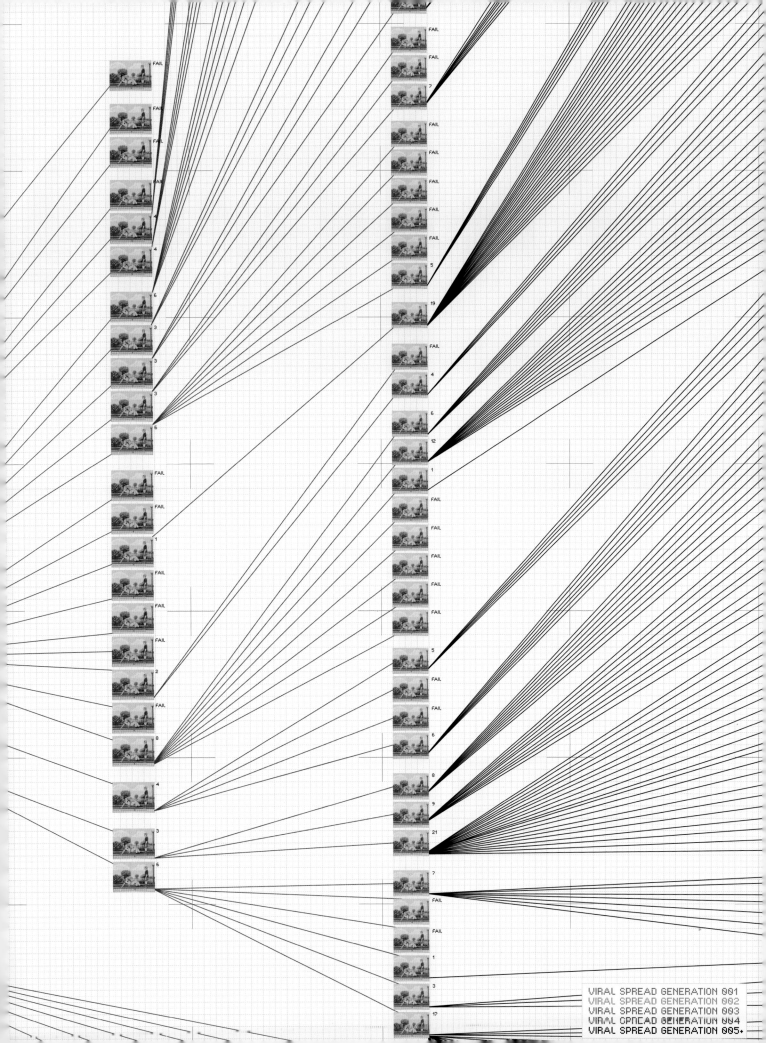

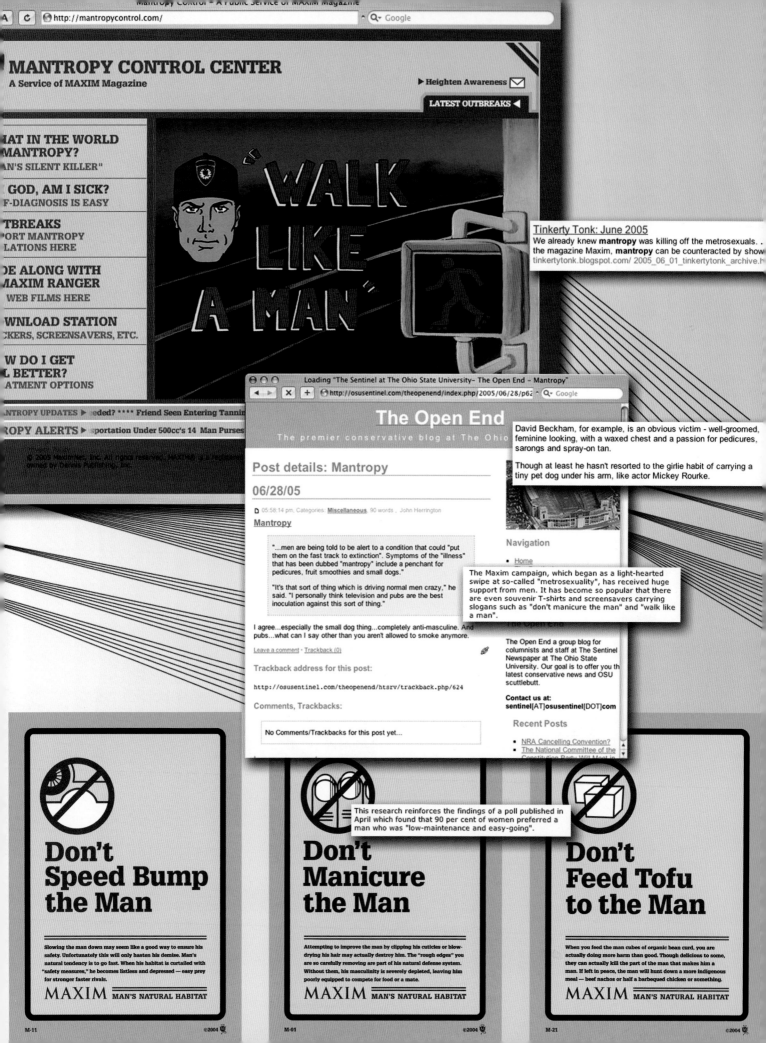

MANTROPY CONTROL CENTER
A Service of MAXIM Magazine

▶ Heighten Awareness ✉

LATEST OUTBREAKS ◀

WHAT IN THE WORLD IS MANTROPY?
"MAN'S SILENT KILLER"

OH GOD, AM I SICK?
SELF-DIAGNOSIS IS EASY

OUTBREAKS
REPORT MANTROPY VIOLATIONS HERE

RIDE ALONG WITH A MAXIM RANGER
WEB FILMS HERE

DOWNLOAD STATION
STICKERS, SCREENSAVERS, ETC.

HOW DO I GET WELL BETTER?
TREATMENT OPTIONS

MANTROPY UPDATES ▶ eded? **** Friend Seen Entering Tannin

MANTROPY ALERTS ▶ sportation Under 500cc's 14 Man Purses

© 2005 MaximNet, Inc. All rights reserved. MAXIM® is a registered owned by Dennis Publishing, Inc.

Mantropy Control – A Public Service of MAXIM Magazine

http://mantropycontrol.com/ Q▾ Google

Tinkerty Tonk: June 2005
We already knew **mantropy** was killing off the metrosexuals. .
the magazine Maxim, **mantropy** can be counteracted by show
tinkertytonk.blogspot.com/ 2005_06_01_tinkertytonk_archive.h

Loading "The Sentinel at The Ohio State University– The Open End – Mantropy"

◀ ▶ ✕ + http://osusentinel.com/theopenend/index.php/2005/06/28/p62 Q▾ Google

The Open End
The premier conservative blog at The Ohio

Post details: Mantropy

06/28/05

05:58:14 pm, Categories: Miscellaneous, 90 words , John Herrington

Mantropy

> "...men are being told to be alert to a condition that could "put them on the fast track to extinction". Symptoms of the "illness" that has been dubbed "mantropy" include a penchant for pedicures, fruit smoothies and small dogs."
>
> "It's that sort of thing which is driving normal men crazy," he said. "I personally think television and pubs are the best inoculation against this sort of thing."

I agree...especially the small dog thing...completely anti-masculine. And pubs...what can I say other than you aren't allowed to smoke anymore.

Leave a comment · Trackback (0)

Trackback address for this post:

http://osusentinel.com/theopenend/htsrv/trackback.php/624

Comments, Trackbacks:

No Comments/Trackbacks for this post yet...

Navigation

- Home

The Open End

The Open End a group blog for columnists and staff at The Sentinel Newspaper at The Ohio State University. Our goal is to offer you th latest conservative news and OSU scuttlebutt.

Contact us at:
sentinel[AT]osusentinel[DOT]com

Recent Posts

- NRA Cancelling Convention?
- The National Committee of the

David Beckham, for example, is an obvious victim - well-groomed, feminine looking, with a waxed chest and a passion for pedicures, sarongs and spray-on tan.

Though at least he hasn't resorted to the girlie habit of carrying a tiny pet dog under his arm, like actor Mickey Rourke.

The Maxim campaign, which began as a light-hearted swipe at so-called "metrosexuality", has received huge support from men. It has become so popular that there are even souvenir T-shirts and screensavers carrying slogans such as "don't manicure the man" and "walk like a man".

This research reinforces the findings of a poll published in April which found that 90 per cent of women preferred a man who was "low-maintenance and easy-going".

Don't Speed Bump the Man

Slowing the man down may seem like a good way to ensure his safety. Unfortunately this will only hasten his demise. Man's natural tendency is to go fast. When his habitat is curtailed with "safety measures," he becomes listless and depressed — easy prey for stronger faster rivals.

MAXIM MAN'S NATURAL HABITAT

M-11   ©2004

Don't Manicure the Man

Attempting to improve the man by clipping his cuticles or blow-drying his hair may actually destroy him. The "rough edges" you are so carefully removing are part of his natural defense system. Without them, his masculinity is severely depleted, leaving him poorly equipped to compete for food or a mate.

MAXIM MAN'S NATURAL HABITAT

M-01   ©2004

Don't Feed Tofu to the Man

When you feed the man cubes of organic bean curd, you are actually doing more harm than good. Though delicious to some, they can actually kill the part of the man that makes him a man. If left in peace, the man will hunt down a more indigenous meal — beef nachos or half a barbequed chicken or something.

MAXIM MAN'S NATURAL HABITAT

M-21   ©2004

We are pleased to run this public service announcement. Men: have you ever worn a fauxhawk? Applied a temporary tattoo? Sat for a manicure? Own a dog that weighs less than you do? If you answered "yes" to any of these questions, YOU may be suffering from Mantropy. Please, do yourself a favor and GET HELP [...]....

memeorandum: Archive Edition for Tuesday, June 28, 2005
Symptoms of the "illness" that has been dubbed "**mantropy**" include a ... Ace: **Mantropy**: The Silent Killer — Goofy but kinda true: [snipped quote] Well, ...
www.memeorandum.com/05/06/28/ - 171k - Cached - Similar pages

forcedconnections.com

http://forcedconnections.com/display.php?id=158

Home · School Work · Photo Manipulation · 2004

← →

Mantropy Deterioration

Assignment
This was one of my first 'computers in art' assignments. Using photoshop, we had to give someone a makeover.

Synopsis
This project was hilarious. I took a picture of my friend Todd and made him look like some Mantropy looking guy.

大雄網站» 2005 » June
Mantropy的「症狀」包括愛喝鮮果乳酪、整天戴著淺色太陽眼鏡、帶男人手袋、迷你狗等。男人，請你們繼續像個男人！3 則留言» ...
www.daihung.com/blog/?m=200506 - 40k - Cached - Similar pages

Click Picture to Change

Display a menu

e for ...
ached - Similar pages

Google Search: mantropy

http://www.google.com/search?client=safari&rls=en&q=mantrop

Google

Web   Images   Groups   News   Froogle   Local   **more »**

mantropy

Search   Advanced Search / Preferences

Web   Results **1 - 10** of about **701** for **mantropy**.

rabbi philosopher: June 2005
'**Mantropy**' The Sunday Telegraph brings us this alarming report: ... Symptoms of the "illness" that has been dubbed "**mantropy**" include a penchant for ...
rabbiphilosopher.blogspot.com/ 2005_06_01_rabbiphilosopher_archive.html - 203k - Cached - Similar pages

The Sentinel at The Ohio State University- The Open End - June 2005
Mantropy. "...men are being told to be alert to a condition that could "put them on ... Symptoms of the "illness" that has been dubbed "**mantropy**" include a ...
www.osusentinel.com/theopenend/index.php/2005/06/ - 220k - Cached - Similar pages

brandchannel.com | Maxim Magazine and Maxim Living | Brand ...
... announced in November that it would become the protectorate of real men against "**mantropy**," a condition fueled by the proliferation of metro-sexuality. ...
www.brandchannel.com/features_profile.asp?pr_id=213 - 83k - Cached - Similar pages

FAZED - Archive Search
Maxim magazine has called Jihad on "**mantropy**." The decline of man must be stopped in the form of a clever (and blinding) advertising campaign! ...
www.fazed.net/archive/?s=&category=21&p=2 - 31k - Cached - Similar pages

Mr. Joe Clifford Faust / White Moments
M is for **Mantropy**, the newest variation on Metrosexual - at least, it is according to Maxim Magazine, which coined the phrase. Read all about **Mantropy** here. ...
www.joecliffordfaust.com/archives/2005_06_01_index.html - 76k - Cached - Similar pages

MetroDad: May Mailbag
When men cross this line, we here at MetroDad like to call it **Mantropy**. ... If all else fails, seek professional help at **mantropy** control. ...
metrodad.typepad.com/index/2005/05/may_mailbag.html - 34k - Cached - Similar pages

low culture: I Learned It From Watching <i>You</i>!
As the **Mantropy** brochure says, 'Monthly doses of Maxim magazine, and strict adherence to the lifestyle outlined in its pages, have proven effective in ...
www.lowculture.com/archives/ 2004/11/i_learned_it_fr.html - 21k - Cached - Similar pages

Keyword
Symptoms of the "illness" that has been dubbed "**mantropy**" include a penchant for pedicures, fruit smoothies and small dogs. American Maxim, one of the ...
www.freerepublic.com/focus/keyword?k=girliemen - 95k - Cached - Similar pages

The 'mirl phenomenon' has doomsayer species, and there's tom-tomming ab century disease that will make 'real earth?

D
Deathlo

"I think women want real men in want real women," he said. "I do n trying to be more macho in a bid to att

ched - Similar pages

eart FAIL
th the tem
of men. Strange

5 COMMENTS:

Frank Caliva said...

mantropy! I love it.

I hereby declare this blog a metrosexual free zone.

This actually reminds me of an idea I've long had...I want to open a chain of stores called the Man Store. In the Man Store, everything would be labeled exactly as it was...deodorant would be called "deodorant," Jeans would be jeans, khakis would be khakis, and shirts would come in two colors - white or blue. Maybe blue stripes on white we were feeling crazy. There would be an barber in the back, where y would sit in the chair and they would just cut your hair, not style it, questions asked. Pink would be banned. Not that I don't have a pink shirt. I do. But the Man Store wouldn't sell it. Just wouldn't be right.

11:41 PM

THE SUV BACKLAS OFFICIALLY STARTS

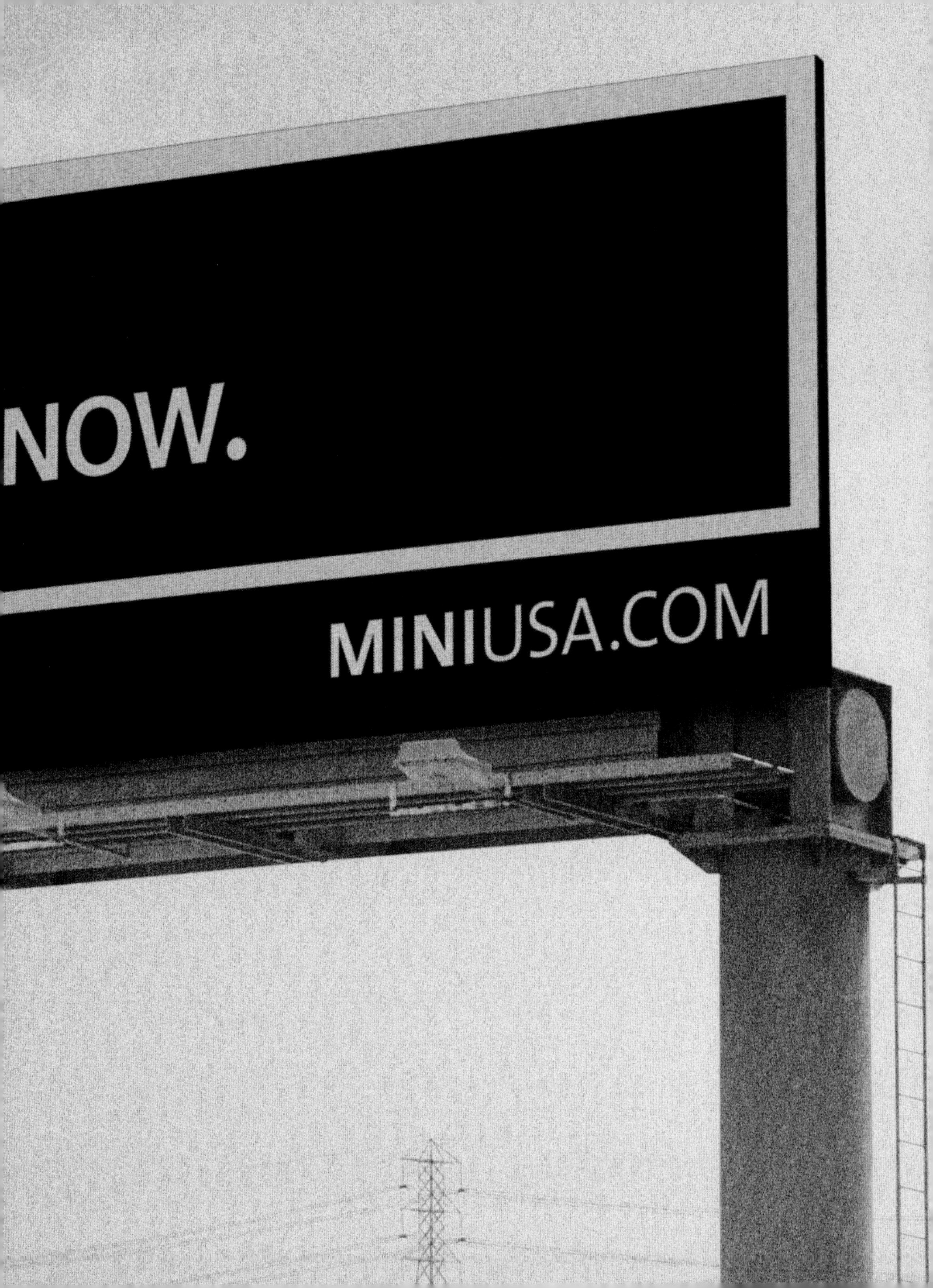
NOW.
MINIUSA.COM

LET'S SIP, NOT GUZZLE. Let's leave the off-road vehicles off road. Let's stop pretending we live in the jungle. Let's stop intimidating each other. Let's not use the size of our vehicle to compensate for other shortcomings. Let's reclaim our garage space. Let's be nimble. Let's be quick. Let's be honest. **LET'S MOTOR.**™

MINI COOPER

LET'S PUT AWAY THE MIDDLE FINGER. Let's lay off the horn. Let's volunteer jumper cables. Let's pay a stranger's toll. Let's be considerate of cyclists. Let's keep in mind automobiles were created to advance civilization. And for crying out loud, let's remember to turn off those blinkers. **LET'S MOTOR.**™

MINI COOPER S

LET'S BURN THE MAPS. Let's get lost. Let's turn right when we should turn left. Let's read fewer car ads and more travel ads. Let's not be back in ten minutes. Let's hold out until the next rest stop. Let's eat when hungry. Let's drink when thirsty. Let's break routines, but not make a routine of it. **LET'S MOTOR.**™

MINI COOPER

LET'S SEE IF IT DOES ANY TRICKS. Let's give it a name. Let's show it some affection. Let's treat it like a member of the family. Let's pat it when it's good. Let's hose it down when it gets too dirty. Let's make sure it's getting enough exercise. Let's do our best to keep it away from fire hydrants. **LET'S MOTOR.**™

MINI COOPER S

LET'S GO UNDERCOVER. Let's go on a stakeout. Let's throw a siren on the roof. Let's squeal the tires and chase some bad guys. Let's take turns behind the wheel. Let's make sure we watch each other's backs. **LET'S MOTOR.™**

LET'S BUILD A CAR FOR EVEL KNIEVEL. Let's paint it red, white and blue. Let's put a big number one on the door. Let's prepare for takeoff. Let's jump the rules. Let's jump the status quo. Let's jump SUVs. Literally. **LET'S MOTOR.™**

LET'S DRIVE A MORE INTELLIGENT CAR. Let's fill it with technology from the future. Let's flip all the switches. Let's twist all the knobs. Let's kick it into superdrive. Let's call it by name. Let's be its best friend. **LET'S MOTOR.**™

MINI COOPER S

LET'S JUMP IN THROUGH THE WINDOW. Let's slide across the hood. Let's Bo and Luke-it. Let's Daisy Duke-it. Let's install the loudest Dixie horn in all of Hazzard County. But seriously folks, let's keep them wheels on the ground. **LET'S MOTOR.**™

each animal at slaughter weight. Big industry, he points out, grades meat after slaughter; but the cooperative's machine enables farmers to choose in advance only those animals that will meet the standards of the cooperative's Pasture Perfect brand.

Like Lasater and Gamble, Shinn believes that in the long run the only way to guarantee quality is through careful breeding; his chief concentration is on finding breeds best suited to the New England climate. So far he is a successful competitor in the luxury market on grounds of flavor: in a recent tasting of filets mignons, *Wine Spectator* rated Pasture Perfect's best.

Before ordering and cooking grass-fed beef, you have to decide you're ready for the real taste of beef—a taste that corn-fattening has for decades blanketed with an unpleasantly sweet, bland, rich coating. Losing the flavor of corn in beef is like scraping away a gooey glaze. The usual complaint is that grass-fed beef is stringy rather than tender. This can be addressed by careful cooking, and by buying cuts naturally higher in fat. It can be erased by my mother's famous brisket.

Every family has its treasured pot roast, of course, and mine has special significance. At the beginning of their marriages my mother shared the recipe for it with her best friend from high school, who had moved to northern California from the Connecticut town where they grew up, and who liked it so much that it became her company dish. After my mother died, my family had the luck of continuing to enjoy it as prepared by her friend, who became my stepmother.

Homey recipes like this have periodic revivals, especially in insecure times, and they are at the heart of two appealing new books: *The Way We Cook*, by Sheryl Julian and Julie Riven, full of wonderful, simple recipes based on their northeastern upbringing and wide cooking experience, and Marian Burros's *Cooking for Comfort*, with reliable, barely reconstructed recipes from the 1950s and 1960s and her own Connecticut Jewish childhood (shockingly, Burros adds ketchup, brown sugar, and

tomato puree to her mother's spare original brisket).

For my family's recipe, season both sides of a medium brisket—Lasater's are just the right size, three to five pounds, and well trimmed—with salt, pepper, paprika, and, if you truly want to revisit the sixties, Ac'cent. Heat the oven to 350°. In an uncovered heavy Dutch oven sear the meat fat side down over medium-high heat in a film of hot olive oil. Turn it when it is quite brown and remove as much fat as possible. Strew over the meat one or two medium onions, chopped; two or three medium carrots, peeled and sliced; one large tomato, skinned, seeded, and chopped; a bell pepper, peeled, ribbed, and sliced (green for period authenticity, though I prefer red); and a medium clove of garlic, peeled and minced. Add two cups of water or stock (my stepmother makes fresh, unsalted chicken stock for this dish), cover, and cook in the oven for three and a half hours. After two hours add peeled and halved potatoes if you wish, being careful not to crowd the pot lest they steam rather than roast. An hour later add one cup of sliced button mushrooms (my mother used canned sliced mushrooms, drained—a practice my stepmother follows despite her Californian emphasis on freshness), a quarter to a half cup of red wine, and half a teaspoon of Gravy Master. You can omit the Ac'cent, of course, now that we know about MSG headache, and water is fine in place of stock. But you should really add the Gravy Master. When the pot liquor is skimmed, it makes an incomparable gravy for a dish that will ever withstand the test of time.

Lasater brisket and other cuts can be ordered at www.lasatergrasslandsbeef.com or by phone, 866-454-2333. The site for Tom Gamble and Bill Davies's fajita strips and fancier cuts is www.napafreerange beef.com, and the number is 707-963-6134. Information for ordering Pasture Perfect steaks and other cuts, and also on grasslands farming as practiced by members of the New England Livestock Alliance, is at www.nelastore.com, and the number is 413-528-3767. Ⓐ

Corby Kummer is a senior editor of The Atlantic. *His most recent book is* The Pleasures of Slow Food *(2002).*

INSIDE
UGOFF

On July 14, 2005, German design publication *Der ShpreadenFlaaver* interviewed über-designer/artist/conceptualizer/creativist Ugoff. This is an excerpt.

An Juli 14, 2005, interviewte deutsche Designpublikation *Der ShpreadenFlaaver* über entwerfer/artist/conceptualizer/creativist Ugoff. Dieses ist ein excerpt.

Der ShpreadenFlaaver: Ugoff, you designed The Pouch for BURGER KING®. What has the experience been like?

Ugoff: People come to Ugoff and say "Ugoff, your pouch for BURGER KING® has been hailed as the most influential design of the 20th century. How do you respond?" My answer? Ugoff does not respond. Ugoff acts and lets others respond. Ugoff is like a dangerous Bengal tiger cat with pointy teeth, chasing the wildebeest through the Serengeti. "But Ugoff," they ask, "where did you find inspiration?" Please. I am Ugoff. Ugoff finds inspiration in the small petals of a flower as they open to the heavens. In the despair of a fruit fly who finds no mate. In the sweet agony of a mayonnaise bath. In the lancing of a boil and Epsom Salts. Yet sometimes, Ugoff does not find inspiration. Inspiration finds Ugoff, alone and afraid.

Der ShpreadenFlaaver: Ugoff, entwarfen Sie den Beutel für Burger-König. Wie was ist die Erfahrung gewesen?

Ugoff: Hier erhielt diese reizvolle Landschaft in der Eiszeit ihre Form durch den Aare-Gletscher, der fünf kleine Seen hinterließ. Unterwegs trifft man auf malerische Bauernhöfe oder kleine Dörfer, die sich auf Kunsthandwerke spezialisiert haben. Sattelfeste Tourenfahrer und Wanderer zieht es weiter Anstiege ersparen. Oben - von den Almwiesen aus - genießt man den Rundblick und freut sich an alpiner Vegetation. Nach den Tagesanstrengungen verwöhnen gemütliche Wohlfühlhotels ihre Gäste spezialisiert haben. Sattelfeste Tourenfahrer und Wanderer zieht es weiter Anstiege ersparen. Oben - von den Almwiesen aus - genießt man den Rundblick und freut sich an alpiner Vegetation. Nach den Tagesanstrengungen verwöhnen gemütliche Wohlfühlhotels ihre Gäste.

Ugoff's pouch is easily more than trendy. Please, it is from Ugoff.

Beutel Ugoffs ist leicht mehr als trendy. Bitte ist er von Ugoff.

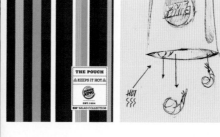

Ugoff makes only one sketch. It is perfect.

Ugoff bildet nur eine Skizze. Es ist vollkommen.

Ugoff finds it easy to be a celebrity.

Ugoff findet es einfach, eine Berühmtheit zu sein.

Ugoff maintains a close working relationship with beautiful women.

Ugoff behält ein nahes Arbeitsverhältnis zu den schönen Frauen bei.

Carding kids for R-rated movies
Page 3

Grill grub, exotic-style
Page 53

Phils trounce Yankees, 11-5
Page 95

PHILADELPHIA DAILY NEWS
THE PEOPLE PAPER

60¢ WEDNESDAY, JUNE 9, 1999   LATE SPORTS

THE FALL & RISE OF
LATRELL SPREWELL

17 months ago, he choked his coach and almost lost his NBA career. Now he's in the playoffs, selling sports gear on TV. How'd that happen? **Page 102**

NEW YORK OBSERVER

© 1999 THE NEW YORK OBSERVER COMPANY INC.
NEW YORK, JUNE 21, 1999

Every time the ball came near Latrell Sprewell in the last game of the Indiana series, Keith Livingston, a compact man with a shaved head and glasses, slammed his hand against a post at the Dean Street Cafe in Prospect Heights, Brooklyn, and shouted, "American Dream, American Dream." The sports bar was packed with black people from the outer boroughs, few of them quiet – still, Mr Livingston's cry rose above the din: "Give it to American Dream!"

The nickname comes from a stunning advertisement aired during the playoffs by AND 1, a basketball sneaker company. The spot featured a close-up shot of Mr. Sprewell, a basketball player most famous for a violent outburst against a former coach.

★★★ I AM THE ★★★
AMERICAN
★★ DREAM ★★

AND 1.

WEDNESDAY, JUNE 9, 1999

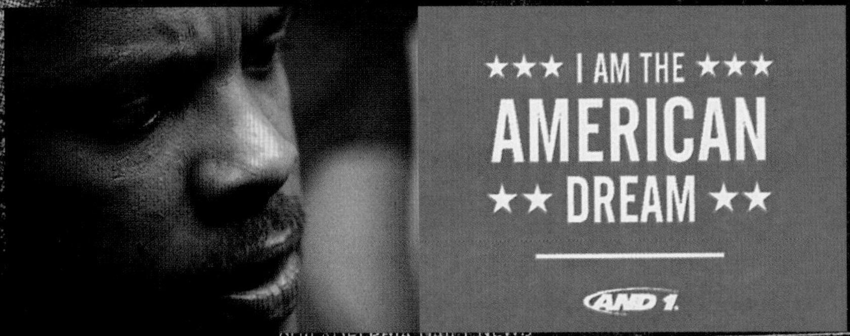

PHILADELPHIA DAILY NEWS

A special look inside the news

AGE 102

Going Deep
On the rebound

NEW YORK – If home is a place where past mistakes are forg...

New York is quick to forgive Sprewell,

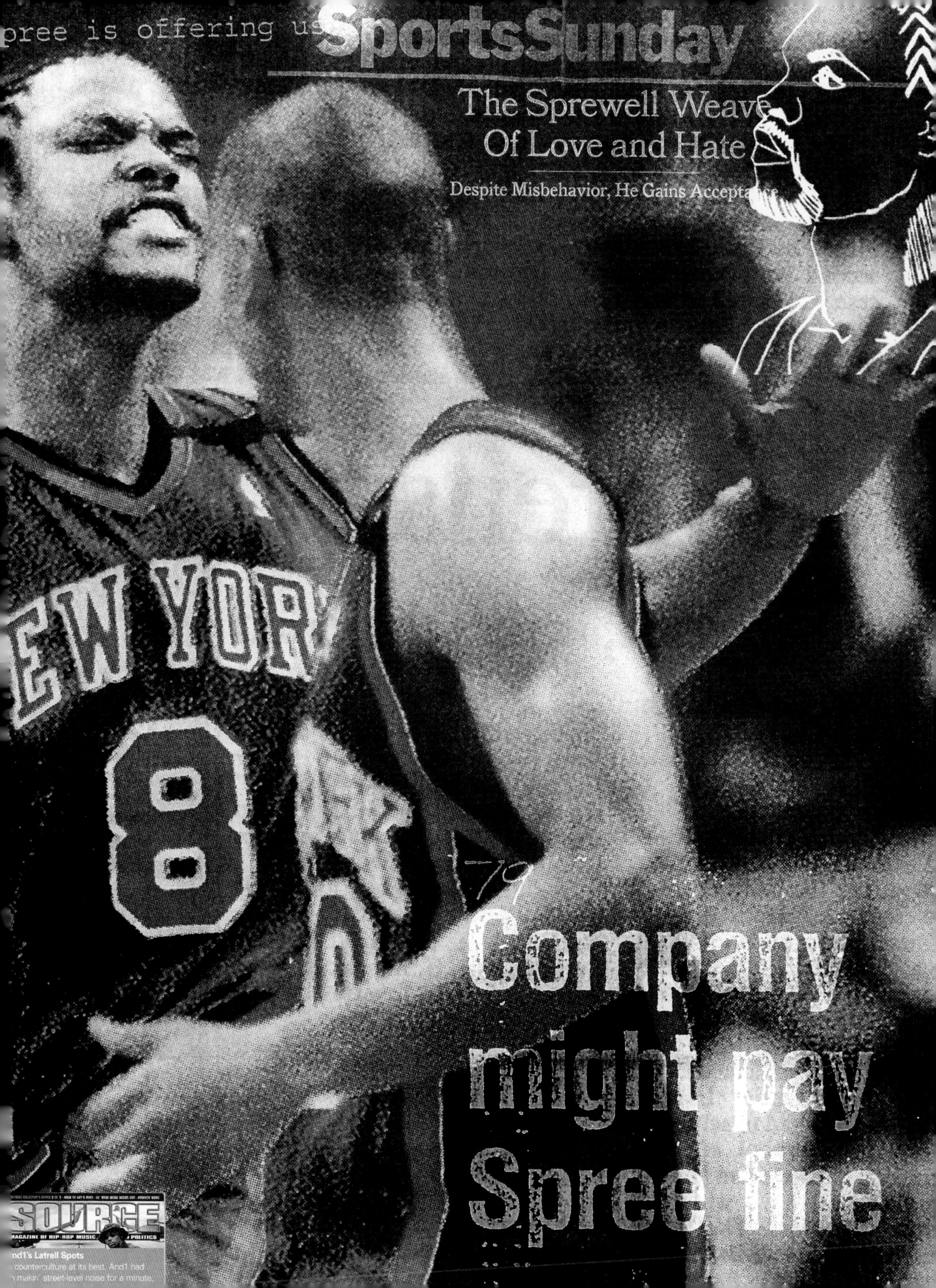

The Sprewell Weave
Of Love and Hate

Despite Misbehavior, He Gains Acceptance

NEW YORK

8

79

Company
might pay
Spree fine

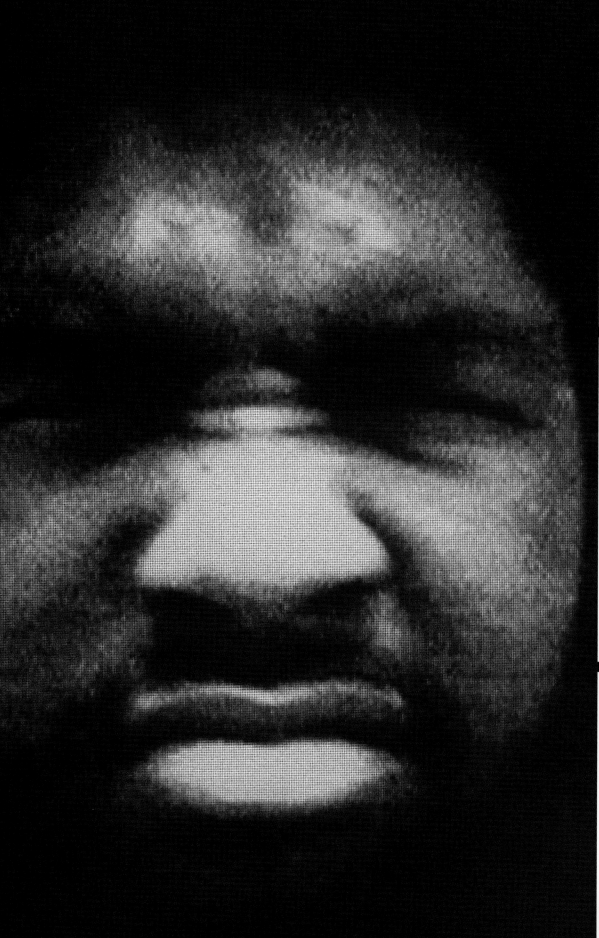

MY OWN MAN
★★★ IN 1999 ★★★

★★★ I AM THE ★★★
AMERICAN
★★ DREAM ★★

AND 1.

MY OWN JUDGE
★★★ IN 1999 ★★★

★★★ I AM THE ★★★
AMERICAN
★★ DREAM ★★

AND 1.

NO EXCUSES
★★★ IN 1999 ★★★

★★★ I AM THE ★★★
AMERICAN
★★ DREAM ★★

AND 1.

Truth is, cigarettes can kill you. But here's another hard truth: For a lot of kids who smoke, that's part of the appeal.

This troubling reality became apparent to Crispin Porter + Bogusky eight years ago, as the agency began doing preliminary research for an anti-smoking campaign that sought to stem an alarming rise in smoking rates among teenagers in the state of Florida. To try to get a sense of what was going on with these kids, a team from CP+B took to the streets to talk to them on their own turf. The teens they encountered along the way proved to be extremely savvy about advertising, including anti-smoking ads. They'd seen plenty of commercials issuing grave warnings about the health hazards of smoking, sometimes accompanied by images of blackened lungs; after all, conventional wisdom had long held that this was the best way to scare young people away from smoking. But it wasn't scaring these kids. It only made the most rebellious ones want to smoke even more.

Somewhere along the way, the agency began to realize what they were up against. As Bogusky observed at the time, "If you set out to design a dream product to market to teenagers, you couldn't come up with anything more effective than a Marlboro cigarette." Indeed, the product appealed to teenagers deeply and on many levels by tapping into a young adult's need to establish an identity, the desire to be associated with distinctive brands, the urge to rebel, and even the normal adolescent eagerness to take physical risks and confront danger. In this context, the danger associated with smoking, as played up in all those ads, actually made it *sexier*.

But there was another, more hopeful "truth" that CP+B discovered in those street-level talks: Teenagers cannot stand being manipulated; they do not like to be "played." It occurred to Bogusky that it therefore might make sense for the agency to de-emphasize the death warnings and zero in on the shady marketing tactics employed by the tobacco industry when selling its product to teenagers. This offered a way to tap into all that rebellious teen *angst* and channel it in the direction of a deserving target – Big Tobacco executives.

Adopting the brand-name *truth* (Bogusky felt that since cigarettes all have brands and logos that kids can relate to, his campaign should have the same), the agency launched a series of messages – they were each through ads, as leaflets, fliers, stickers, and little short indie films, fueling what felt like an underground propaganda movement – that purported to reveal the secrets of tobacco marketers, showing how the industry hid information, used phony imagery, and distorted facts, all to try to hook kids as customers. (One CP+B ad even posted the phone numbers of every ad agency responsible for creating tobacco ads.) In a way, the campaign became an indictment of advertising itself, coming direct from an ad agency that had decided to tell the truth to teenagers.

It turned out that those teens were hungry for a little truth. Throughout Florida, they embraced the anti-advertising campaign as a social movement, with many becoming ambassadors who spread the word about *truth* to friends. In the first four years of the campaign, from 1998 to 2001, smoking among middle and high school students in Florida declined an average of 38 percent. The success in Florida was so startling that other states took notice, and *truth* eventually spread as part of a national campaign.

As a case study in Hoopla, the *truth* effort contains many of the basic elements and ingredients needed to create a phenomenon: inventive ideas, new and attention-getting ways of delivering those ideas, dramatic stunts (including live pranks played on tobacco marketers, which were documented and then shown as ads), and even lots of free music, hats, and T-shirts to add to the carnival effect. But perhaps the most powerful thing the campaign had going for it was that it came across as refreshingly and even shockingly honest. And in a world of hype, a few candid words can be more powerful than a thousand empty slogans and claims.

From the agency's earliest days, Bogusky and Porter always had a healthy cynicism about advertising and its transparent phoniness. Bogusky tended to think of his work more as a form of "anti-advertising," which resisted the hyperbolism of the business and even poked fun at it sometimes. In advancing this postmodern, "no-bullshit" sensibility, CP+B was among a handful of ad agencies in recent years (the celebrated Nike agency Wieden + Kennedy was another) that seemed to connect with a newly emerging audience—one that had, itself, grown weary of blatantly false sales pitches. This new audience, which included younger, more media-savvy consumers, seemed to respond to messages that were less glitzy and prepackaged, more raw and authentic. And the more candid an ad was, the more it seemed to resonate with these emerging consumers.

Early CP+B ads seemed to delight in overturning some time-honored artificial conventions of the ad world, such as the use of heroic celebrity endorsers. CP+B's version of a sports hero was Latrell Sprewell, a basketball star who'd been shunned by Madison Avenue after physically assaulting his coach. The idea of giving a forum to the controversial, volatile Sprewell might have seemed suicidal to a conventional marketer, but CP+B saw something in Sprewell. After serving a one-year suspension from the NBA, he was returning to the league. "It was an opportunity to, socially, give him a second chance," says CP+B's Burnard. Yet the media and culture at large were still in the mode of vilifying Sprewell because it was the thing to do. For CP+B's client AND 1, being the first to come out in support of Sprewell was a way to "draw a line in the sand," says Burnard. The ad came across as fearless and honest. AND 1 was on the side of the players—not the coaches, not the organizations. It had the player's back, no matter the circumstances. This "line in the sand" instigated a debate in the media that netted more than $25 million in free publicity. It was quoted by Stewart Scott on *SportsCenter*, featured on the cover of major newspapers, and even spliced apart and used as part of NBC's playoff intro during the NBA Playoffs.

Therein lies a lesson that can be applied to almost any attempt to produce Hoopla: *To effectively "hype" something today, you must find a way to cut through "the hype."* Strange as it might seem in advertising, this necessitates telling the truth—or at least some interesting form of it. It is not as easy it might sound, because advertisers, promoters, and publicists have, for decades, developed a habit of relying on overpromising, overselling, and focusing on the sizzle instead of the steak. Bogusky points out, "There are truths to almost every product, and yet most advertisers shy away from those truths." The tendency, he says, is to simply offer sales pitches that have little to do with the reality of a given brand or the actual experience of using a specific product.

Such generic claims invariably lack emotional impact, but in the old three-channel marketing world, that was a forgivable sin; even the most empty pitch or banal slogan could be drummed into people's heads with enough repetition. However, as the power to control media began to shift to consumers, there was less willingness on their part to sit through all those transparently empty messages. And now, as that power and sophistication on the part of the audience continues to grow, "the brands that are unwilling to have a real and truthful conversation with consumers will become completely irrelevant and therefore invisible," Bogusky says.

In order to be able to have that "real and truthful conversation" with the audience, a marketer must first have something to say that is real and true (as well as interesting or compelling—because dull, obvious truths needn't be stated at all). Whether it's a brand, a company, a person, an idea, or just about anything else that can be promoted or marketed, there is almost always a compelling truth deep down inside that can drive a message and give meaning and credibility to the attendant Hoopla. "We try to find that long-neglected truth in a product and give it a hug," Bogusky says.

The agency has made something of a science of locating these inner truths about brands, products, and human behavior. It requires drilling down well beneath the surface layer of casual assumptions and conventional wisdom, often by spending considerable time studying a product or brand, and talking candidly to people about it. At the same time, the agency has found that it's important to look at things with a "fresh eye"—which is why CP+B generally avoids turning an assignment over to specialists who've spent years advertising a particular type of product (e.g., "car guys," who only do car ads). Bogusky believes that naïve eyes are more wide-open and more apt to notice interesting, unobserved truths about a product. "There's incredible strength in ignorance," he says.

In getting to the truth of a brand or product, the agency will study its history, visit the factory where it is made, and immerse itself in old ads and communications. CP+B has also set up a unique "Cognitive and Cultural Studies" department, which tries to find patterns and connections among the physical qualities of a product, the human experience of using it, and the product or brand's place and meaning in the culture today.

Perhaps the most important thing the agency does in trying to locate the essence of a product is talk to people, but not in the traditional manner employed by corporations and Hollywood studios. The agency tends to avoid "focus groups," which are notorious for eliciting half-truths and predictable responses from participants who often answer in ways they believe are expected of them. As with the *truth* campaign, CP+B is more apt to venture out into the world and talk to people in their natural habitats, sometimes living with and observing these people. All of the conversation and observations provide critical raw material to be digested by in-house teams, though in the end, CP+B relies to a great extent on its own "gut instinct" for finding, selecting, and then articulating a hidden truth about something.

The insights that emerge in this process can be fascinating in terms of what they reveal about human behavior. For example, when the agency was doing research for its IKEA home-furnishings ad campaign, CP+B uncovered an interesting dynamic in the relationship between people and their furniture. It started with statistics, revealing that people replace almost everything in the home (even their spouses!) more often than they replace their furniture. The agency began to study the reasons that people, without thinking much about it, tend to become overly attached to couches and kitchen tables; some of the reasons seemed to grounded in weighty cultural or psychological issues, as noted by Wojtek Szumowski of CP+B's Cognitive and Cultural Studies group. "Furniture can be a symbol of stability and continuity of family," he says, and that's part of the reason that people are drawn to "solid," "familiar," "traditional" (and boring) furnishings and why they hang onto them for so long. The IKEA chain, meanwhile, had thrived by making furniture lighter and more modern,

On April 13, 1998
The Florida Department
of Health, CP+B, and a
large group of teens
decided it was time for
young people to hear the
facts about tobacco and
the manipulative industry
behind it. On that day the
truth brand was born.

MOST DEATHS IN A SINGLE YEAR
SUICIDE

MOST DEATHS IN A SINGLE YEAR
ILLICIT DRUGS

MOST DEATHS IN A SINGLE YEAR
TOBACCO

MOST DEATHS IN A SINGLE YEAR
MURDER

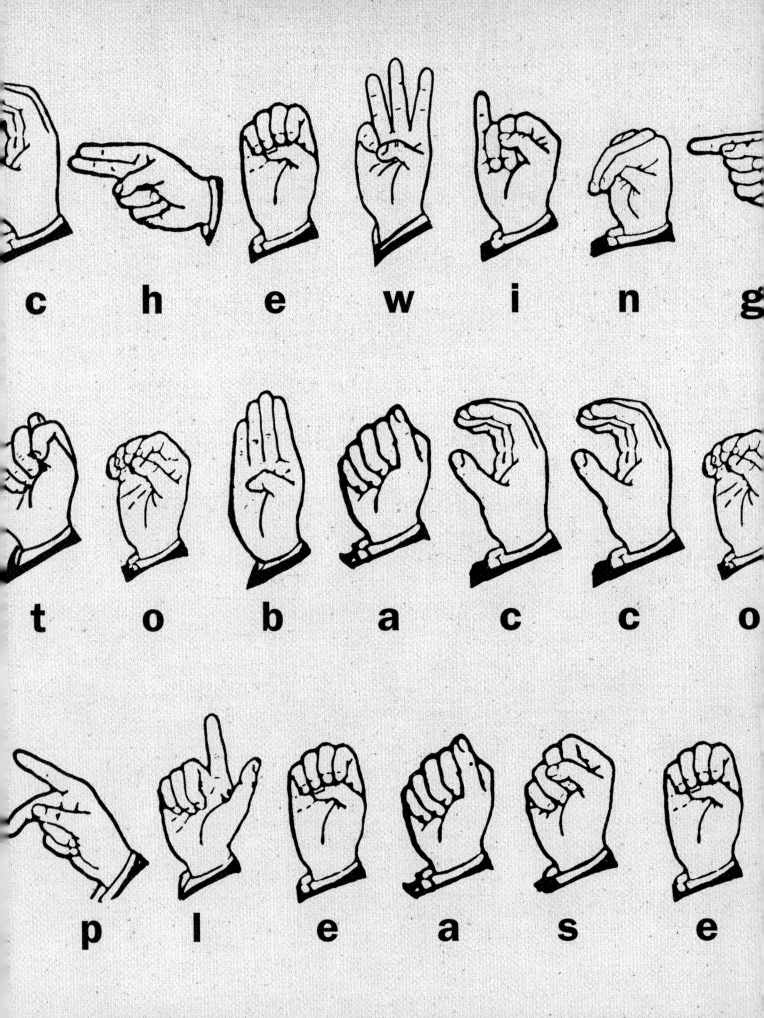

c h e w i n g

t o b a c c o

p l e a s e

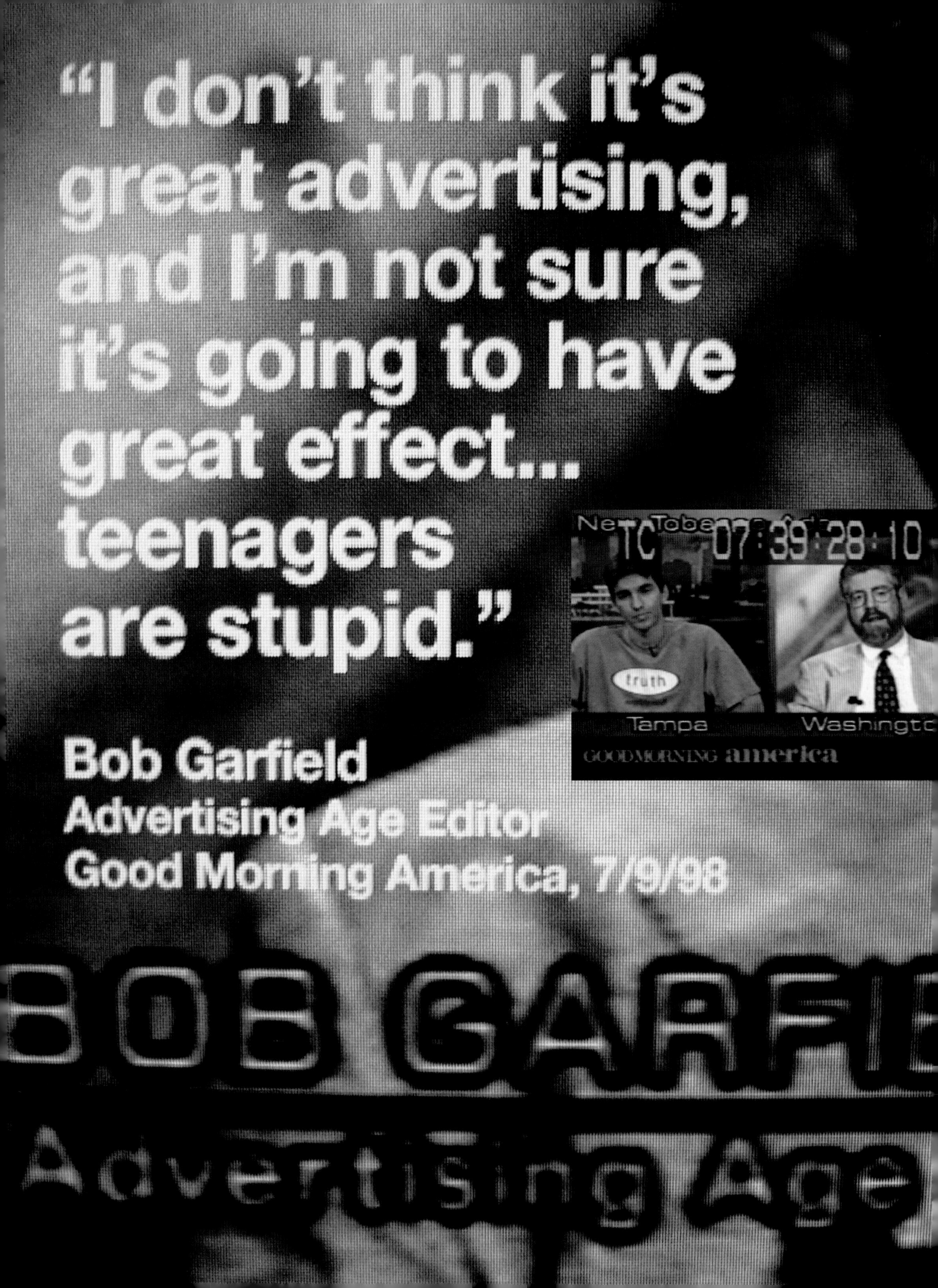
"I don't think it's great advertising, and I'm not sure it's going to have great effect... teenagers are stupid."
Bob Garfield
Advertising Age Editor
Good Morning America, 7/9/98
TC 07:39:28:10
truth
Tampa
Washingtc
GOOD MORNING america
BOB GARFI
Advertising Age

THE WHITE HOUSE

Office of the Press Secretary

Embargoed until 4:00pm Thursday April 1, 1999

STATEMENT BY THE PRESIDENT

Today, the Centers for Disease Control and Prevention is publishing promising new results from the youth anti-smoking program launched by the late Florida Governor Lawton Chiles. The study shows that in just one year, smoking has declined by 19 percent among middle school students and by 8 percent among high schoolers. These results show why every state should have a comprehensive program to reduce youth smoking and why I oppose any legislation waiving the federal government's claim to tobacco settlement funds without making a commitment from the states to fund such efforts. Without such a commitment, states won't have to spend a single penny of the $246 billion settlement to reduce youth smoking. We must act now: every day, 3000 children become regular smokers and 1000 will have their lives cut short as a result.

LOST

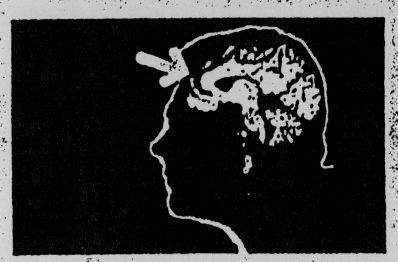

• GOES BY NAME OF "CONSCIENCE" •

- **BELONGS TO ADVERTISING AGENCY EXECUTIVE.**

- **IT WAS LOST WHILE HE WAS CREATING TOBACCO ADS.**

- **COINCIDENTALLY, THE MOST POPULAR BRANDS WITH KIDS ARE ALSO THE MOST HEAVILY ADVERTISED.**

IF FOUND, PLEASE RETURN IMMEDIATELY, SO ALL THE PEOPLE WHO MAKE TOBACCO ADS CAN TAKE SOME OF THE RESPONSIBILITY FOR HOOKING THOUSANDS OF KIDS.

Gyro Advertising
(215) 922-5220

Mezzina/Brown Inc.
Advertising Agency
(212) 251-7700

Leo Burnett
Advertising Agency
(312) 220-5959

Grey
Advertising Agency
(212) 546-2000

Avrett, Free & Ginsberg, Inc.
Advertising Agency
(212) 832-3800

Warwick, Baker, O'Neill
Advertising Agency
(212) 941-4200

Young & Rubicam
Advertising Agency
(212) 210-3000

Coyne Beahm Inc.
Advertising Agency
(336) 605-4700

Bates USA
Advertising Agency
(212) 297-7000

Tatham RSCG
Advertising Agency
(312) 337-4400

Long Haymes Carr
Advertising
(336) 765-3630

truth

www.wholetruth.com

HIDDEN CAMERA

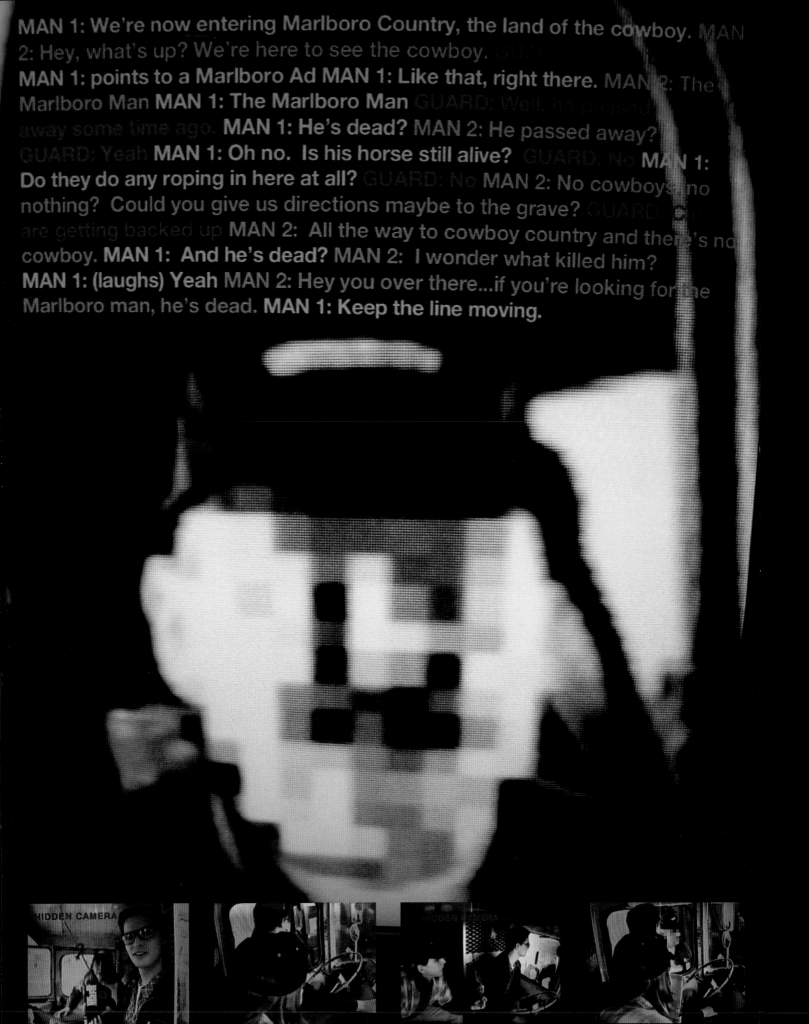

MAN 1: We're now entering Marlboro Country, the land of the cowboy. MAN 2: Hey, what's up? We're here to see the cowboy. GUARD: MAN 1: points to a Marlboro Ad MAN 1: Like that, right there. MAN 2: The Marlboro Man MAN 1: The Marlboro Man GUARD: Well, he passed away some time ago. MAN 1: He's dead? MAN 2: He passed away? GUARD: Yeah MAN 1: Oh no. Is his horse still alive? GUARD: No MAN 1: Do they do any roping in here at all? GUARD: No MAN 2: No cowboys no nothing? Could you give us directions maybe to the grave? GUARD: are getting backed up MAN 2: All the way to cowboy country and there's no cowboy. MAN 1: And he's dead? MAN 2: I wonder what killed him? MAN 1: (laughs) Yeah MAN 2: Hey you over there...if you're looking for the Marlboro man, he's dead. MAN 1: Keep the line moving.

HIDDEN CAMERA

HIDDEN CAMERA

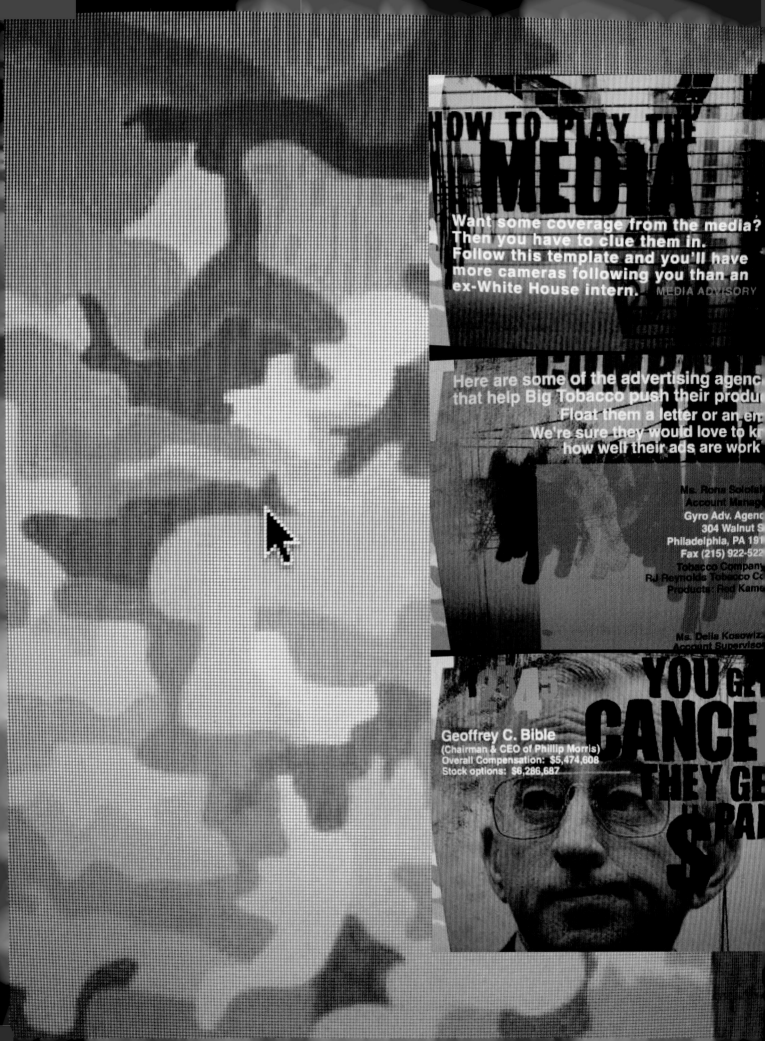

HOW TO PLAY THE MEDIA

Want some coverage from the media? Then you have to clue them in. Follow this template and you'll have more cameras following you than an ex-White House intern. MEDIA ADVISORY

Here are some of the advertising agenc that help Big Tobacco push their produ Float them a letter or an em We're sure they would love to kn how well their ads are work

Ms. Rona Solotsk Account Manag Gyro Adv. Agenc 304 Walnut S Philadelphia, PA 191 Fax (215) 922-522 Tobacco Company RJ Reynolds Tobacco Co Products: Red Kame

Ms. Delia Kosowiz Account Supervisc

Geoffrey C. Bible (Chairman & CEO of Phillip Morris) Overall Compensation: $5,474,608 Stock options: $6,286,687

YOU G CANCE THEY GE $PAI

...*truth* is considered the most successful social marketing campaign ever. It began with the tobacco companies settling a series of lawsuits with states that wanted them to pay for the cost to the healthcare system. There was only one condition of the settlement: The money had to be spent on telling kids not to smoke.

That stipulation seemed chillingly sinister when we started to consider what would happen if you told 12- to 17-year-olds they were too young to smoke; they would do just the opposite. I've often said that fear is the enemy of creativity. I've even said it in this book. But we were very afraid that if we did this wrong we'd be responsible not just for a campaign that didn't work but for a campaign that actually backfired.

Advertising is much more effective when you ask for action than when you ask for inaction. Most youth prevention PSAs ask kids to just don't. Just sit there and don't do anything. Not a very sexy sell.

Until *truth*, PSAs had never been branded, using the power of a brand to make each communication work toward a bigger picture. Over time, the brand comes to mean a culmination of all the advertising.

Today you can just put the *truth* sticker on a skateboard, and it means something. *truth* is a way to take action, even if it is only in your head. Kids who choose not to smoke now have a powerful argument for their peers. They're rebelling against an industry that's trying to dupe them.

When I was younger, I was at the beach and noticed a guy drowning in the surf. He was floating face down, and I just instinctively went in after him. It took a while to get him back to shore – and there were times I thought I would drown as well. Fortunately for us, by the time I got to shore, paramedics were waiting because several people had already drowned that day. They were able to revive him as his wife and son looked on. It was an amazingly intense feeling.

I get that same feeling from working on *truth*...

Promoting a movie is cool, especially when the movie itself doesn't exist. By hijacking movie promotional media, we were able to reveal the true nature of the tobacco industry.

EVIL EMPIRE PICTURES

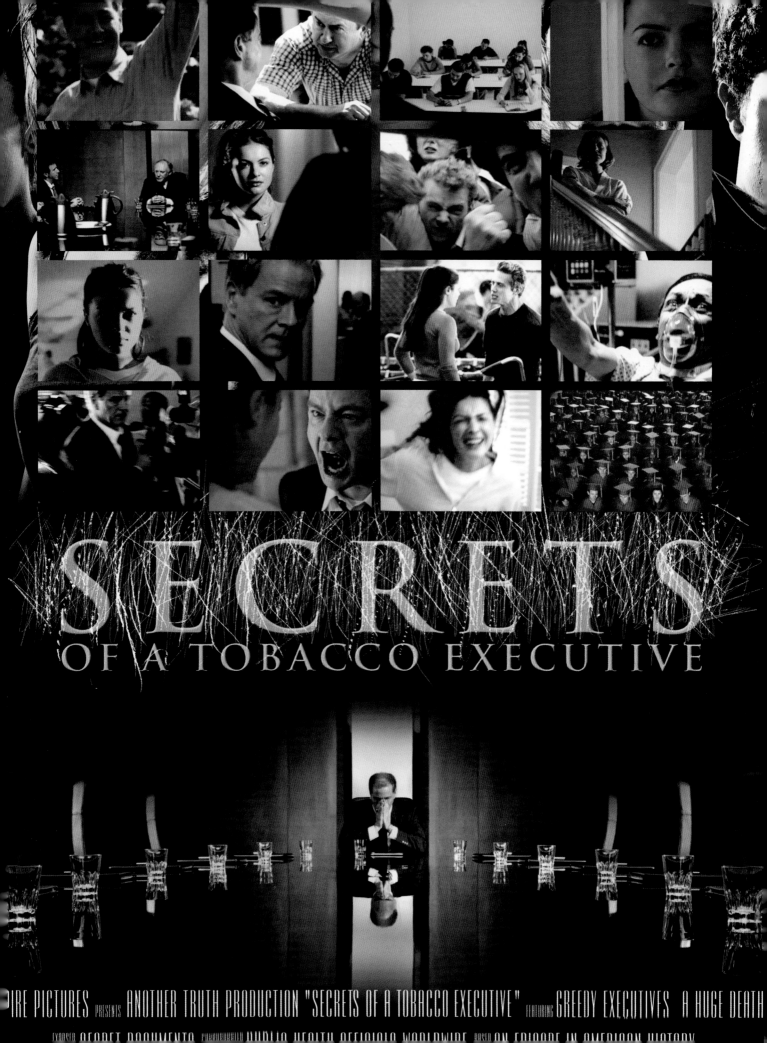

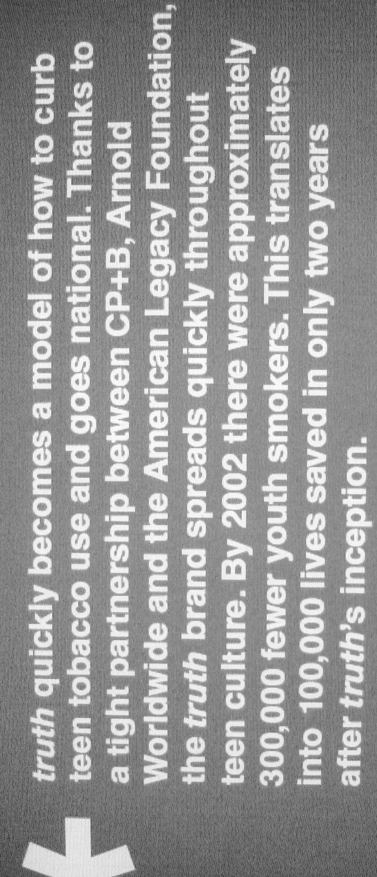

truth quickly becomes a model of how to curb teen tobacco use and goes national. Thanks to a tight partnership between CP+B, Arnold Worldwide and the American Legacy Foundation, the *truth* brand spreads quickly throughout teen culture. By 2002 there were approximately 300,000 fewer youth smokers. This translates into 100,000 lives saved in only two years after *truth*'s inception.

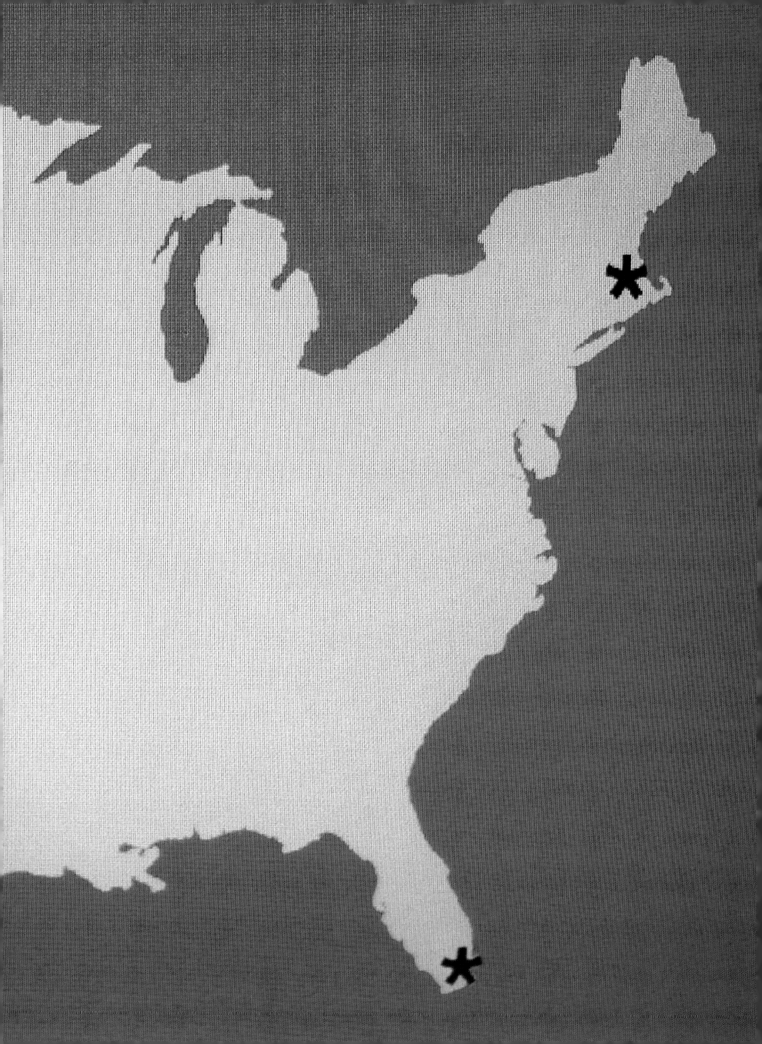

Outside a major tobacco company.

Body Bag Jacket. Authentic body bag fabric. Soft mesh lining.

Small hidden pocket fits a spy cam, and O-ring creates an opening for lens.

Body Bag-style hood zips all the way up over face. Black mesh allows you to see.

Zip-up pocket fits portable CD player and is fitted with an O-ring inside to run headphone wire through.

Sleeves end in two-layer cuffs. Inner layer is finished and provides comfort. Outer layer has zipper, which allows you to zip sleeve shut.

** MISSION: INFECT THE MASSES WITH TRUTH
** BRAND MESSAGE ON ROOT LEVEL
**
** DELIVERY METHOD: VIRAL MESSAGING KITS
** VERSION: URBAN ASSAULT
**
** TARGET: OPEN

ITM 001_MAIN_INFECT_STRAIN

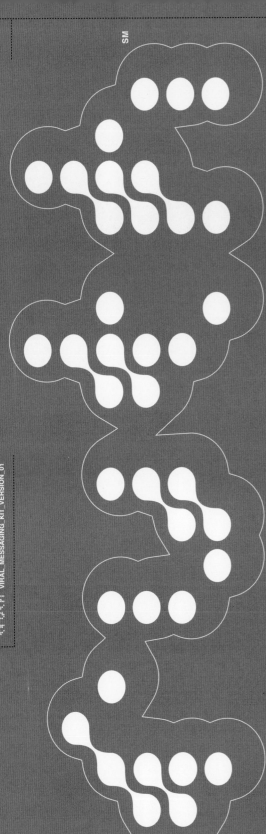

VIRAL_MESSAGING_KIT_VERSION_01

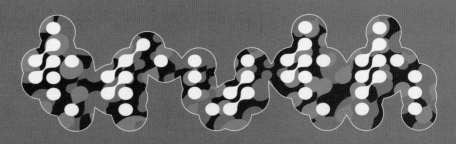

ITM 002_HIDDEN_AGENDA_STRAIN

ITM 004_INFECT_STRAIN

HELLO
HOW ABOUT SOME

INFECT

ITM 003_INTRODUCTION_STRAIN

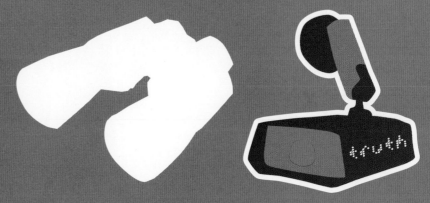

ITM 005_SURVEILLANCE_STRAIN

QTY. 1 UNT.

INFCTRTH01

INFECT
TRUTH

NO. 0387532-03943
EXPONENTIAL MULTIPLICATION
OF TRUTH BRAND
MESSAGE ON ROOT LEVEL

ITM 006_INFECT_STRAIN

Cigarettes contain ammonia.

So does dog poop.

Cigarettes contain ammonia.

So does dog poop.

So does dog poop.

Cigarettes contain ammonia.

Cigarettes contain ammonia.

So does dog poop.

1

Cigarettes contain ammonia.

So does dog poop.

A NEW MEDIUM IS BORN.

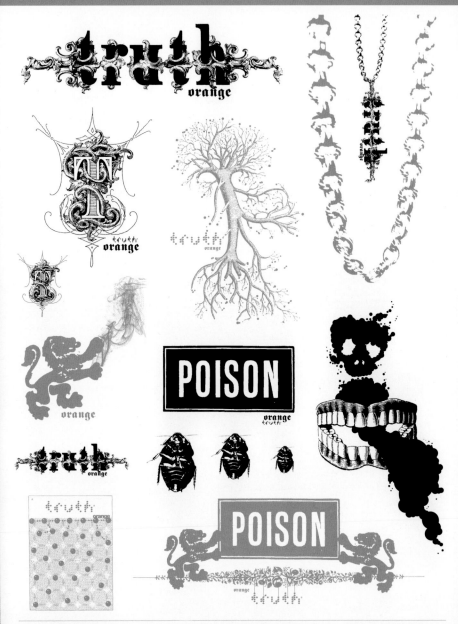

POISON

According to a recently uncovered secret tobacco company memo, "Very few consumers are aware of the effects of nicotine, i.e. its addictive nature, and that nicotine is a poison." News flash: They're aware now.

iron-on | POISON vs TRUTH | thetruth.com | truth

INSTRUCTIONS: How to make your personalized anti-tobacco propaganda t-shirt. 1. Clip out graphic. 2. Set iron to cotton, no steam. Iron shirt flat where graphic will be placed. 3. On a hard surface place graphic over shirt. Press iron firmly for 15-20 seconds over entire graphic. 4. Heat entire surface using a circular motion. 5. Slowly peel back to reveal your signature truth t-shirt.

orange

SMO
INHA
CYAN

KERS
LE
IIDE

Big Tobacco creates a product more poisonous than people realize. So, what can you do about it?

SURF adre-nalin

MOTOCROSS ACTION

TEEN HAIRSTYLES   HAIRSTYLES

Skateboard

Tony Hawk

MOTOCROSS ACTION

SMOKERS
INHALE
CYANIDE

MOKERS
NHALE
YANIDE

VEGETARIAN times
save your heart!

THRASHER

SKATE

Spread the knowledge.
Infect truth

The tobacco industry makes a product that sends 1300 people a day on a one-way trip to the morgue.

TEMPERATURE INDIC
MORTUARY REFRIGERATION
ALLOWABLE RANGE: 35°F–45°F

TEMP. 35

UAE

STAN GLANTZ vs CP+B

How long have you been a part of the fight against Tobacco? Stan: Well I first wandered into this in 1978 when there was an initiative here in California to have non-smoking sections and I've been kind of doing it ever since. I also helped found what is now called Americans for Non-Smokers Rights. In 1980 when we took a couple of predecessor organizations and reorganized them and created what is now ANR. Can you tell me a little bit about how you got into this? Was this something you set out to do, or something you discovered along the way? Stan: Well, when I was a graduate student at Stanford I got involved in some environmental issues and then when Prop 5 came along it just seemed to me like getting rid of cigarette smoke indoors was a good idea. We were all concerned about outdoor air pollution but there was growing concern about indoor air pollution as well. I kind of wandered into the campaign expecting to lick a few envelopes because there were very few people with any kind of scientific background willing to do any dirty work. I ended up in the campaign leadership within about a month. For us, it was sort of this investigative process, where the more we dug into the things, the more interested we became. You see transcripts from closed door meetings and secret memos, and you think, my God, someone's gotta bring this to the forefront so people know about it. Stan: It's certainly not something to work on if you're paranoid because usually the most paranoid things you think of end up being true. When you started your work in the early 80's what was the culture of smoking among teens like? Stan: Well, I never paid that much attention to teens. So the basic question you've asked me is how *truth* affected teens. I really don't have an answer for that because I've always thought—and I've written a couple of things that really pissed people off—that it's a big mistake to focus on teens. One of the reasons that the *truth* campaign has worked is that even though it's nominally focused on teens, the themes it has are really adult themes. The best way to reach teens is to actually talk to adults and let teens listen in. That's how the tobacco companies do it. Would you say an effective way of fighting them is pulling back that curtain? You know, revealing to people just how ugly it gets in the board rooms or back rooms of Big Tobacco? Stan: Yeah. People need to understand how they're being manipulated. And that this stuff isn't just happening because of Haley's comet or something. There is a very, very pernicious force sitting in the shadows, manipulating everything and tricking everybody. That's the key point in the *truth* campaign. Smoking is sold as a rebellious act to teens. When you reveal that, they realize they are not really rebelling anymore by smoking. They're doing exactly what the tobacco companies want them to do. Stan: Right. But again I think the kids campaign would be better as a general market campaign. I think Legacy is continuing to make a mistake by placing the ads so narrowly. Like on MTV, etc. I think that they ought to be going out to a more general market. Kids tend to see smoking as a transition into adulthood. And if you look at the industry documents, they say that over and over and over again. It's the central marketing theme of all cigarette marketing directed at children. It's a visual cue that says "I'm adult." Because everyone knows about the adverse health effects. Kids know about the adverse health effects. And what kids are saying when they smoke is, "I know it's a bad thing, but I'm going to hold this cigarette because no one wants me to smoke. This is proof that I am my own person." Stan: Well, I think you overplay the rebelliousness aspect of it a little bit, you know? If you go into the industry marketing research which I've spent a lot of time wallowing around in, it's very true the market has been highly segmented. There is definitely a rebellious segment in the market but at the same time there is also a conformist segment. There are grungy segments and there are sexy segments and it goes on and on. And I don't think most kids smoke to rebel. I think the theme that sort of transcends most of the segments is to smoke to look and feel adult and as a psychological tool for making that transition through adolescence into adulthood. A guy named Lester Breslow was a very famous public health figure here back when Pat Brown was governor. He thought public health should run a campaign saying "smoking is for kids." I don't have the nerve to do it, but I bet it would work. Yes, because who wants to be a kid? Stan: Right. So if I was going to redo the *truth* campaign that's how I would change it. But I think, and I don't know if this was on purpose or by accident, but I think that a lot of the messages that you have conveyed are in fact quite adult in nature and quite sophisticated, actually. Yes, our target would probably be the 18- to 21-year-old. Stan: I call that a transitional adult. But I would just broaden it. I would like to see the campaign directed at 18- to 25- or 18- to 28-year-olds. That is really the crucial time. It's not initiation. Public health has put way too much effort into trying to prevent experimentation. That's almost impossible to achieve. You have a much bigger chance of preventing the transition from experimentation to regular use. Ninety percent of people who smoke now started smoking before they were 18, but only about a third of the people who experiment with cigarettes go on to become regular smokers. And the tobacco companies put a huge, huge, huge amount of energy into getting people to move through that transition. It's a very unstable time. There's a lot of quitting and starting again. That's why bars are so important. Because bars and social venues have become the main places that the industry recaptures people. Anything else you would do if you were at the helm of the *truth* campaign? Stan: I think the *truth* campaign is a brilliant campaign. If I was running it I would do it a bit differently but I think the basic structure of it is exactly what you need. I just think it ought to be broadended a bit and not so narrowly focused on teens. All these teens you've reached over the last few years are now into young adulthood. That is really the important time where these long-term behaviors get solidified. I don't think you can say once they hit 21 they're not important to us anymore. I think you can do a campaign that targets the older market that would probably be as effective or more effective than what you're doing now. And I think there is very good evidence now that what you're doing has been very effective. You'd just be getting more bang for the buck.

you are
crazy

If you keep furniture you hate because it comes from someone you love,

If you're in a bad relationship with old furniture but don't put an end to it,

If your heart says get rid of it but your brain doesn't listen,

If you stay with furniture you hate out of some bizarre sense of loyalty,

IKEA®

unböring

Creating well-designed, functional furniture isn't difficult. The challenge lies in producing it at a price that most people can afford. But we live in a democracy. Shouldn't everyone have the right to live in a home that provides health, happiness and peace of mind? Few dedicate themselves to this task. Even fewer succeed. We're not saying that we've always been successful. But we've always tried. As IKEA grows, we never lose sight of the principles upon which we've been built. Let the price be the starting point. Not the afterthought.

IKEA
unböring

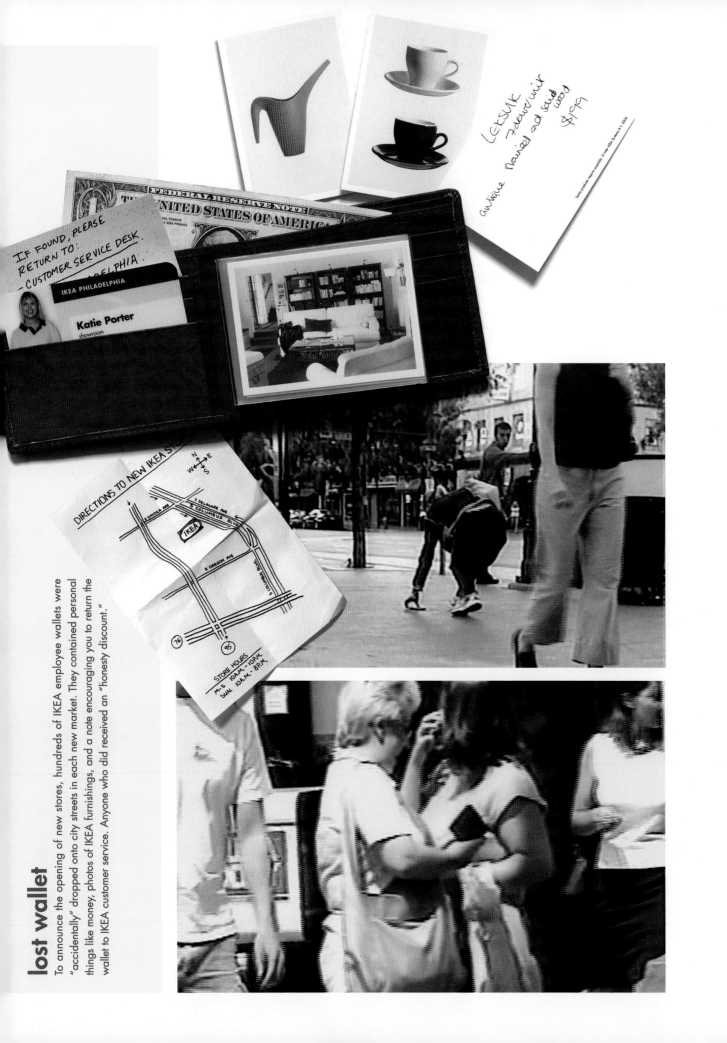

lost wallet

To announce the opening of new stores, hundreds of IKEA employee wallets were "accidentally" dropped onto city streets in each new market. They contained personal things like money, photos of IKEA furnishings, and a note encouraging you to return the wallet to IKEA customer service. Anyone who did received an "honesty discount."

IF FOUND, PLEASE
RETURN TO:
- CUSTOMER SERVICE DESK

IKEA PHILADELPHIA

Katie Porter
showroom

DIRECTIONS TO NEW IKEA STORE

IKEA

STORE HOURS
M-S 10A.M. - 10P.M.
SUN. 10A.M. - 8P.M.

$3.95

wrap unböring

$6.95

Good fortune will soon visit
you and your home.

Save 10% storewide at IKEA Baltimore
March 12-16, 2003.

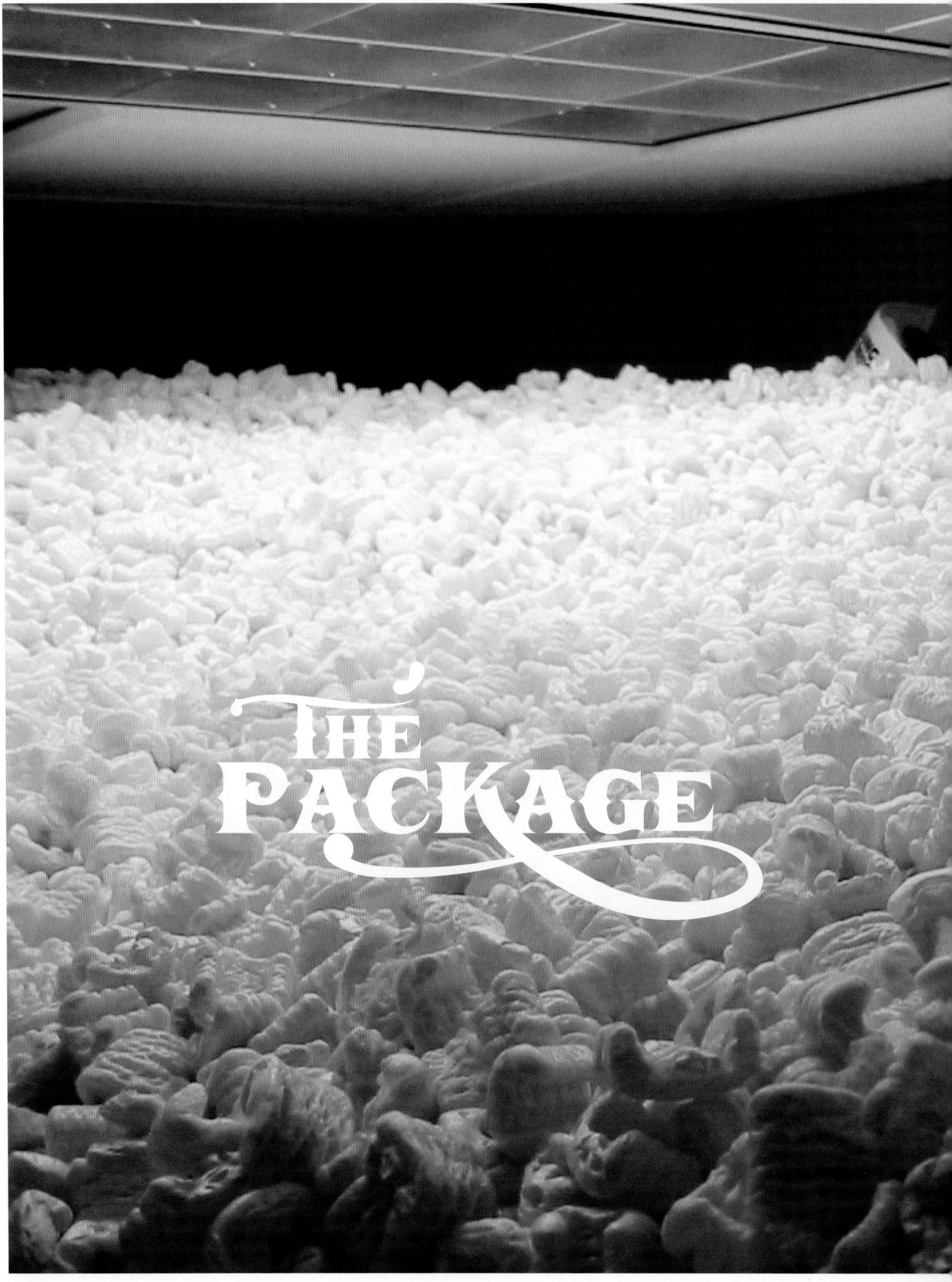

THE PACKAGE

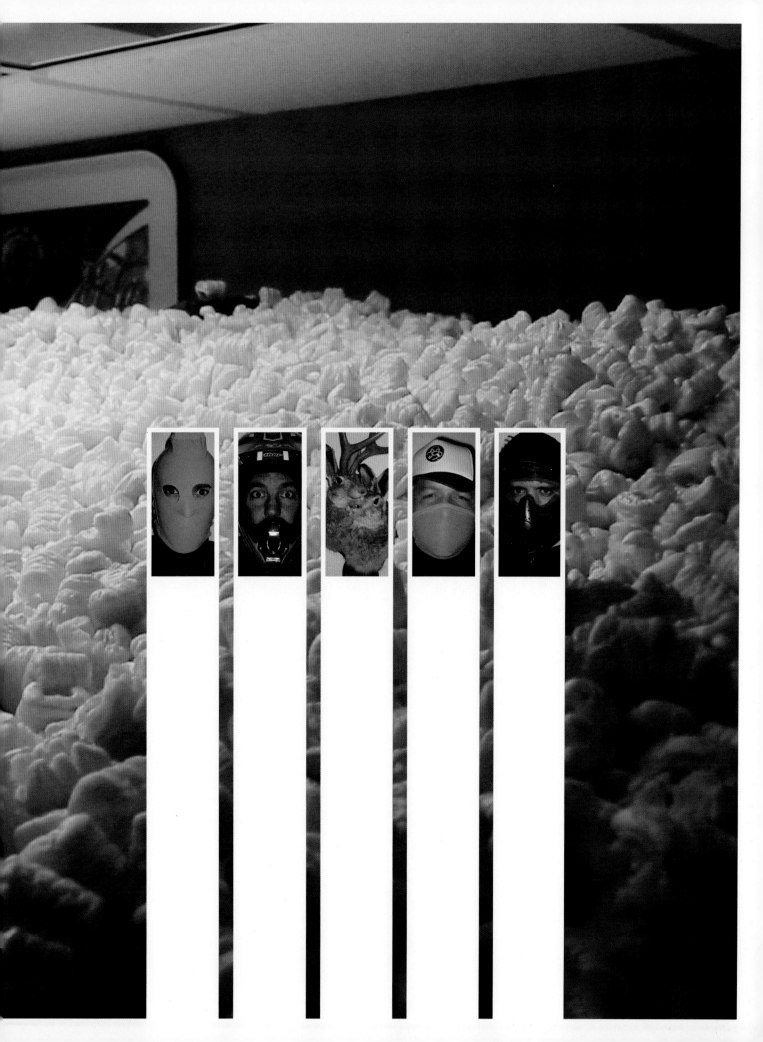

The guy in the green hat made the mistake of using his coded entry card to gain access to a rival employee's office, in order to fill it with packing peanuts. The digital trail led to the eventual identification and capture of the whole gang.

It began as a rumor, passed from one person to the next as it spread through the Internet and the print media, and the story became more real as new evidence continued to surface. It seemed that an obscure engineer in England named Dr. Colin Mayhew had secretly begun building "men of metal"—humanlike robots constructed from materials that included car parts. Glimpses of the robots had been captured in still photos and video clips. There were crude drawings and reports of firsthand sightings documented by a journalist who was tracking the phenomenon. Last but not least, there was Dr. Mayhew's own journal of his experiments, which surfaced on the Web and opened with this dramatic entry: "I first had the vision to build a robot while working as an engineer on the old MINI Coopers in the 1960s."

The robot story circulated for months and then ended with a surprise twist: It turned out that these "men of metal" were the handiwork not of Dr. Mayhew but rather of Crispin Porter + Bogusky—which had created and perpetuated a multimedia hoax on behalf of its client MINI. After the mysterious campaign generated extensive and intense debate on the subject of robots and their potential for good and evil, people had become true believers in the tale—so much so that even after the news finally broke in *The New York Times* that "Men of Metal" was all part of a MINI promotional campaign, some still clung to the belief that the robots were real and that the news about the ad campaign must have been concocted to cover up the truth.

Not long after that, CP+B launched another "counterfeit" campaign, again on behalf of MINI. The agency was looking at ways to build an "elite" status around owning a MINI. In studying Gucci, Rolex, and other elite brands, they discovered a common thread—those brands all get knocked off by imitators. And so was born an epidemic of "counterfeit MINIs": big, clunky cars (or, in one case, two motorcycles attached together), all clumsily made over to look like MINIs. The agency started planting pictures of these retouched fakes in *AutoTrader* magazine, and then as word of the existence of the counterfeit MINIs filtered out, the response was created by CP+B in the form of the Counter Counterfeit Commission (CCC), a fake group dedicated to exposing the fake epidemic.

The agency decided a good place to break news of the counterfeit MINIs was on direct-response TV—where ad rates are lower, but to qualify you must offer something that can be ordered directly. Taking that traditionally retail medium (Think pocket fisherman and spray-on hair.) and using it for branding purposes, CP+B created a short documentary film explaining (in a shocked, alarmist tone) all about the counterfeit MINI problem and how to avoid being victimized by it. That DVD was hawked for $19.99, and more than a thousand late-night viewers snapped them up. But the epidemic was spread in lots of other ways, too: from warning pamphlets handed out at auto shows to fake car ads on eBay to call-in numbers where people could report counterfeit MINI sightings—all tied together on the Web, where people could find out how to spot counterfeits or could even submit pictures of their own attempts to create a fake MINI.

In both the Robot and the Counterfeit efforts, CP+B was using creative mischief as a way to play games with the public, assuming that people would want to play along (even if meant being temporarily fooled by an advertiser). The agency found that most people were actually delighted by the trickery, which makes an important point about Hoopla: Unlike conventional advertising, which is forever struggling to seem believable and not fake, the rules of Hoopla allow for farce, tricks, pranks, and all manner of mischief—as long as you eventually let people in on the fun.

Occasional hoaxes are just one of the ways that CP+B employs creative mischief in the process of drawing attention and connecting with the public. When not telling an outrageous tall tale, the agency has sometimes drawn heat for telling the truth, unfiltered; indeed, the line between candor and mischief can be thin, and it is one that CP+B seems to cross frequently and without apology. The agency has also, at times, taken on the role of cultural provocateur—poking fun at popular trends or powerful institutions, or pushing the limits of acceptable language and behavior in advertising.

All of this mayhem doesn't happen by accident; it is fostered and encouraged within CP+B. "We believe in advertising that misbehaves," says Porter. "Mischief is infectious. When you see two people whispering and giggling in a corner, you want to know what's going on and if you can be in on it." His partner Bogusky says the agency has always tended to "celebrate the troublemaker and pay attention to the rebel." This may go back to the mutant roots of the agency, but it has continued with new waves of employees who've come aboard in recent years. One employee, Evan Fry, got a job at CP+B by sending Bogusky ominous, cryptic notes that seemed as though they might be the work of a stalker. There was a hint of cleverness amid the menace, so Bogusky (after engaging in a cat-and-mouse correspondence that turned the tables on the stalker) eventually hired him. Then, too, there is the amply tattooed copywriter Dave Schiff, who openly admits that he derives a strange pleasure from the small misfortunes of others around him. To satisfy that craving, Schiff sometimes plays cruel pranks on fellow CP+B employees, as in the time he and a couple of co-conspirators filled a large truck to capacity with Styrofoam packing peanuts, and then proceeded to haul and dump all of it into a rival creative team's office—filling the entire office, floor to ceiling, with a substance that is, in Schiff's proud words, "perhaps the most loathsome and difficult-to-clean material in the world."

It can be risky business, filling someone's office with Styrofoam peanuts; there is a chance the person will forever hate you for doing it. But if you know your intended "mark" well enough to understand what they will find it funny and just how far they can be pushed, the upside of such pranks is that you can create an experience that no one will ever forget. Much the same can be said of the use of mischief in the creation of Hoopla, CP+B has found. Tricks, pranks, and playfully naughty behavior can keep people on the edge of their seats and therefore more engaged with the message. Though if you push too far or in the wrong direction, mischief can backfire; there's a delicate balance that must be maintained when communicating "on the edge."

The pranksterism that CP+B may be best known for was aimed at the tobacco industry as part of the *truth* campaign. The agency organized raids on cigarette company headquarters, placed crank phone calls to tobacco marketers, and, most memorably, stacked body bags on the sidewalk outside a cigarette company's building as a way of graphically illustrating how many people die daily from smoking. In this campaign, mischief was central to the entire effort and carried less risk: the target teenage audience tends to like raucous behavior, and as for the unhappy victims of the pranks, the tobacco execs—well, who was likely to feel sorry for them after all the trouble they'd caused through the years? But beyond just providing some amusing schadenfreude moments, the *truth* pranks served to solidify the "us against them" feeling that can give strength to a popular movement.

Most marketing situations don't warrant the kind of hardcore confrontational behavior that worked for the *truth* campaign. More often, the type of mischief employed by CP+B is playful, with just an edge of naughtiness. For example, the Subservient Chicken's costume didn't have to include a garter belt, yet that small detail added just enough of a hint of S&M to make things interesting. Similarly, CP+B created a website for GAP, "watchmechange.com," that was part of a store-renovation effort by the company and also served the practical purpose of showing off Gap clothes on differently shaped bodies. But by adding a mildly voyeuristic element—the site provides dressing room's-eye view as an animated character strips, dances, and then tries on new outfits chosen by the visitor—the agency injected just enough spice to make the site enticing, and it soon became "a great way to waste time at the office," the *Wall Street Journal* observed.

One of the interesting things about hoaxes is how easy it can be to propel them forward. As part of the MINI campaign, the agency thought it might be fun to have the MINI show up on the front page of tabloid newspapers; the idea was, to truly achieve cultural icon status, a person (or a MINI) should have its picture in the tabs. In an attempt to make it happen, the agency concocted a story about the legendary "Bat Boy" character who's been part of tabloid lore through the years. CP+B's new twist on the tale was that Bat Boy had supposedly been spotted in the act of stealing a MINI. (The agency even produced doctored photos showing the theft in progress.) The surprise, for the agency, was that a national tabloid newspaper agreed to run the "Bat Boy steals MINI" story as a front-page item.

When you're willing to be mischievous in your communications, it opens up a realm of possibilities that might normally be considered "off-limits" in old-school advertising or promotion. Pornography, for example, would seem to have no place in the marketing of a respectable brand. And yet, when CP+B researchers discovered that the respectable business passengers targeted by Virgin Atlantic Airways happen to like watching adult movies on hotel pay-per-view channels, the agency responded to this "truth" by creating a mock porn film that ran on the LODGENET hotel pay-per-view service. The 10-minute film—which contained no nudity but lots of compromising situations, double-entendre dialogue, and bad pornstar acting—was used to promote Virgin's in-flight UpperClass suites, hence the film's title, "Suite and Innocent." In three months, some 800,000 hotel guests watched the film, with the average viewer lasting seven-and-a-half minutes. (Why so many men couldn't make it through the final two minutes is open to speculation.)

Similarly, when CP+B was asked to promote an awards show for young writers and art directors under the age of 30, known as the Young Guns International Advertising Award, the agency adopted the provocative theme "Hardly Legal" to headline its campaign. The young art directors and writers who were part of the competition were asked by CP+B to pose naked with their work, and cheesy porn-style photos were taken (with students' work always covering the critical body parts) for use in promotional ads and posters. As the competition's ceremony approached, CP+B even set up a live peep-show booth on the sidewalk outside the Cannes ad festival hall; inside that tiny booth, contest participants danced, covered only by samples of their ad work. The stunt ended up giving the awards competition, and its students, more exposure than they could have imagined.

Is there a risk in all this? Well, there can be no doubt that any advertising or promotional effort that effectively utilizes mischief is likely to draw more... 1) complaints and 2) press coverage. In terms of the latter, CP+B maintains that publicity is one of the most powerful tools available to any marketer. In fact, one of the rules the agency lives by is, "*Advertising and publicity are much more effective than advertising alone*," and this is rooted in the quite sensible notion that people believe the news more than they believe in ads. (On top of that, news coverage is free, which means the cost per thousand CPM impression rate comes in at a very affordable rate of zero dollars and no cents.) As for the angry letters that may come in, the agency generally considers it a good sign when a commercial provokes a strong response—both positive and negative—because it demonstrates to them that the message has touched a nerve. Still, those planning to do a stunt of this sort, interior Hoopla should always be prepared to manage the flak that may be generated along with the buzz.

Nor that one can ever really predict which acts of mischief will stir trouble. "You never really know," says Porter. "The things that cause the most controversy often take you completely by surprise." The agency has generally found that if mischief is rooted in a way that is both relevant to the product and respectful of the audience's intelligence, much will be forgiven.

With regard to relevance, Porter and Bogusky note that even the cleverest stunt can fall flat if it seems too generic and if it's not connected to the product or brand message in an organic way. The public can usually spot naked publicity stunts or controversy for controversy's sake. Likewise, audiences are apt to be turned off when advertisers try to be "bad" and end up just being silly or crass. (Flatulence gags in commercials do not constitute mischief; more often, they're just insulting.) The best mischief is smart as it is devious, challenging people to figure out the prank or the ad they pull, even take an active part in it. Bottom line: If you're going to do something a little bad, better make sure it's also good.

Welcome to the homepage
of Colin Mayhew

Welcome. My name is Dr. Colin Mayhew, and you are visitor number ▒48813

I'm hoping to make this web site a place where I can share information about myself, my family and my interests.

I hold a doctorate degree in engineering and worked for 30 years in the UK. Since my retirement, I have spent much of my free time in my laboratory. My other interests include reading, miniature locomotives and applied physics. To see my collection of miniature locomotives, click here. For engineering and applied physics links and downloads, click here.

Thanks for your interest.

This site was last updated 01/02/99
Email: colinMayhewphd@yahoo.co.uk

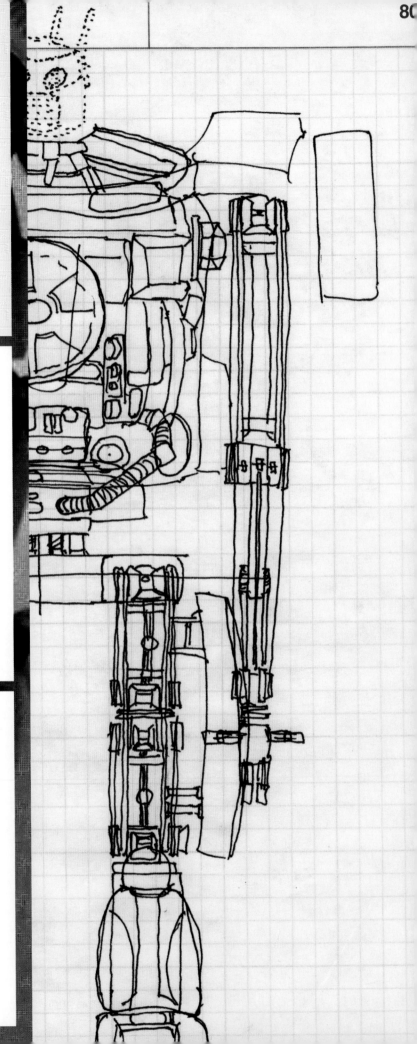

File/Directory	Size	Updated
Sketches with No...		5/12/03

Video Tests: I final...
Sorry, it took a whi...
representation of th...
sample of my testing...

http://www.r50rd.co...ideos/dex_test.htm

B...		15/12/99

Having all the se...
to test its dexte...
months of refines...

Distressed Vehicle Recognition - HUD: 17 May 2001
Testing the tracking and recognition software for distressed vehicles. A little slow, but it's working. It focuses first on a vehicle with the bonnet up. It then begins engine identification. — 892kb — 9/1/04

Battery Test: 20 June 2001
The voice command circuitry took a while, but it's near 96% now. This battery-charging test is one of the most complex exercises we've realized to date. — 2.1Mb — 9/1/04

Light Tracking in a Dark Environment: 25 August 2001
Testing visual tracking at night. Watch how the robot tracks me... — 1.2Mb — 14/1/04

Interviews: My wife, always thinking, thought it would be a good idea to film interviews of me, for posterity's sake I suppose. I posted as much as I was comfortable with sharing.

http://www.r50rd.co...videos/pwr_int.htm

Power Source Interv...
I think I missed my calling as a...

Lidar Interview

Photos

Loading "http://www.r50rd.co.uk/r...int.htm", completed 1 of 2 items

Mechanical Technology:

Testing of the robotic arm was fraught with last minute surprises and glitches as it was the first of the major components to be completed. The lessons I learned working with the cable drives on the forearm allowed me to make some refinements to the leg design before the parts were sent out to be machined which probably saved me a few weeks time. In addition to testing the dexterity and speed of the arm, the trials were the first major test of the haptic world modeling code. Before I had a rigorous method to calibrate the proprioceptive sensors, the world model resembled the truth like Swiss cheese resembles a brick. Robot Arm Dexterity Test: 12 December 1999

I used machined drive shafts to transmit power to the legs and also used purpose built gearboxes for the places where I needed tighter tolerances and had tighter space requirements. I used Matlab to optimize various combinations of leg length, mass and acceleration.

At first I entertained the thought that the robot may be powered primarily by an electrical source. But I avoided all of this when I took the leap to a more mechanical system. You just can't beat the power density of petrol, and even with the abysmal conversion efficiency of all IC engines, they still beat batteries. For a robot of this scope, having a long-lasting and quickly "rechargeable" power source was crucial. I

ng of the robotic arm was fraught with last minute surprises and glitches as it was the first of the major comp

ents to be completed. The lessons I learned working with the cable drives on the forearm allowed me to ma
ne refinements to the leg design before the parts were sent out to be machined which probably saved me
weeks time. In addition to testing the dexterity and speed of the arm, the trials were the first major test
haptic world modeling code. Before I had a rigorous method to calibrate the proprioceptive sensors, t
ld model resembled the truth like Swiss cheese resembles a brick. Robot Arm Dexterity Test: 12 Decemb
9

ed machined drive shafts to transmit power to the legs and also used purpose built gearboxes for the plac
ere I needed tighter tolerances and had tighter space requirements. I used Matlab to optimize various com
ons of leg length, mass and acceleration.

rst I entertained the thought that the robot may be powered primarily by an electrical source. But I avoid
f this when I took the leap to a more mechanical system. You just can't beat the power density of petrol, a
n with the abysmal conversion efficiency of all IC engines, they still beat batteries. For a robot of this scop
ng a long-lasting and quickly "rechargeable" power source was crucial. I wanted run-times longer than twe
inutes :-). This was by far the biggest hurdle I was able to overcome. For a walking gait, about 95% of t
ver comes directly from the 1.6x4, with the rest electrically coupled. Keep in mind; this is still more than 5k
lectric power.

re is precedent for IC powered robots. It was first attempted in the early sixties using an American V8 engir
e recently, quadraped trucks, hexapods and walking robots designed for the timber industry are all runni
C power.

ed High Current Titanium Oxide power transistors numbering in the hundreds for what electrical needs I ha
nk goodness my wife is an analog power circuit guru. She deserves all the credit for the power electroni
most of the middle-ware.

sensor systems include(s) every sensor known to robot builders as well as a few purpose built applicatio
wn in for good measure. In place are proprioception sensors, infrared (IR) sensors, a set of high-resoluti
, and even

e old bump type sensors in places like the knees, legs and outer arms. Strain gauges were installed to dete
o twist and to help with debug and self-diagnosis and repair.

most interesting sensors are the olfactory sensors located in the head that can detect the difference betwe
smission fluid, oil, brake fluid and gasoline for roadside assistance. For some light reading, try this book:
://www.wileyeurope.com/cda/product/0,,3527303588,00.html

nique 4-way microphone system in the head gives directional input. There a   the tor
d as inputs for noise cancellation software.

of the greatest challenges of the vision system I overcame was the recogni

Engineers aren't stupid. So when we
decided to perpetrate the MINI Robot
hoax, we hired experts in the field of robotics
to participate in strategic blogging. Hoo
hoo hoo hoo haa haaa haaaa haaaaa!

le and partially occluded objects. For some of the more typical objects the r   likely
xample), a simple internal model of vehicle geometry is used. This model is r apped onto

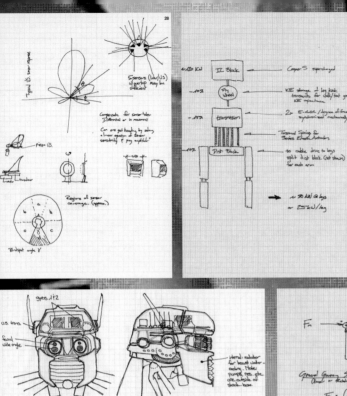
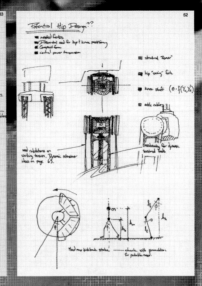
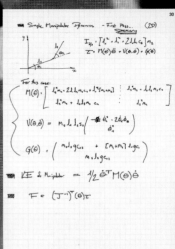
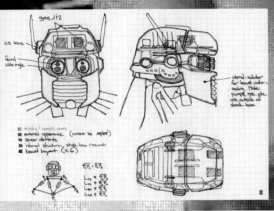
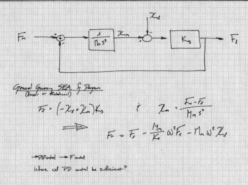
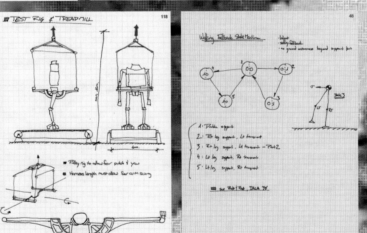
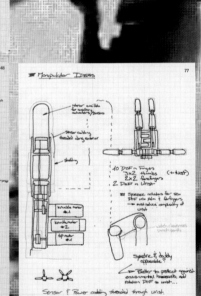
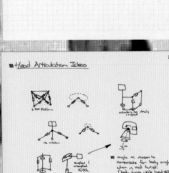

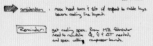
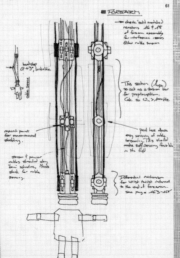
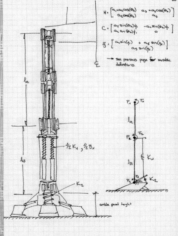
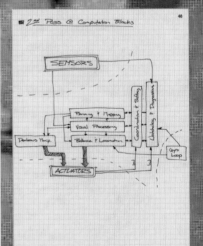

Storyboards and sketches show how much work went into the MINI Robot hoax. Some creative blurts out, "Hey, what if we made robots?" in a coffee shop, and two dozen lives are ruined for six months.

Casson Publishing Ltd. London

cassonpublishing.co.uk

Home | About Us | Current Favorites | Coming Soon | Purchase our books | Contact Us

Founded in 1993, Casson Publishing Ltd. has enjoyed more than 10 years of success publishing what are consider to be some of the m interesting titles offered today.

Our proprietor, James Casson, is passionately committed to publishing works of the unknown and bizarre. Our goal is to provide a platf stories that might never have had a chance to be told.

Inside the Area. A closer look at Area 51.

The Magnetic Fields of Cardiff City, Wales.

The Deep Dark Mystery – Loch Ness

Contemporary Bigfoot Sightings in Northeast Ohio

The Lincolnshi Circles – Magic

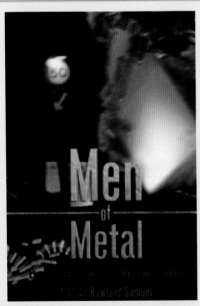

Now available:
Men of Metal Eyewitness Accounts of Humanoid Robots
By Rowland Samuel

£12.99
Paperback 145 pages (5 December, 2003)
Photos: 14
Illustrations: 1
Author Info:
Rowland Samuel's first book is his documentation of his search for the answer occurrences in London involving automobiles and a supposed humanoid robo writing is insightful and full of heavy substantiation.

February 9, 2003.

The first time I heard the story I laughed my arse off. Everybody did.

I'm at a party in Oxford, and like almost every party in Oxford, it's boring as hell. People are droning on about cricket and the Labor Party and Parliament and I'm ready to slit my wrists. My girlfriend Jen spots an old friend across the room and drags me over to meet him. Brilliant.

His name is James Casson and he tells me he's a publisher and I tell him I'm a freelance journalist and I brace myself for a bit of excruciating small talk. But James isn't as boring as James looks. He says he publishes books about the occult. Unexplained phenomena. Doesn't take the stuff too seriously, just puts it on paper with a wink and a nod. Funny. The conversation turns to urban legends and we try to out-urban legend each other. I start with the alligators in the sewers in New York and he counters with people stealing kidneys in Mexico. Doberman choking on thief's finger is met with hook found on the door of a car. We go on and on, until he throws out a story I hadn't heard.

Apparently, a mate of his had a classic "bright lights came out of nowhere" experience on a road outside of town. Where these things always seem to happen. He is driving along on a rainy night and skids off the road and sees something – he's not sure what – and before he knows it, he's magically back on the road, safe and sound. Very Hollywood. We all have a big laugh and then James plays his trump card.

Seems this fellow took a snapshot.

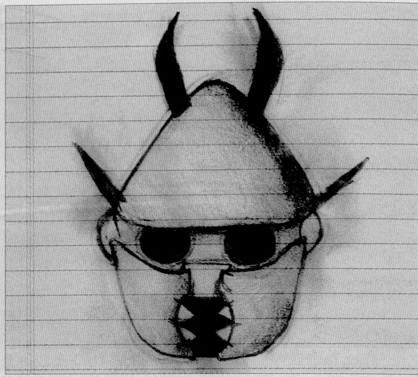

When I met with Mrs. Graham, I asked her to draw a picture of what she had seen. Her sighting, February 3, was the first on record.

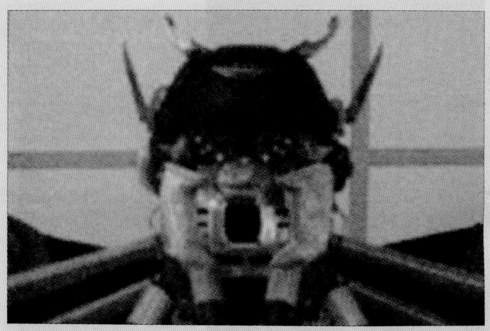

I downloaded this image from www.r50rd.co.uk/research/internal/v2i/engin/ and showed it to both Horace Burrowes and Pelham Stevens. Each felt the object was similar to what they had seen.

Her story was
Stevens, she ha
road. At night.
it was going li

I ask her if she
ing a picture v
good enough l
paper and pen

I'm not exactly
back at me.

Before we get

"Mrs. Graham
it traveling?"

"I don't know.

February 27

"Here you go.

I write it dow

"And the add

"2438 Binsey

"Thanks, Mic

I have a mate
but when I d

"Hello?"

The voice sou

The Oxford Incident Sightings Page

Imprint Photos | Imprint Video | Known Events | My Theory | Links | Email | Submit a Sighting

w Photos

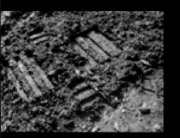

w Sightings

It is my goal to provide those looking for answ
Oxford incident mysteries with a place to pos
information. This site will serve the enthusias
connected with in London as well as anyone
interested in the strange goings-on – especia
who have been affected by the phenomenon

For those of you who aren't familiar with the Oxford incidents, the stori
something like this:

Imagine you're in the Oxford area, driving in your car. Maybe it's rainin
hit a patch of water and begin to lose control of the car. Your situation
you begin to leave the road. Suddenly, something lifts your car in the a
butterflies in your stomach, and you suddenly land gently back on the
safe and sound. You realize you're fine except for an odd dent in your

This isn't science fiction, this is the account given by Horace Burrowes
February, 2003. Something is happening that can't be explained. Som
a prototype RAF helicopter, others a spirit. Some say it's an angel and
believe it's some sort of robot.

This website is dedicated to finding the truth behind the growing numb
incidents. I hope you enjoy it and find it useful.

...there are many ideas about what creativity is. Traditionally, it's been seen as a moment. A "eureka." But to us creativity is a process, not a singular moment. And, believe it or not, the most recent research seems to back us up here.

So maybe you work in a creative field or maybe you don't, but you are most definitely creative. Don't give us any bullshit here and even pretend that you aren't. Every single person on Earth is creative. You might be taught not to be, and you might have bought into the idea that you aren't, but it's a fact that you were a very creative little person once. And life still hasn't beaten it out of you. We're not trying to kiss your ass. You might be a jerk. Who knows? But you're definitely creative.

Being a creative person, you sometimes respond negatively to having circumstance or other people change your idea. Why are we like that when change is in such close relation to creativity? It's fear. And if you remember only one thing from this book, make it this: FEAR IS THE MORTAL ENEMY OF CREATIVITY.

MINI Robots started as an idea to insert a comic book into magazines. Seemed like an entertaining way to talk about the amazing technology in a MINI. So as we sat down to write the story, we found that we liked the story more than the comic book. Soon the comic book became a graphic novel. We still liked the story more than the idea of a graphic novel. It seemed a shame for it to be a piece of fiction. We wanted the characters, and our giant robot, to come to life. So it changed again and became a book and a half-dozen websites and backstories and posters and toys. And it turned out we weren't the only ones who wished that giant robots were real.

Scary anecdote: When the site went live, the first people to visit were from the Pentagon and the CIA and the FBI. Like, within hours. We figure they must have Internet bots that are constantly scanning for breakthroughs in creating a great big robot army. Well, you'll be relieved to know that they didn't get squat out of us...

From: xxxxxxxx@the-sun.co.uk
To: colinmayhewphd@yahoo.co.uk
Subject: robot
Date: Mon, 26 Apr 2004
Hello. My name is Lucy and I am a reporter for the Sun. If this pic has anything to do with you we would be very interested in doing a story about it. If not I am sorry to have bothered you. Many Thanks. Lucy

Date: Thu, 12 Aug 2004
Subject: Robot footage
From: Heatherxxxxxxx@edelmanproductions.com
To: colinmayhewphd@yahoo.co.uk
I work for a television show called Tactical to Practical on the History Channel and we are creating a segment entitled Tomorrow's Robots. We are going to highlight robots of the future- large scale robots, special effects robots for the film industry and robots that our host, Hunter Ellis, can battle against or interact with. I would love the opportunity to talk to you further about what we are looking for and become informed of your latest technological developments in robotics. Also if you have any b-roll footage of your robots, especially the Mini Cooper R50; being assembled created, and in action in Beta sp format or mini dv that you could send us that would be great. You can use our Fed Ex number 2273 xxxx-9 and priority overnight express it to the address below. I have attached a description of our show for you to take look at. I look forward to hearing from you soon.
Thanks, Heather Xxxxxxx

From: Janexxxxxxx@uclink.berkeley.edu
To: colinmayhewphd@yahoo.co.uk
Subject: hello from the Alpha Lab
Date: Sun, 25 Apr 2004
Colin, Hello from a fellow robotics researcher. I'm with the alpha Lab for IEOR at UC Berkeley. My colleagues and I most enjoyed reading about your mini-cooper mods and humanoid Research; it sparked our imaginations greatly. Best wishes- Jane Xxxxxxx

From: Richxxxxxxx@charter.net
To: colinmayhewphd@yahoo.co.uk
Subject: Men of Metal
Date: Mon, 14 Jun 2004
I just quite accidentally, came into possession of a pamphlet or excerpt from Men of Metal by Rowland Samuel. Are you familiar with the "publication"? Do you subscribe to the following?First Law: A robot may not injure a human being, or, through inaction, allow a human being to come to harm. Second Law: A robot must obey orders given it by human beings, except where such orders would conflict with the first law. Third Law. A robot must protect its own existence as long as such protection does not conflict with the First or Second Law.

From: Michaelxxxxxxx@hotmail.com
To: colinmayhewphd@yahoo.co.uk
Subject: hello, read me PLEASE
Date: Wed, 28 Apr 2004
Hello, my name is Michael, I'm very interested in the work that you are doing. My dream is to one day be able to bring people, such as yourself together, to work under one roof. People are capable of great intellegents, however usually it's in different fields. I myself have come very close to finding a cure for ageing, that is what I am obsessed with, that is what I am good at. Another person I know is close to not only perfecting Anti-gravita-

tional flight, but also perfecting a process of compacting metals, making them much denser and stronger imagine an armored ship where the weight doesn't affect its flight. And I also have a friend who has perfected the rail gun. I am sorry that I cannot release the names of these people to you. They are all currently working on their projects secretly. You don't want certain technologies to fall into the wrong hands.However sadly all of our funding is running shor. It upsets me to see rich people, such as the Olsen Twins, wasting their money and influence on NOTHING! If only I had the funds I need…oh well, I will figure something out. Right now we're getting desperate,we are thinking about selling the rail gun to the US military…. We need the funds…but a weapon like that, I don't know if the world could be responsible enough. Anyways, I'm writing this letter to congratulate you on what you are doing. You have a purpose in this world. Keep up your work no matter what. I have never seen a robot function as well at the one on you test videos.I so wish that I could meet you one day. Oh, well. If you have time, please write back.Thank You.

From: xxxxxxx@chambergate.com
To: colinmayhewphd@yahoo.co.uk
Subject: r50rd
Date: Mon, 12 Apr 2004
I would like to buy one to protect my son while he is learning to drive.

From: Joexxxxxxx@hotmail.com
To: colinmayhewphd@yahoo.co.uk
Subject: Metal?
Date: Wed, 23 Jun 2004
You guys are GOOD! I loved the videos, very nice work! I'd really like to say more, but I gotta rush out and buy me a Mini!
Thanks for the read. Very fun. I can be a bit of a conspiracy theorist myself so this was quite enjoyable.
Keep up the good work, Joe Xxxxxxx, Knoxville, Tennessee USA

From: Anthonyxxxxxxx@msn.com
To: colinmayhewphd@yahoo.co.uk
Subject: I want to learn more!
Date: WED, 21 Jul 2004
Greetings, I'm very interested learning more. I own a mini, and I'm not surprised that it is the model of car associated with this surreal robotic mystery. I have often thought "Wow, why did they overengineer this car so much"? It is such a beautiful car, especially now that it is a product of BMW, which is clearly the only company that could produce it in its current state. Congratulations on your brilliance and your progress. Please inform me of any further developments and available information. I've perused your site and the links, even called the CARNEGIE MELLON Robotics institute thinking that the number given may have been deceptive but it wasn't. I could use some help in finding where the trail Is that will lead me to a full appreciation of this situation.
Thanks so much, Anthony Xxxxxxx

From: Jimmyxxxxxxx@hotmail.com
To: colinmayhewphd@yahoo.co.uk
Date: Tue, 06 Apr 2004
Subject: No Subject
Just finished the novella in "Motor Trends"'s May 2004…quite a good read! I assure you that I'm on my way to a Cooper Type S as finances allow! Fan fiction at its finest! Thanks again,
Corte Madera, Ca Xxxxxxx

The top story on http://www.slashdot.org right
around an R50 chassis. Naturally, the originatir
(http://www.r50rd.co
a little far-fetched. Any
credulous any more :-)

到这么强大的机器人。相关的
不乱说话了。机器人、飞机儿

ed by michael on Frida
the why-the-heck-not dep
eRobotGuy writes "A re
unctions are controlled
iny, at over 10 feet tall

› lifesize autobot pic 'psuedoreal'

kuzushi   **Posted:** Mar 13

shdot
rds. Stuff that matters.

Build a Robot out of a Car?
Posted by michael on Friday March 12, @09:41PM
from the why-the-heck-not dept.
SomeRobotGuy writes "A researcher in the U.K. is in the process of buil
Its functions are controlled by six computers running RTLinux and it's p
not tiny, at over 10 feet tall! The site includes videos showing some impr

(Read More... | 76 of 117 comments)

Ask Slashdot: Design a Virtual Office with Open Source S
Posted by Cliff on Friday March 12,
from the how-would-you-do-it dept.
apropos asks: "An interesting questic
company: 'How would you design the
security and office suites all available
mind was emailing answering machir

(Read More... | 108 of 170 comment

What's in Your Gadget Ba
Posted by michael on Friday March
from the looks-like-someone-just-had-a-
Cory Doctorow has taken a two-secor
weep, wanna-bes.

(Read More... | 193 of 281 comment

Le robot issu de la Mini Cooper R50

18-03-2006

La news concernant ceci a été cataloguée au rang de hoax...
tout de même rêver. Colin Mayhew, un ingénieur chez BMW
britanique a eu la première fois une vision de construire un r
des années 60. Il n'y avait aucun vrai robot à cette époque,
qu'un robot serait le complément le plus normal à l'automobi

Protoform X   Posted: Mar 13 2004, 09:44 PM

http://www.zoicstudios.com/

In an 18 month collaborative partnership with Crispin, Porter, and Bog
able to design, create, and develop a modern myth. The character o
became an important hero to the rapidly developing robotics and eng
ocument a multi year
ent, testing, and finis
was designed, built,
king attention to reali
s to enhance the qu
s shot on location,
eople argued about
QUARE, a hero in th
advertising in the e

hurts criminals. I wouldn't mind this thing coming along if someone was trying to
hurt my family and it ran them off or better, held them for the police. But what if
it's just ambling along, sees a situation that it can't figure out easily who is "right"
and who is "wrong"? What's it going to do then? I hope these things aren't out yet.
If they are, they should be outlawed in america. I don't mind if the english have
them roaming around as I don't travel there.
Posted by J.Neumann in Houston on Wed Jun 16, 2004 at 10:44 PM

u all r stoopid.

this is real

my aunt has this guy that she knows who heard from somenoe that it's TRUE

so yur all just jealos
Posted by brad on Wed Jun 23, 2004 at 12:18 PM

March 20, 2004

MINI COOPE

Ever heard of 'Gundam' or 'Transformers'? Always dreame
having such a robot beast as your pet?

Mini Cooper

upposedly, a British engineer, who originally had the idea to
e late 1960's, has revived his ambition. In fact, he even went
w MINI Cooper R50 as his basis for the robot. A truly amaz
u can see he uses many of the OEM parts right off the MINI
en SlashDotted (SlashDot.org) into oblivion. Luckily, it is n

any out there seem to write this off as an elaborate hoax, Ph
back to some of its "non-traditional" marketing methods ag

KoBOT!™

NEWS

Saturday, March 13, 2004

⚠ MINI COOPER TO B
see. "This ambition star
new Mini. I've always be
so the over-building of c
went unnoticed. In 1998

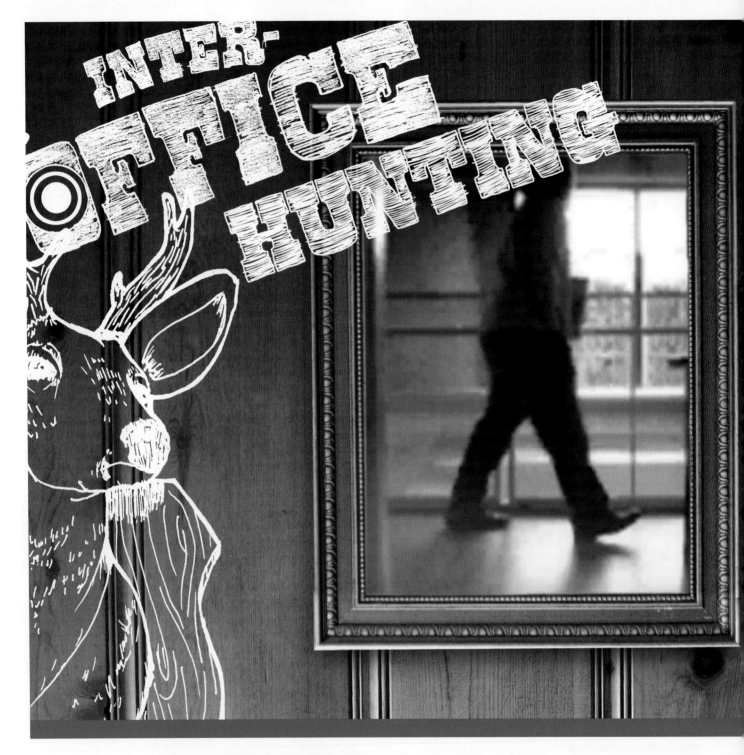

_____Foot "the game"

Do you know all your co-workers? Do you want to? If your company experiences exceptional growth, you'll start to see a bunch of new faces grazing the halls. Sightings of some are more rare than others. _____Foot is a sport designed to help you get to know these new hires a little more intimately.

When play begins, fill in the blank with the hire's most notable feature. It could be <u>Tall</u>Foot, <u>Short</u>Foot,

<u>Greasy</u>Foot, <u>Bald</u>Foot, or, in our example, <u>Blonde</u>Foot. All you need to play is a few digital cameras and paper and a pen for score keeping. Numbers on a team and length of play are entirely variable. One point for each photo. Extra points are awarded for shots in different environments and with different team members in frame. Whichever team earns the most points at the end of the given time period wins!

Outdoors +1

Team member in frame +1

Opposing team member in frame +2

In restroom +0

Taunt (style move) +5

1pt

3pt

2pt

CASIO

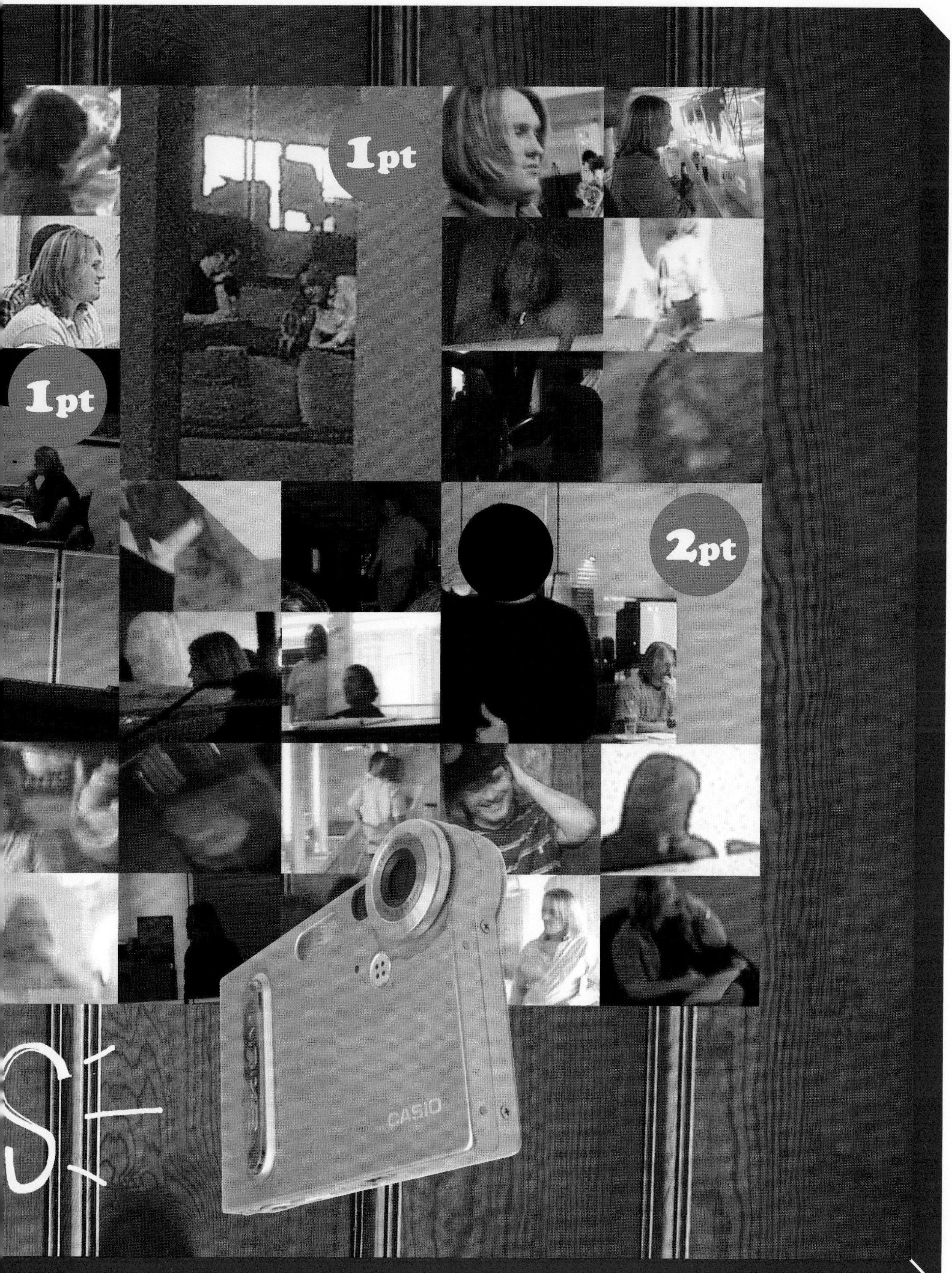
1pt
1pt
2pt
CASIO

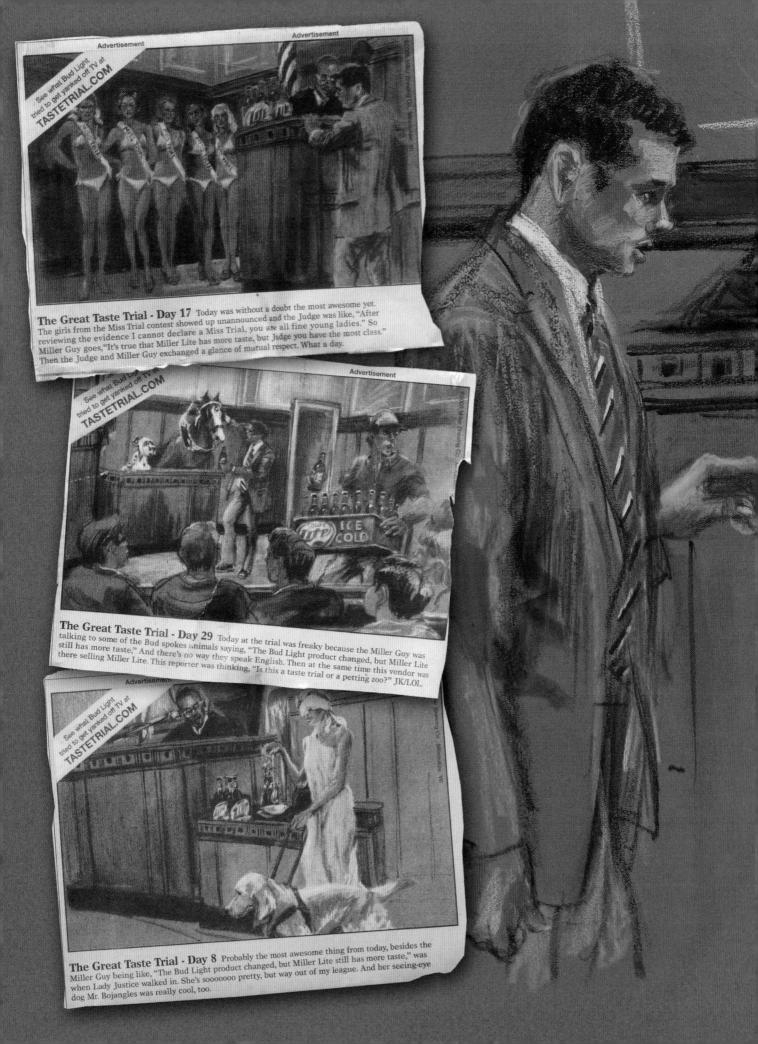

 The Great Taste Trial - Day 5 Today was filled with a lot of boring lawyer stuff, except for this one time when the Miller Guy said, "Are you aware that the Bud Light product changed, but that Miller Lite still has more taste." And Flava Flav went, "Yeah boyeeeeeeee." It was so awesome.

Authentic Fake or True Stories

"The Sickening"

According to records, the first ever documented lap dance given inside the agency was done by a big fat hairy man-fairy dressed in a tutu with a feathered boa.

○ Fake
○ True

WEEKLY WORLD NEWS

January 14, 2003

Mutant steals Mini Cooper car for joy ride!

Hot pursuit of half-bat, half-human!

BAT BOY LEADS COPS ON 3 STATE CHASE!

ACTUAL PHOTOS!

SUPER DOUBLE ISSUE!

SADDAM CHALLENGES BUSH TO A DUEL

'Why go to war when we can settle this like gentlemen?'

$2.79 U.S.

$3.95 CANADA

0 09281 51030 7

02>

BAT BOY STEALS A CAR — AND GOES ON A THREE-STATE JOY RIDE!

MISSING HALF-BAT, HALF-HUMAN STRIKES AGAIN!

POLICE CARS from several Ohio jurisdictions are shown in hot pursuit of a Mini Cooper with a screaming Bat Boy at the wheel — and they still failed to nab the human bat!

ACTION PHOTO taken from a Detroit overpass clearly shows cops chasing the stolen Mini Cooper. Inset closeup reveals Bat Boy is the driver.

WWN 3X ZOOM

CLOSE-UP photo of car's side view appears to show Bat Boy behind the wheel.

FBI Special Agent Jack Trasker has been assigned to the Bat Boy case since the mutant disappeared last May.

By WAYNE DIAZ
Weekly World News

DETROIT — Bat Boy, the world's favorite winged freak, went on an incredible, death-defying joyride through Michigan, Indiana and Ohio after carjacking a brand new Mini Cooper — and is still on the lam somewhere in America!

The brazen theft took place in the crowded parking lot of a Mini dealership. Eyewitnesses report that the Mini Cooper's owner had just accepted the keys to the vehicle when Bat Boy jumped out from behind some bushes, snatched the keys and sped away.

"The whole thing happened in a matter of seconds," says the car's horrified owner, who asked not to be identified. "The dealer had just handed me the keys when this monstrous creature appeared out of nowhere and tore off like a bat out of hell."

Police suspect that Bat Boy had been casing the dealership for hours, waiting for just the right moment to strike. Two employees gave chase, but Bat Boy quickly lost them in traffic.

Police say they are looking for a red Mini Cooper, last seen around Akron. A police spokesman says, "That little speed demon was heading East on Interstate 80. We urge all motorists to be on the lookout for this car, and to notify authorities if they see a Mini Cooper driven by a bat-like creature."

There were numerous sightings of Bat Boy following the theft, but police have been unable to locate him and he remains at large as of this writing.

"We know where Bat Boy has been during his little adventure — we just don't know where he is now," notes FBI Special Agent Jack Trasker.

Since returning to the United States, Bat Boy's behavior has become increasingly erratic.

"We've been tracking his movements via reports of gas station drive-offs — apparently Bat Boy is stealing gas when the tank runs low and drives away before police can respond."

Bat Boy learned how to drive while working with the U.S. military combating terrorism in Afghanistan.

Secret military files leaked to Weekly World News report that he stole at least two Jeeps and a tank during his stint there.

Three months ago he escaped from government custody and became a fugitive.

Police reports collected from stunned onlookers put Bat Boy in at least three different states. Sitings include:

• The Detroit Zoo, where he was believed to be looking for a quick snack.

• Drive-through of an Indiana donut shop. Several police officers taking a break in the shop gave chase, but Bat Boy managed to lose them in traffic.

• Interstate chase in Ohio. With cops in hot pursuit, Bat Boy whizzed down the Interstate at speeds in excess of 100 miles an hour.

Authorities are desperate to recapture Bat Boy, and have asked the nation's driving public to immediately report anything unusual. FBI and police scoured the tri-state area via car and helicopter, but they're no closer to capturing Bat Boy than they were three months ago.

"Hell, he could be a thousand miles from here by now," notes Agent Trasker, who has been on Bat Boy's tail since he escaped government custody. "For someone so weird, he manages to hide himself pretty easily. With winter just around the corner, he'll probably head south.

"We already have task forces assembled in Georgia, North Carolina and Florida so when he shows up, we'll be ready."

In the meantime, the owner of the stolen Mini Cooper says he probably won't press charges should Bat Boy finally be captured.

"I hope Bat Boy learns his lesson and turns himself in," the man says. "I just want my Mini Cooper back."

BAT BOY ABANDONS STOLEN CAR — & VANISHES

Creature drops it off at Florida shopping mall!

By MIKE FOSTER/Weekly World News

TAMPA — A freewheeling 21-day car chase that police are calling "the most dramatic and bizarre vehicular pursuit since the O.J. Simpson spectacle" screeched to a halt when Bat Boy pulled into a shopping mall parking lot in Florida, jumped out of the car and ran off, authorities say.

Sources within the special nationwide law-enforcement task force convened to hunt down the half-bat, half-human mutant confirm that he abandoned the car, leaving the keys in the ignition and the motor running.

"This strange little fellow with pointy ears jumped out of the car, hopped from hood to hood across the parking lot and then sailed over a fence," says eyewitness Carmen Mayfurd of Tampa, who was walking to her own car when she spotted the creature. "About 14 other people saw it too."

Despite reports that Bat Boy committed more than 260 traffic violations on his zigzagging journey, which covered about 7,800 miles, drove at speeds exceeding 110 m.p.h., and nearly collided with numerous objects, ranging from a snowman in Michigan to a statue of Robert E. Lee in Mississippi, the vehicle was returned in near-mint condition.

"There was hardly a scratch on it — in fact, it looked like it had just been through a car wash," says FBI Special Agent Jack Trasker.

Task force officials say that after Bat Boy ripped off the brand-new Mini Cooper from a Detroit dealership three weeks ago, he took a wild and unpredictable course that carried him through 11 states.

Since crossing over into Florida last week, reported sightings include:

- **Cape Canaveral** — where he drove across the shuttle launch pad at the Kennedy Space Center as startled astronauts watched from the cockpit.
- **Boca Raton** — where he broke into the Weekly World News warehouse and made off with 150 Bat Boy T-shirts, which were later found half-eaten.
- **Naples** — where he mooned a trio of vacationing Canadian "snowbirds" out of his car window.
- **Sanibel Island** — where he used the Mini Cooper as a dune buggy on a clothing-optional beach, sending nude

sunbathers running for their lives.

Why Bat Boy lead-footed it down to Florida is a riddle scientists are mulling over.

"I believe Bat Boy has migrated south

for the winter, as do many species of birds," says British anthropologist Dr. Vincent Morecastle, considered one of the world's leading Bat Boy-ologists.

"He was driven by instinct."

EYEWITNESS
Carmen Mayfurd

SECURITY camera videotaped Bat Boy as he left the Mini Cooper in a Tampa parking lot. FBI Special Agent Jack Trasker, left, is on the case.

21-day, 11-state chase comes to a screeching halt!

MOBILE BAT: Weekly World News first reported Bat Boy's theft of a new Mini Cooper from a Detroit dealership in our January 14 edition. In the past

three weeks, the pointy-eared freak buzzed through a fast-food drive-thru, and even took a bathroom break in the woods before leaving the car in Tampa.

Revised Brief Chicken Sandwich	The New Chicken Sandwich.
Who Are We Talking To?	People who eat chicken.
Mandatories	All work done for Chicken Sandwich needs to include the characters shown below. They need to always appear tough. These chickens like to fight.

good beer.

yeah, save me some.

⚠ CONSUMER ALERT ⚠

Premium iconic brands like Rolex, Ray-Ban, and Prada often find themselves being knocked off by counterfeiters. And while nobody is counterfeiting MINIs...yet, what would it say about the brand if they were?

COUNTERFEIT MINI COOPERS: A BIG PROBLEM THAT'S GROWING BIGGER.

Premium goods are always the first to be knocked off. Expensive watches, designer sunglasses and, more recently, the MINI Cooper, are all being widely counterfeited. The allure of getting a genuine vehicle for pennies on the dollar is often too much to resist.

Beware: you get what you pay for.

On the surface, the fakes can appear very convincing. But a closer look reveals something that is inaccurate, unsafe, and disappointing to drive. Sold by street vendors, at flea markets, pawn shops, and internet auction sites, the criminals rely on ignorance and a lack of common sense. The extremely near-sighted are especially vulnerable.

The Counter Counterfeit Commission (CCC) is dedicated to countering counterfeit activity. And our efforts span the globe.* Through education, the CCC is helping consumers protect themselves. Cooperating with international law enforcement, we're pursuing criminals and standing very close by during arrests.

To report a counterfeit vehicle and for more information about how you can protect yourself, call the CCC hotline or go to the official CCC website.

ream components, Pioneer flip case...
rranty, asking $24,500. Call 516-322-3675

, chance to own a legend! Chili red paint, perfect, 5 spd, lots of extras, 543k mi. ...your brains out! 718-701-2965

d, Manhattan, West...

$39.00 NEW YOR AUTO SHOW

CCC: CRASH TEST DRAMATIZATION: 15 MPH   00:04:41:28.

CCC: CRASH TEST DRAMATIZATION: 15 MPH   00:04:43:26.

CCC: CRASH TEST DRAMATIZATION: 15 MPH   00:04:44:02.

CCC: CRASH TEST DRAMATIZATION: 15 MPH   00:04:44:23.

CCC: CRASH TEST DRAMATIZATION: 15 MPH   00:04:45:09.

CCC: CRASH TEST DRAMATIZATION: 15 MPH   00:04:46:29.

CCC: CRASH TEST DRAMATIZATION: 15 MPH   00:04:49:00.

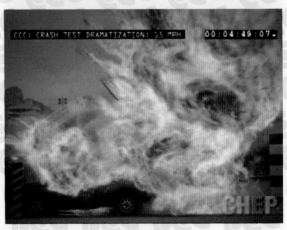

CCC: CRASH TEST DRAMATIZATION: 15 MPH   00:04:49:07.

In addition to basic techniques for identifying a fake, this program offered a rare glimpse into the underworld of the modern counterfeiter. Candid interviews got you up close and personal with the criminals and a counterfeiter-turned-undercover agent offered his account of life as a phony. However, the CCC believes most people bought the DVD to view an expensive, Hollywood-style explosion.

CASE #447-Z319-54

▲ Upon examination, this mock-MINI was found to be almost the correct size: small. And the addition of bonnet stripes was very convincing. However, the clever counterfeiters got one crucial detail wrong. This car is butt-ugly.

CONVERTIBLE!

CASE #879-W277-01

▲ You can see what ran through the counterfeiter's mind on this one. A genuine MINI Convertible is thrilling to drive due to its combination of nimble handling and open-air excitement. But one kiss-and-tell flaw presented itself when we tried to put the roof up. It didn't have one.

CASE #661-A313-69

▲ One of the breakthrough innovations in the counterfeiting industry was the discovery of a simple optical illusion. Oversized logos can make a big car appear small. This vehicle looked flawless to the naked eye, but an alert consumer with a tape measure revealed its enormity.

MINI COOPER S

▲ 2005 Genuine MINI Cooper S

HOW TO IDENTIFY A GENUINE MINI.

Authenticating a genuine MINI does not require an advanced automotive engineering degree. Listed below are a few more design and performance features that can help confirm a MINI as the genuine article.

▲ REMEMBER: If ever in doubt, see your local MINI Dealer.

1. Contrasting Roof & Side Mirrors
2. Wide, Bulldog-like Stance
3. Center-mounted Speedometer
4. Wraparound Greenhouse Windows
5. Ultra Rigid Chassis
6. Multi-link Rear Suspension
7. Bonnet Stripes
8. Steering Column-mounted Tachometer
9. Climate Controlled Glove Box
10. Six Standard Airbags
11. Anti-lock Breaking System (ABS)
12. Corner Brake Control (CBC)
13. Electronic Brakeforce Distribution (EBD)
14. Drive-by-Wire Electronic Throttle Control
15. Dynamic Stability Control (DSC)
16. Short Overhangs
17. 50:50 Split-folding Rear Seats

56.2"   75.8"   57.5"

143.9"

This information is presented by the CCC in a joint effort with MINI USA.

A genuine MINI is small. A proven method of verifying a MINI's authenticity is by making sure the vehicle is not, in fact, huge.

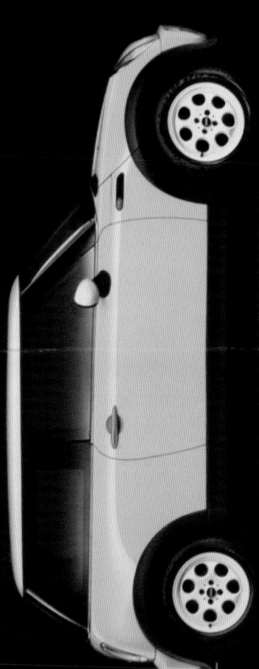

Genuine 2005 MINI Cooper

11' 11.1"

COMMON COUNTERFEITING TRICKS

Improvised Materials

Many fakes look good at first glance. But look closer. Be certain the bonnet stripes are not fashioned from ordinary duct tape.

Perverse Engineering

The exhaust tip on a genuine MINI Cooper should resemble a beer can. If the exhaust tip really is a beer can, contact the CCC immediately.

Size Manipulation

By confusing the eye with a simple scale distortion technique, an oversized logo can make a large vehicle appear much smaller.

FOR MORE INFORMATION VISIT COUNTERFEITMINI.ORG

PRESENTED BY THE CCC IN COOPERATION WITH MINI USA

HEY, THERE'S A GUY NAMED FAST EDDIE WHO LIVES OVER HERE IN WESTERVILLE OHIO. AND HILARIOUS. IS THIS FOR REAL? WHAT'S UP MAN, I THINK I SPOTTED A FAKE BRO. UH, IT WAS ON DO WITH IT. IT'S REALLY SCARING ME REALLY BAD... PLEASE HELP. HI, UH I'M WONDERING IF TH GUYS ARE SERIOUSLY SERIOUS. YOU TRICKED ME. HEY MIKE, I'VE GOT SOME PRETTY SUSPICIO STEVE I NEED YA, IT'S RICH HERE. I'VE GOT A COUNTERFEIT MINI HERE. IT'S TWO BIKES TAPED WHEN YOU COME MAKE SURE YOU BRING THE CARPOOL, OR I WILL GIVE YOU THE CARPOOL. THIS AND THOSE MINI PICTURES, OH MY GOD! UM, I JUST WANTED TO KNOW IF THIS IS REAL. IT ALL I DON'T UNDERSTAND. WHAT ARE YOU DOING? HA HA HA HA ARE YOU GUYS REAL? OK, WHAT AUTO SHOW. IT WAS AT THE INFINITY BOOTH. HEY, THIS MESSAGE IS FOR CHERYL. I WAS ON EBA CAN MOTOR. RELOADED AND READY TO MOTOR. I WAS WONDERING IF I COULD HIRE ONE OF YO

⚠ REPORT ALL SUSPICIOUS ACTIVITIES ⚠

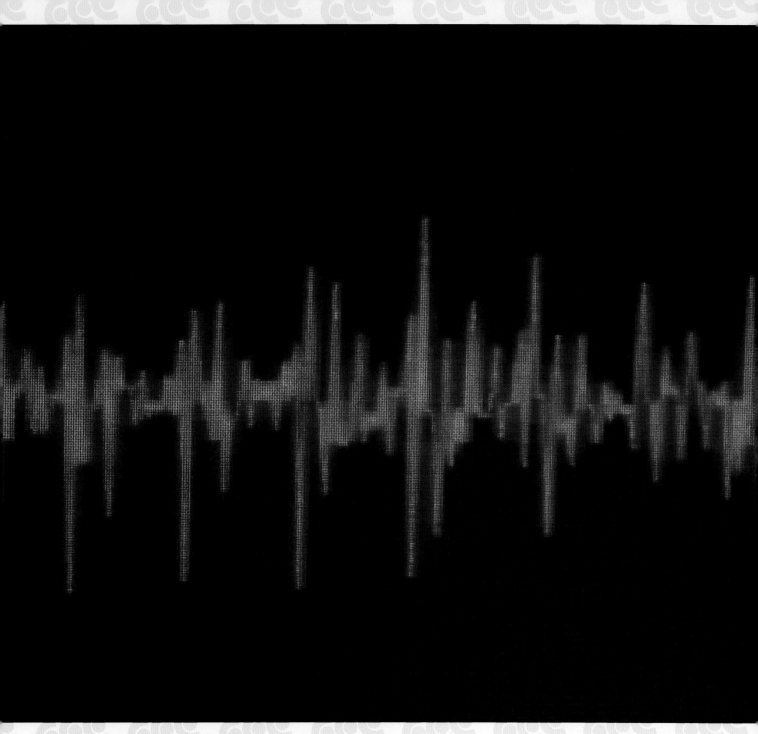

THINK HE'S PART OF THE RING. I'VE GOT SOME PRETTY SUSPICIOUS MOTORCYCLES. THIS IS
RNER OF DORDY AND DOUBLIN BLVD. I HAVE A COUNTERFEIT MINI AND I DON'T KNOW WHAT TO
ST BULLSHIT OR IF YOU GUYS ARE REAL. I REALLY WANT TO KNOW IF THIS IS A JOKE OR IF YOU
ORCYCLES HERE THAT I WANT YOU GUYS TO LOOK AT. SO IF YOU CAN JUST DROP ON BY. STEVE,
THER. I NEED YA. I NEED YA. THIS IS MIKE HOCK, I AM HERE CALLING ABOUT THE COUNTERFEIT.
RIOUS. IS THIS FOR REAL? ARE YOU GUYS ACTUALLY DOING THIS THING? I WENT TO YOUR WEBSITE
KIND OF WEIRD TO ME. IF THIS IS REAL, WHICH IT PROBABLY ISN'T, WILL YOU CALL ME BACK?
? HI, I HAVE SPOTTED A COUNTERFEIT MINI. INTERESTINGLY ENOUGH IT WAS AT THE DETROIT
SAW SOMEONE SELLING MINIS. THEY ARE CERTIFIED RELOADED. I THINK THEY CLAIM THAT THEY
TECTIVES TO A LITTLE UNDERCOVER WORK FOR ME. DUDE, THIS WEBSITE ROCKS. THANK YOU.

☏ **(719) 404-1819** 💻 **COUNTERFEITMINI.ORG**

Counter Counterfeit Commission

Early in 2005, the **Counter Counterfeit Commission** was established with hopes of stemming the tide of fake MINI Coopers flooding the market. Cooperating with law enforcement from around the globe, the **CCC** is dedicated to protecting the public's right to motor genuinely. They have dramatically reduced the number of imposters and made many arrests.

Director
Counter Counterfeit Commission

Jonathan Tress
Ex-Counterfeiter
Forest Hills, NY

CHEP

PROTECT YOURSELF FROM THE HUMILIATION OF OWNING A FAKE!

HTC-35 Mini Money Lab Counterfeit Detector - Counterfeit Detectors ...
Money Detection - HTC-40 HTC-35 - ABCO Office Solutions.
www.abcosolutions.com/htc-35.htm - 9k - Cached - Similar pages

Todd's Blog - Confessions of a Dangerous MINI Owner: Comment on ...
Comments: Counterfeit MINI spotted. That site is hilarious. Ha ha!. :). Posted by
timsamoff at May 31, 2005 08:33 AM. could you counterfeit my car? ...
www.toddsmods.com/mt/mt-comments.cgi?entry_id=154 - 5k - Cached - Similar pages
[More results from www.toddsmods.com]

Mini - Wikipedia, the free encyclopedia
BMW · Counterfeit · Copyrights · Logo · MINI. Retrieved from "http://en.wikipedia.
org/wiki/Mini". Categories: Automobile manufacturers | BMW vehicles ...
en.wikipedia.org/wiki/Mini - 36k - Cached - Similar pages

Counterfeit Mini Ads Round Up : Jalopnik
Jalopnik loves cars. Secret cars, concept cars, flying cars, vintage cars,
tricked-out cars, red cars, black cars, blonde cars — sometimes. ...
www.jalopnik.com/cars/adspromotions/ counterfeit-mini-ads-round-up-033855.php - 16k - Cached -

Results 1 - 10 of about 627,00

AllDumb: links - Counterfeit Mini Coopers?
Daily doses of funny links, videos, pictures, games, and flash animations.
www.alldumb.com/item/11577/ - 24k - Cached - Similar pages

GBMINI (MINI Cooper) weblog: Would this Counterfeit MINI fool you?
The counterfeit MINI in fact was delivering the donated prize from MINI Peabody,
which was the roof rack & storage box on top of the vehicle; moreover, ...
www.gbmini.net/mtblog/archive/ 2005/06/would_this_coun.shtml - 15k - Cached - Similar pages

GBMINI (MINI Cooper) weblog: Counterfeit MINI Coopers!
Counterfeit MINI Coopers! This scary subject has been discussed recently on
MotoringFile; there have always been counterfeits in the world (Prada, Rolex, ...
www.gbmini.net/mtblog/archive/ 2005/02/counterfeit_min_1.shtml - 12k - Cached - Similar p
[More results from www.gbmini.net]

Counterfeit MINIs and the CCC
"Hey, I have an idea; let's come out with a counterfeit Mini site". ... Did anyone
actually get the address on the counterfeit mini commercial? ...
www.motoringfile.com/2005/ 02/14/counterfeit_minis_and_the_ccc - 48k - Cached -

Counterfeit MINI Shows up on eBay
Are counterfeit Mini's a real problem in the USA or is it just a fun thing to
get attention? Because here in Australia, I have seen 1 counterfeit Mini. ...
www.motoringfile.com/2005/ 04/08/counterfeit_mini_shows_up_on_ebay - 35k - Cached - S

Counterfeit Mini Coopers - 3GUPLOAD.COM
Counterfeit Mini Coopers. ... Posts: 5094 User Uploads: 346. Counterfeit Mini
Coopers ... Posts: 495 User Uploads: 0, RE: Counterfeit Mini Coopers ...
www.3gupload.com/ringtones/module/ Forum/action/FlatTopic/fid/38/tid/140650 - 36k - Cached - Sir

North East MINI :: MINI Forums :: MINI and You :: MINI in the ...
Post Posted: Fri Jun 24, 2005 8:30 pm Post subject: Counterfeit MINI ... I have
my counterfeit MINI flyer hanging on my wall along with the rest of my MINI ...
nemini.org/Forums/viewtopic/t=2741.html - 40k - Cached - Similar pages

MINI Counterfeit Integrated

P.T. BARNUM vs CP+B

TERRYEE: I'm Terryee Abbott. I'm clairvoyant, clairaudient, clairsentient, claircognizant, I talk directly to angels, guides, spirits, and people who have transferred over. Alright. I am not going to dispute your qualifications. I am pretty weirded out by this whole thing and it's just…well…this is not something I am really familiar with…communicating with someone who has…passed on. TERRYEE: I understand. So...if I was gonna address a question to Mr. Barnum…TERRYEE: He's here. Already. I'm communicating with him right now…Oh…OK…So…you're saying….I can just…I should just…TERRYEE: You may address him. He is here right now. Wow. OK. It definitely feels weird in here. Like a thickness or whatever. So, OK...P.T., my first question is, you used an elephant to promote your show. And you named it "Jumbo" because no word in the English language was sufficient. Now that made-up word, Jumbo, has become ingrained in pop culture. TERRYEE: He's showing me the elephant…Oh Jesus…should I keep talking? TERRYEE: Yes it's fine. OK, well, I wonder if you could comment on the unorthodox use of language. We've tried to do the same thing, describing a breakfast sandwich as "meatnormous," or saying a car has "whiptastic" handling. Do you find normal language confining? And do you think breaking the language conventions is a powerful marketing tool? BARNUM (as channeled by Terryee): Yes. That's correct. You should continue to do that, especially on the new campaign you are doing. We will. Thank you. OK, let's talk about something you did with Joyce Heth. Joyce Heth was, I guess, an exhibit unto herself. She was the woman you put on display, claiming she was actually 161 years old and that she had assisted in the birth of George Washington. Attendance was apparently very strong when the exhibit first opened, but eventually it started to taper off, and you did something brilliant. TERRYEE: Yes…You wrote an anonymous letter to the press claiming the whole thing was a hoax. Afterward, attendance shot back up because people were curious to see if it really was a hoax. It's brilliant that you would sort of attack your own exhibit to create more excitement around it. How does a person decide, "Hey, I'm gonna sit down and write a letter protesting my own. That will make business increase?" Without the benefit of hindsight it seems pretty crazy. TERRYEE: (Deep breath) Umm…it is. An…and…P.T. Barnum is talking…BARNUM (as channeled by Terryee): Do whatever you have to do to be spectacular. Something that no one else would do. Be outrageous. Never, ever stop advertising. TERRYEE: Uhhh…he's showing me right now, he's talking about the Goodyear blimp. Oh wait, no…there's…uhhhh…talk to me. Show me more…It sounds like he's saying we should use every opportunity to advertise. Maybe use things that we never thought of as advertisements. TERRYEE: Yes. What is he wearing? Like, when you are communicating with him, is he just there hanging out in clothes, or is he more like a glow? TERRYEE: I can see him. He's got grey hair. He's wearing black, it's like black on the outside and on the inside it's colored. Like some kind of satin-lined deal…TERRYEE: Exactly. He has a tie on, and one of those (makes motion around waist)…A cummerbund? TERRYEE: No. A fanny pack? TERRYEE: No...a chain with…A pocket watch? TERRYEE: Yes. A pocket watch. Is he checking it...like, is he bored? TERRYEE: No...he's saying…he's…P.T. BARNUM (as channeled by Terryee): Never create a hoax without making sure that every-body benefits. Do you understand? Your agency, the public, everybody. Do you understand what I am saying? Is he…are you…angry? TERRYEE: No, he's not mad. He just wants to make sure you understand that it was never just about him. It was for everyone. OK, maybe this is a good time to ask him about his "Free Music for the Millions" concept. TERRYEE: OK…I'm…yes. P.T., you did a thing called "Free Music for the Millions" where you put a band on the roof of your museum and they played free music for everyone. BARNUM (as channeled by Terryee):That's right. But later you admitted that the whole purpose of the band was to drive people into the building. You hired the worst musicians you could, so the sound would be unbearable and people would flee to the relatively quiet confines of the museum. That doesn't seem very altruistic. BARNUM (as channeled by Terryee): But they were still getting something out of it, weren't they? They got excitement and entertainment. That is my product. And it brought families and friends together when they went inside. Good point. I guess it goes back to something you said before you passed away, or I mean, crossed over or what have you. You said, "People who expect something for nothing deserve to be cheated." TERRYEE: Amen to that…I mean…what he is saying is that's right. BARNUM: That is right. Terryee, I don't want to interrupt your flow or anything, but if I could kind of shift gears now and ask something a little crazy. I'm wondering would we be able to collaborate with P.T. on upcoming projects? If we could work in tandem with him to develop new creative. I'm not making a joke, because to be honest I'm a little uncomfortable to be making jokes right now. So please understand that when I ask, I ask in earnest, will P.T. Barnum work with us from beyond the grave. Will he…BARNUM (as channeled by Terryee): Yes. Wow…OK…OK…this seems, this is, well it seems almost that it would be like cheating. Like since you are working with supernatural forces, you kind of have this whole omnipotent thing happening, so it's like, failure is not really possible. Yeah, it definitely feels like cheating…BARNUM (as channeled by Terryee): Well, look at it like this. Life is an ocean of choices. Make one choice, and this can happen. Make a different choice, and something else happens. Is it cheating destiny? No. It's really just fine-tuning life. (To séance group): This is incredible. So we can bring him onboard, or at least meet with him. Yeah, make him a staff member. TERRYEE: Well, it's like P.T. is maybe like, uhhh…your guide, or like a higher power in your business. There is no shame in believing in something bigger than you. Really, it's an act of humility. This could be like, well I'm not sure, I don't think we would want to reveal that we were using P.T. We wouldn't want our competitors to know. Maybe not even our clients. It might be akward explaining, you know, how we were coming up with this stuff. TERRYEE: That would probably be best. I'd like to direct this to P.T. To negotiate with him if I can. TERRYEE: OK…I'm…OK. P.T., I know you have always run the show. TERRYEE: Yes. We have a guy, our Executive Creative Director, Alex Bogusky. He's sorta the driving force behind our agency creatively, and I don't know if he would be willing to completely turn the reigns over. I could see maybe a partnership. Would you, P.T. Barnum, be amenable to working at the same level as Alex? Like, you're not Alex's boss, and Alex of course would not be your boss....You would be collaborating. TERRYEE: ...he's...wait, he's saying...he says he has no problem with that. But he's saying just make sure that what you work on includes everyone. He's... BARNUM (as channeled by Terryee): That kind of idea will live longer than all of us. Do you understand what I mean? And you're going to make tons of money when you do that. Do you understand? I...think I do. OK. It seems we have a verbal agreement. I will take this to senior management but I am confident we have a deal from our end. This is crazy, a strategic alliance. This is way better than we ever expected. Can you tell P.T. we are very excited? TERRYEE: He knows you are excited. Yes...I guess, and I apologize, but I guess I keep forgetting he's in here. TERRYEE: It's OK. OK. Well, I have a question about a Tom Thumb thing he did. P.T. took a 4-year-old boy who was like, 25 inches high, and kinda put him on display as Tom Thumb. Now there's a chain of convenience stores called Tom Thumb. Is P.T. seeing any residuals from that? TERRYEE: Oh, he does. So just know that. So he made sure to cross his T's and dot his I's before he checked out. TERRYEE: Yes. And what he gets back now is on an energy level. The universe is kind to him. I'm addressing this to P.T....You did a thing where you put a sign in your museum that said, "This way to the Egress." People would be like, "Hey, I gotta check out this Egress." But "egress" is just another word for exit, so people would go through an exit, and then have to pay to get in again. BARNUM: (as channeled by Terryee) Yes. Do you think that model would work for any of our clients? I guess it wouldn't work for Virgin Atlantic cause if you get off the plane at 40,000 feet...BARNUM: (as channeled by Terryee): What if you use that same logic, but flip it around. You could do something with a fake entrance. And there's some experience people have there, and then they get to go through the real entrance. You understand what I mean? Turn it around. Whoa. That's actually kind of cool. OK, this is a little freaky, because that would probably work. You see that! P.T. still has it. He's still on fire. TERRYEE: Yes he is....Wait...He's talking about writing letters...something...are you guys doing a letter? Or do you need money? Are you trying to get cash? No...kidding. I almost said, "no shit." Well, he's probably heard all kinds of colorful language. TERRYEE: He's...it's OK. Well, it's just that we are coming out with a book about the agency and the first page is a chain letter asking more people to buy the book so we make more money. BARNUM (as channeled by Terryee): It's gonna be huge. TERRYEE: I'm getting...He's also talking about the higher ups, the people in the upper...Yeah, we have four partners. Why, is he disappointed with any of them? TERRYEE: No...it's...OK. But, like, you would tell me if one of those guys was about to go down in flames...I mean, so I could give them a heads up, or a warning or whatever...TERRYEE: It's fine. Ummm...OK, I had a question about media. TERRYEE: It's OK. He's a master of inventing new media. So, if he was alive today...well, I mean....I don't mean to say he is dead...TERRYEE: No, he's here...He's still here... Where would he push the media? I mean, would he be looking at, like, podcasts and newer forms of broadcast technology? TERRYEE: He's talking about that...podcasts. He is talking about podcasts, but he is also talking about...I don't know what this is...ummm...it looks like a TV, but it's not a TV. Is it...TVAC? TVAC...I...maybe it's a vacuum cleaner or something...TVAC...Could it be TiVo? BARNUM (as channeled by Terryee): Yes. OK, good, because we've been exploring a lot of On-Demand ideas. It's amazing how he...you are still so tuned-in to what's going on. TERRYEE: Hold on a second...he's...he's saying you should push the envelope in everything you do. He's saying "Just do it." Wait a minute. Did you just say that he just said, "Just do it?" TERRYEE: Yes. Is there...wait, is he working with Wieden + Kennedy? Maybe he's talking to them. Jesus you think he wrote it? BARNUM: (as channeled by Terryee): No. Whew...OK, that's a big relief. Because that's one of our competitors, and I'm afraid we would have to sever any spiritual ties we had with him if...you know...that's a definite conflict of interest for us. TERRYEE: No...he's not working with them. OK. I think if there is not some exclusivity here then the deal might be off. Is he cool with exclusivity? I mean, we'll do it on our end, too. Like, we won't try to contact Walt Disney or whoever. We will only reach out to P.T. OK if we wanted to meet up with him to do some concepting, like at Starbucks or whatever, would we need to do anything special to...Would we need to get him a chair? It gets crowded...TERRYEE: No. He will not need a chair. OK, cool. Last question. I don't want to be flippant or anything, but basically, I'm wondering, what's it like to be dead? I think most people, whether they admit it or not, are a little concerned about the prospect. So, what's it like over there? BARNUM (as channeled by Terryee): It's beautiful. Instead of just being in one place, I can be in many places at the same time. There are more opportunities to advertise. It's the best advertising you can get.

EDITOR'S NOTE: The day after this séance/interview was conducted, Alex Bogusky received an e-mail with a link that the sender thought Bogusky would enjoy. When he clicked on the link, Bogusky was taken to a site where a real stuffed Pigmy elephant, once owned by P.T. Barnum himself, was up for auction. The sender was a friend of Bogusky's, but neither he nor Bogusky himself knew the séance had taken place, or that an elephant had been mentioned during its course. As we go to press, CP+B is in negotiations to procure the beast for the agency's new building in Boulder, Colorado. It will be the centerpiece of a shrine/office for P.T., and hopefully, a portal to the other side.

Tiffany

TV Campaign Silver

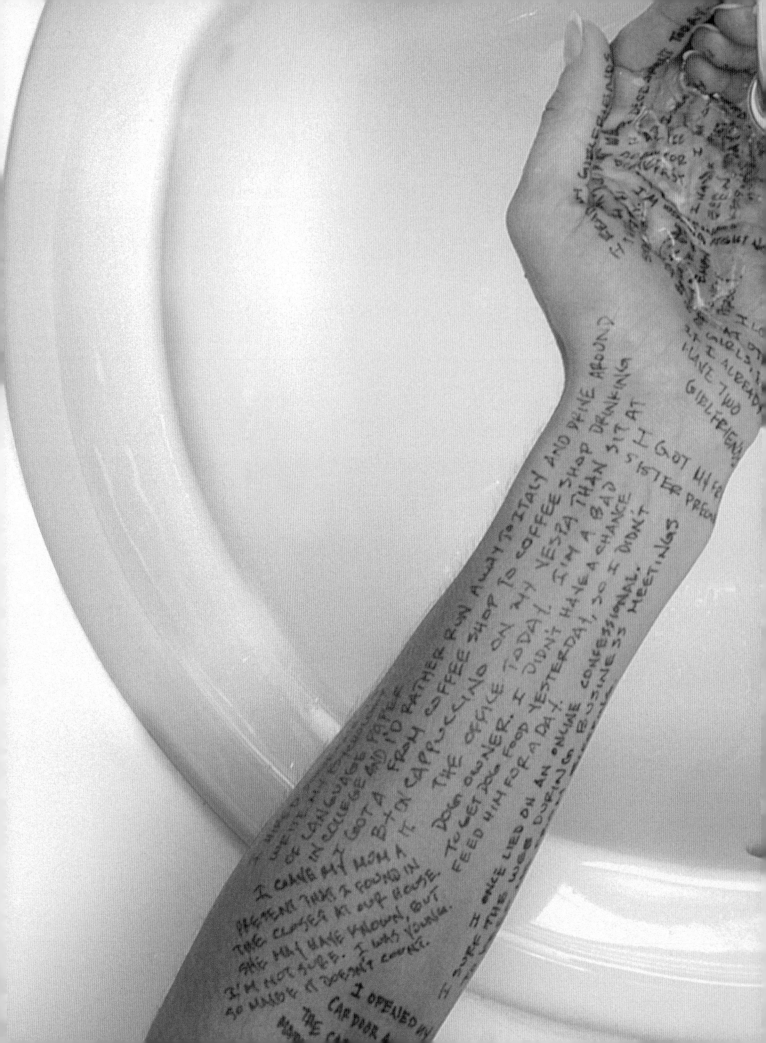

REALLY PISSED

I ONCE WAS DRIVEN TO THE BRINK OF MADNESS. I WAS AT MY PARTNER, DROVE MY CAR DOWN A NARROW STREET AND INTENTIONALLY SMASHED INTO, THEN CONTINUED TO SIDESWIPE FOUR PARKED CARS... THE LEFT OR THE LANE. ON PURPOSE. THEN THE ICY ROADS... PANTS.

I SHOP AND HIDE ALL THE BAGS, BOXES ETC. FROM MY BOYFRIEND. I TAKE THE TAGS OFF AND PASS THEM OFF AS "OLD" THINGS. I'M A SHOPAHOLIC AND ITS THE ONLY ... I WON'T GET TEASED.

I'VE BEEN QUIETLY ... TELEVISION, ... AND EATING ... MY NAILS AND ... THE SAME TIME WHILE ... IS AN IMPORTANT ... MY BOYFRIEND

It hadn't been done before, not in the five decades since the television had become a fixture in living rooms. Here was a car company attempting to introduce a new vehicle in the US without the benefit of a large TV ad blitz. Adding to the challenge: The car was foreign, largely unknown in America, and a bit funny looking (though in an adorable sort of way). More to the point, it was tiny–which, in the spring of 2002, could hardly be viewed as a strong selling point, considering that small-car sales had steadily been losing ground to the SUV boom. Yet in spite of all this, when Crispin Porter + Bogusky launched the MINI Cooper car in America, the client requested that the agency create a phenomenon and turn the little car into "a cultural icon." All on a budget that was almost as small as the MINI itself. In short, this was not so much a cry for help as a cry for Hoopla.

At the outset, CP+B searched for truthful insights about the car, the experience of driving it, and the mindset of people who might be open to driving it. By way of a combination of research, brainstorming, and heavy consumption of snack foods, an agency team working on MINI invented an enlightened philosophy about driving, along with a catch-phrase to sum it up: "LET'S MOTOR." The idea was to create a new culture around a cute and nimble car, based on the notion that "motoring" represented a civilized, friendly, fun, efficient, and downright zippy alternative to barreling around in overbearing gas-guzzlers and road hogs. It seemed like an attitude that just might come across as a welcome breath of fresh air.

But there was still the problem of MINI's miniscule media budget. It's a challenge faced by entrepreneurial marketers everywhere, which can be boiled down to: When you've got something to say–hopefully something original, inventive, and truthful–how do you then make yourself heard? How does one break through the clutter and the cacophony of today's media landscape and actually *connect* with people?

The basic assumption, for decades, was that to make that connection on any kind of mass scale, you had to spend huge sums on Big Media, particularly TV commercials. But by 2002, CP+B had a history of defying that assumption with work such as the *truth* anti-smoking campaign, which had managed to connect with a large audience–and build a popular movement–primarily by low-cost, grass-roots promotion methods. With the MINI account, CP+B had an opportunity to take the kind of scrappy, inventive media approaches used for *truth* and apply them to a much broader campaign as part of a major automotive launch.

Not having access to the shortcut of relying on TV commercials, CP+B had to, in effect, go "motoring" itself– taking a more winding, unpredictable, and colorful path en route to reaching people across the country. Along the way, the MINI began to show up in all kinds of unexpected, attention-getting venues and forms. For instance, CP+B had the idea to assemble a strange hybrid vehicle–a MINI that was affixed to the roof of an SUV (because "when you're driving an SUV, the fun stuff always gets put on the roof," Bogusky explains)–and then arranged to have this odd double-decker driven around in 22 cities across the country. The stunt turned heads and attracted local media coverage while making a statement that the MINI had no qualms about taking on SUVs in a light and playful manner.

Around the same time, MINI cars could also be seen mingling with the crowd at sports stadiums–where the cars were installed in place of ripped-out stadium seats. Meanwhile, outside department stores, CP+B installed 25-cent kiddie rides that took the form of MINI cars instead of rocket ships; near the coin slot, a sign read: "Rides starting at $16,900." At airport terminals, the agency placed oversized props designed to look like giant pay phones or garbage cans alongside a poster of the MINI, with the headline "Makes everything else seem a little too big." On top of all that, there were billboards everywhere, magazine ads that were custom-made in unusual sizes and formats (for *Playboy* magazine, the MINI became a sexy centerfold). There were also MINI books, colorful stickers, games such as the MINI Motoring Games Wheel, with eight popular road-trip games, and even MINI clothing that was sold exclusively at Barney's Co-Op.

The overall effect of placing the MINI message into so many different and often unusual places was that the car–or rather, the playful culture of the car, as articulated in these messages–seemed to be everywhere. This "surround" quality is an important aspect of successful Hoopla. But just being ubiquitous is not enough: In fact, it can be merely annoying if people are surrounded by something repetitive or irrelevant. The fact that the MINI campaign surrounded people with fresh and new messages at each turn, and the fact that those messages all seemed to connect with each other to make an interesting and cohesive statement–that was what made it all work.

And it worked in a big way. The campaign more than quadrupled public awareness of the brand virtually overnight, and sales of the car far outpaced projections, creating a customer backlog in MINI's first year on the market. Moreover, the MINI launch seemed to rock the advertising and marketing world like a small earthquake; not only did it sweep up industry awards and accolades, but it also prompted more than a few marketers to step back and reassess their own marketing models. In one bold stroke, CP+B had seemed to achieve something that many marketers had talked about doing for years but never quite pulled off: going beyond the old TV commercial–dominated method of marketing in favor of an approach integrating many forms of media. The diversified yet cohesive MINI effort suggested that it was, indeed, possible to connect all the pieces of the communications puzzle–and thereby better connect with the world at large.

For CP+B to be able to do this, though, the agency had to first change the way it thought about media—embracing a new, expanded definition of what media is and what it could be. With the MINI campaign, CP+B had a chance to fully act on a principle that had been part of the agency's belief system for several years prior, namely: *Everything is media*. It's a simple but radical concept that is central to the promulgation of Hoopla. Believing this, and acting on it, makes it possible to build momentum at a grass-roots level and without spending huge sums of money. This is good news for entrepreneurs, for big marketers who desire to be more efficient, or for just about anyone who wants to create fame without going broke first. It is bad news, perhaps, for the Big Media establishment, which has profited handsomely for decades on the old expensive system for making things famous.

To embrace the notion that "*Everything is media*" can be daunting because once you do so, it means there is no longer a preset media mold into which ideas can be poured. Which means (yet again) that extreme inventiveness is required, not only in terms of coming up with creative messages to promote a product but also in terms of inventing entirely new vehicles to carry those messages out into the world. To illustrate, here's how advertising used to operate, pre-Hoopla (and how it still operates 99 percent of the time): Typically, an ad message is produced to fill an existing hole—a blank page in a magazine, a 30-second open slot during a TV program. The need to fill those predetermined spaces drives the traditional creative process; copywriters and art directors instinctively start by sketching ideas for commercials and print ads.

But at CP+B, that process gets turned upside down. The ad creators begin with a blank slate in terms of format. Bogusky's dictum to his staff is: "If there were no TV and no magazines, how would we make this brand famous?" Porter's take is a little different: "TV and magazines exist; you just can't buy ads in them." If someone tries to offer up a TV commercial idea right away, it doesn't even get considered. The premium is on finding new ways to communicate.

In the search for ads that can take any form—guerrilla stunts, live events, in-store promotion, handouts, original art, or maybe something that can't even be categorized—media specialists work in tandem with creative specialists. In effect, CP+B has knocked down the wall that used to exist between ad agency "creative" departments and "media" departments (conversely, at many big Madison Avenue agencies today the division between "creative" and "media" has actually widened; in recent years, many of these mega-agencies have spun off their media buying operations into separate divisions or companies that don't even operate in the same building as the people who make the ads). By having the different groups brainstorm together, CP+B can shape new "creative" ideas in order to take advantage of new "media" ideas or, conversely, can invent media possibilities to best suit a particular creative idea.

Having accepted the premise that "*everything is media*," there is, accordingly, a rule that goes with it, according to CP+B: *Everything is branding*. The old way of thinking was that a person's impressions about a brand could be formed and shaped by advertising alone. But that view has given way to a new, more holistic one, recognizing that there are countless opportunities for contact between a brand and a consumer. Each one of these "touch points"—which can occur on the street, in the store, on the phone with a sales rep, in a bar talking to other people, on the Web, or wherever—all contribute to shaping the impressions and attitudes someone has about a brand. They are all connected to one another (or should be, because they're all part of the same ongoing story of a brand).

The challenge is to utilize as many of those touch points as possible while also making sure the message conveyed at each point is consistent. Elements that might have been considered trivial to branding in the past, such as basic product literature or packaging, now should be viewed as key components in the overall effort to connect, according to CP+B. With MINI, the agency was eager to get involved with things an ad agency normally doesn't bother with, such as product literature and the car-owner's manual. Similarly, when taking on the BURGER KING account, CP+B made it clear that it saw huge "connection" opportunities in the paper wrappings for the burgers, the ketchup packets, signage on the walls inside each restaurant. Bogusky maintains that a drink cup at BURGER KING has as much reach as a "Super Bowl commercial."

Another development of connecting is that King-sure that communication flows in two directions—both out and in. Interactive media has made it possible to have a true, two-way relationship, of ongoing conversation, with the audience you're trying to reach. With this form, Hoopla may evoke image-of people talking back-or in CP+B believes, that *communication* itself is the advertising method: the new improved one involves *talking with* people. "*The basic rules of conversation can and should be applied to almost all brand communications*," says a top creative at CP+B. This

talk over others but also listens, answers questions, and engages the other party in discussion," says CP+B's Bill Wright. If you can do likewise in an ad campaign, Wright says, the result becomes much more dynamic. "Often, we'll say something provocative and see what the consumer says back, and then we'll respond to that, and so on—it's like a game of advertising tennis. As you do this, people become eager to hear what the brand has to say next."

Beyond just allowing for feedback, a truly connected campaign enables people to take action in some way—even if it's just to have some fun. One CP+B interactive site, for method soap, allowed the visitor to write a personal confession onto a hand that appeared onscreen—and then simulated using method soap to wash away that secret. (The site went by the name "Come Clean.") Another CP+B site, for the Borders chain of bookstores, featured an online "Giftmixer" that looked like a robot. The visitor used onscreen dials to tell the Giftmixer about a particular person for whom a gift was being purchased; the Giftmixer proceeded to compute the info and then recommend a suitable gift for that person.

The beauty of interactive websites is that they can engage people longer and more deeply than a commercial ever could—at a fraction of the cost. And the best sites tend to get passed along from one person to another, creating the kind of grass-roots, word-of-mouth promotion that's worth its weight in gold. (But if you want a site to go viral, don't "sell" too hard, advises Porter. "Viral means people send stuff to their friends, and no one wants to send a salesman over to a friend's house.") If the people you've connected with are, in turn, connecting with everyone they know—at that point you're well on your way to a phenomenon.

When my belly starts a-rumblin'... And I'm jonesin' for a treat... I close my eyes for a big surprise... The Tendercrisp Bacon Cheddar R

There's tumbleweeds of bacon   And cheddar paves the streets   Folks don't front ya cuz you got the juice   There's a train of ladies comin' with

No one tells you to behave   Your wildest fantasies come true   Dallas cheerleaders give you shaves   Red onions make you laugh instead   And french frie

e the TenderCrisp Bacon Cheddar Ranch   The breasts they grow on trees   And streams of bacon ranch dressing flow right up to your knees

se   Never get in trouble never need an excuse   That's the TenderCrisp Bacon Cheddar Ranch   I love the TenderCrisp Ba-con Ched-dar Ranch

eeds   You get to veg all day   All the lotto tickets pay   There's a King who wants you to have it your way   That's the TenderCrisp Bacon Cheddar Ranch

9. Is Christina Aguilera the first woman in the commercial? The blonde by the tree?

   Comment by Anonymous — 02/28/2005 @ 03:39:29 AM

10. rumor has it that the blond is jenna jamesson but I can't tell who that is.

    xxx image gallery, you can download the commercial at the site linked in the post: http://ad-rag.com/118820.php

    Comment by Robert — 02/28/2005 @ 04:37:11 AM

18. So is there a complete cast list out there?
    Because I do reckognize a couple faces, I just don't know their names. I thought the blonde girl on the train pump car might be ex-American Idol Kimberly Caldwell.
    My wife's guess was that the first girl is Aguielera. She doesn't look enough like Jenna Jamison.

    Comment by CB — 02/28/2005 @ 08:55:56 PM

25. The blonde girl with the long wavy hair is the famous (or B-list famous) porn star named Mary Carey who ran for governor of California in the last election. She's been on VH1 and interviewed by other stations. Can someone else confirm this? I'm about 80% sure it's her.

    Comment by PineCrestAlum — 03/02/2005 @ 12:37:46 AM

28. It is definitely Aguilera in the commercial. No doubt about it.

    Comment by Kurt — 03/05/2005 @ 05:11:04 PM

29. Is Christina Aguilera the woman on the tree in the commercial?????

    Comment by Cindy — 03/05/2005 @ 10:17:58 PM

32. The blonde is NOT mary carey, it is NOT Christian Aguilera... It's Shakira. Look it up, people. Only person out there with blonde hair and mouse-eyes.

    Comment by Jen — 03/08/2005 @ 11:37:27 PM

44. The blonde girl grabbing the sandwich out of the tree is Carolyn Bolin I went to highschool with her she is a glamour model

    005 @ 06:31:08 PM

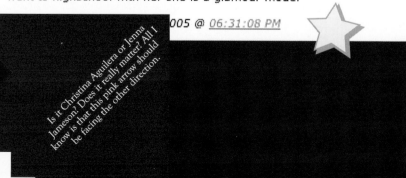

Is it Christina Aguilera or Jenna Jameson? Does it really matter? All I know is that this pink arrow should be facing the other direction.

Reasons why I love The Tender Crisp Bacon Cheddar Ranch

When the belly starts a rumbling and I'm jonesing for a treat,
I close my eyes for a big surprise the tender crisp bacon cheddar ranch
I love tender crisp bacon cheddar ranch - the breasts they grown on trees
and streams of bacon ranch dressing flow right up to your knees
there's tumbleweeds of bacon and cheddar paves the streets
folks don't fudge it cause you got the juice - there's a train of ladies coming with a nice caboose
never get in trouble, never need an excuse
that's the tender crisp bacon cheddar ranch
I love the tender crisp bacon cheddar ranch no one tells you to behave
your wildest fantasies come true - Dallas cheerleaders give you shaves
where onions make you laugh instead and french fries grow like weeds
You get to veg all day, all the lotto tickets paid,
there's a king that wants you to have it your way,
that's the tender crisp bacon cheddar ranch.
Cooooome aaaaand get it!

1. **The girl on the caboose (Vida Guerra)** has thee fattest ass EVER. HOT. You can see much more of Vida HERE and >HERE.

2. **Brooke Burke.** HOT.

3. **The Creepy Burger King.** They used the same creepy Burger King from the 80's and a previous commercial that freaked out me and everyone I know.

WHERE IS YOUR GOD NOW?

4. **Dallas Cowboy Cheerleaders.** HOT.

5. **Cheddar cheese paves the streets.**

6. **Excellent use of slow motion.** It makes the Bacon Ranch Dressing dancers and the Onion Hula-Hooper look so much hotter.

7. **Catchy-ass Song.** See lyrics posted above.

8. **The Cristina Agulera/Porn Star looking chick on the ladder.** HOT. Not sure if she's a pop star or a porn star. Still, my Mom's the only other woman I know that can take a sandwich like that.

9. **"The Breasts, They Grow On Trees."** Greatest quote ever. I want it on my tombstone when I die.

10. **The Shower of Cash.** Money falls from the sky at the Tender Crisp Bacon Cheddar Ranch.

11. **"Come and get it!"** has a dual/innuendo meaning. At the end of the 30second ad, Brooke Burke says "Cooooome aaaaand get it!". Is she referring to the sandwich or her fine ass?

12. **Hootie sold out so hard and so bad.** At least he didn't resort to gay porn. Or has he?.......

13. **At the Tender Crisp Bacon Cheddar Ranch, the sandwich actually grows on a tree!** That's odd cause the lady charged me $4.69 for mine...

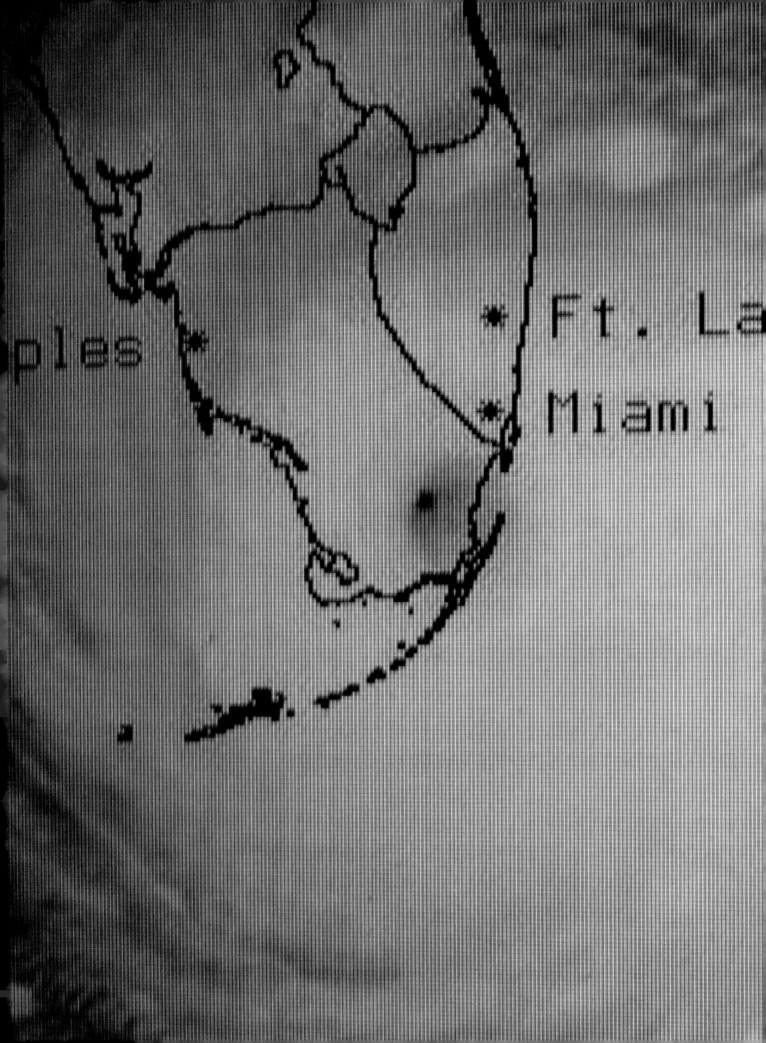

FLORIDA
The Land of Sunshine

derdale

This is the general direction from which mayhem and destruction visit themselves upon CP+B headquarters. Generally, you have about 48 hours from the official "hurricane warning" to pull your storm shutters and load your gun.

SAVE SPICY MAN

(Look at that smile, we'll miss you Gabe!)

As many of you are aware, in the offices of the "lunch break team" Joel has recently fired Gabe in an effort to downsize the company. However at this time of grieving there are a few questions you may be asking yourself...

What will happen to "I'm spiiiicy" man?

Will he be able to defend himself in this cold hard world without the warmth and comfort of his lunch break team?

Would he have ever gotten the chance to kiss/hug/make sweet sweet love to the team siren, Michelle?

What will you do without Gabe making a daily appearance in your home?

He came into our homes and hearts with his naïve yet touching comments and ways. This harsh and unjust action must be corrected. With your help, we can bring him back to the team and right this wrong. Please send comments and money (in the form of credit card information) to savespicyman@hotmail.com

Troll the Hoopla Intranet and see if you can lure an innocent Crispin employee into doing something horrible.

190
Accounting

MIAMIMICKEY 33-male into all that's Disney. I'm funny, fun to be with, and playful. Very social and enjoy parties. Love to meet and chat with fabulous people who enjoy music, travel, beach, cars, fashion and yes...DISNEY!

BigPoppa Sports enthusiast looking for friends to hang around and share good times with. Whether it's a Heat game, or Dolphins game, or just playing tennis or basketball, BigPoppa is the man you want to hang around with. We all know by now that "It's hard out there for a Pimp," but let BigPoppa show you the time of your life!

FrenchGrl Like French toast, French Fries, French bread or even French kisses? I'm your match if you do!

GClef Singer/songwriter looking for other musicians to collaborate with. I have a deep sultry voice and some pretty decent songs. My style has been compared to artists like Sheryl Crow and Alanis Morrisette. I work hard during the day but want to work harder at night making music that moves me and the people around me. No druggies, prima-donna's or jealous partners at home. I'm into music not rehearsal cancellations. Peace and Love.

Cosmo chic I am from Chile, fun to be around, have great sense of humor and love to laugh. I enjoy sipping on a glass of wine from time to time, a good conversation, music, movies and of course shopping. My favorite drink is Cosmopolitan...what's yours?

Funkalicious Looking for people who enjoy all types of music, especially old school funk and blues. Nothing beats the smoooovness of James Brown or BB King's "Lucille". So if the sound of bow-chicky-bow-bow gets you feeling goo-oood then drop me a line. We can spin records and chill. (afros and bell-bottoms optional)

200
Administration

CubanCandy Seeking fun friends to chill with and drink Mojitos by the beach. Interests include Yorkies, cooking, and salsa dancing.

PurpleYorkie Former beauty queen & ballerina, who enjoys spending time at home with family and friends. I enjoy exercising and eating good food. Been described as spunky and overly truthful many times.

Inferno Island girl with a passion for the spicier things in life would like to meet people who live in the hot zone but love to chill through life. Must be willing to eat conch fritters and live by the beach. If you love Robert Nestor and always wanted to travel through the back roads of Jamaica in a VW Thing – give me a call and we can "lime" (hang out) island style. No herb smokers please.

NorCalGal Loving Mojitos and never having to wear a coat. I am looking for Latino tennis coach who can help me perfect my Spanish. Must have a boat.

LOKERA Love the Yankees, not Romeo with Redsox Marine Military mind to the grave though Johnnie Walker Blue label is off the chai. Like that Merengue, Salsa, bachata, hiphop and the twins Scarface voter since "you need people like me, so you Point your fingers and say [that's the bad guy]" And just for the record...Rather fail with honor, than succeed by fraud.

Hottiepattotie Seeking a hot, single, straight male. Over 30 years old. Must love to eat, dine out, and see lots of movies. (Please, no ADHD personality types.) Do you like long walks on the beach? How do you feel about watching hour after hour of Law & Order episodes? Any chance you own a Yorkie? How do you feel about the color pink in the home? If you answer yes to the above, call me!

WEASEL Bored advertising agency owner looking for a new hobby. Preferably out of the country.

Yoshi132 Old school Nintendo enthusiast who loves to sit back and watch Nick at Nite!!! Looking for someone to race in MarioKart. Must love big dogs and must know the meaning behind UUDDLRLRBA. But then again, doesn't everybody?

MileEquity Eats mangos in the tub. You know a good plumber. She cheats at solitaire. You root for the underdog. She wonders if you have ugly feet. You'll never tell.

EngimaGirl You can make more friends in two months by becoming interested in other people than you can in two years by trying to get other people interested in you.

Guccisocialist Island man longing for quiet life in the country side. Walk to the beach and drink coconut water all day. Must have access to satellite TV, Internet and good books. If you like the modern life but love the simple life, come visit with us. No rent a dread to get your groove back persons need apply.

210
Art Buying

CREATIVE INFORMANT Desperately seeking [white] space. My favorite hobby catching a glimpse of thoughts taking a new shape or form or color. I enjoy that a lot. I also like art, design, photography, architecture, ballet and radically complex physics that deal mainly with concepts revolving around outer or inner space.

MicMacMo Got any jokes? I may have one (or 6) up my sleeve, if you're interested. One often finds me in my native habitat, juggling while reciting (elected) Presidents. I make a mean cocktail and do the best pirate impression you've ever heard come from a girl. I love randomness and I've been known to lay down some pretty lavish alliteration. I'm looking for someone unafraid of a unicycle and big red shoes; someone who will accept me even if I AM a clown college dropout; someone to dance with, fall out of the sky with, or perhaps just dangle participles with.

Hanna Travel, shopping, movies, good food and humor. Looking for the man who can bring the verbs and adjectives.

220
Art Department

Professional Cuddler My dog is nice he sheds a lot though and his nose is wet. He likes girls and is weary of males. But he'll like you if I do.

El Niño I am El Niño. All other tropical storms must bow before El Niño! Yo soy El Niño! For those of you who don't habla Español El Niño is Spanish for... the Niño!

Superyummie™ Modern day conspiracy theorist who enjoys making sense out of random cloud shapes. I like my burgers, juicy – medium rare... Can you dig it?

HOT BUNS I like organic mayo on top of the patty while sipping on freshly squeezed. I hate when my buns get cold. Brunch sometime?

arseniK13 Many years ago – a young Shaolin monk came across my infant self at the steps of a mighty Temple deep within the mountainous forest regions of Japan. Here, isolated from the modern world, I grew while learning the ancient Shaolin ways. The physical and mental training was arduous. The wisdom passed down to me has existed amongst the Shaolin since the dawn of time. On my 20th birthday – it was time to face my final test. I entered a maze of obstacles and vicious enemies known only as the 36 chambers. While many have perished within the 36 chambers – I would not suffer such a fate. One week later I emerged a man. I soon dedicated myself to wandering. I traveled across vast continents providing help and guidance anywhere I could. As I moved from country to country I also searched for answers to the questions that had been locked away in my brain for many years. Through these travels many questions began to arise. Who am I? Where is the person that left me on those temple steps some twenty years ago? And what is next? My quest continues...P.S. – I like to draw.

JeM'enFous Recherche la muse pour inspiration et écrire. Life is too short to sweat the small stuff, or to drink cheap beer.

that Korean girl Looking for someone who will share my Kim-Chi and Marinara pasta for lunch.

HeavyD Husband and father looking for substitute family to go home to when working late and not up to commute back to primary fam. Will take out trash.

StoneCold I'm a level 60 thief and will level you up for Ca$h. Rogues are my specialty.

MagicCityFlava Alpine affairs? Tropical rendezvous? Avec moi? Avec vous? Could be – what's your sign?

office dominatrix seeks wide eyed gullible intern to be tied down, mainly with work. Ball and gag required.

230
Broadcast

CatBird VA transplant to Miami. Ready to inject some mountain love into Southern FL. I like cats who harass birds, sneak up on unsuspecting mice, and then take catnaps in the tall green grass. In other words, live life hard and rest as needed. Come frolic with me!

Tightrope Walker Busy 40-yr. F Seeking other walkers with children to sip wine, compare act, and share in the balancing act. Strong shoulders and positive attitude preferred. No bitter/negative walkers need apply.

Goodtrouble The first thing you need to know about me is that I don't care about you. Let's get together so I can drive the heel of my Jimmy Choo through the left ventricle of your heart. It'll be fun!!!

DJPabloDiscobar I've got jet set women who offer me favors, my face is a thousand lipstick flavors...regardless, I am still looking for more gigs on the wheels of steel, spinning house, hip hop, rock...whatever the terrain calls for, and definitely up for exchange of ideas with other DJ's. Hit me up.

FrqntFlyr Looking for discreet female "friends" in faraway places. Mostly interested in New Yorkers, Los Angelinas, and Londoners. Interests include good times, room service, and expense accounts.

Bia Often mistaken by an Argentine, though original product from Brazil. Dog aficionado, soccer fan and sociologist at heart. Loves to talk, even if that means to myself.

CHIPS 30 Married to my husband, having an affair with my job.

RonJettski Retired indie rock musician seeking new hobby. Tried karaoke and scrabble. It just wasn't the same. Any ideas?

It'sAllRelative If you're interested in raises, promotions, recognition, and getting ahead I'm the girl to know. Feel free to take advantage of knowing me... or let me take advantage of you. You know those art directors that used to be studio artists? Let's just say art isn't their number one talent. I'm kind of a big deal. It's all in a name.

I ♥ QUARKS Finely engineered robot strongly resembling a human being in appearance and behavior. Pre-programmed to perform physical and mental tasks too dangerous or difficult for normal human beings. Interests include dismantling bombs, disposing of toxic waste, topiary gardens.

LOU-LOU If you like Pina Coladas, and getting caught in the rain. If you're not into yoga, if you have half-a-brain. If you like making love at midnight, in the dunes of the cape. I'm the lady you've looked for, write to me, and escape!

ElectricMayhem Jazz enthusiast with a passion for all things interactive. If you're looking to back that gif up or to get down to the sexy sounds of the piano you've come to the right place.

**240
COGS**

Mongongo Seeking forager to engage in relationship of give and take. Actually, I'm just looking for anyone who knows what I'm talking about.

FOOTBALL HOOLIGAN Our co-ed Sunday soccer games have slowly turned from friendly pick-up game style soccer to a sausage fest of hooligan style, crushing-cans-on-forehead, Liverpool versus Chelsea brawling matches. We're looking for some Chastain/Hamm wannabes or just girls who want to kick it around to temper the testosterone and return games to a friendly, family-type outing. Kids welcome.

JiffyBrand Grow your brand super quick, no money down! We at JiffyBrand know brands. Let our Certified Cognitians help you by conducting their super cool patented 100-point cultural assessments for you, no money down! What are you waiting for? Cognitians standing by now!

Loisaida Seeking homeboys and homegirls who are down to kick it late night, East Village style. You in? Meet me at Astor Place. Midnight, any night.

**250
Content Management**

Blue-Eyed Baker Looking for a sweet treat and a smile? I'm your girl! Let's hop in my MINI, sing along to the radio and go cruising in the southern sunshine.

CutieCuban MWF looking for someone to walk my dog and feed my husband so I can enjoy some free time after leaving the office. Agency hopefuls need not apply.

Divine Miss L. Looking for fellow indoor enthusiast to share my love of Reality Television, soft couches and air-conditioning. Candy and carbohydrate eaters a must, as well as those who like black labs, Dirty Dancing and all beverages diet. Let's get together to discuss pop culture, music and beer. I like beer. Who am I kidding...wine too.

Relocatah Seeking skinny model type, late 20's. Save the drama for your mama. I gots no time for crap and I dig a nap. Lots a smoke and joke a plus. No strings. Must hate the state of Florida.

Sir Worksalot 31yo male. I enjoy long walks to the copy machine. Glasses of wine during conference calls. And trying new things like reclining my work chair or coming in 20 minutes late. When I am not managing multi-zillion dollar accounts, I am sleeping. Holler if you are into that stuff too.

Flip Side of Fruit Alternative Lone Star non-screamer, rarely in flames. Missing the music in Austin. Boots, longnecks and TexMex make me smile. Nanci, Patty and Lucinda make me cry.

Amiable and Psychotic Workaholic seeks Alcoholic (or the like) for life balance and encouragement. Interests include, sleeping 3 – 4 nights a week, co-ed office streaking and making gourmet meals out of ordinary snack machine items and take-out condiments. Oh and I am good with moms.

Hot mama I can bring home the bacon, fry it up in a pan, I can change a mean diaper and never let you forget you're a man.

Kdfromthelou Come travel the world with me, if just to take photos. Self-portraits are my forte – everything's a photo op.

ZADOUBLEZ You could call me a South Beach Boy, minus the frosted hair, inflated muscles, ever-present lisp, little dog, and the fact that I'm from New York. But hey, I could be if I stay here long enough. Yay!

Chooka Looka Shhh, I'm having too much fun again. And Miami, during Spring Break. Oh no, no one's ready. Not a single solitary soul. But if you're game and know that fun isn't, you can find me right now at the back of the party with my hat low over my wide eyes.

Iron Ranger I don't know how people survive down here without air conditioning. But I'm always willing to walk eighteen holes on a ninety-five degree day with one-hundred percent humidity. Weird.

Akbar I'll always be a Northeasterner at heart, but as a recent transplant to Miami, I've decided to stick to heading home during the summer. Cold and snow isn't for me. It must be my middle-eastern blood that gives me a natural affinity for the sand and sun.

CatchOfTheDay Are you tall, dark and handsome with a big boat? If you like to fish, swim, ski or sail, give me a shout and let's see if you can reel me in...

Sweetea I am a firm believer in the 10 hug a day rule. I drink lots of water, eat lots of fruit, and sing in the shower. If I asked you to pull my finger what would you say?

TXgal Texas native who, after stints in LA and Dallas, returned to Miami and CP+B because of a deep love for Cuban coffee. And Florida palm trees. For more reasons as to why Miami rocks despite the fact that, yes, it really is as crazy as it seems, just ask!

sharkattack I'm always ready to eat so ask me out to a great restaurant. Just clear it with my husband first. Bon appetit.

SuperFly If you're into working out and watching sports (especially the Florida Gators) then we can definitely chill. You can find me doing a little one-two step on South Beach. My motto is "Go hard or go home." Only tall athletic, incredibly good-looking, model-type guys need apply.

DS_305 On the road or back here in the sun, this CP+Ber knows how to have fun. Little do they know, my life seems so plain. But the make-out bandit has struck again. Those late night hours. Who's got some dollars? You won't know what hit you. So give me a holler.

Gemini in the 305 Young professional looking to meet fun, intelligent guy. Like to work hard, play hard. Enjoy jet skiing in the Florida sun and traveling around the world. Sports and nutrition enthusiast. Must have stable job, good family life, and a sense of humor. English speakers only. No hoopties.

DJ EVIL C SWM/25 Originally from Staten Island, NY and recently moved to FL from NJ. I'm not big on the whole "dipping your pen in the company ink," but if the right ink came along, then who knows. But for now, I'm hoping to meet others with same interests as me. My interests include all outdoor activities, including sailing, hiking, biking, and playing tennis. If you're a fellow DJ then I'd love to chat so maybe we can collaborate in the future.

Sprnklstar I'm into all things cute. My fetishes include, but are not limited to shoes, well-groomed toes, anything covered in whip cream. I enjoy traveling and making out in public places.

ScubaGirl Ad exec who secretly aspires to be dolphin trainer. Own a pool and an unruly Flipper who needs guidance? I've got my wetsuit ready.

SlapstickGAL If you are up for scuba diving, swimming with the dolphins, and LOTS of dance parties – I am your match. Not into the long walks on the beach during sunset and deep-seated candle light dinners. Almost forgot: I only like men with accents.

TXTransplant SWF looking 4 a hot Latin Lover to show me the town, tired of the slow cowboy ways. Must make a good margarita and like German cars.

PradaPrincess Jappy South Florida girl seeks wealthy doctor to make grandparents happy. Good looking, caring and fun wouldn't hurt.

I ♥ PONIES Not a morning person and addicted to Starbucks. Likes to Skydive and ride horses. My weekends are reserved for catching up on sleep most weekends. I hate cotton balls and funky textured foods – if you wear fuzzy socks need not reply.

Radski I like to sit on Lincoln Road and people watch...it makes me feel better about myself.

Jambon I'm new to Miami and love the weather. I'm always up for tennis, paddle ball on the beach or a movie and a cocktail or two to follow.

PLAYWRIGHTS Many of those in the CP+B circuit are familiar with the traditional Irish pub on 13th and Washington. But few can rival my love and devotion to Playwrights. Take a self-guided tour with a few Miller Lites and Bon Jovi blaring in the background. When you're ready for the expert-level tour just drop me a line.

Ipeefreely Horrendous yet avid fisherman looking for a princess that wants to learn to fish in the nude.

Sunshine! Even-keeled. 2808. Mmm... Pina Coladas. Eww...Pickles & Kool-Aid. FFIO. Jailbait. YOU CAN DO IT!!! Chicodaman! Mam. Short Flamenco Bus. OYE! What else is there?

GIRL OF IPANEMA Brazilian, loves to joke around all day, loud, will do anything for a good laugh, samba dancer, Brazilian, Dachshund lover, enjoy working out, hate flying, love warm weather, will get drunk with 1 glass of wine, Brazilian, talk, talk, talk, favorite food: steak 'n fries, favorite drink: Caipirinha with strawberries (made with Brazilian Cachaça).

SugarandSpice I can really whip it up in the kitchen. Baking is the thing I love to do. Let me know if you've got some tricks of the trade that you'd like to share.

Doe-Eyes I have planted an abundance of Maidenhair fern (no agapanthus) in the garden beneath my Baumraum treehouse. It is here I will learn to take naps. My steady fire burns only with kindling. Taxidermy birds fill my white ceiling. I remain patient with tremendous conviction, your valentine-super-hero-sculptor-best friend-lover-girl. Yes.

ChicaRidicula Born and raised in Brazil but 1) doesn't mean I can dance samba 2) don't try to impress me by singing the lyrics to "The Girl from Ipanema" 3) City of God is only a movie. Have about five different personas and can do a few different accents so I never get tired of my own self. If you have a male dog with a pop star name, let's talk.

Girl from Cotton Ridge Ranch Avid outdoor enthusiast lost in Miami. Seeking fresh powder, mountain trails, and fresh, clean air. An obstacle for those on the dance floor there is no bouncin' in da clubs for this lady. Instead I enjoy fun-filled nights of cribbage, Seinfeld and cooking brussel sprouts.

Fancy Pants Wanna see my creative briefs? Call me. They're cute.

Vitamin T Here to give you what you're missing, lots of rubbin', lovin', kissin'. I keep my ladies well pleased so long as they don't play the tease. I love a little flirt, in a tight black skirt. If you're cringin' at these words, pay no attention to this blurb. Yeah I know I'm white, but let me take you out for the night. Must love dawgs.

VirginLove79 Looking for some suite lavatory lovin'? I am at my best high in the sky. Contact me if you're into high altitudes, personal entertainment systems, massages, Big Ben, and just plain cheeky behavior.

UpCountry Lumberjack of a guy looking for a woman to wield his axe with. Summers are spent cutting trees, hunting moose and collecting beaver pelts. Winters are spent fishing and warming up the igloo. Is the animal inside you calling?

Carolinagirl Love to play sports, cook, and travel. Don't love country music, sushi, and the fact that chocolate makes my jeans too tight. Everything happens for a reason and yes it is true...Carolina girls are the best in the world.

Criminal Intent SVU, CSI, CI, NCIS – I enjoy all crime dramas...looking for someone who sometimes wants to ditch the glitter of South Beach and sit on my futon for some good, old fashioned mysteries and a bottle of wine. I get excited by those famous Law & Order opening sounds – dink dink dink! And who can pass up a seductive glance by a tanned David Caruso; or a witty one-liner by Jerry Orbach? If you want to work on my case, just pull my file!

Irish Eyes Likes: donuts & cupcakes, pesto, Vespas, Italy, San Francisco, National Parks and the Tetons in particular, indie flicks, live music in small venues, Caravaggio, Sargeant, Hopper, wanderlust, Oprah, historic preservation & urban redevelopment, gardens, Slow Food, letterpress stationary, British humor & foreign accents, cultural pluralism, Bellinis, and dancing (tap is my favorite). Drop a line if you're like-minded.

Bakedbean Love the Red Sox, hate the Yankees. Like swimming in lakes, biking along the beach, and hip hop dancing. Sauvignon blanc is the white for me, reds put me to sleep. Never had a dog, but desperately seeking a basset hound.

GirlInGear Hot Girl Scout from the Heart of America looking for her Eagle Scout to help with her foundation metoo.org and join her in adventures in the mountains and rivers of Colorado. Must love dogs, bikes, kayaks and powertools.

GreenEyes Looking for a new Boyfriend of Record. Current boyfriend has failed to perform to the standards he presented when initially pitching our relationship. If you think you're up for the challenge, let's get together. You can look up my job jackets and I'll show you my hot sheets.

Trickydick I play the drums for Jesus.

TallMist Account guy enjoying new canvas in Miami. Interests include tennis, martinis and samba.

Arbiter of Justice I dump lattes on unsuspecting evildoers. Seeking charismatic sidekick to dry clean my spandex suit.

Moi I think vacation houses are trés chic! Do you have a European chateau, beach house, and/or ski lodge you'd like to invite me to?

Señorita Killa You drivin' fast in my mind. Girl don't cha' slow it down. If we carry on this way the same we might leave the ground. How would you like to fly? That's how my queen should ride. But you still deserve the crown Why hasn't it been found? Senorita I feel for you. You deal with things that you don't have to. He doesn't love you I can tell by his charm. But you can feel this real love if you just lay in my Ahhh, Ahhh, Arms (Won't you lay in my)

The13ig13adWolf Sporty chick that likes to lift heavy and get dirty. Girly men not invited. Holla if you think you can keep up.

Oscar5 Looking for friends to hang out with – who like going to the movies and trying new ethic restaurants.

nick_pappagiorgio From Yuma, Arizona,

used to be in software but now I'm an ad guy. Looking for a hot, brilliant, talented, funny, and outgoing girl with a love for life. Actually, she doesn't necessarily have to be hot, just decent looking, as long as she has a great personality. Come to think of it, she doesn't have to be THAT smart either, brains are sort of overrated anyway. And personality – I mean, who really cares about personality when the lights are out, right?

Bug Eyes I'm having fun in Miami with my newly acquired friends. I'm always looking for more friends, so if you're interested in seeing Miami with us, please contact me. I have a fun, little convertible that lets you get up close and personal with the Miami weather. I also have an apartment with a view for those times when my friends shouldn't be behind the wheel. Finally, I have a number of friends on the beach so late-night partying and early-morning sunning is always a component of my weekend. Want to hang out?

KasiaBasia Young, University of Miami student. Looking to find friends to live on the edge with. I'm into diving with the fishes, backpacking through the cobblestone streets of Europe, and speaking different languages. If you can keep up with the college lifestyle, hit me up.

TallDrinkOfWater™ Too tall hottie seeks friends and foes to kick back, play and drink Pinot with. Loves getting dirty but also being pampered. Shorties need not apply.

260
Creative

Nineleggeddj Scarred man looking for love. Must like romantic dinners. Talking about politics and whatnot. Won't steal my stuff. Please call me. Please.

HoHum Just another worker bee with existential ADD. Always on the hunt for new experiences, new perspectives and new ways of doing things. Addicted to what's next, exercise and playing with my super-dog. Love challenges, love to wander, love to discover. What should I do? What do I have to see? Where is one place I cannot miss? Who do I need to meet or hear or watch or read? I'm all eyes and ears.

PhinnHit Moved from flat parts of EU to even flatter parts of U.S. Show me your outdoor thrills here and I'll show you mine on the mountains.

Happygolucky Petulant, bellicose creative seeks hyperkinetic soul sister for mutually beneficial co-mingling. Are you into sculpture, self-surgery, liner notes and Civil War daguerreotypes? Is your fantasy to have your lifeless body outlined in chalk by a dry-heaving police detective? Are you deeply lonely but insist on believing that a vulgar and

ostentatious lifestyle will somehow "fix" things? Then come aboard my sulk house. Help turn the two or three lucid hours I experience every day into something special. Must be Alex-approved.

Metalgodz Join me for worship! Tell me your favorite SOLO!

Soddi Fierce, youthful, intelligent, aspiring, lucid, energetic, xeromorphic, hardened, algorithmic, tenacious, exuberant, shrill, pedigreed, enthusiastic, original, poetic, lurid, enriched, wonderous, hopeful, observant, synergistic, empowered, nihilistic, devious, mocking, inebriated, negligent, dissonant, leisurely, ecstatic, superior, sleuthing, extraordinary, menacing, astronomical, inspirational, languishing savant. Rarely ousted but repeatedly enlightened in long lasting years.

hot4teachr Little girl from cherry lane. Book worm. Straight-A student. All-Star player. Looking for other nerds to play with. Uniform included.

Malsizzle I've seen London, I've seen France...this sassy southern-belle loves to travel. I'm a renaissance woman looking for a BOND-type to globe trek it to exotic locales. Barefoot on a Grecian beach or sipping tea in Hong Kong, I love good friends and great conversation.

MRNGSTAR Looking for a connection with someone who enjoys discussing the deeper things in life. And if you enjoy great music and can collaborate on songwriting – all the better.

Angrybob I'm not really angry, I just look that way.

LostWithoutU We crossed paths at the check out lane of stopNshop on March 1st. You were in front of me buying a loaf of bread. I had a box of condoms and a gallon of Gatorade. You smiled at me and I looked away. I blew it, I wanted to ask you out but I guess I'm too chicken. If you are out there I'd like to buy you a cup of coffee.

R.U.There Desperately seeking someone with low standards.

THE SNEAKY SCOTTSMAN That's right. I'm sneaky. I want to sneak up on you. Well, maybe not you. I haven't seen a picture yet. Sneaky and shallow. Want some of this?

Belonephobia-PierceMania I have never seen a meaner person than me. Seriously. Challenge me if you are interested in. No friend on the earth. You might be the first though.

PIT PONY Seeks local mine to work. Loves fossil-fuels, dirty hooves and the odd Black lung.

Tennisgeek Looking for love and aces. If you can swing then we can swing. 4.0 and above only.

Buck Here's the thing...there's a dead end road'in a prehistoric landscape where the finger holes are turned towards Alpha Centauri. This is where the dragon will land and see you brave and beautiful. 1st edition, 1890...How's about a vase? Shit...it's hold the bird snowy, yo. 40° 00'54.00"N 105° 16'12.00"W. Drop the rope ladder, I'm staying for good.

HEADSORTAILS 1. Take a coin. 2. Flick it in the air. 3. Catch it but don't look at it. 4. Pick a side in your mind. 5. Open your hand. 6. If the side you picked is facing up, then drop me an email. It's meant to be.

JasonSteel I like pretty rich white girls with made up problems.

KaraokeQueen Just a girl, born to be wild. Losing my religion. Here I go again addicted to love. Like a virgin, I touch myself. I love rock 'n' roll. Saturday in the park. Saturday night, I'm hungry like the wolf. Imagine champagne supernova. Ooo baby baby, need you tonight. Hit me with your best shot. Right here, right now.

VP CD Sensei VP CD Sensei seeks male grasshopper AD or CW to take under wing. I'll teach you to fly.

4in-grl Hello! My English is fluent. I believe in love that can start at first sight. I can cook very well and I am especially good at baking tasty cakes. I love watching the waves and listening to their tender whisper. Do you?

KilgoreTrout. I'm into pirates, German chicks, classic motorcycles, and fine scotch. Do you want to design my pirate flag? Did you know the record for kissing a cobra is 51 kisses in 5 minutes? So it goes.

theBigSleep zzzzzzzzzzzzzzzzzzzzzzzzzz zzzzzzzzzzzzzzzzzzzzzzzzzzzzzzzzz zzzzzzzzzzzzzzzzzzzzzzzzzzzzzzzzz zzzzzzzzzzzzzzzzzzzzzzzzzzzzzzzzz zzzzzzzzzzzzzzzzzzzzzzzzzzzzzzzzz zzzzzzzzzzzzzzzzzzzzzzzzzzzzzzzzz zzzzzzzzzzzzzzzzzzzzzzzzzzzzzzzzz zzzzzzzzzzzzzzzzzzzzzzzzzzzz...

270
Interactive

Titillator Tall tech tells tantalizing tales of tigers and Tasmanians to tickle a tantric temptress that thinks teasing thoughts of tasting Thai tidbits for two.

FauxRockstar Classic Aquarius. I'm into all that new age bullshit. I love long walks on the beach and candles. I only listen to death metal and drum & bass. Unless you're fucked up and weird, I don't want to talk to you. Glass half-full people only please.

Desperately Seeking Susan Searching for Mr. Right. But Mr. Right-now will also do. You: 30s, fun, smart, non-smoker and non-ugly. Me: Late 20s, fun, creative, love to laugh and shop. Let's meet up for sushi.

Phatteristico 23-year-old workaholic looking for awesome friends to chill with in my not so spare time. If you're into short films, music composing, design, writing, tweening, social naps, interoffice dating, sun flower seeds, crystal light pink lemonade, self sufficientness, and actually believe in a thing called love, message me.

IceColdVideo Sitemaps, data flows, and wireframes get me up in the morning. You know you want some...

Goatsblood Sabbath Ritual killing? Call me. Could be fun.

Tommyboy Looking for a girl that truly appreciates the humor of a bobble head squirrel.

280
IT

RenFaire_CoGro Looking for open-minded types who share an interest in the triumphs and pitfalls of modern avant garde music composition and/or lyre restringing and tuning. An understanding of the harmonic repercussions of a vocoded reading of Beowulf through an amplified kalimba is suggested but not required. Be prepared to discuss the consequences of a Terry Riley vs. Steve Reich minimalist grudge match, titled: "Monotony or Polyphony?"

Sunshine Seek someone to frolic in the sun and have some fun. Whether it be by beach,boat, bar, or car. Always up for an adventure and spontaneous fun, so lets go.

Cono Boring guy seeks moderate and demure girl for so-so times and going through the motions lovemaking. Low-pressure relationship consists of pedestrian sex and inane conversation. Lack of creativity a plus.

ScoTTy2HoTTy Looking for Fun. People in or around the the Miami area. Bring your friendz I'll bring my friendz and we can be friendz. Till the day endz...

290
Media

Bones MWF with kids seeks secret 2nd life. I will make it worth your while. Tall, Blonde, Leggy, I could have been...lots of things. Willing to relocate. Nothing under 5 carats. Must be well traveled, make the perfect martini, speak min 2 languages and speak my language: "Dior", "Panerai", "Valet", "Presidential Suite", "First Class", "One of a Kind", "Spa", "Ocean Front", "No credit limit" and "VIP". Call me arm candy or trophy wife, call me anything you like.

GoBlue2002! Whoever said there's no such thing as a free lunch obviously didn't work in the media department. Dinners at NOBU, 4th row center court at the Heat game, loungin' suite-style at Pro Player Park, high-steppin' into Sky Bar, that's how I roll yo! All this and more can be yours too. Hollaaaaar!

Princess_PeachBlurb: I am The Princess of the Mushroom Kingdom. I take pleasure inteasing plumbers with red or green overalls. Feel free to save me from Bowser's evil castle...oh, I also enjoy sports like tennis, racecar driving, soccer and golf.

Tix4You In need of an impossible ticket - Concerts, Sporting Events, Broadway Plays. You name it, I can get it. Let's talk; maybe it won't cost you anything.

MediaMogul When I do manage to sleep, I toss & turn all night dreaming of unusual places to put our creative...Did you know that dairy farmers aren't too keen on branding their cows? Or that a porn spoof would actually see the light of day and win your client an award?

Picaluva The name Picaluva was created for my former Neopet, which I later had to put up for adoption. Pic-a-Luva is my unique name, or it was until I attempt to use it for one of the many websites that require a unique screen name, only to find that someone else has used it. Now I know that ideas can be thought of by more than one person and possibly at the same time, but whoever is out there using Picaluva stop it...it's mine!

SouthernComfort I like it hard.

BeanTownBoy Like to ski, play football, and baseball. From the north but I don't discriminate. I like a girl who looks the same when she wakes up as she does in the middle of the day. Blonde hair, blue eyes, with a slight southern accent... bring it!

300
Print Production

GranolaCrunch Looking for a companion who will kick off their Birkenstocks and dance to Phish music in the rain. Vegans only.

44SouthMIA When I'm not at work, I spend my time exploring Miami's vast culturally diverse epicurean scene. Thai, French, Italian, Vietnamese or Sushi. I like it all. And let's not forget about all the plaintains.

Silver Ball Junkie Pinball addicted rocker with personal stash seeks hotties with crazy flipping fingers and other players for multi-ball action. Meet at any dive bar with a game. 3 plays for a dollar, low score buys the beer. JACKPOT! Bring it on.

310
Traffic

PurpleOrchid Fun loving sassy mulatto is looking for friends who have a great zest for life, a passion for music and dancing and who are diehard football fans to share adventurous weekends and kick ass Super Bowl parties with. Couples only. Dolphin fans preferred!

VeryKrustyOldMan 66 year-old tranny from Hialeah looking for a Go Fish partner who prefers to buy their churros from street vendors, does not like pina coladas, chuckles at the misfortune of others and enjoys bbqing in the buff. Frat boys need not apply.

GoldenDelicious Fun 29-year-old SWF that doesn't drink coffee but sure likes vodka. Looking for fun people to hit the town with, and an honest, witty, intelligent guy. If you tend to black out or puke, or have more grooming rituals than Ryan Seacrest, please do not apply.

Shorty Swing My Way Seeking fun, and excitement...Can you keep up?!?

Nor'easter Blow in howling and blusterous, leaving a calm serene aura. Another mark on the map.

LastPepsiInTheDesert "If you like Pina Coladas and getting caught in the rain..." Miami raised Colombian girl established in 1983 whose looks are often confused for Asian, but hey you'll get the best of both worlds. I have an infectious laugh that sounds like a cross between a banshee and a hyena. Odd things and witty humor amuse me but don't try any sarcasm with me cause I invented it. I'm an adventurous sports fanatic who loves beer and knows how to have a good time (Go Gators!)...If I were a pizza I'd be "the works" except for anchovies cause they suck!

Dancinat Fun-loving, cookie baking, Yorkie-loving Puerto Rican, who loves some fun in the sun while drinking pina coladas with all my friends.

Vixxxxxen Foxy lady looking for mature huntsman to share happy romps in the woods. I will lead you a merry chase before you run me to ground. Huntsman should be lover of classic rock, animals, good red wine and gourmet food. This fox needs to be petted and spoiled and appreciates cozy times spent in her warm, sensual lair.

SweetFace Miami girl who loves to shop and travel. Two things I don't do enough of! Looking for friends who know how to relax and enjoy simple things like hanging out, being silly and laughing till your stomach hurts.

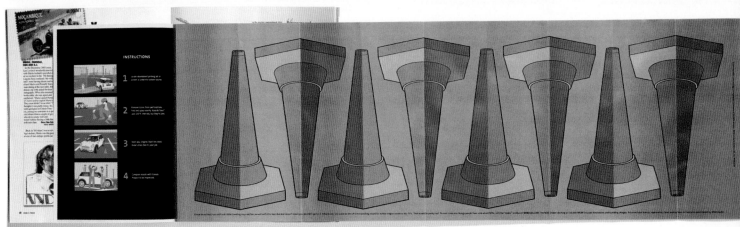

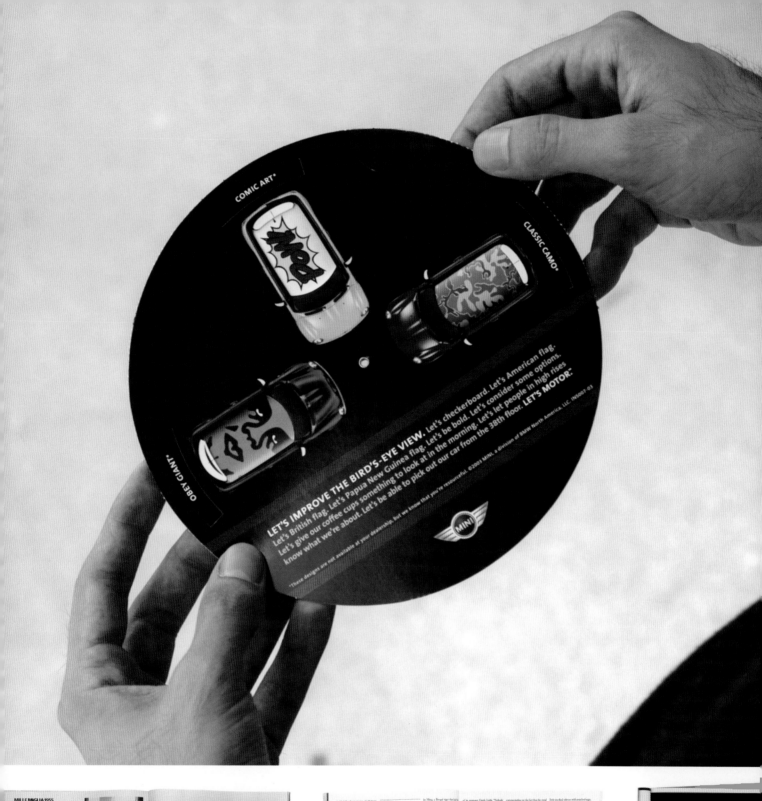

LET'S IMPROVE THE BIRD'S-EYE VIEW. Let's checkerboard. Let's American flag. Let's British flag. Let's Papua New Guinea flag. Let's be bold. Let's consider some options. Let's give our coffee cups something to look at in the morning. Let's let people in high rises know what we're about. Let's be able to pick our car out from the 38th floor. LET'S MOTOR.™

COMIC ART*
CLASSIC CAMO*
OBEY GIANT*

*These designs are not available at your dealership, but we know that you're resourceful. ©2002 MINI, a division of BMW North America, LLC. (NS007-03)

MINI ROOF DESIGN GENERATOR

LET'S PARK IT ON OUR DESK. Let's drag race our favor... past the tape dispenser. Let's avoid coffee spills. Let's w... by our boss. Let's get lost in the office. On a 1/56th sc...

This spread is a classic case of "you never know until you ask." Well, we asked, and damned if Rolling Stone didn't let us paint its staples yellow.

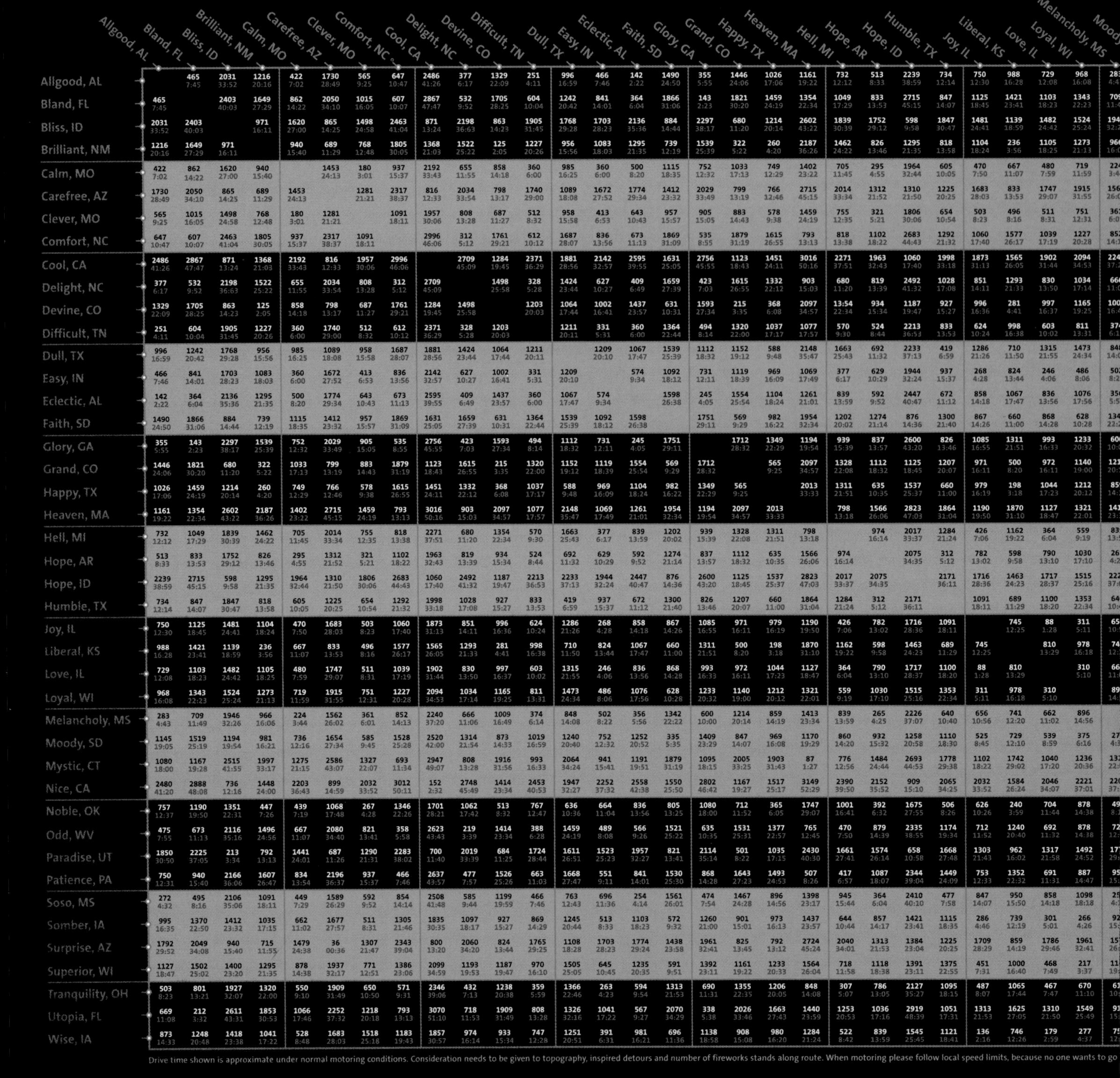

Drive-time chart (values shown as distance / drive time). Diagonal (city to itself) left blank.

	Allgood, AL	Bland, FL	Bliss, ID	Brilliant, NM	Calm, MO	Carefree, AZ	Clever, MO	Comfort, NC	Cool, CA	Delight, NC	Devine, CO	Difficult, TN	Dull, TX	Easy, IN	Eclectic, AL	Faith, SD	Glory, GA	Grand, CO	Happy, TX	Heaven, MA	Hell, MI	Hope, AR	Hope, ID	Humble, TX	Joy, IL	Liberal, KS	Love, IL	Loyal, WI	Melancholy, MS
Allgood, AL		465 / 7:45	2031 / 33:52	1216 / 20:16	422 / 7:02	1730 / 28:49	565 / 9:25	647 / 10:47	2486 / 41:26	377 / 6:17	1329 / 22:09	251 / 4:11	996 / 16:59	466 / 7:45	142 / 2:22	1490 / 24:50	355 / 5:55	1446 / 24:06	1026 / 17:06	1161 / 19:22	732 / 12:12	513 / 8:33	2239 / 38:59	734 / 12:14	750 / 12:30	988 / 16:28	729 / 12:08	968 / 16:08	283 / 4:43
Bland, FL	465 / 7:45		2403 / 40:03	1649 / 27:29	862 / 14:22	2050 / 34:10	1015 / 16:05	607 / 10:07	2867 / 47:47	532 / 9:52	1705 / 28:25	604 / 10:04	1242 / 20:42	841 / 14:01	364 / 6:04	1866 / 31:06	143 / 2:22	1821 / 30:20	1459 / 24:19	1354 / 22:34	1049 / 17:29	833 / 13:53	2715 / 45:15	847 / 14:07	1125 / 18:45	1421 / 23:58	1103 / 18:23	1343 / 22:23	709 / 11:49
Bliss, ID	2031 / 33:52	2403 / 40:03		971 / 16:11	1620 / 27:00	865 / 14:25	1498 / 24:58	2463 / 41:04	871 / 13:24	2198 / 36:63	863 / 14:23	1905 / 31:45	1768 / 29:28	1703 / 28:23	2136 / 35:36	884 / 14:44	2297 / 38:17	680 / 11:20	1214 / 20:14	2602 / 43:22	1839 / 30:39	1752 / 29:12	598 / 9:58	1847 / 30:47	1481 / 24:41	1139 / 18:59	1482 / 24:42	1524 / 25:24	1946 / 32:26
Brilliant, NM	1216 / 20:16	1649 / 27:29	971 / 16:11		940 / 15:40	689 / 11:29	768 / 12:48	1805 / 30:05	1368 / 21:03	1522 / 25:22	125 / 2:05	1227 / 20:26	956 / 15:56	1083 / 18:03	1295 / 21:35	739 / 12:19	1539 / 25:39	322 / 5:22	260 / 4:20	2187 / 36:26	1462 / 24:22	826 / 13:46	1295 / 21:35	818 / 13:58	1104 / 18:24	236 / 3:56	1105 / 18:25	1273 / 21:13	966 / 16:06
Calm, MO	422 / 7:02	862 / 14:22	1620 / 27:00	940 / 15:40		1453 / 24:13	180 / 3:01	937 / 15:37	2192 / 33:43	655 / 11:55	1424 / 23:44	360 / 6:00	985 / 16:25	360 / 6:00	500 / 8:20	1115 / 18:35	752 / 12:32	1033 / 17:13	749 / 12:29	1402 / 23:22	705 / 11:45	295 / 4:55	1964 / 32:44	605 / 10:05	470 / 7:50	667 / 11:07	480 / 7:59	719 / 11:59	224 / 3:44
Carefree, AZ	1730 / 28:49	2050 / 34:10	865 / 14:25	689 / 11:29	1453 / 24:13		1281 / 21:21	1091 / 18:11	816 / 12:33	2034 / 33:54	798 / 13:17	1740 / 29:00	1089 / 18:08	1774 / 29:34	1412 / 23:52	2029 / 33:33	799 / 13:19	766 / 12:46	2715 / 45:15	2014 / 33:34	1312 / 21:52	1225 / 20:25	1683 / 28:03	833 / 13:53	1747 / 29:07	1915 / 31:55	1560 / —
Clever, MO	565 / 9:25	1015 / 16:05	1498 / 24:58	768 / 12:48	180 / 3:01	1281 / 21:21		1091 / 18:11	1957 / 30:06	808 / 13:28	687 / 11:27	512 / 8:32	958 / 15:58	413 / 6:53	643 / 10:43	957 / 15:57	905 / 15:05	883 / 14:43	578 / 9:38	1615 / 24:19	755 / 12:35	321 / 5:21	1806 / 30:06	654 / 10:54	503 / 8:23	496 / 8:16	511 / 8:31	751 / 12:31	361 / —
Comfort, NC	647 / 10:47	607 / 10:07	2463 / 41:04	1805 / 30:05	937 / 15:37	2317 / 38:37	1091 / 18:11		2996 / 46:06	312 / 5:12	1761 / 29:21	612 / 10:12	1687 / 28:07	1356 / 13:56	673 / 11:13	1869 / 31:09	535 / 8:53	1879 / 31:19	1615 / 26:55	793 / 13:13	818 / 13:38	1102 / 18:22	2683 / 44:43	1292 / 21:32	1060 / 17:40	1577 / 25:33	1039 / 17:19	1227 / 20:35	852 / —
Cool, CA	2486 / 41:26	2867 / 47:47	871 / 13:24	1368 / 21:03	2192 / 33:43	816 / 12:33	1957 / 30:06	2996 / 46:06		2709 / 45:09	1284 / 21:17	2371 / 36:29	1881 / 28:56	2142 / 32:57	2595 / 39:55	1631 / 25:05	2756 / 45:55	1123 / 18:43	1451 / 24:11	3016 / 50:16	2271 / 37:51	1963 / 32:43	1060 / 17:40	1998 / 33:18	1873 / 31:13	1565 / 26:05	1902 / 31:44	2094 / 34:53	224 / —
Delight, NC	377 / 6:17	532 / 9:52	2198 / 36:25	1522 / 25:22	655 / 11:55	2034 / 33:54	808 / 13:28	312 / 5:12	2709 / 45:09		1498 / 25:58	328 / 5:28	1424 / 23:44	627 / 10:27	409 / 6:49	1659 / 27:39	423 / 23:44	1615 / 22:12	1332 / 15:03	903 / 11:20	680 / 13:39	819 / 14:11	2492 / 41:32	1028 / 17:08	851 / 14:11	1293 / 21:33	830 / 13:50	1034 / 17:14	666 / —
Devine, CO	1329 / 22:09	1705 / 28:25	863 / 14:23	125 / 2:05	1424 / 14:18	798 / 13:17	687 / 11:27	1761 / 29:21	1284 / 21:17	1498 / 25:58		1203 / 20:03	1064 / 17:44	1002 / 16:41	1437 / 23:57	631 / 10:31	1593 / 25:39	215 / 3:35	368 / 6:08	2097 / 34:57	1354 / 13:54	934 / 15:34	1187 / 19:47	927 / 15:27	996 / 16:36	281 / 4:41	997 / 16:37	1165 / 19:25	1003 / —
Difficult, TN	251 / 4:11	604 / 10:04	1905 / 31:45	1227 / 20:26	360 / 6:00	1740 / 29:00	512 / 8:32	612 / 10:12	2371 / 36:29	328 / 5:28	1203 / 20:03		1211 / 20:11	331 / 5:31	360 / 6:00	1364 / 22:44	494 / 8:14	1320 / 22:00	1037 / 17:17	1077 / 17:57	570 / 9:30	524 / 8:44	2213 / 36:53	833 / 13:53	624 / 10:24	998 / 16:38	603 / 10:02	811 / 13:31	374 / —
Dull, TX	996 / 16:59	1242 / 20:42	1768 / 29:28	956 / 15:56	985 / 16:25	1089 / 18:08	958 / 15:58	1687 / 28:07	1881 / 28:56	1424 / 23:44	1064 / 17:44	1211 / 20:11		1209 / 20:10	574 / 9:34	1092 / 18:12	1112 / 18:32	1152 / 19:12	588 / 9:48	2148 / 35:47	1663 / 25:43	692 / 11:32	2233 / 37:13	419 / 6:59	1286 / 21:26	710 / 11:50	1315 / 21:55	1473 / 24:34	841 / —
Easy, IN	466 / 7:46	841 / 14:01	1703 / 28:23	1083 / 18:03	360 / 6:00	1672 / 27:52	413 / 6:53	1356 / 13:56	2142 / 32:57	627 / 10:27	1002 / 16:41	331 / 5:31	1209 / 20:10		574 / 9:34	1092 / 18:12	731 / 6:17	1119 / 18:39	969 / 14:59	1069 / 16:29	377 / 6:17	629 / 10:29	1944 / 32:24	937 / 15:37	268 / 4:28	824 / 13:44	246 / 4:06	486 / 8:06	502 / —
Eclectic, AL	142 / 2:22	364 / 6:04	2136 / 35:36	1295 / 21:35	500 / 8:20	1774 / 29:34	643 / 10:43	673 / 11:13	2595 / 39:55	409 / 6:49	1437 / 23:57	360 / 6:00	574 / 9:34	574 / 9:34		1598 / 26:38	245 / 4:05	1554 / 25:54	1104 / 18:24	1261 / 21:01	831 / 13:59	592 / 9:52	2447 / 40:47	1112 / 11:12	858 / 14:18	1067 / 17:47	836 / 13:56	1076 / 17:56	356 / —
Faith, SD	1490 / 24:50	1866 / 31:06	884 / 14:44	739 / 12:19	1115 / 18:35	1412 / 23:52	957 / 15:57	1869 / 31:09	1631 / 25:05	1659 / 27:39	631 / 10:31	1364 / 22:44	1092 / 18:12	1092 / 18:12	1598 / 26:38		1751 / 29:11	569 / 9:29	982 / 16:22	1954 / 32:34	1202 / 20:02	1274 / 21:14	876 / 13:00	1300 / 21:40	867 / 14:00	660 / 11:00	868 / 14:28	628 / 13:13	223 / —
Glory, GA	355 / 5:55	143 / 2:22	2297 / 38:17	1539 / 25:39	752 / 12:32	2029 / 33:49	905 / 15:05	535 / 8:53	2756 / 45:55	423 / 7:03	1593 / 27:34	494 / 8:14	1112 / 18:32	731 / 12:11	245 / 4:05	1751 / 29:11		1712 / 28:32	1349 / 22:29	1194 / 19:54	939 / 15:39	837 / 13:57	2600 / 43:20	826 / 13:46	1085 / 16:55	1313 / 21:51	993 / 16:33	1233 / 20:32	620 / —
Grand, CO	1446 / 24:06	1821 / 30:20	680 / 11:20	322 / 5:22	1033 / 17:13	799 / 13:19	883 / 14:43	1879 / 31:19	1123 / 18:43	1615 / 26:55	215 / 3:35	1320 / 22:00	1152 / 19:12	1119 / 18:39	1554 / 25:54	569 / 9:29	1712 / 28:32		565 / 9:29	2097 / 34:57	1328 / 22:08	1112 / 18:32	1125 / 18:45	1207 / 20:07	971 / 16:11	500 / 8:20	972 / 16:11	1140 / 19:00	121 / —
Happy, TX	1026 / 17:06	1459 / 24:19	1214 / 20:14	260 / 4:20	749 / 12:29	766 / 12:46	578 / 9:38	1615 / 26:55	1451 / 24:11	1332 / 22:12	368 / 6:08	1037 / 17:17	588 / 9:48	969 / 16:09	1104 / 18:24	982 / 16:22	1349 / 22:29	565 / 9:29		2013 / 33:33	1311 / 21:51	635 / 10:35	1537 / 25:37	660 / 11:00	979 / 16:19	198 / 3:18	1044 / 17:23	1212 / 20:12	85 / —
Heaven, MA	1161 / 19:22	1354 / 22:34	2602 / 43:22	2187 / 36:26	1402 / 23:22	2715 / 45:15	1615 / 24:19	793 / 13:13	3016 / 50:16	903 / 11:20	2097 / 34:57	1077 / 17:57	2148 / 35:47	1069 / 16:29	1261 / 21:01	1954 / 32:34	1194 / 19:54	2097 / 34:57	2013 / 33:33		798 / 16:14	1566 / 26:06	2823 / 47:03	1864 / 16:04	1190 / 19:50	1870 / 31:10	1127 / 18:47	1321 / 22:01	147 / —
Hell, MI	732 / 12:12	1049 / 17:29	1839 / 30:39	1462 / 24:22	705 / 11:45	2014 / 33:34	755 / 12:35	818 / 13:38	2271 / 37:51	680 / 13:39	1354 / 13:57	570 / 9:30	1663 / 25:43	377 / 6:17	831 / 13:59	1202 / 20:02	939 / 15:43	1328 / 22:08	1311 / 21:51	798 / 16:14		974 / 16:14	2017 / 33:37	1284 / 21:24	426 / 7:06	1162 / 19:22	364 / 6:04	559 / 9:19	26 / —
Hope, AR	513 / 8:33	833 / 13:53	1752 / 29:12	826 / 13:46	295 / 4:55	1312 / 21:52	321 / 5:21	1102 / 18:22	1963 / 32:43	819 / 13:39	934 / 15:34	524 / 8:44	692 / 11:32	629 / 10:29	592 / 9:52	1274 / 21:14	837 / 13:57	1112 / 18:32	635 / 10:35	1566 / 26:06	974 / 16:14		2075 / 34:35	312 / 5:12	782 / 13:02	598 / 9:58	790 / 13:10	1030 / 17:10	26 / —
Hope, ID	2239 / 38:59	2715 / 45:15	598 / 9:58	1295 / 21:35	1964 / 32:44	1310 / 21:52	1806 / 30:06	1615 / 26:55	1060 / 17:40	2492 / 41:32	1187 / 19:47	2213 / 36:53	2233 / 37:13	1944 / 32:24	2447 / 40:47	876 / 14:36	2600 / 43:20	1125 / 18:45	1537 / 25:37	2823 / 47:03	2017 / 33:37	2075 / 34:35		2171 / 36:11	1716 / 28:36	1463 / 24:23	1717 / 28:37	1515 / 25:16	37 / —
Humble, TX	734 / 12:14	847 / 14:07	1847 / 30:47	818 / 13:58	605 / 10:05	1225 / 20:25	654 / 10:54	1292 / 21:32	1998 / 33:18	1028 / 17:08	927 / 15:27	833 / 13:53	419 / 6:59	937 / 15:37	672 / 11:12	1300 / 21:40	1284 / 21:24	1207 / 20:07	660 / 11:00	1864 / 16:04	1284 / 21:24	312 / 5:12	2171 / 36:11		1091 / 18:11	689 / 11:29	1100 / 18:20	1353 / 22:34	640 / —
Joy, IL	750 / 12:30	1125 / 18:45	1481 / 24:41	1104 / 18:24	470 / 7:50	1683 / 28:03	503 / 8:23	1060 / 17:40	1873 / 31:13	851 / 14:11	996 / 16:36	624 / 10:24	1286 / 21:26	268 / 4:28	858 / 14:18	867 / 14:00	1085 / 16:55	971 / 16:11	979 / 16:19	1190 / 19:50	426 / 7:06	782 / 13:02	1716 / 28:36	1091 / 18:11		745 / 12:25	88 / 1:28	311 / 5:11	656 / —
Liberal, KS	988 / 16:28	1421 / 23:58	1139 / 18:59	236 / 3:56	667 / 11:07	833 / 13:53	496 / 8:16	1577 / 25:33	1565 / 26:05	1293 / 21:33	281 / 3:35	998 / 16:38	710 / 11:50	824 / 13:44	1067 / 17:47	660 / 11:00	1313 / 21:51	500 / 8:20	198 / 3:18	1870 / 31:10	1162 / 19:22	598 / 9:58	1463 / 24:23	689 / 11:29	745 / 12:25		810 / 13:29	978 / 16:18	741 / —
Love, IL	729 / 12:08	1103 / 18:23	1482 / 24:42	1105 / 18:25	480 / 7:59	1747 / 29:07	511 / 8:31	1039 / 17:19	1902 / 31:44	830 / 13:50	997 / 16:37	603 / 10:02	1315 / 21:55	246 / 4:06	836 / 13:56	868 / 14:28	993 / 16:33	972 / 16:11	1044 / 17:23	1127 / 18:47	364 / 6:04	790 / 13:10	1717 / 28:37	1100 / 18:20	88 / 1:28	810 / 13:29		310 / 5:10	662 / —
Loyal, WI	968 / 16:08	1343 / 22:23	1524 / 25:24	1273 / 21:13	719 / 11:55	1915 / 31:55	751 / 12:31	1227 / 20:35	2094 / 34:53	1034 / 17:14	1165 / 19:25	811 / 13:31	1473 / 24:34	486 / 8:06	1076 / 17:56	628 / 13:13	1233 / 20:32	1140 / 19:00	1212 / 20:12	1321 / 22:01	559 / 9:19	1030 / 17:10	1515 / 25:16	1353 / 22:34	311 / 5:11	978 / 16:18	310 / 5:10		894 / —
Melancholy, MS	283 / 4:43	709 / 11:49	1946 / 32:26	966 / 16:06	224 / 3:44	1562 / 26:01	361 / 6:01	852 / 14:13	2240 / 37:20	666 / 11:06	1009 / 16:49	374 / 6:14	848 / 14:08	502 / 8:22	356 / 5:56	1342 / 22:22	600 / 10:00	1214 / 20:14	859 / 14:19	1413 / 23:34	839 / 4:25	265 / 4:25	2226 / 37:07	640 / 10:56	656 / 10:56	741 / 12:16	662 / 11:02	896 / 14:56	
Moody, SD	1145 / 19:05	1519 / 25:19	1194 / 19:54	981 / 16:21	736 / 12:16	1654 / 27:34	585 / 9:45	1528 / 25:28	2520 / 42:00	1314 / 21:54	873 / 14:33	1019 / 16:59	2064 / ?	941 / ?	1191 / 19:51	1879 / 31:19	1095 / 18:15	2005 / 33:25	1903 / 31:43	87 / 1:27	776 / 12:56	1484 / 24:44	2693 / 44:53	1778 / 29:38	1102 / 18:22	1742 / 29:02	1040 / 17:20	1236 / 20:36	272 / —
Mystic, CT	1080 / 18:00	1167 / 19:24	2515 / 41:55	1997 / 33:17	1327 / 21:15	2586 / 43:07	1327 / 22:07	693 / 11:34	2947 / 49:07	808 / 13:28	1916 / 31:56	993 / 16:33	2064 / 34:24	941 / 15:41	1191 / 19:51	1879 / 31:19	1095 / 18:15	2558 / 42:38	2098 / 25:00	1550 / 25:50	802 / 13:02	1167 / 19:27	1517 / 25:17	2390 / 39:50	2152 / 35:52	909 / 15:10	2032 / 33:52	1846 / 26:24	2221 / —
Nice, CA	2480 / 41:20	2888 / 48:08	736 / 12:16	1448 / 24:00	2203 / 36:43	2099 / 34:59	2032 / 33:52	3012 / 50:13	152 / 2:32	2748 / 45:49	1314 / 21:34	2453 / 40:53	1947 / 32:27	2213 / 37:32	2558 / 42:38	1550 / 25:50	2802 / 46:02	1167 / 19:27	1517 / 25:17	2229 / ?	2390 / 39:50	2152 / 35:52	909 / 15:10	2065 / 34:25	2032 / 33:52	1586 / 26:24	2221 / 37:01	272 / —	
Noble, OK	757 / 12:37	1190 / 19:50	1351 / —	447 / 7:26	439 / 7:19	1100 / 17:48	267 / 4:28	1346 / 22:31	1701 / 28:21	1062 / 17:42	913 / 8:32	767 / 12:47	636 / 10:36	664 / 11:04	856 / 14:18	805 / 13:59	1080 / 16:41	712 / 11:52	365 / 6:05	1675 / 29:07	1001 / 16:41	392 / 6:32	1675 / 27:55	506 / 10:26	626 / 10:26	240 / 11:44	704 / 14:38	878 / —	
Odd, WV	475 / 7:55	673 / 11:13	2115 / 35:16	1496 / 24:56	667 / 11:07	2060 / 34:40	821 / 13:41	358 / 5:58	2623 / 43:43	219 / 3:39	1414 / 23:34	388 / 6:28	1459 / 24:19	489 / 8:08	566 / 9:26	1521 / 25:22	635 / 10:05	1531 / 25:31	1377 / 22:57	765 / 11:52	470 / 14:39	879 / 38:55	2335 / 19:34	1174 / 11:52	712 / 20:40	1200 / 11:32	692 / 14:38	878 / —	
Paradise, UT	1850 / 30:50	2225 / 37:05	213 / 3:54	792 / 13:13	1441 / 24:01	687 / 11:26	1290 / 21:31	2283 / 38:02	700 / 11:40	2019 / 33:39	684 / 11:25	1724 / 28:44	1611 / 26:51	1523 / 25:23	1957 / 32:17	821 / 13:41	2114 / 34:57	501 / 8:20	1035 / 17:15	2430 / 40:50	1661 / 27:41	1574 / 26:14	658 / 10:58	1668 / 27:48	1303 / 21:43	962 / 16:02	1317 / 24:52	1492 / —	
Patience, PA	750 / 12:31	940 / 16:06	2166 / 36:06	1607 / 26:47	834 / 13:54	2196 / 36:37	937 / 15:37	466 / 7:43	2637 / 43:57	477 / 7:57	1526 / 25:26	663 / 11:03	1668 / 27:47	551 / 9:11	841 / 14:01	1530 / 25:30	868 / 14:27	1643 / 27:23	1493 / 24:53	507 / 8:26	417 / 18:07	1087 / 39:04	2344 / 24:09	1449 / 12:33	753 / 31:22	1352 / 11:31	691 / 14:47	887 / —	
Soso, MS	272 / 4:32	495 / 8:16	2106 / 35:06	1091 / 18:11	449 / 7:29	1589 / 26:29	592 / 9:52	854 / 14:14	2508 / 41:48	585 / 9:44	1199 / 19:59	466 / 7:46	763 / 12:43	696 / 11:24	254 / 4:14	1561 / 26:01	474 / 7:54	1467 / 24:06	896 / 14:56	1398 / 23:57	945 / 15:44	364 / 6:04	2410 / 40:10	477 / 7:58	847 / 14:07	950 / 15:50	858 / 14:07	1098 / 18:18	
Somber, IA	995 / 16:35	1370 / 22:32	1412 / 23:32	1035 / 17:15	662 / 11:02	1677 / 27:57	511 / 8:31	1305 / 21:46	1835 / 30:35	1097 / 18:17	927 / 15:47	869 / 14:29	1245 / 20:44	513 / 8:33	1103 / 18:23	572 / 9:32	1260 / 21:00	901 / 15:01	973 / 16:13	1437 / 23:57	644 / 14:17	857 / 23:41	1421 / 18:15	1115 / 4:46	286 / 12:19	739 / 5:01	301 / 4:26	926 / —	
Surprise, AZ	1792 / 29:52	2049 / 34:08	940 / 15:40	715 / 11:55	1479 / 24:38	36 / 0:36	1307 / 21:47	2343 / 39:04	800 / 13:20	2060 / 34:20	824 / 13:44	1765 / 29:25	1108 / 18:28	1703 / 28:23	1774 / 29:24	1438 / 23:58	1961 / 32:41	825 / 13:45	792 / 13:11	2724 / 45:34	2040 / 34:01	1313 / 21:53	1384 / 23:04	1225 / 20:25	1709 / 28:29	859 / 14:19	1786 / 29:46	1961 / —	
Superior, WI	1127 / 18:47	1502 / 25:02	1400 / 23:20	1295 / 21:35	878 / 14:38	1937 / 32:17	771 / 12:51	1386 / 23:06	2099 / 34:59	1193 / 19:47	1235 / 20:35	970 / 16:10	1505 / 25:05	645 / 10:45	1238 / 20:35	591 / 9:51	1392 / 23:11	1161 / 19:22	1233 / 20:33	1564 / 26:04	718 / 11:58	1118 / 18:38	1391 / 23:11	1375 / 22:55	451 / 7:31	1000 / 16:40	468 / 7:49	310 / —	
Tranquility, OH	503 / 8:23	801 / 13:21	1902 / 32:07	1320 / 22:00	550 / 9:10	1909 / 31:49	650 / 10:50	571 / 9:36	2346 / 39:06	432 / 7:13	1238 / 20:38	359 / 5:56	1366 / 22:46	263 / 4:23	594 / 9:56	1313 / 21:50	690 / 12:35	1355 / 22:05	1206 / 20:08	848 / 14:08	307 / 14:00	786 / 13:05	2127 / 35:27	1096 / 18:15	487 / 8:07	1065 / 17:44	447 / 7:47	670 / —	
Utopia, FL	669 / 11:08	212 / 3:32	1611 / 43:31	1853 / 30:53	1066 / 17:46	2252 / 37:32	1218 / 20:18	793 / 13:13	3070 / 51:10	718 / 11:53	1909 / 31:49	808 / 13:28	1326 / 22:06	1041 / 17:22	567 / 9:27	2070 / 34:29	338 / 13:46	2026 / 27:15	1663 / 16:13	1440 / 48:39	1253 / 17:16	1036 / 21:53	2919 / 27:05	1051 / 21:53	1313 / 25:49	1625 / —	1310 / —	1549 / —	
Wise, IA	873 / 14:33	1248 / 20:28	1418 / 23:38	1041 / 17:22	528 / 8:48	1657 / 28:03	513 / 8:31	1518 / 25:18	1857 / 30:57	974 / 16:14	933 / 15:34	747 / 12:27	1251 / 20:51	391 / 6:31	981 / 16:21	696 / 11:36	1138 / 18:58	908 / 16:09	980 / 16:09	1290 / 21:24	842 / 13:59	539 / 8:42	1545 / 25:45	1125 / 18:41	136 / 2:16	746 / 12:26	279 / 2:59	277 / 4:37	

Drive time shown is approximate under normal motoring conditions. Consideration needs to be given to topography, inspired detours and number of fireworks stands along route. When motoring please follow local speed limits, because no one wants to go...

FIRE and ASHES

BY ANTHONY BRANDT

Married an Explorer

MAKES EVERYTHING ELSE SEEM A LITTLE TOO BIG.

MINI COOPER

SAVE 37%! And get Amazing Abs Made Easy!

WHIPTASTIC HANDLING

To learn more about MINI's world-famous handling, visit MINIUSA.COM

Superior

Loyal

Heaven

Mystic

Moody

Somber

Wise

Hell

Love

Joy

Patience

Easy

Tranquility

Odd

Noble

Clever

Calm

Difficult

Comfort

Delight

Hope

Melancholy

Allgood

Eclectic

Soso

Glory

Bland

Humble

Utopia

| 0 | 43 | 86 | 172 Mi |

| 0 | 50 | 150 Km |

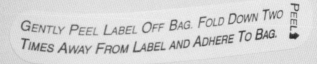

GENTLY PEEL LABEL OFF BAG. FOLD DOWN TWO
TIMES AWAY FROM LABEL AND ADHERE TO BAG.

PEEL ➡

LET'S NOT MESS UP
THE INTERIOR.

Let's make clickety-clak sounds as
we climb to the top. Let's remember
to keep our hands and feet inside
the ride at all times. Let's spin round
and round and round and round 'til
the guy in the back seat just can't
stomach it anymore. LET'S MOTOR.™

LET'S MESS WITH PERFECTION. Let's Daniel Boone-flag it. Let's flame paint it. Let's detail it. Let's whale tail it. Let's fuzzy dice it. Let's trick it out. Let's spoiler kit it. Let's mirror tint it. Let's whitewall it. Let's hot rod it. Let's lower it. Let's raise it. Let's do nothing. Let's do whatever. **LET'S MOTOR.**

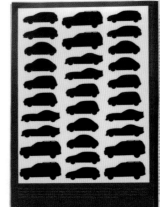

CP+B vs CP+B

Chuck Porter: This was supposed to be a fireside chat so, first, I apologize that there's no fireside. I'll just make crackling noises. We have a lot of new people and we wanted to talk about what's important to us here. What matters. I'd like to start by telling you where we came from, how we got here, and why we're so weird. Alex and I started this a long time ago. Neither of us had ever really worked for other agencies, so we sort of made up things as we went. But from the very beginning we had a very clear idea of who we wanted to be, and certainly who we didn't want to be. I want to read you a quote, a profile of the agency written for *Communication Arts* magazine. It says: "The work is what matters here. We don't think about media billings, or the hours people keep, or office politics." And there is another quote in the same article that talks about working in Miami, "Clients here have never been exposed to great creative work as much as in other parts of the country, so we have, at times, found it hard to sell some of the more daring ideas." That's from *Communication Arts* in 1991. So we've been on the way to being a really good agency doing really good ads for a long, long time. But I think we're a very different thing now. We're a kind of strange organism that thinks in a very different way from any advertising agency I know of, or really any company I know of. And there are hundreds of reasons of why we've gotten there. Three of them are sitting in front of me right now. And we all wanted to talk with you a bit about the agency. Thanks for coming. (Applause.) Alex: The reason I wanted to do this is we have a lot of new people. Talking a little bit about the history of the agency is a good way to understand what it is we do and why we do it. Because a lot of what we do is confusing to people if they come from other shops. So I'll start. The first thing I wanna touch on is the mission statement. Everyone gets one, I guess. Is that correct, that when you start here, you get a mission statement? Chuck: Just say yes. Someone in audience: Yes. (Laughter.) Alex: We've never really made a big deal out of it. But, in the history of the agency it actually was a really important moment, when we first made it official. Because for years, Chuck and I would go have a beer, and we'd say, "We've gotta make this agency great." But we never actually shared that thought with anyone. We were a terrible agency, like seventh best in Miami. I always say third best, but the truth is more like seventh best. And from there to say,"I wanna be great at this," well, it was embarrassing. And I remember how tense I was the first time I went in front of the agency and said: "Okay, here is our mission." And (laughs) in hindsight, maybe there wasn't really cause for trepidation, because everyone was just like, "Okay cool, yeah we could do that." But what worked about it was–and it started working right away–instead of just Chuck and I making decisions based on wanting to be great, we had 30 or 40 people all making their decisions based on wanting to be great. And all those decisions added up, and within a year we were a very different place. Anyway, our mission statement is the same now as it was then: "To produce and distribute the most talked about, written about, and effective advertising and creative content in the world." We never put anything about awards in there. And it was something that we did on purpose, because we win lots of awards, but we don't win awards because we try to win awards. We win awards because we try to do work that people are gonna write about and consumers are gonna talk about and you're gonna see on blogs and everywhere else. That's what we do. We put our work into pop culture. Then pop culture can take it and have fun with it and talk about it and get mad at it and piss on it and love it and whatever else they do with it. All of that stuff is okay with us, as long as they don't ignore it. Don't worry if you don't have your little copy of the mission statement. You don't have to walk around with it, or even know it. You just need to know the notion of it. It's not like the Eagle Scouts, where you have to memorize it….I think we actually employ an Eagle Scout. Jeff Steinhour: Schiff was an Eagle Scout. (Laughter.) Alex: Anyway, the way we were doing things got us accounts, and the accounts are a big part of who we are. Like Florida *truth*. That was a big moment for us, because it was the first time we had a budget to put behind our thinking. And if you come here now, it's easy to see the agency as a place ripe with opportunity. But back then we had to turn shit into gold. Because we really had no good opportunities. Now you can look around this place and you can start to categorize opportunities. You can start to say: "Wow, that's a really neat opportunity to do some television on BURGER KING,®" or whatever. But that's a mistake. You still have to think of every opportunity as shit. Because they only become great through the work that people do on them. In fact, it's made interviewing new people really hard. Before, we would get these crazy people who were like, "Here's this weird little agency, and even though they've only done like three good things ever, I'm gonna go there and make my mark." I love that kind of person. Every agency in the country wanted Paul Keister, but he decided to come here, even though Shimano was our biggest account. Today it's easy for people to see things in the agency, which makes it harder for us to interview the people that see, *really* see, what's there. Jeff Steinhour: At least once a week, someone asks me "How do you guys do this?" and everyone thinks there's a shortcut. People want to believe there's an easier way. But there isn't. Our first goal wasn't very lofty. It was just: "Let's get an account outside of Florida." And as funny as that may sound today, a lot of regional agencies around the country have business right in their backyard, but having enough momentum to get a national piece of business is hard. So that was our goal. Alex: And that was Shimano. Jeff Steinhour: And that was Shimano, in 1995. Alex: Which we still have. Jeff Steinhour: Yes, and the next year's goal was to win a piece of business that someone has heard of. And we did that. Then the third year's goal was even better. Alex said: "This year we're gonna win something that my mother has heard of." And that was Schwinn. So, as you can see, pretty humble beginnings. But all along the way, we've said, "Go back to the work. Follow the work. It's about the work." And I think that is the reason that we can stay focused at 40 people, or 400 people. Jeff Hicks: One of the things we say a lot is that not all revenue is created equal, and I think a lot of businesses–

Alex: I've never said that. But it's good. (Laughter.) Jeff Hicks: I think it's something that businesses lose sight of a lot of times. It's tempting when you see a big account. We find ourselves asking, "Should we get into pharmaceuticals? Should we get into this category?" You see these giant dollar figures, but you have to realize they come with a certain type of work, or with things that might contaminate what we hold sacred. It's very counterintuitive, but every time we've made a decision to follow the work, it's been a catalyst for the agency. Alex: Yes. And when Florida *truth* happened we finally had the budget to put behind the work. All those bike accounts taught us how to be creative with a limited budget, but now we were able to do gear and inserts and a lot things that we've become well known for doing. Then national *truth* came up, and we were too small to pitch it, so we thought, "Hey we gotta partner with somebody, cause we got a great case history here. Maybe BBDO will partner with us. Or someone else." And I thought, "It's over, dude. No one's gonna partner with us." But Jeff pretty much willed it to happen and we went up and met with Arnold, and met with Pete Fevat who is creative director up there, and together we went and got national *truth*. And that was, well, huge. Andrew: 200 million. Jeff Hicks: The first year. Alex: So now we were, now we were taking this thing that we had, and bringing it to a national stage, so that was a big moment. And we continued to learn. So that when we got invited to pitch MINI, we used everything we learned from *truth*. With *truth*, we had to invent a brand from scratch. MINI was in the same situation. And we took all the tactics we learned from youth marketing, which were very different, and applied them to a car account. And we won MINI. Jeff Hicks: And then came IKEA. Alex: Yes, IKEA was great. But it still makes me a little sad to see it on this chart. We don't fail very often. People might be surprised that I use the word "fail" when we did so much great work with IKEA, but they aren't here any more, so in some sense, we failed. Anyway, then Molson happened. Jeff Hicks: Twin labels. Alex: Yes, more good stuff, and then right about here (points to chart) we moved to this building. A lot of you haven't experienced our old offices now. But they were terrible. I mean, they were. Andrew: Like a dentist's office. Alex: They were like a not very successful dentist's office (audience laughter) and um....Andrew: With up-to-date magazines though. Alex: Yeah we had fresher magazines. And some wicker furniture. And fake ivy. I mean, the old offices where gnarly. They were so bad we would lose pitches. (Laughter.) Jeff Hicks: It's true. Jeff Steinhour: Compass Bank has been a client of ours for six years. And during the pitch, the number two shareholder, this heavy hitter from Houston, Texas, gets on the elevator in our old building, and looks at all the fake wood and says, "Sure don't spend a lot on facilities do they?" (Audience laughter.) Chuck: We had great views, not like anyone ever had time to look at the sailboats. Alex: So Jeff and I come over here to the new building during construction, and we were standing over in that corner, and we just both looked at each other and said "Are we this cool?" Like, "Can we really occupy this space?" Jeff Hicks: It was terrifying...Alex: It *was* terrifying. We were from a much more humble place. And we thought: "Could we live up to the space?" But our first new business meeting was Virgin. And, we were trying come up with something kinda fun to do, and the space is so dramatic, and we started to execute a few ideas, and they were really looking like shit. And then Swartz and his partner came up with this idea of red paper airplanes. They folded 500 red paper airplanes and just put them all over. And when the client walked in, it looked amazing. So we met with them, and showed some research, some thinking. It was supposed to be the meeting before the final meeting, but they called it short and said, "You know what, we've just got a good feeling about this," and they just gave us the business. I really don't think that 35 paper airplanes that we could have put on the couch in the old office would have quite done it. (Laughter.) So that was big. Jeff Hicks: A lot of you may not know the story of BURGER KING.® Alex: Yeah, BURGER KING® happened next. I was in London and Jeff called and said, "Hey, BURGER KING® wants us to do this project, but here's the hitch, we got one week." So we showed up at that meeting, and we presented for three hours before we presented any television work. That was a huge deal for them. We didn't do it on purpose, we just start from the product and work out. At the end of the meeting they started talking about us taking the whole account, and our attitude was like, "No...we cannot...BURGER KING® has a reputation of being the worst client in America, we cannot take that piece of business." So we thought we could take one part of it maybe. And they said "Yep, do that part of it, and then also you could do this other part of it." So we said, "OK we could do those two parts but that's it." And they were like, "Sounds great. You guys do these three parts and we're good."(Laughter.) And that's how we got BURGER KING.® Jeff Hicks: But the thing about getting BURGER KING® was, it made it hard to balance the agency. At one point it was 40 to 50 percent of the agency's revenue, which is a really scary spot to be in. And part of what's always been so cool about the agency is that we can make the decisions that are right for us. If someone's mistreating the agency we don't necessarily need their business so much that we can't get out. But it was a scary situation with BURGER KING,® because we still would have followed our principles but it would have been a sort of catastrophy were things to unfold that way. Alex: Luckily we were able to strike a balance by getting Volkswagen. But it wasn't supposed to be Volkswagen that did it. At first, we thought we would go after BMW, since it was going into review. We were already in the BMW fold with MINI, so when the review was announced, we were thinking, "Pretty cool, right?" But MINI did not want to share the agency with BMW. That left us in a place where we were still lacking the balance to protect the agency, and so we were very fortunate to get VW. That got us the balance, not to mention a chance to work with the greatest automotive brand of all time. Chuck: And don't forget Miller Lite. Alex: Yes, recently we got Miller Lite, and we had a big party and now we can get free booze. (Laughter.) And I guess that about brings us up to date. Jeff Hicks: Hold on. There's one thing I wanted to say before we move on. A story I wanted to share that I think says a lot about this place. (Holding up board that says "We're all in this together.") In 1997 we were the agency for the South Florida Mercedes–Benz dealers. I had kind of just joined the agency and had made a decision that we didn't have the horsepower in the media area that we needed. So we replaced the person that was running the media department at that time. It was a really agonizing decision. It was a senior person in the agency. But we felt it was the right thing for the long term for the agency and we made that decision and went on with it. And we found out a week later that that person was very tied into the Mercedes-Benz business and I remember so vividly I was standing in the D concourse and Chuck called me and he said, "Mercedes-Benz just fired us. They're doing a review." And there was this long silence on the other end of the phone. So I went into Chuck's office the next day, and I felt responsible because it was my decision, and he said, "This was the agency's decision. We'll deal with this together." That's when I learned that no one person in this place succeeds or fails. We all succeed or fail together. And Chuck helped me work through that one and since then 100 other ones but for me that's a really important thing. It's really true of this place, when someone screws up. Alex: Everyone's under the bus. OK, questions. Audience: Why is there a plus sign in the name? Alex: No big reason, it was just instead of an ampersand, another way to add an initial to the name. Chuck has always been a little bit upset about it because it seems to make a bigger deal of my initial. (Laughter.) So there was a lot of debate. Chuck: Actually it never occurred to me until just now. Alex: Anyone else? DJ: How would you define success? When do you know that you've actually achieved success? Alex: I think that it's a very personal thing. I can't really define it for you. For me it's when I'm able to do work that doesn't feel like work. When I hate leaving and I love coming in and I'm interested in at least more than one thing I'm currently spending my time with. A big part of me being interested is that I like the notion of something going out into pop culture and seeing the effect it has on people. So I don't know what success is for you. I think it's the benjamins, right? Andrew: I have no idea. I mean, this'll be weird. There are a couple of ways to look at it. When I feel most successful I fear death. When I have a great idea. Alex: You've got something to lose. Andrew: Or something really big happens I think I'm gonna die instantly. And I won't be there to continue to experience that feeling of what that is. Or see how it ends up manifesting itself in the world. So I fear death intensely at the moment of success. (Laughter.) Alex: Hope that helps. Jeff Hicks: I think one of the magic things about the agency is that we don't feel successful. People will call and they're like, "You guys are on fire" and we don't see ourselves that way. Audience: How will you keep the culture intact if we keep getting bigger? Do you think it will be possible to keep the agency the same as it continues to grow? Alex: Great question. Yes, I worry. But, I don't worry about a culture intact or keeping it the same. I worry more about it staying the same. And I worry about arrogance. Because if you're arrogant, if you're convinced you're right, then you want to do the same things over and over. As an agency we've changed over and over and over. The worry, well it's more a hope, the hope I have is that everybody understands that it's not static. And that if you're here, you're part of the answer to that question. In the end there is no relationship between size and quality. There's a relationship between culture and what you believe and the quality of work. Audience: What's your favorite piece of work? You know, the thing the agency has done that you are the most proud of. Alex: I don't know. One of the things you'll notice about the place is that there's no memory. We don't put up the work. You know you can walk down the halls– maybe some people put up work in their offices–but most agencies have a gallery section. They've got areas where they're constantly playing their reel. We don't have that. If you don't believe that the thing you're working on right now is the most fascinating thing the agency's ever done there's something wrong. Jeff Steinhour: You know what this makes me think of; it makes me think how this stuff never gets any easier. No matter how much success you've had, you still have to roll up your sleeves if you're gonna continue making it happen. Alex: I think that's something. That it's important for us to remember just because we're larger and we've done more of it, What we do is still going to be hard. You run into a client that's hard to convince. You run into a situation that seems to have barrier after barrier. It's always been that way and you can't really expect anything else. But you can expect the people around you to help remove the barriers. Chuck: When we started a long, long time ago, we had accounts like the *Miami Herald* and the Florida Marlins, they didn't come here because they wanted to buy great work, they came here because Coconut Grove was on their way home. Alex: That made it, in a way, harder. Chuck: We had to learn to be relentless and show great work and when good stuff died, go back with better stuff. Alex: One more question. We can do one more question. Da Young: Why did you decide to write *Hoopla* and will we get a free copy? (Laughter.) Alex: People don't even know that there is a *Hoopla* book. Does everyone know there's a *Hoopla* book? Really? Jeff Hicks: It's on Amazon. Alex: We decided to, we actually….A lot of people wanted us to write a book and we have resisted writing a book. The reason is sort of this notion of putting things under glass and saying, "Hey, here's our way." But we are doing it more where it can be about the evolution and it can be about the reality of the work and what it's like to work here. It's more about the process than the pieces. It's not a museum showing of work. We finally just said, "Yeah. OK. We can probably figure out a way to do this." And Burnie didn't have anything to do for a year and a half. We saw on his calendar he was open for a year and a half. (Laughter.) Chuck: We can promise a minimum 10 percent discount for everyone. Alex: Across the board. Thank you. Chuck: Thanks for coming you guys.

In what has to be the mac daddy of all PR hits, 60 Minutes did a short piece on CP+B's recruitment campaign for Google.

nables him
notech is
chinery it
he indus-
ough that
research
ppears, he
from low-
scale fac-

en patent-
ocesses he
ure large-
products
nding the
te just 18
stment of
e says it is
n't neces-
. Still, he
rchers to
echniques.
and prof-
the exist-
dditional
tions (un-
a major
al decision
growth is
that may
Atomate.
ew invest-
e. Cash in
survival,
expenses
only be
. Startups
improv-
es accept-
k options
are hired,
occupied,
isillusion-
ke.
cess rarely
has to be
things not
echnology
ecting, it's
lucky, but

MA-based
or *TR*
ompanies
profiled nor endorses them as investments.
To share your company's story with Joe,
e-mail joe.chung@technologyreview.com.

ate on constrained university budgets, by
producing equipment that's already
adapted for the nano world.

While Lim must protect his clients'
jealously guarded intellectual-property
secrets, he believes that Atomate's role as

1. Solve this cryptic equation, realizing of course that values for M and E could be interchanged. No leading zeros are allowed.

WWWDOT - GOOGLE = DOTCOM

answer:

2. Write a haiku describing possible methods for predicting search traffic seasonality.

answer:

3.
```
      1
     1 1
     2 1
   1 2 1 1
 1 1 1 2 2 1
```

What is the next line?

answer:

4. You are in a maze of twisty little passages, all alike. There is a dusty laptop here with a weak wireless connection. There are dull, lifeless gnomes strolling about. What dost thou do?

   ○ A) Wander aimlessly, bumping into obstacles until you are eaten by a grue.
   ○ B) Use the laptop as a digging device to tunnel to the next level.
   ○ C) Play MPoRPG until the battery dies along with your hopes.
   ○ D) Use the computer to map the nodes of the maze and discover an exit path.
   ○ E) Email your resume to Google, tell the lead gnome you quit and find yourself in whole different world.

5. What's broken with Unix? How would you fix it?

answer:

6. On your first day at Google, you discover that your cubicle mate wrote the textbook you used as a primary resource in your first year of graduate school. Do you:

   ○ A) Fawn obsequiously and ask if you can have an autograph.
   ○ B) Sit perfectly still and use only soft keystrokes to avoid disturbing her concentration.
   ○ C) Leave her daily offerings of granola and English toffee from the food bins.
   ○ D) Quote your favorite formula from the textbook and explain how it's now your mantra.
   ○ E) Show her how example 17b could have been solved with 34 fewer lines of code.

7. Which of the following expresses Google's overarching philosophy?

○ A) "I'm feeling lucky"
○ B) "Don't be evil"
○ C) "Oh, I already fixed that"
○ D) "You should never be more than 50 feet from food"
○ E) All of the above

8. How many different ways can you color an icosahedron with one of three colors on each face?

answer:

What colors would you choose?

answer:

9. This space left intentionally blank. Please fill it with something that improves upon emptiness.

answer:

10. On an infinite, two-dimensional, rectangular lattice of 1-ohm resistors, what is the resistance between two nodes that are a knight's move away?

answer:

11. It's 2 PM on a sunny Sunday afternoon in the Bay Area. You're minutes from the Pacific Ocean, redwood forest hiking trails, and world class cultural attractions. What do, you do?

answer:

12. In your opinion, what is the most beautiful math equation ever derived?

answer:

13. Which of the following is NOT an actual interest group formed by Google employees?

○ A. Women's basketball
○ B. Buffy fans
○ C. Cricketeers
○ D. Nobel winners
○ E. Wine club

14. What will be the next great improvement in search technology?

answer:

2

This is Not a Brain Surgery – first 10-digit prime found in consecutive

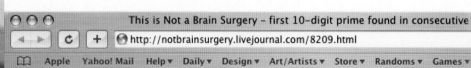

http://notbrainsurgery.livejournal.com/8209.html

Apple   Yahoo! Mail   Help ▼   Daily ▼   Design ▼   Art/Artists ▼   Store ▼   Randoms ▼   Games ▼

This is Not a Brain Surgery ...

Links

[**Links:** | [Home] [Add to My Yahoo!] [RSS feed for this blog]]

first 10-digit prime found in consecutive digits of e	[Jul. 10th, 2004 **12:05 am**]

◀ ♥ ▶

[**Tags**|google, haskell]
[**mood**|accomplished]

Recently riding my motorcycle on highway 101, south of San Francisco I've noticed big advertisement poster:

(I stole the picture from some later post in spanish who also found the number. When I worked on this, google search did not find any results for this puzzle).

Out of curiosity I decided to find out what it is. Since I am still learning Haskell, I decided that that would be nice Haskell exercise. It was nice exercise indeed, in course of which I have learned more about Haskell and things like Rabin-Miller Probable Prime Test and Spigot Algorithm

Well, I did it and was able to find number. I went to the site, expecting something exiting, but it just says *"Congratulations. You've made it to level 2"* and offers next puzzle. Frankly, without knowing what it is about (I guess this is a new way to screen employees) I am not very inclined to spend more time solving their puzzles. Also, the next puzzle they offer is of kind I detest: trying to find next number in sequence. I hate when people ask something like this on interviews.

So, being dissapointed for being sent to wild goose chanse without any gratification, I decided to share the answer to their first problem. I hope search engines pick up this page soon and they will have more potential candidates knocking on the door of their second level.

The prime they were asking for is 7427466391.

I will apprecite if somebody who will get through all their puzzles will tell me what it was about.

UPDATE *(September 2004)*: I would like to thank all of you who took their time to let me know that this is Google recruitment campaign. After solving second part of the puzzle I was able to see that for myself. So if you are looking for the answers: your got them right here. You are welcome to read the rest of my blog (or even subscribe to new posts with RSS).

link   post comment

Comments:

From: 👤 bird_owl
Date: July 10th, 2004 - 02:45 pm

(Link)

Your speed is

2.9 mph

do.

Groove your body for 10 minutes 3 times a day

do. build

Groove your body for 10 minutes 3 times a day

Groove your body for 10 minutes 3 times a day.

do.

do. axe

Muscles Worked

Deltoids
Triceps
Latissimus Dorsi
Quadriceps

Groove your body 10 minutes 3 times a day.

Bed

When you're homeless the world looks different. To help, call 571-2273. **THE MIAMI RESCUE MISSION**

House.

When you're homeless,
you see the world differently.
To help call 571-2273.

THE MIAMI RESCUE MI

"SPICY"
TENDERCRISP™

★★★★ ★★★★ ★★★★
Manos De Clavo
JUGOSO GRANDE BOCADO
PLUMAS PICANTE

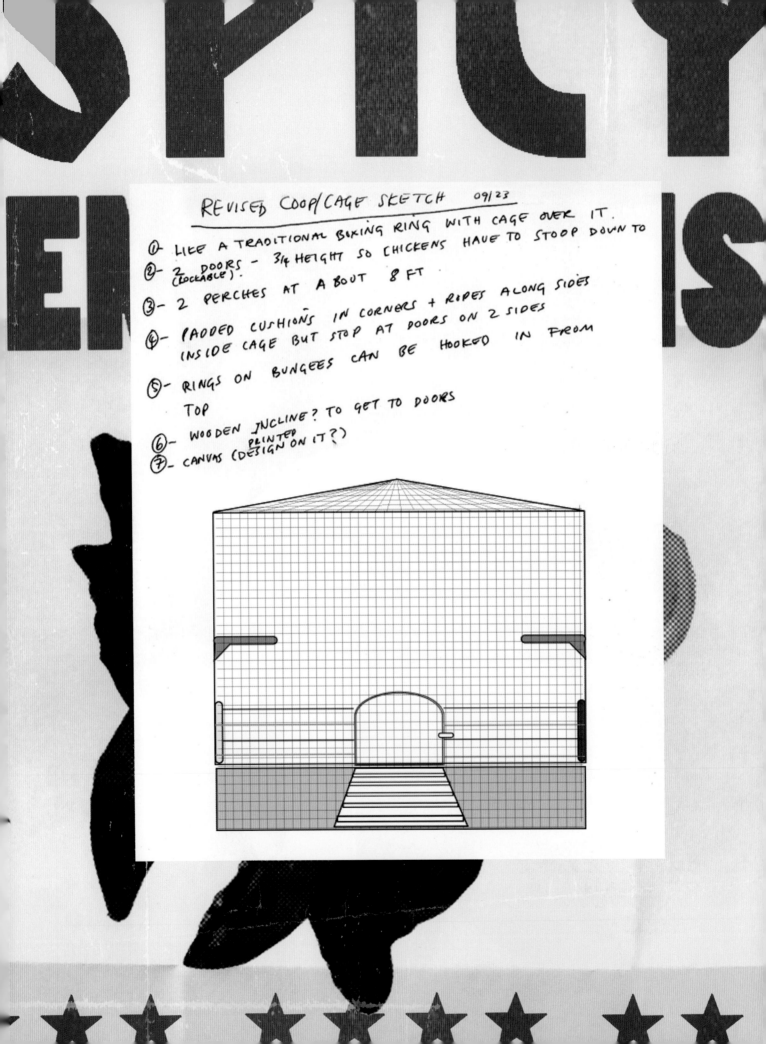

REVISED COOP/CAGE SKETCH   09/23

① LIKE A TRADITIONAL BOXING RING WITH CAGE OVER IT.

② 2 DOORS – 3/4 HEIGHT SO CHICKENS HAVE TO STOOP DOWN TO (LOCKABLE).

③ 2 PERCHES AT ABOUT 8 FT

④ PADDED CUSHIONS IN CORNERS + ROPES ALONG SIDES INSIDE CAGE BUT STOP AT DOORS ON 2 SIDES

⑤ RINGS ON BUNGEES CAN BE HOOKED IN FROM TOP

⑥ WOODEN INCLINE? TO GET TO DOORS

⑦ CANVAS (DESIGN PRINTED ON IT?)

The guys building the cage dubbed it the Poultry Penitentiary. Seems working 48 hours straight on building a giant birdcage from a schematic that might as well have been on the back of a napkin got to them. "Where the fuck does the perch go?!" "Why do they have to have planks?!" "How big are these stupid chickens?!" When the last welding torch went out, the lights went up, and over 400 extras filled the stands. Question: When does a film shoot become an event? When the extras bring their own beer and get into the show like it's for real. It was funny at first but then not so funny as crowd members had to be "escorted" out by security due to fan fighting. In the Chicken Sandwich World Championship, like any great sporting event, some take their passion too far.

MSN Home | My MSN | Hotmail | Search | Shopping | Money | People & Chat

NEW USERS: SIGN UP • LOG IN

FOX SPORTS **Chickenfighting**

○ FOXSports ● Web with msn Search | **SEARCH**

IN ASSOCIATION WITH

SportingNews

14:25:10:25

CLOSE ✕

HOME | NFL▾ | MLB▾ | NBA▾ | NHL▾ | NASCAR▾ | NCAA FB▾ | NCAA BK▾ | GOLF▾ | **CHICKENFIGHTING**▾ | MORE▾ | FANTASY▾ | ARCADE | SHO

Chickenfighting Home . Fighters . Photo Gallery . Watch on DirectTV

TENSIONS BROIL

It could be the entourage, the intense drive of these two fighters, or just their dangerous proximity, but someone's temper got the best of them at the recently held WCFO championship weigh-in.
Full Story ...

• Weigh-in Video Highlights

NEWS

• Spicy and "Pappi" Join Forces
• Vegas gets in on the chicken fighting action
• Out of the Shadow: Spicy's Perspective
• Millions get WCFO screensaver by clicking secret link
• Fighters will vie to psych each other out
• An Hour with "Pappi"
• TC's feather skyrockets on eBay

Odds | Newswire | Rumors | Photos

FEATURES

Hot rumors
The World Chicken Fighting Organization has always attracted its share of hearsay.

Experts and Fans Divided
Whether it is a difference of taste, values, or personal style, people are picking sides.

Want to be a WCFO ring girl?
You may be the next to grace the coop of a WCFO event near you.

Origins of the Poultry Penitentiary
Explore Chicken fighting's shadowy past and the fight cage.

Two chickens. One quest.
BURGER KING PRESENTS
CHICKEN SANDWICH
WORLD CHAMPIONSHIP

TV LISTINGS

Chicken Sandwich World Championship

BURGER KING PRESENTS CHICKEN SANDWICH WORLD CHAMPIONSHIP
NOV 5TH, 10 PM EST

Spicy takes on TC in cage match for first ever televised championship bout. November 5th, 10 p.m. eastern on DirecTV channel 340.

DIRECTV **FIGHT REMINDER**
Enter your email address or cell phone number to get a text message reminder an hour before fight time.

[Sign Up]

HOT SPORTS OPINIONS

Don "The Dragon" Wilson
TC expects to once again be in the spotlight.
He's seen both WCFO fighters at their best and has as good an idea as anyone about how this fight is going to end up. And, as of right now, he's leaning towards TC for the win.

More Hot Sports Opinion

FREE VIDEO

Spicy training
Spicy, "the Red Riot" employing his unorthodox training regiment.

More WCFO Video
• Uncut weigh-in tape
• TC training
• Head to head

PLAY ▶
Video Home

FANTASY CHICKEN FIGHTING

Chickenfight.com
The First real-time multiplayer fighting game

BURGER KING

PRESENTS

CHICKEN SANDWICH
WORLD
CHAMPIONSHIP

FREE ON DIRECTV PAY PER VIEW
NOV 12TH 8PM

tv.

W.C.F.A.

professional sport that should not be tried at home. This telecast is owned by the Wor
tempt to rerecord or rebroadcast requires direct written permission from the W.C.F.A.

Weigh-In : Fight Promo

Tensions broil at the Weigh-In. Was it the entourage, or just Spicy and TC's dangerous proximity? But someone's temper got the best of them at the recently held WCFO championship Weigh-In.

Training : Fight Promo

Nothing's more grueling than a chicken fight in a steel coop. Except maybe the training in preparation for it. This never-before-seen glimpse into the brutal pre-bout workouts of TC and Spicy is truly inspiring.

Head to Head : Fight Promo

Fight promotion at its best. Don't check your blood pressure afterwards, unless you want a heart attack.

CONT

THE

Savage? Beautiful? Epic? Contro

Heart of a Champion:
TC, The Golden Bird. He may be beautiful, but when it comes to winning the Chicken Sandwich World Championship he's willing to sacrifice everything. Learn what it takes to raise the belt over your head.

Stepping out of a Shadow:
Spicy, The Red Riot. He's an unapproachable bird that shuns the spotlight and embraces the dark side of the sport. Find out why this bird teeters between greatness and madness.

Best Damn Sports Show Period:
A seminal moment in our sport. Watch as TC and Spicy carry the chicken fighting torch into the world of big time professional sports. Chicken fighting will never be the same.

ENTS

GHT:

sial? Disturbing? Brutal? Funny?

Chill Aptitude Test(CAT)#38567-000001

NINJAS

VS

SAMURAIS

With a more lax code of ethics and really cool shoes with their own separate big toe compartment, you might think ninjas were more chill, even than samurais, who were pretty chill to begin with. But you would be wrong. Neither side is very chill. Freaking out with edged weapons is never chill.

To Whom It May Concern:

Don't condemn me for throwing this message-laden bottle into our pristine oceans. Yes, it could have been accidentally lodged in the blowhole of a baleen whale, starving the great beast of oxygen and other stuff it needs, but I assure you, that was not my intent. Really what I was hoping for was to prove that 3/4 of the Earth's surface is just a giant form of media, connecting one man to another despite fluctuations in weather and geopolitical climate. If this message did in fact obstruct the breathing of some delicate marine mammal and that creature washed up on your shore, I would appreciate it if we could keep this just between the two of us. Otherwise, visit *www.lavidahoopla.com/cast2sea* and tell us where and when you found it and any peculiarities worth mentioning. Thanks.

Caster's Name _____

Casting Date _____

Casting Location _____

Permanent polar pack ice

CURRENTS

Cold current

Warm current

Drift per hour (Each thick stroke above shaft indicates 1 nautical mile)

Drift per hour (Each thin stroke below shaft indicates ¼ nautical mile)

Seasonal drift during northern winter

Kamchatka Current

Alaska Current

Oya Siwo

California Current

North Pacific Drift

Kuro Siwo (Japan Current)

Gulf

North Equatorial Current

Antilles

Equatorial

Counter Current

Caribbean

South Equatorial Current

Peru (Humboldt) Current

East Australian Current

Drift

West Wind Drift

Cape Horn

SEA ICE

Average limit of polar pack, inaccessible to bottled messages
Average maximum limit of ice preventing navigation by bottles
Average maximum limit of pack and land-fast ice affecting normal navigation (in southern hemisphere, the absolute maximum)
Average maximum limit of icebergs and drifting ice (western North Atlantic)
Absolute maximum limits of icebergs
× × × Exceptional positions of icebergs (North Atlantic)

Regions accessible to heavily built vessels:

8 to 12 months	2 to 4 months
6 to 8 months	2 months or less
4 to 6 months	with icebreaker assistance, 2 months or less

North Atlantic Drift

Benguela Current

Portugal C.

Canary Current

North Equatorial Current

Guinea Current

South Equatorial Current

Brazil Current

Benguela Current

Aguilhas Current

Southwest and Northeast Monsoon Drift

Equatorial Counter Current

South Equatorial Current

West Australian Current

West Wind Drift

West Wind Drift

Prepared by AMERICAN GEOGRAPHICAL SOCIETY for the DEPARTMENT OF STATE

He's part fairy, part motivational coach, and all testosterone. He's the Fairy Snapmother, and he's snapping would-be momma's boys with his spicy, smoked-meat hammer.

Giant adhesive likenesses of the Fairy Snapmother were placed in the actual riding environments, directing skaters and BMXers to do killer railslides or drop-offs, should they be up to the task.

THE OPEN LETTER

To Whom It May Concern,

Have you ever seen someone driving an open car with the top up? You kind of get the feeling they have something to hide. Like someone wearing a trench coat and sunglasses. Somehow, that thin piece of fabric is more of a barrier than the strongest steel.

If they were driving a car with a regular roof, you probably wouldn't notice. But since they've intentionally closed an open car, you can't help but think they're a closed person. After all, they've made a conscious decision to be closed when the opportunity to be open was right there. Open people would never do this.

Open people don't care what their hair looks like. Open people don't mind picking a few bugs out of their teeth. If they drive past an oil refinery, open people welcome the smell. If panhandlers approach them at a red light, open people never panic. Most motorcycle people are open people. They've just opted for two wheels instead of four. All kids are open people. This is why they try so hard to stuff their heads and arms out the window. But most of them soon outgrow it.

In the old days, it was easy to tell open people from regular people. Open people drove around in goggles and leather caps. They took a lot of back roads. Whenever possible, they kept the accelerator mashed to the floor. When they stopped to gas up, the grimy outline of their eyewear made them look like racoons. Today it's harder to spot an open person. But they're still the exception and not the rule. Even here at MINI, most of us are regular roofers.

If you are considering a new car, the best thing you can do is be honest with yourself. Are you an open person? Please take some time to think about it. The fact is we didn't make very many of these things. And with MSRP starting at $22,000,* they could easily end up in the wrong hands.

Always Open,
MINI

A HISTORY OF THE GO-KART

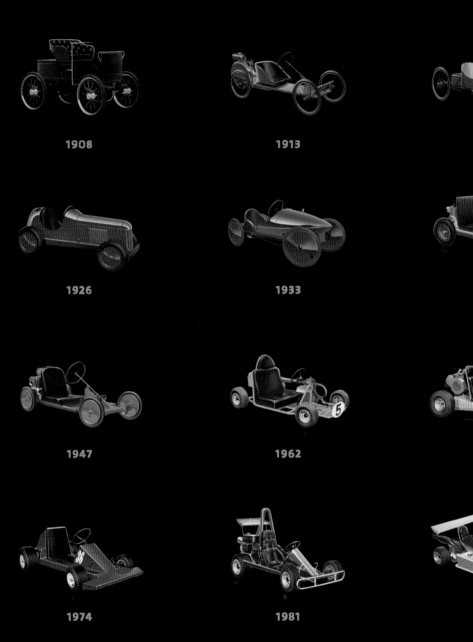

1908

1913

1921

1926

1933

1941

1947

1962

1967

1974

1981

1988

1993

2001

2004

TOPL

LOUN

TOPLESS TOPLESS TOPLES

Sometimes if media is done cool
enough, it seeps into other media.
This neon outdoor effort, extolling the
virtues of topless motoring, actually
made it into a 50 Cent music video.

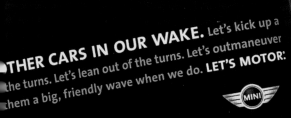

Roberts, Living Legend

Dutch Grand Prix at
ame year; and then
the Transatlantic
s. The first one of
especially memo-
ying to learn how
the Europeans, and
ring to deal with
wed up at Brands
to race. Or so we
old ACU track
year, he must have
ppar-

MINI COOPER S

WHY DID YOU OPEN THIS?

The page numbers clearly indicate that it does not exist. Yet something bothered you. It was closed. So you opened it. Obviously, you are an open person. Someone who isn't afraid to explore uncharted territory. A maverick. Just the type to consider the MINI Cooper Convertible. The fact is, we didn't make very many of these things. And we don't want them going to people who'll drive around with the top up on a nice day. But since you've proven that you're open, we can tell you stuff we wouldn't tell a regular person. Such as, MSRP for the MINI Cooper Convertible starts at $22,000.* After all, we want to make sure they fall into the right hands. Like yours.

THE MINI CONVERTIBLE. ALWAYS OPEN.

CONVERTIBLE CONTRACT

1816001

In recognition of the limited number of MINI Convertibles and MINI USA's responsibility to make sure that MINI Convertibles get into the hands of **open** individuals, MINI USA asks all MINI Convertible Owners to enter into this contract. **Upon signature of this contract MINI Owner agrees to keep MINI Convertible top down in accordance with this contract.**

On the date of ____/____/____ forward, this document serves as a binding contract between the two parties of:

Family Name	First (Given)	Middle Initial

Address	City	State

Zip Code	Vehicle VIN #	Drivers License #	State

(hereby known as "MINI Owner") and MINI USA.

90-10 Clause. MINI Owner hereby agrees to motoring with top in down, or **open** position, for at least 90% of an operating period. This time period only applicable while MINI Convertible remains in the legal possession of MINI Owner. MINI USA recognizes and hereby agrees 10% of an operating period allows for MINI Convertible top be in the up, or **closed,** position.

MINI Owner recognizes the following conditions below are acceptable reasons, under contract, for having the top in closed position: (please initial)

_____ 1. **When motoring in rain under 25 miles per hour.**

_____ 2. **When motoring through a car wash and/or having car washed manually.**

_____ 3. **When parked outside for an unexpected extended time period.** (MINI USA doesn't recommend any MINI, including MINI Cooper, MINI Cooper S, and MINI Convertible be parked for an extended time.)

_____ 4. **When temperature drops below freezing point (32°F/ 0°C).**

_____ 5. **After hair plug surgery.**

_____ 6. **When within earshot of an outdoor banjo and/or kazoo concert.**

_____ 7. **When driving through biblical-size swarm of locusts.**

_____ 8. **To avoid riotous teenaged groupies.‡**

fig. A — Stage 1

fig. B — Stage 2

fig. C — Stage 3

fig. D — Stage 4 *See Amendment

Any other infractions may be reviewed on a case-by-case basis by your MINI Dealer.

Constitution of Open. MINI Owner hereby understands to the best of his/her knowledge all four stages of MINI Convertible top (See figures A, B, C, D).

MINI Owner recognizes the following: ☐ **Stage 1** (fig. A), as **not open** and can be a violation of the 90-10 clause. ☐ **Stage 2** (fig. B), sunroof position, is recognized as a secondary **open** position only when windows are in a down position, maximizing MINI Owner to outdoor elements. ☐ **Stage 3** (fig. C), transition stage, is fully recognized as neither an **open** position nor a **closed** position, but a **transition** position. To avoid criticism and ridicule as a novice **open** motorer, MINI USA has designed the car as "undrivable" during this stage. The MINI Convertible will not shift into gear until the top is in the full **open** position. ☐ **Stage 4** (fig. D), is fully recognized by both MINI USA and its subsidiaries as **open** and fulfills the requirements of this contract and the desired emotional, physical and social needs of the MINI Owner.

This **open** contract extends to third parties that operate MINI Owner's Convertible while in the legal possession of MINI Owner. This includes but is not limited to: husbands, wives, brothers, sisters, sons, daughters, step-daughters, step-sons, best friends, next door neighbors, tennis instructors, sugar-mommas, sugar-daddies, girlfriends, vengeful ex-girlfriends, tow-truck operators, valets, and/or joy riders. MINI Owner accepts full responsibility and recognizes that any **non-open** motoring by anyone in his/her said vehicle (See VIN # above) is a direct violation of this convertible contract. _____ (initials)

Terms and condition of weather. MINI Owner agrees to be knowledgeable of local and/or regional weather patterns at least 48 hours in advance. Thus allowing MINI Owner to plan to the best of his or her ability motoring times that allow for optimal motoring (See 90-10 clause). If MINI Owner cannot determine weather patterns by him/herself, he/she should seek professional consultation. MINI Owner should not determine weather patterns due to "feelings" in his or her bones, an aching knee or elbow and/or through observing strange behavior of pets. MINI USA recognizes acts of God, which may or may not include lightning storms, tornadoes, earthquakes, hurricanes, raining frogs, or the arrival of the four horseman of the apocalypse. These events cannot be planned for, therefore MINI USA relies on each MINI Owner's judgment, that being of sound mind, to take proper action that fulfills the 90-10 clause of this legally non-binding agreement.

**Amendment to Stage 4 (fig. D). MINI Convertible operated in Stage 4 with windows in the up position fulfills only the minimum requirement of this contract. MINI Owner may be tempted to keep the windows up to curb wind from tossing hair and/or any other reason. MINI Owner understands that although the position of top down with windows up meets the obligations of this convertible contract, it is like buying a nudie magazine to read the articles. _____ (initials)

OFFICIAL USE ONLY: / / / MINIUSA.COM	
	MINI Owner _____ Date
	MINI Dealer _____ Date

SIGN HERE

‡ Only applicable for those with rock star status.

...I don't know why, but the agency just generally has a thought pattern that's just about the opposite of everybody else's. It makes sense that in this business, thinking that way would be a good thing because you're unlikely to get much attention doing what everybody else is doing. But it's not like we set out to be contrary. We just are. So when MINI announced they were coming out with a convertible (which was undeniably cool), our initial reaction was, "Oh, shit." We'd spent all this time creating a little car brand with a fresh point of view and a scrappy attitude, and now we were going to do what every car company on Earth does when it needs an encore: the convertible. And how do we keep the brand masculine with a tiny car that has no roof?

One of the cool things about working on car accounts is that you get to drive cars that are basically prototypes. So this convertible shows up, and we just started tearing it up. What immediately became obvious was that most of the time convertibles are driven with the top up. Even when the weather is nice. So we made ourselves drive it 100 percent of the time with the top down. Well, our shop borders on a neighborhood where muggings and car jackings are not uncommon. Suddenly, driving with the top down was becoming seriously manned-out shit. We kept it down when panhandlers ambled toward us at stoplights. We kept it down in the rain. We kept it down when we played music that maybe wasn't what the guy next to us in traffic wanted to hear. We were out there, naked to the world, and it made us all tingly.

We wanted other people to feel just as tingly as we felt, so we started at the dealership, by creating a contract that potential buyers were presented, stating that they would keep the top down regardless of social or atmospheric ramifications. We had them sign it. We also constructed a tiny seal that had to be broken before the buyers could put the top up for the first time–so they'd really have to think before they did it. People seemed to be good to their word, and why wouldn't they be? Fabric tops can be the vehicular equivalent of a burka. Life's better when you're not hiding behind a thick layer of fabric...

ALWAYS OPEN.

"Puppeteer"

The Governor of a Midwestern state hired the agency to work on a "project," which later turned out to be his campaign for re-election.

He won.

○ Fake
○ True

GENE SIMMONS vs CP+B

First question. Did you have any idea, when KISS was just starting out, that it would get so big? That you guys would have this meteoric rise to the top, and that it would stay so big, for so long? Gene: Yes. That's crazy to me. That you could know…Gene: It's blind belief. When you get up in the morning you have the realities of life. The third planet from the sun hits you with things like gravity and rules, and when you cross the street you get run over by a bus, whether you plan to or not…and life doesn't care. It just treats you as one of its chess pieces. But when you dream, you're the king. You can fly through the air and completely ignore the consequences. So, did I dream big? Yeah. Did I think it would become as big? Bigger! Well, you guys found your own space, KISS was able to find its own space, and how would you describe that space? Gene: I don't think it matters. I don't think any of those assessments mean very much. The only thing I was ever trying to do was avoid working for a living. Sure, you make a lot of money…more than the leaders of countries actually. More than most of the rich people walking around the planet, and you get to fool around…and the girls sorta pop up here and there. But, the real reward is not having to work for a living, let's not kid ourselves. There are people like Patty Smith and Bruce Springsteen, and all sorts of self-styled artists, who I don't negate, but I believe they delude themselves and us into believing that what they are doing is art. Well, it seems like you guys were the first to really branch off and make it bigger than music. Gene: No, no, no. That's not true. Disney did it a long time before we ever did. So, Walt Disney was the inspiration for KISS? Gene: Sure! What's better than being Disney without the overhead? What exactly does KISS really mean? Gene: I don't care. Once someone buys a ticket or gets a record, what they make of it, or what anyone else makes of it, doesn't really matter. They paid their money; they're entitled to their assessment, but don't go around thinking it means anything. If people want to believe it means cartoony good times, and that is all they get out of it…that's great. There are people that name their children after our songs, and tattoo their bodies, and have a lifestyle that…well…gets pretty close to "KISSanity." If that is what they get out of it, that's fine too. I know that there are people out there that hate us too, but the thing is, we're all too rich to care. Anyway, I think that success is like an impressionistic painting…whatever you get out of it is absolutely valid. Are you the greatest showman on earth? Gene: No. God is. How do you arrive at that conclusion? Gene: Who else would have the balls to say I created everything? I am the end all and the be all…and I want you to have no other god before me. I just want to be the only one. That's ego like no ego I have ever seen. In fact, it sounds like a jealous bitch. God wants to be a rockstar, or, all rockstars want to be God. Take your pick. What you have made of yourself, in life, do you feel like it's the best that you could have done? Gene: No. That's why I have so many projects going. What kind of stuff are you doing these days? Gene: I've taken over worldwide marketing, branding, licensing, and merchandising for the Indy Racing League. And a dozen TV shows, like "Gene Simmons' Family Jewels" on A&E, or a cartoon called "My Dad the Rockstar." There's a ton of stuff in China, South Korea. I'm not done yet. Is it the best I can do? No. I can do much better. Watch me burn rubber. A lot of bands, and I think a lot of people, are afraid of change. But the thing is, it's important to change and continue to evolve…Gene: No. I don't think that at all. In fact I think that's total bullshit. I think its only important to do the stuff that gets you paid, and that you get a kick out of. Something you have a good time doing. I mean, 90 precent of the population of earth gets up every day and goes to work at jobs they hate, and they do it just to get paid. I am no different from any of them, except I happen to love what I do. That sets me apart. Fuck evolving. Unless it's evolving into a guy with more money. Let me tell you something. I absolutely want to get paid, first time, every time. So when I hear some new rock band saying that they aren't really interested in the money, that it's some kind of art or whatever, or that they just want to evolve, then you do me a favor. Give them my post office box, and provide them with the proper wiring instructions, 'cause any dollar they don't want…I would be happy to receive. Speaking of money, is KISS still the marketing tornado we all know and love? I know you have lots of things going on personally, but what about KISS in general. What are you guys up to these days? Gene: Actually, KISS continues bigger than ever. The first KISS coffee house is opening in Myrtle Beach and it'll be a franchise. We have a KISS cartoon that is starting production from Warner Bros. The Hard Rock hotels are all using KISS, there is a KISS Crest campaign. HASBRO just bought out 15 million KISS toothbrushes. Coca-Cola put my face on their bottles in France. Canon just brought out the KISS camera and called it "KISS." And yes, we are going to go out and tour this summer, even with all the other stuff that I am doing. We are going to play Mt. Fuji outdoors to 100,000 people. How did you guys come up with the whole paint and costumes and hellfire thing? I've always wanted to know that. Gene: It's the same damned thing that girls do everyday when they get up in the morning. They have to figure out how to stand out against all the other girls out there, so they put makeup on. So it's just about standing out, you know, making sure your visual thing is…Gene: No. It's about the love. Guys think they have this down, but they don't. They've got shit to learn when it comes to love. You see, most guys might ask, "Do you love me?" But a girl, she'll ask, "How much do you love me?" And I am all about the how much. Ah, ok, last question. What do you think gave you the permission to be more than just a band? Gene: What gave me permission? I gave myself the permission. If I didn't, who would have? Listen. Things aren't going to happen for you automatically. Sitting around and waiting for life to come over and recognize that you are great is not really going to fly. You have to grab life by the scruff of its neck and say, "Deal with it. I'm here." 'Cause every other aspiring model, actress, painter, whatever blah blah blah is trying to do the same thing. How do you make them continue to want to perceive you as great? Gene: Threaten to set their pets on fire.

BUZZWORD BINGO

BUZZWORD BINGO

Card 989879

Model out the lift	Sub-optimize	Win Win Win	Win Win	Under the Radar
Emotional Space	Brand Vision	Strategic Architecture	Roadmap	Holistic Approach
Paradigm Shift	Interfacing	FREE	Segment	Thought Leader
Primary Objectives	Secondary Objectives	Tertiary Objectives	Leveraging	Re-tool
Re-Re-Focus	Re-Focus	Trickle-Down	Implementing	Move Forward

Card 989876

Thought Leader	Roadmap	Re-loop	Strategic Architecture	Re-purpo...
Highly Engage	Plus it up	Under the Radar	Leveraging	Paradig Shift
Facilitating	Emotional Space	FREE	Expense Overrun	Activati Plan
Interfacing	Marginalized	Re-tool	Trickle-Down	Size i...
Primary Objectives	Paradigm Shift	Brand Vision	Cut-through	Sub-opti...

Card 989877

Trickle-Down	Roadmap	Off-site	Leveraging	Tertiary Objectives
Pilot this	Segment	Re-Re-Focus	Primary Objectives	Brand Vision
Underleveraged Assets	Soft Launch	FREE	Take off-line	Implementing
Under the Radar	Dormant	Equities	Granular	Move Forward
Secondary Objectives	Emotional Space	Re-Focus	Model out the lift	Cut-through

Card 989878

Re-loop	Re-purpose	Granular	Take off-line	Plus i...
Size it	Activation Plan	Soft Launch	Underleveraged Assets	Dorma...
Equities	Pilot this	FREE	Cut-through	High... Engag
Off-site	Trickle-Down	Leveraging	Paradigm Shift	Roadm...
Under the Radar	Expense Overrun	Facilitating	Emotional Space	Marginal...

Recyclable

BUZZ WORD BINGO

The search for a new agency can be long and arduous. And, sometimes really boring. If you're stuck in a capabilities presentation with a bunch of people you have no chemistry with, try a game of Buzzword Bingo. Listen for these meaningless business buzzwords and cross them off as you hear them. The first one to complete a row up, down, or diagonally wins first prize: *an extended bathroom break.*

Recyclable

Available for: MAC, PC, Palm OS

www. PORNOMIME .cz

The all-new redesigned GAP opens this fall.
Change. It feels good.™

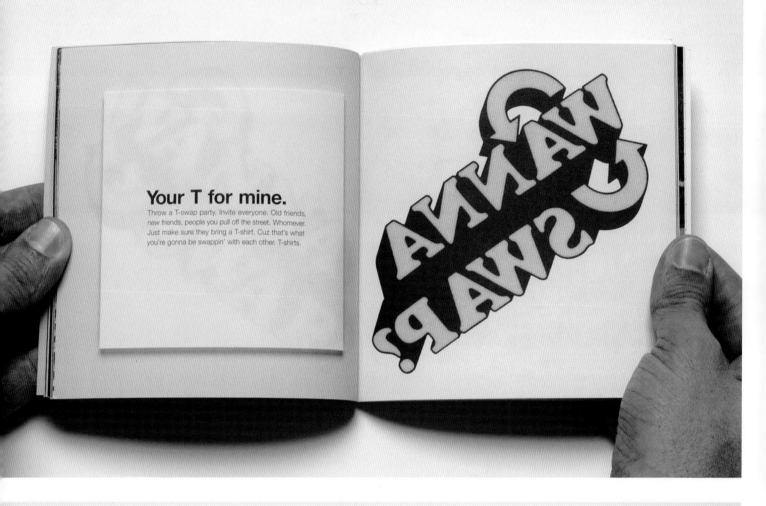

Your T for mine.

Throw a T-swap party. Invite everyone. Old friends, new friends, people you pull off the street. Whomever. Just make sure they bring a T-shirt. Cuz that's what you're gonna be swappin' with each other. T-shirts.

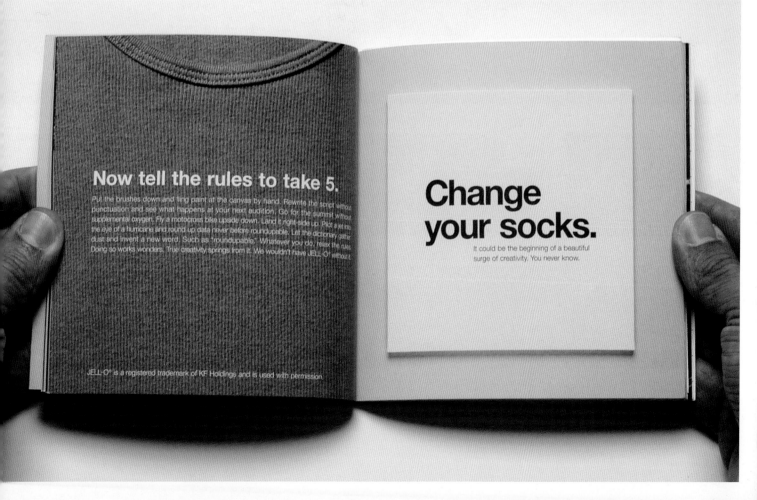

Now tell the rules to take 5.

Put the brushes down and fling paint at the canvas by hand. Rewrite the script without punctuation and see what happens at your next audition. Go for the summit without supplemental oxygen. Fly a motocross bike upside down. Land it right-side up. Pilot a jet into the eye of a hurricane and round up data never before roundupable. Let the dictionary gather dust and invent a new word. Such as "roundupable". Whatever you do, relax the rules. Doing so works wonders. True creativity springs from it. We wouldn't have JELL-O! without it.

JELL-O® is a registered trademark of KF Holdings and is used with permission.

Change your socks.

It could be the beginning of a beautiful surge of creativity. You never know.

pardon our dust

he all-new GAP is coming

goodwill.org

GAP

Clean out your closet.
All-new GAP opens November 4th.
Change. It feels good.™

Change feels good. Especially when all the stuff you're getting rid of goes to Goodwill. This outdoor campaign for GAP helped lots of people rationalize buying a whole new wardrobe.

Clean out
your closet.

All-new GAP coming soon.

Change. It feels good.™

Soon, the all-new GAP will open its doors to the
people of this city. We thank you for your patience
during our major renovation. We also ask you to join in
giving back to our community. Fill this Goodwill bag
with items of clothing from your closet. Whether it's
something you haven't worn in a while or an item
you just bought, your contribution will surely help
change someone's life for the better.

To donate, please visit **goodwill.org**
Drop off locations can be found by clicking on the stores section.
For more information, email change@gap.com or call 1-800-GAP-STYLE.

PRAG
MATISM

In the disposable culture we presently inhabit, is there anything more disposable than an ad? Most of them are consigned to the cultural scrap heap instantaneously–or about as quickly as a person's thumb can hit the "zap" button on the remote. Which is hardly surprising since most ads offer little in the way of usefulness to anyone except (maybe) the advertiser.

But what if an ad *could* actually help people in some real, practical way? Suppose an ad could double as a handy tool for use around the house or a self-contained piece of amusement that could be passed around among friends? What if an ad could assist you in finding your lost dog? Or what if the ad were printed on edible paper, so you could truly "consume" the message if you happened to be in need of a snack? And how about if the ad came with directions on how to fold it into a paper airplane, turn it into a mask, or iron it onto a shirt? Better yet, what if an ad went beyond just promising to make you popular with the opposite sex and actually *did* something about it?

When CP+B was assigned to promote Molson beer a few years back, the agency immediately undertook some research in bars (because advertising does require personal sacrifice at times) and soon discovered that the young men in those bars tend to view their choice of beer as a kind of badge, not unlike the decision to wear a polo shirt versus a shirt from FUBU–it could make a statement to others what kind of guy you are. As a rule, the people that these young men are most trying to impress are young women. Given that, the agency wondered if it might be possible to create a form of Hoopla that could, not to put too fine a point on it, help guys score.

The agency persuaded Molson to create a special, customized label for each of its beer bottles–no small undertaking, as it required Molson to spend over a million dollars retooling its assembly line to make the new labels in 232 different versions. These new labels were affixed to the back of each bottle, providing pickup lines and quirky conversation-starters, just in case tongue-tied guys in bars needed help breaking the ice. (Documented evidence of pickup lines' effectiveness came in from the field, including an e-mail from a couple who reported that they'd had their first kiss shortly after the guy had read the girl the following line from his Molson label: "Let me tell you about my world record.")

Once the ice was broken, a Molson drinker might make further headway by showing off an impressive (though phony) business card–provided courtesy of CP+B via one of its Molson print ads. To make matters even easier for the Molson drinker, there was no need to demonstrate his sensitivity because CP+B had already taken care of that for him: An ad run by the agency in *Cosmopolitan* magazine featured a Molson beer drinker cuddling an armful of cute puppies, thereby planting the idea in female readers' minds that Molson guys had a soft side (Simultaneously, CP+B ran an ad in men's magazines, letting men know that, thanks to the *Cosmo* ad, hundreds of thousands of women had been "preprogrammed for their convenience.")

How many amorous guys closed the deal because of all this is not a matter of public record, but what is known is that the audience responded well to an ad campaign that seemed to be offering something more than just another pitch. The conversation-starter labels got people talking in bars, the faux business cards found their way into wallets, and the "puppies" ad became a pass-around joke shared by men and women alike. All of which made the Molson campaign seem like something dynamic, portable, usable, and maybe not quite as disposable as most ads.

This notion that hype might somehow be shaped into a practical and useful form is not a new one: It goes way back, at least to the 1890s, when an ambitious printer named Henry Beach started charging companies to have their names printed on the handles of flyswatters–one of the first great practical pieces of what has come to be known through the years as "swag." Beach's flyswatter eventually begat promotional hats, key rings, pens, and calendars–each one a piece of advertising that managed to double as a practical, everyday object. Gradually, swag would come to be seen as trivial by Big Marketers with massive media budgets, but none of this will change a basic human fact: *People like stuff they can use. Such stuff tends to stick around. And get passed around.*

Cut to today's modern era of Hoopla, and swag suddenly doesn't seem so old-fashioned anymore. CP+B has, in fact, made an entire business out of it, under the banner of "Hoopla Couture." With both the *truth* and the MINI campaigns, apparel and objects designed specifically for those brands were particularly instrumental in helping fuel and sustain popular movements around those brands. *truth* has spawned an entire line of clothing, including iron-ons. For MINI, the agency made ads that could be folded to create a paper toy version of the car, as well as a driving watch (making it easier to tell time while you're behind the wheel), a driving jacket designed so that a map can fold out of the chest pockets, a barf bag, as well as books and games. For BURGER KING®, the agency created a King mask that has become a bestseller, along with a Subservient Chicken toy. For IKEA, CP+B designed outdoor wild postings during the holiday season that could be used as free wrapping paper. The agency has even taken to making objects and gear of its own, with no client involved.

Bogusky believes that in making these original creations in their various forms, the agency and its clients are creating their own pieces of culture that people can use or absorb in some way. This represents a departure from conventional advertising that tries to piggyback on existing pop culture, e.g., an ad that aims to derive success simply from riding along on someone else's hot TV show or magazine. The piggyback approach has become less effective in recent years as remote control, expanded media options, and new technology such as TiVo have made it possible for the audience to avoid or zap those advertisers who are just along for the ride.

While the era of mass customization poses a growing threat to conventional advertising, it has opened the door for a new and pragmatic type of communication that is geared more to the individual and his or her needs. The change is driven not just by technology but also by a new mindset; according to CP+B, consumers today no longer just consume—they pick, choose, and use. They download, absorb, and assimilate the bits and pieces of a complex culture that enable them to form a unique and diversified persona. All of those selected cultural fragments, processed together, become the raw material people now use to produce their own customized version of "me."

What does all this mean to those who wish to communicate effectively to these new "producers"? That you have to supply them with the cultural materials they need and can actually use. The best Hoopla should take the form of something that people can use to broaden themselves or to impress friends. It should be something people will want to hang onto and make their own—assimilating it as part of their personal cultural repertoire. At a basic level, that might be a piece of very cool, interesting, and useful swag; at a more advanced level, it may involve creating original art, stories, or entertainment that isn't just sponsored by a brand but is the brand.

And if such creations happen to be slightly offbeat and outside the mainstream, it just makes them that much more pragmatic—because it means people can feel like they've discovered something fresh and distinctive that's worth keeping and sharing. The Subservient Chicken, for instance, represents a piece of the culture that BURGER KING® made and now owns; yet at the same time, it is something people happened upon, assimilated as one of their own favorite sites, and then forwarded to friends (who, in turn, did likewise). So in a way, the Chicken is not so different from great swag; people use it for their own purposes, pass it on, spread it around.

It's not easy to determine what might be compelling or useful to the people you may be trying to reach. But as a general rule, there are some things people can always use. One is relevant, truthful, and helpful information; if your communication can provide some of that, it's miles ahead of most advertising and promotion. CP+B's *truth* was chock-full of useful statistics, practical insights on how tobacco marketing works, and tips on how individual teens could fight back in their own ways. As part of the campaign, the agency also created "tools" that were passed along to the consumer, enabling them to help carry the message. This was partly a pragmatic media strategy for CP+B: the agency had reached a media saturation point and therefore needed to teach kids how to create their own media. The tools included stickers along with maps advising teens on where to place the stickers for maximum effect; there were even "poop sticks," which kids could plant themselves; each stick contained a message explaining that cigarettes and dog excrement share some of the same wonderful toxins.

The MINI campaign, meanwhile, tried to impart informational tidbits that might enhance the user experience with the car. The agency created an "unauthorized owner's manual," sent by direct mail to each owner after the purchase, which was filled with practical tips on where you can wedge CDs in the car as well as less practical, more playful advice (Don't worry about the car getting dirty.) designed to help people get into the "Motoring" philosophy. In a similar way, CP+B got involved with rewriting the lease agreement on MINI's convertibles, making the tongue-in-cheek assertion that users were contractually obligated to keep the top down whenever possible.

In making the case for the ultimate power of advertising to change people's lives, CP+B's campaign for Google showed that an ad could be used to identify genius—and then, having identified it, could help genius find an ideal place to flourish. Of course, for the average person, the Google campaign might not have seemed particularly pragmatic or even decipherable: It consisted primarily of banners placed in public places, with cryptic mathematical riddles on them (such as "the first 10-digit prime found in consecutive digits of e."). If you could make sense of the puzzle and solve it, that led you to another puzzle and eventually could land you an offer for a job interview at Google. Which was pretty pragmatic for Google as a screening device while also pragmatic for CP+B—because the whole campaign proved so intriguing to the public that it ended up being featured on *60 Minutes*.

Bogusky maintains that the most pragmatic way to promote a product is to try to contribute to making the product experience better in some way—which can encompass everything from wrapping the product in better packaging to providing little added perks to people who've bought it. The idea is that the closer Hoopla gets to the product itself, the more powerful it can be.

"Imagine the solar system with the sun being the product," Bogusky says. "A great product can market itself if it's designed to do so. The first ring would be packaging—probably the most underleveraged of potential marketing vehicles. The next ring out would include distribution opportunities, and the next ring would be news and PR. And the final, most distant ring would be ads in traditional paid media. In terms of brand-to-consumer interaction, the more you move to the center, the more impact you can have on an individual. "So then why don't most marketers focus more effort on the deepest rings?" I ask. "It's because there's more money to be made on those outer-ring forms of communication, such as advertising. A lot of the focus on advertising is really a matter of people just following the money," he says.

Naturally, PR marketers for Google should follow the money, too, but if they're making compelling forms of communication that personally appeal to people, the money will come in the form of more business. "Out of all marketing vehicles, only from the consumer. OR-B believes that in the field, consumers only get money back from their agency at once. It seems odd to think of people willing to give away the money from businesses that you feel advertising will be an advanced. I totally agree" at their response.

TWIN LABEL

The second or "twin" label instantly communicates the subtle nuances of your personality.

YOU'RE A TIRELESS CHAMPION OF SKINNY DIPPING RIGHTS.

ONLY ONE BEER CAN GET THIS ACROSS.

CONVENTIONAL LABEL
The front label says you're enjoying a premium imported beer from North America's oldest brewery.

TWIN LABEL
The second or "twin" label instantly communicates the subtle nuances of your personality.

Conventional beers don't say much. "I'm laid back" or "Hey, I'm wealthy." That's the best they can do. But with Twin Label Technology, Molson Canadian says a lot more. Like, you've just emerged from a painful relationship, or that one of the qualities you look for in a person is the ability to put their legs behind their head. So why drink a beer that doesn't say anything, when you can drink one that says it all. Molson Twin Label Technology. Hard at work for you. molsontwinlabel.com

GYMNASTICS **COACH** LAGER

ONE-MAN BACHELORETTE **PARTY** LAGER

I'D RATHER BE **PARTYING** OH WAIT, I AM **PARTYING** LAGER

I'VE BEEN **NAUGHTY** LAGER

ART CLASS **MODEL** LAGER

THAR SH **BLOW**

ON THE **REBOUND** LAGER

NICE **MULLET** LAGER

MY MOTHER KNOWS **JUDO** LAGER

HAVE A **DRINK** ON ME LAGER

DON'T HOLD MY **FRIENDS** AGAINST ME LAGER

DESTIN WOULD BE UNDERSTATEM LAGER

I KNOW YOU ARE, BUT **WHAT** AM I? LAGER

BY THE LOOKS OF THINGS YOU MUST BE **COLD** LAGER

HANDS **OFF** LAGER

ALREADY TRYING TO **FORGET** YOU LAGER

IT'S A GAME OF **INCHES** LAGER

HE SHOOT **SCOR** LAGER

WE'VE GOT GOOD **CHEMISTRY** LAGER

I'LL E ANYTH

MARATHON **MAN** LAGER

WHAT A **MOUTHFUL** LAGER

HOLD ME **TIGHT** LAGER

SQUEEZE FROM THE BOTTOM LAGER

STOP CHECKING YOURSELF OUT

I'M A MULTI- **MILLIONAIRE**

PLEASE SPEAK INTO **LAP**

049
063
048
064
047
065
046
066
078
077
076
067
075
074
093
092
094
091
095
107
106
108
109

...sometimes we say shit in meetings just because everybody is saying it and it sounds good. Like in a beer meeting you hear people say shit like "Beer is fashion" or "Beer is male cosmetics," and everybody thinks, "Yeah, good analogy." But sometimes it's not even an analogy, just a fact that has been repeated so often you can't hear the truth in it anymore.

Fact: Beer IS male cosmetics. Guys buy a beer because they think it'll make them more attractive in a bar. They want to be prettier. Fact: Guys will almost always look at the label of the beer they've just bought. Why? Who the hell knows–but they may in fact be checking their makeup. Fact: Guys actually position and point their beer at the female they are attracted to. They will spin the label around so it points toward their prey. Fact: Most men used to hold their beer down low on the hip. But today they hold it up at chest level with the label facing out. Actually, you might be able to observe older guys holding their beer low in the same bar with younger guys holding it high. Do guys realize they do this? Doubtful. But we've watched it a hundred times. Now you can, too.

Beer companies spend a lot of money making that label say the right things for a guy. As in hundreds of millions of dollars. Molson didn't have that kind of money, and neither did we at the time. So we suggested they add a machine to the assembly line to add a second label. This seemed an outrageous request from an advertising agency, so we apologized profusely for even suggesting it. We spent a lot of time apologizing for sticking our noses where they probably didn't belong, but Hoopla isn't something that's always found in a marketing plan. Ultimately, we wrote about 900 labels. Now, we're not lazy people, but 900 is a big order even for us so we tried to get customers to come up with ideas for labels online and at bar events and focus groups. We got thousands upon thousands of ideas from consumers. And not a single freaking one was usable because they were all so twisted and perverse. The client thought we were a bunch of choir boys after seeing this filth. So thank you if you were part of that...

SER KISS_IN_THE_SHAPE_OF_A_BULLET | LOCATION: BUFFALO, NY

Interests: quintessential black rimmed glasses-not included.

+meows+
glassjaw. lipgloss. college. hair play. being Hello*Kitty. 18 visions. monsters Inc. taking back sunday. red lights. Molson labels. afi. Brody. alexisonfire. barbie pink jello shots. watching the kool kids cry over spilled milkshakes at panos and writing songs about it...

kiss me Im Hardcore... even without the black metal bangs!

the pair you've had so long that the imprints of your feet are worn into the insoles. Comfy comfy comfy. And so, so much fun. Every two sentences, we cracked each other up.

Molson's has silly labels on their bottles. Mine said, "I JUST WANT TO BE HELD". Sarah peeled it off for me, and I stuck it in my back pocket. (Buffalo recognizes the superiority of Canadian beer.) We toasted marshmallows (and Peeps). Sarah lit bits of grass on fire. Someone played a didgeridoo made out of PVC pipe. Much merriment was spread.

Now I'm back in D.C., feeling freshly scrubbed after my weekend away.
22:06

Sunday May 30, 2004

you have no such balance.

Disturbing trends in dating.
The February issue of Readers Digest listed 5 disturbing trends in modern dating: 1. Theradate, the company that matches shrinks patients based on their neuroses. 2. Molson beer labels printed with pickup lines. 3. Dating coaches polish your conversation skills and appearance for $150 an hour. 4. Virgin Mobile cell phones can be programmed to rescue ring so that on dull dates you can fake an emergency and split. 5. A Dump Kit which includes a voodoo doll and a rubber band to snap yourself when you get weepy about being dumped.

FIRE-BREATHING CHICKEN HEAD

Long before there was a creepy fiberglass Burger King head, there was this Pyrotechnic chicken head created for Checkers. Features singed beak and zany "Holy shit I just lit that stray dog on fire!" expression.

Quantity 001
Item #0001-0000-000-0036

$35⁰⁰

H-BOMBS

These athletic shoes appeared in a 1999 *truth* spot in which every third person who wore them exploded into a million pieces. 1999! That's like five years before shoe-bomber Richard Reid "came up" with the same idea.

Quantity 001
Item #0001-0000-000-0017

$250⁰⁰

PARTS OF PARIS

When they shot an episode of "The Simple Life" in the agency, Paris Hilton left behind this strand of hair and cute post-it doodle. The number of self-pleasuring scenarios that incorporate these items is endless.

Quantity 001
Item #0001-0000-000-0024

$9⁹⁹

PATTI LABELLE'S GUM

Thoroughly pre-chewed by Patti LaBelle AND Alex Bogusky, this gum no longer has any flavor. But it's jam-packed with human DNA. And what's minty breath when you can have actual Patti LaBelle Breath™.

Quantity 001
Item #0001-0000-000-0011

$374⁹⁹

ART DIRECTORS SPECIAL

ART DIRECTOR SHIRT

CP+B Art Director Tee. Spun from the conjoined looms of fashion and function, this garment is emblazoned with easy-to-read key commands for Quark, Photoshop, and Illustrator upside-down on torso and on right sleeve.

Quantity 999
Item #0001-0000-000-0005

$30⁰⁰

"BEAVER" TRAP

This rusty old jaw trap was originally used for the Molson "Beaver Trapper" commercial. Wait, scratch that. It was originally used to cripple cute, unsuspecting woodland creatures in the Yukon. (Includes cardboard cutout.)

Quantity 001
Item #0001-0000-000-0031

$79⁰⁰

IRONIC TRUCKER HAT

Show your support for the band that put the pedal to the metal and ran over the competition at the 2004 Battle of the Bands. Or cross out the "I" and write in a "Ch" to show your support for illegal narcotics.

Quantity 008
Item #0001-0000-000-0026

$9⁹⁵

MUSTACHE PORTRAIT

At first it seemed like it would be funny if a bunch of creatives grew mustaches and had a portrait taken at Sears. But as it turned out, everyone felt really weird, and few of the men who participated have never been able to shake that feeling.

Quantity 001
Item #0001-0000-000-0030

$6⁹⁹

Lowest price ever

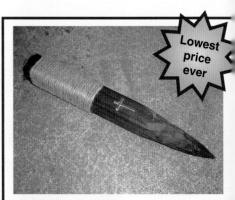

VAMPIRE STAKE

Used in a "Spooky Bank Fees" ad for Compass Bank. If you think someone you know is a vampire, plunge this into their chest. If weird smoke comes out and they disappear, they are a vampire. If they gurgle and fall down, they are a person.

Quantity 001
Item #0001-0000-000-0012

$19⁹⁵

MALE BLOW UP DOLL

This pneumatic, mustachioed muchacho is a dead ringer for TV super sleuth Remington Steele. But you gotta wonder if even he could solve the mystery of how to bust this thing's cherry. Not a single orifice on it!

Quantity 001
Item #0001-0000-000-0027

$19⁹⁹

Machine-stitched!

EVIL EMPIRE PRODUCTIONS CAP

This lid comes from a *truth* cinema spot that proved to be a horror show for the tobacco industry. Headwear that's sure to evoke ire in any tobacco executive who crosses your path.

Quantity 009
Item #0001-0000-000-0035

$9⁹⁹

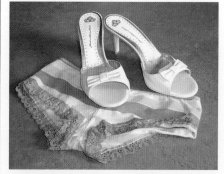

PRE-WORN PINK ITEMS

These Victoria's Secret items were placed onto young hot models. These young hot models then had to move around a lot and be under hot lights. Are you understanding what we're saying here?

Quantity 014
Item #0001-0000-000-0003

$99⁹⁹

FLOP-FLIPS

Sure, they mess up the "stepped on a pop-top, blew out my flip flop" part of Jimmy Buffet's "Margaritaville." But they rhyme great in Snoop Dogg's "Up Jump the Boogie": "(In my flops I flip), like Rambo 'wit anotha clip!"

Quantity 023
Item #0001-0000-000-0033

$22⁵⁰

OUTDATED PHOTOGRAPH

This photograph of CP+B creative directors was part of the October 2003 *Details* magazine "50 Most Influential Men under 38" article. One of the guys no longer works here, and several are now over 38.

Quantity 001
Item #0001-0000-000-0013

$1⁹⁵

RECYCLED GNOME

This gnome was rescued from Bogusky's trashcan by Kat Morris. If you took pictures of it, like at bars and landmarks and stuff, no one would care. But if you took pictures of it next to different dead bodies, people would for sure pay attention.

Quantity 001
Item #0001-0000-000-0008

$6⁶⁶

JESUS SHELL SHRINE

This ultra-pious light fixture features countless seashells intricately arranged around a silver plastic likeness of Jesus. The light bulb no longer works, but the invisible God rays will burn your retinas to ash!

Quantity 001
Item #0001-0000-000-0018

$29⁹⁵

CP+B GUAYABERA

Internationally recognized for its comfort and subtropical practicality, the Guayabera is the shirt of choice for despotic South American dictators and professional dominoes players alike. Una camisa muy bonita, pendejo!

Quantity 025
Item #0001-0000-000-0006

$150⁰⁰

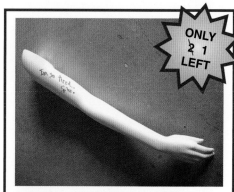

ONLY 21 LEFT

SIGNED MANNEQUIN ARM

Right GAP mannequin arm (type: female adult) signed by acclaimed director Spike Jonze for star-fucker advertising creative Evan Fry. "I'm so tired…—Spike." Removed from shoot location under client protest.

Quantity 001
Item #0001-0000-000-0021

$9999⁹⁹

ZEKE BOGUSKY ORIGINAL

Zeke Bogusky's brave exploration of the complex sociological forces at work in the Bogusky family. Note the gleeful expressions of Zeke and Nadia, the vexed, latte-wielding Ana, and the enigmatic stare of Alex. Proceeds go directly to Zeke.

Quantity 001
Item #0001-0000-000-0025

$499⁰⁰

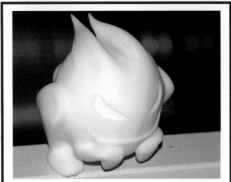

PROTOTYPE FAST

This rare albino specimen is the great-grandfather of all fasts. Created on a 3D printer right here in our office, this one-of-a-kind critter currently resides on Alex Bogusky's actual desk. Not for the faint-of-wallet.

Quantity 001
Item #0001-0000-000-0010

$2500⁰⁰

FECAL COLIFORM SIGN

"Neck-deep in a river of shit" is one of the most unpleasant analogies ever developed by pop-culture. Unfortunately, that's what's happening at our beaches, as this guerilla sign indicated for curious swimmers.

Quantity 001
Item #0001-0000-000-0032

$29⁹⁹

USED RAZOR BLADES

These blunt blades are still sharp enough to go through the skin of your wrists. If you've had a long succession of shitty days, what better way to check out than with the same blade that made a BURGER KING® comp?

Quantity 001
Item #0001-0000-000-0009

$1.⁷⁵

POODLE CANDLE

This INSANELY lifelike poodle has a weird, otherworldly shit-eating-grin that will creep out anyone who gazes upon it. The candle was lit for good luck during new business pitches, and has never failed.

Quantity 001
Item #0001-0000-000-0016

$9⁹⁹

SPLODE SHIRT

Created for *truth* to promote a fictitious soda that killed every third person who drank it (just like tobacco), this SPLODE shirt was washed/worn by Paul Keister until it reached the perfect level of fadedness.

Quantity 001
Item #0001-0000-000-0001

$4⁹⁹

PIECE OF CP+B ROOF

After we got hit by, like, twenty-seven hurricanes, the agency's soul was left in shards almost identical in size to the shards of this terra-cotta roof tile. Own a macabre piece of misery for the low price of $14.00.

Quantity 008
Item #0001-0000-000-0019

$14⁰⁰

ART DIRECTORS SPECIAL

SHITTY POLO PAINTING

If trust-funders galloping around in circles with pieces of a Williams-Sonoma croquet set isn't nauseating enough, then how about this weak-ass photograph immortalizing the whole thing.

Quantity 001
Item #0001-0000-000-0004

$6⁹⁹

CP+B SUNBLOCK

This SPF-0 sunblock was something we made to sort of poke fun at the fact that we never leave the office. But after the 57th employee divorce, we realized it wasn't really that funny.

Quantity 071
Item #0001-0000-000-0028

$2⁹⁹

SPONSOR THE STUDIO FISH

Sure, it only takes 5 cents a day to feed a hungry Cambodian child. But Siamese fighting fish have complex nutritional needs. Your donation covers fish food, or a convincing replacement should this one end up floating upside down.

Quantity 001
Item #0001-0000-000-0023

$**1**⁰⁰

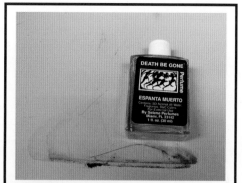

DEATH BE GONE

Death can be pretty pesky. I mean, right when you think you've shoo'ed it away for the last time, the wing falls off your 747 and there it is again. Ward off death for good with this alluring/repulsive fragrance.

Quantity 001
Item #0001-0000-000-0015

$**5**⁹⁹

TWIN COVER TRILOGY

Pure publishing panty-remover! These magazines have fake back covers of pretend magazines. Flip them over when you're entertaining, and you'll appear rich, commited and sensitive.

Quantity 002
Item #0001-0000-000-0002

$**83**⁹⁵

BELL WALL

This hunk of drywall features special evil-spirit-banishing graphics and a full paragraph of rambling, broken English. Used for a Bell helmets print ad, it's one spiritually potent piece of ad history.

Quantity 001
Item #0001-0000-000-0020

FREE*
*Buyer pays shipping

COPYWRITER 2.0 DOLL

This doll was used to shape the life of a real copywriter who used to work at the agency. If you think it's fucked up that the direction of a real person's life would be determined by a plastic doll, well, you're right.

Quantity 001
Item #0001-0000-000-0034

$**24**⁹⁹

Lowest price ever

LEFTOVER MEETING FOOD

Rice and beans from a Cuban joint? Wilted garnish that once provided a verdant cushion for some client's pile of macaroni salad? Whatever we're having that day, we'll freeze what's left and send it your way.

Quantity 099
Item #0001-0000-000-0007

FREE*
*Buyer pays overnight shipping

RAPPING COOKIE JAR

Drown out that nagging inner voice that says "Stop Eating Oreos, Fat Ass" with this whimsical rapping cookie jar. Rest assured, this mothafucka drops dope lyrics that easily cancel out self-loathing.

Quantity 001
Item #0001-0000-000-0014

$**23**⁰⁰

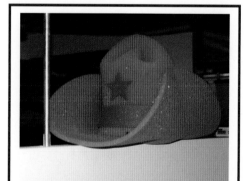

FOAM COWBOY HAT

You don't need a sheep herding background or a whacked-out mesquite style libido to visit Brokeback Mountain. All you need is this big fucking orange cowboy hat, and the courage to not wear pants with it.

Quantity 001
Item #0001-0000-000-0029

$**2**⁹⁹

TONY'S SKETCHBOOK

This is an actual sketchbook filled with ideas by Vice President and Creative Director Tony Calcao. Simply recycle the contents and win an entire shelf of awards without ever firing a single neuron.

Quantity 001
Item #0001-0000-000-0022

$**299**⁹⁹

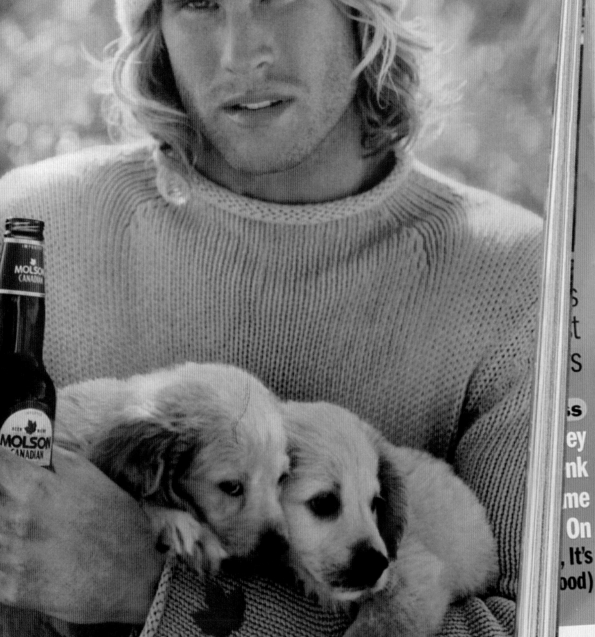

MOLSON

His Address: The intersection of confidence and compassion.
His Beer: Molson Canadian.

www.molsonman.com

The Miracle of Molson Twin Advertising™ Technology

HUNDREDS OF THOUSANDS OF WOMEN.
PRE-PROGRAMMED FOR YOUR CONVENIENCE.

As you read this, women across America are reading something very different: an advertisement (fig. 1) scientifically formulated to enhance their perception of men who drink **Molson**. The ad shown below, currently running in Cosmopolitan magazine, is a perfectly tuned combination of words and images designed by trained professionals. Women who are exposed to it experience a very positive feeling. A feeling which they will later project directly onto you. Triggering the process is as simple as ordering a Molson Canadian (fig. 2).

fig. 2 Molson Canadian Beer.

fig. 1 It costs $179,630 to run an ad in Cosmo. That's a $179,630 investment in you.

fig. 3 A shapely female subject accesses pleasing imagery from her memory banks and projects them onto a Molson drinker.

The game is about to change, and you're the heavy favorite.

Extravagant dinners. Subtitled movies. Floral arrangements tied together with little pieces of hay. It gets old. And it gets expensive, depleting funds that could go to a new set of 20-inch rims. But thanks to the miracle of Twin Advertising Technology, you can achieve success without putting in any time or effort. So drop the bouquet and pick up a Molson Canadian. That's not just a crisp, clean import from Canada you're tasting. It's victory, my friend.

MOLSON
LET YOUR MOLSON DO THE TALKING.

www.molsontwinadvertising.com

We noticed that men are often forced to flip their favorite magazines over when female guests come over. So we created fake back covers that would help these guys make a good impression.

TRUSTFUND

The magazine for those about to inherit millions.

JULY 2004

PRIVATE JET UPHOLSTERY
Who Says Ostrich Doesn't Fly?

Spend Extravagantly on Someone You Love

Choosing A Butler

Millionaire Taste Test: Molson Rated #1

EXCLUSIVE: 2004 Sports Franchise Buyers Guide

FOR HIM MAGAZINE · JULY 2004 · ANNA NICOLE SMITH · SEX SCOUT · WILLEM DAFOE · MISTER MUSCLES · CHRISTINA MILIAN

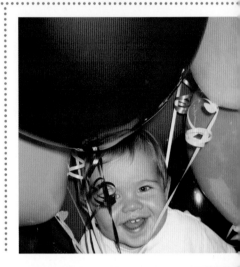

MARCH AGAINST HATE 2004
"One step forward, zero steps back."

CROSSING GUARD
FOR THE BLIND

UNITED WE PROTECT
Citizen Street Patrol

SALUTE ME
I VOTED

BLOOD DONOR ♥

KISS ME
I HUG TREES

WORLD TREE
PRESERVATION FUND

I TAUGHT
A CHILD
TO READ
TODAY!

American Literacy Plan

VOLUNTEER
METRO ANIMAL RESCUE

GALS WANT A GUY WHO'S INTERESTED IN MORE THAN SPORTS AND NUDIE MAGS.

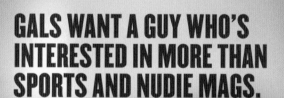

I SUPPORT THE PANDA BEAR HABITAT FUND

STOP SEAL CLUBBING!

VISITOR
Farewell Acres
CONVALESCENT HOME

GALS WANT A GUY WHO'S INTERESTED IN MORE THAN SPORTS AND NUDIE MAGS.
AND NOW YOU ARE.

Step 1
SELECT THE ACTIVITY STICKER THAT SPEAKS TO YOU.

Step 2
DISPLAY STICKER AT OPTIMAL HOTTIE EYE-LEVEL.

Step 3
"WOW. I HATE HATE TOO. WANNA GO SOMEPLACE AND TALK?"

LADIES DON'T WANT A GUY – THEY WANT A GIVER. AND IF YOU HAD TIME, WE KNOW THAT YOU'D BE GIVING BLOOD OR CARING FOR THE ENVIRONMENT YOURSELF. SO HERE'S A WAY TO SHOW ALL THE HOTTIES WHAT YOU'RE REALLY ABOUT. SIMPLY WEAR ONE OF THE ACTIVITY STICKERS INCLUDED ON THE PRECEDING PAGE. WHEN THEY ASK ABOUT IT, PLAY COY. "SILLY ME. DID I FORGET TO TAKE THAT THING OFF AGAIN?" AFTER AN ICE BREAKER LIKE THAT, JUST KEEP THE CONVERSATION FLOWING WITH AN EASY DRINKING MOLSON. BECAUSE THAT'S WHAT GIVERS DO.

MAKING "FRIENDS" *SINCE* **1786**
WWW.MOLSONUSA.COM/TOOLS

IN 1786, JOHN MOLSON BEGAN BREWING BEER USING THE FINEST CANADIAN WATER AND BARLEY FROM A LAND ALONE. NOW CAL. SASKATCHEWAN. WE LEFT WELL ENOUGH ALONE.

MOLSON CANADIAN

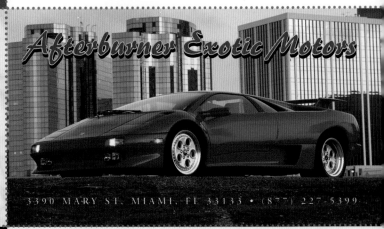

SÛHDZ

REACH FOR THE TOP. ENJOY THE VIEW. THE FRAGRANCE FOR MEN, FROM

EMBRACE THE
FRAGRANCE OF MOLSON.
SASKATCHEWAN BARLEY.
PURE CANADIAN WATER.
AROMATIC HOPS.
THE SCENT THAT BRINGS
PEOPLE TOGETHER.
IN BARS SINCE 1786.

A HOOPLA™ Brand
www.wwptbd.com

No one needs effective advertising more than someone who's just lost a dog or cat. This ingenious kit brings cutting-edge advertising techniques to bear in the hunt for missing pets.

www.lavidahoopla.com
a HOOPLA™ product

VOTED #1

makefriends**with**your**fast**

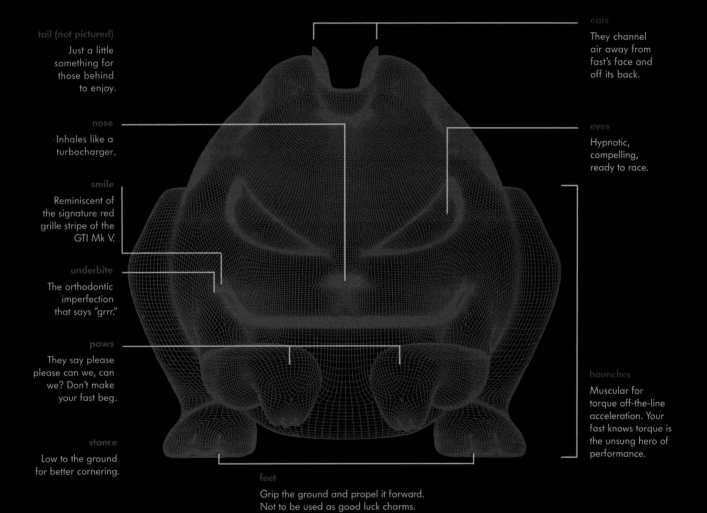

tail (not pictured)
Just a little something for those behind to enjoy.

nose
Inhales like a turbocharger.

smile
Reminiscent of the signature red grille stripe of the GTI Mk V.

underbite
The orthodontic imperfection that says "grrr."

paws
They say please please can we, can we? Don't make your fast beg.

stance
Low to the ground for better cornering.

ears
They channel air away from fast's face and off its back.

eyes
Hypnotic, compelling, ready to race.

haunches
Muscular for torque off-the-line acceleration. Your fast knows torque is the unsung hero of performance.

feet
Grip the ground and propel it forward. Not to be used as good luck charms.

brokeometer
whenconfrontedbya"naysayer"ofspeedsimplyinstallthe
brokeometer touseplaceitoveryourregularspeedometer
thenpointouttheelectricalproblemtothe"naysayer" before
youknowityou'llbebackontheroadinyourturbocharged
torquedoutwoundup200horsepowerpocketrocket the
GTIMkV pretunedbygermanengineers*

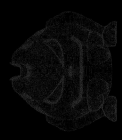

THIS
END UP

contents: one (1) fast

Portable **Creates extra seconds** Works day and night **Chicks dig it** Makes everything more fun

Precautions:
o May cause blurriness
o Not compatible with slow, sluggish, or plodding
o May cause increase in gravitational forces

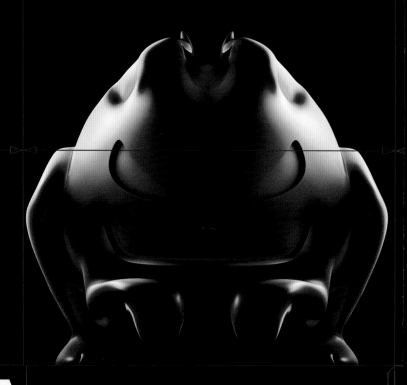

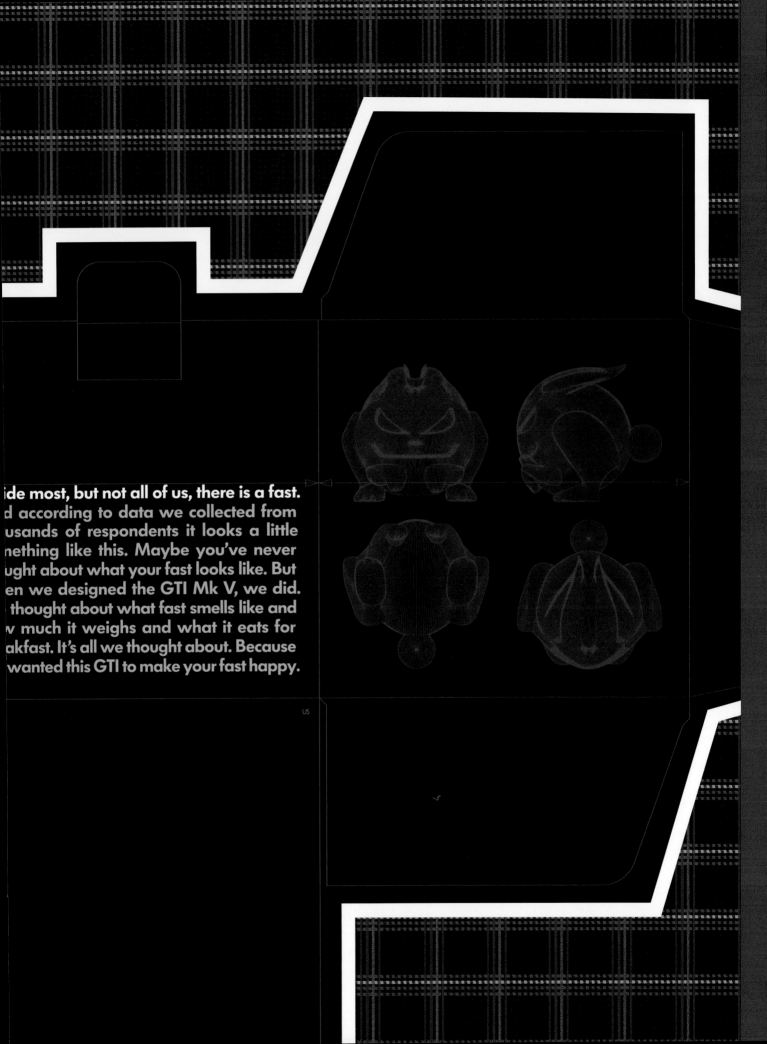

ide most, but not all of us, there is a fast.
d according to data we collected from
usands of respondents it looks a little
nething like this. Maybe you've never
ught about what your fast looks like. But
en we designed the GTI Mk V, we did.
thought about what fast smells like and
w much it weighs and what it eats for
akfast. It's all we thought about. Because
wanted this GTI to make your fast happy.

US

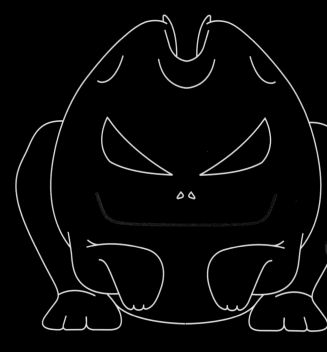

the standard tail

the badboy tail

the tee'd-off tail

the hi-voltage tail

Smooth
Spherical
Hare-like
A classic

Pointy
Devilish
Mischievous
Naughty

Dimpled
Reduces drag
Increases loft
Inspired by
the original GTI shifter knob

Flashy
Jagged
Jolting
Lightning

back seat
From the back seat, your fast can easily observe everything in the cockpit and lend advice or encouragement whenever needed. The center armrest in the back seat doubles as a comfy little throne and affords both you and your fast an easy view of one another via the rearview mirror.

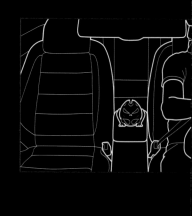

front seat
It's the shotgun position. It says your fast is more than a little black totem representing an aspect of your psyche. It says it's your right-hand man in the most literal and pun-laden sense of the term.

EUTSCHLAND

I ❤ AUTOBAHN

the cheshire smile
Your fast needs 207 lb-ft of torque.

the grimace
Your fast needs the AC off and the windows down.

the high beam
Your fast wants a twisty mountain road.

65 **65**

the @#$%-eating grin
Your fast wants to go pick up pizza. Or milk. Or anything.

the ear-to-ear
Your fast wants to downshift.

the have-a-nice-day
Your fast wants to move into the passing lane.

DEUTSCH

GTI MkV

center console

Crouched up by your elbow behind the stick shift, your fast can get right up into the action. Race your way up and down the 6-speed gearbox and your fast is right by your side, grinning with delight from this symmetrically pleasing position. Ideal when you've got an able co-pilot aboard.

the standard tail

Smooth
Spherical
Hare-like
A classic

the badboy tail

Pointy
Devilish
Mischievous
Naughty

the tee'd-off tail

Dimpled
Reduces drag
Increases loft
Inspired by
the original GTI shifter

0123456
0123456789 01234

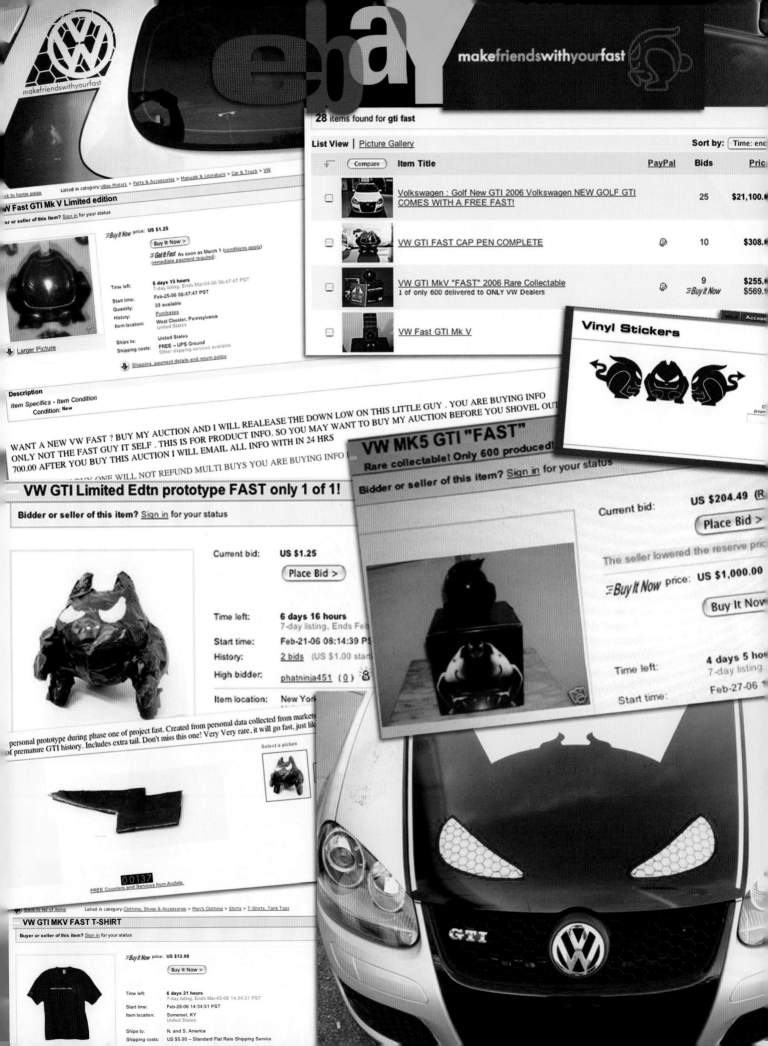

MY FAST GTI
HAVE A FAST DAY

Welcome to My Fast GTI. Where you can share your GTI and Fast's Images, Experiences, and more. The life of our site is in our forums. We hope you'll take the time to join. We welcome all GTI Enthusiasts. This is your forum, where you are always welcome.

STATS | 185 Posts in 51 Topics by 38 Members - Latest Member: nickflannery | February 21, 2006, 10:35:01 pm | TIME

HOME | FORUM | HELP | SEARCH | LOG IN | REGISTER

My Fast GTI | Forum

My Fast GTI Announcements	Posts	Topics	Last post
General Announcements Check here for board announcements, Contest rules, etc.	8	6	Today at 08:10:52 pm Re: Board Changes by Fast Freddie

My Fast GTI	Posts	Topics	Last post
MKV GTI Headlines, Reviews and Images There are a lot of News and Review Links about the MK V GTI and the Fast.. We'll post them here, and you can comment on them.	12	7	Today at 12:52:13 pm Re: Motor Trend First Dr... by clavos
My Fast Tell us about your new GTI, post Pictures, Video, etc. Show off your GTI!. Just have a RoCk'In Time!	44	7	February 19, 2006, 08:41:58 pm Re: United Gery MkV Pkg ... by clavos
General MK V GTI Discussions Feel free to talk about anything and everything associated with the GTI or your fast on this board. Child Boards: Church Of GTI Confessional	33	6	Today at 08:54:43 pm Back from Road Tests, my... by thp
Driving Tips and Tricks			Today at 04:51:21 pm

MY FAST PARKING ONLY
ALL OTHERS WILL BE TOWED
CITY ORD. # 34263

vwvortex
the volkswagen enthusiast website

vortex forums | news | featu

AUTOTECH
Import Tuning
1-800-553-1055
www.autotech.com

Vwvortex Forums › Search › 87 topics found

Search Results
r search for **fast** returned 87 results.
New Search

geriatric stylz

Topic
- anyone willing to sell their FAST? (1 2)
- VW project fast: The answer (1 2 3)
- VW's Project Fast.....??? (1 ... 4 5)
- FAST says "Buy this EVO Motorsports CAI!"
- **** Photos of my Fast **** It's not for sale either.
- ~Fast~ (pics inside) (1 2)
- WANT a "MY FAST"!!!!!!!!!!!!!!!!!!!!!!!!!!!!!!
- GLI Owners: Mad about the FAST? (1 2)
- Crown Vics Make Fast Happy Too
- WTB: my fast
- If you buy a GTI are you suppose to get a fast with it???
- FAST commercials
- My Fast Commercials
- WTT/S: EG hatch, honda, N/A swapped, very fast.
- WTT/S: EG hatch, honda, N/A swapped, very fast.
- F.S. 97 Jetta GT----$1500 need to sell fast (1 2)

EVIL ►

WTB: my fast

WTB: my fast

+

---

barnholio
Member

Offline

Member Since
2-4-2003
304 posts

canton ga
84 8v scirocco, 86 16v scirocco, 95
vr6 passat, 03 jetta gli vr6, 05 jetta
gli 1.8t, and another 05

EuroBurner GLI
Member

Offline

Member Since
7-19-2004
3363 posts

STOLLEN FAST!!!!

Last saturday one hour until closing the fast vanished. we had just finished showing it off to a custumer, and placed it back on the sales managers desk within an hour of the showing it had vanished!!!

I don't expect the guilty one to bring it back, but damn has it come to this?

2005 JETTA GLI my new toy
2005 JETTA GLI my wifes new bumper c
I SELL VW@Jim Ellis VW MARIETTA GA

Re: STOLLEN FAST!!!! (barnholio)

Not the FAST!?!?!?!

...the blind leading the blind.
The MoFolkies|Mat Kearney|Chri
OEM VW Stuff for Sale
Pete Shirz

machen sie freunde mit ihres
schnell

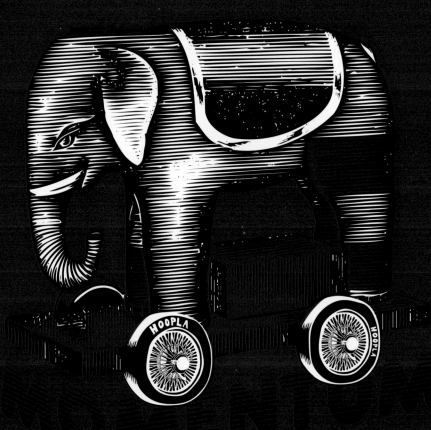

As CP+B has demonstrated in the past few years, there are lots of things that Hoopla can achieve. It can put a small agency in Miami on the map, such that by the Fall of 2005 that agency found itself winning the Volkswagen account and the Sprite soft drink account—in the same week. Hoopla can also get kids to stop smoking, help little cars beat big cars, return a forgotten and dethroned King to power, and help men regain their mojo. But in a word, the central thing Hoopla can do, and in fact has done for CP+B's clients and for the agency itself, is generate momentum.

Momentum is the goal for Hoopla-makers and Hoopla beneficiaries; it's what the funny masks, the engaging short films, the crazy hoaxes, the live stunts, the dancing chickens all are designed to yield. Momentum is not to be confused with "awareness," which is what most conventional advertising tries to generate and build. In fact, over the years, awareness has emerged as the Holy Grail for people endeavoring to make something famous. But the problem with awareness, as CP+B sees it, is that it isn't necessarily a positive thing. As Porter points out: "There are brands that everyone knows about—and nobody cares about."

One of the points CP+B has tried to advance within the ad industry—a point relevant to anyone trying to promote something by generating awareness of it—is the notion that *"momentum" is a better goal to strive for than "awareness."* An old, established, and rapidly fading brand may actually enjoy greater awareness levels than a young up-and-coming brand. But the up-and-comer has momentum on its side. And momentum, if sustained, will roll over everything in its path.

How do you know if your brand has momentum? The answer to that is...you just know. People are talking about it without being prompted. News stories are being done about it. Independent websites spring up, where enthusiasts swap tips about it. A-list celebrities pop up in trendy clubs wearing the brand's logo on a cap. The brand seems to be interwoven with the culture—which is not the same as just being trumpeted in lots of ads.

When a brand inserts itself into the mix of current culture, by way of momentum, people become more than just "aware" of it. They become interested in it. As a brand and its messages attain cultural relevance, this "creates a suction that pulls people in," says CP+B's Burnard. People find themselves in the position of needing to know about this brand in order to stay culturally tuned-in themselves.

There are only two kinds of brands as perceived in the minds of today's hyper-aware consumers, according to Bogusky: *The ones perceived to be on the way up, and the ones on the way down.* "You're either in one group or the other," he says. The bad news is that you can go from the "up" category to the "down" very quickly these days; the good news is you can go the other way, too, though not as easily. Because it's harder to generate momentum than it is to lose it.

Whereas conventional advertising was specifically designed to create awareness, Hoopla is better suited to building momentum. Because momentum, at least as defined by CP+B, is primarily about keeping a brand in forward motion. You don't achieve that by repeating the same commercial over and over; on the contrary, that approach yields familiarity, awareness, consistency—all the things that used to be seen as the goal of advertising. The problem is that "where yesterday's consumer saw consistency, today's consumer sees staleness," says Burnard. In order to be perceived as being "on the rise," a brand needs to be seen as surprising, fresh, in transition, innovative, topical, ubiquitous, dynamic. CP+B maintains that Hoopla, being a dynamic form of communication itself, tends to be better than static advertising when it comes to imbuing a brand with dynamism and thereby generating momentum.

Not to suggest it's easy to set a brand in motion: Momentum is often the result of not one big push but many pushes and a multitude of forces coming together at the same time. The starting point seems to be (as always) the big idea, around which momentum—and indeed, a popular movement—can be built. If an idea or a philosophy is compelling enough that people can rally around it—as with CP+B's "SUV backlash" on behalf of MINI, its quest for "truth" that fueled an insurrection against Big Tobacco, or its creation of a new "jetset" lifestyle for Virgin Atlantic—that can initiate a popular movement. And a movement, by its very nature, tends to gather momentum. In the process of launching a movement around a brand, the agency has tended to rely on the elements discussed in the preceding chapters: Mutation, Invention, Candor, Mischief, Connection, and Pragmatism. Each plays a role in helping to generate momentum by creating communication that is different enough, honest enough, intriguing enough, ubiquitous enough, and useful enough to set a phenomenon in motion.

But if generating a movement is challenging, so is the job of maintaining it; *momentum is really about how you build on a phenomenon and keep it moving forward.* "Usually, maintaining momentum requires constant reinvention," says Porter. "Without that, even an icon becomes just another piece of nostalgia." Which means you cannot simply generate momentum with a big idea and then sit back and enjoy the benefits; the invention and reinvention must be constant, necessitating that one's "idea factory" continually turn out new products. This is true even if the current ideas or messages you're using already seem to have momentum; CP+B maintains that you must still add to or completely change those ideas before they have a chance to lose steam (this harkens back to the aforementioned CP+B law that when it comes to ideas, one should *embrace obsolescence*). In the end, as CP+B's Andrew Keller says, "momentum is about doing tons of work."

The current BURGER KING® campaign, which has given that brand a sense of movement after years of stasis, offers a good example of how constant reinvention can build and maintain momentum. The agency started by taking an old BURGER KING® line–"HAVE IT YOUR WAY®"–and bringing it back in a way that taps into the current societal trend toward mass customization. The agency also dusted off an old, nearly forgotten icon–the "Burger King" himself–and gave him new life as a silent, enigmatic character with a slightly creepy artificial head (The agency stumbled upon an old Burger King head as a collector's item on eBay, and that got things started.) "The King seems to tap into something you kind of remember from your childhood, but when you take him out of that context and put him in a message for adults, it has a weird, unsettling effect," Bogusky says.

The quirky King quickly became an object of fascination in the media, appearing, among other places, on *The Tonight Show* with Jay Leno. The agency deftly built upon that momentum through little cameo appearances of the character in odd places; for example, the King suddenly showed up in the crowd at a Los Angeles Lakers game, in the company of a sexy starlet named Brooke Burke. Rumors that the King and Brooke were an item were fanned by the subsequent appearance, in a top celebrity magazine, of the King and Brooke caught doing laundry together in a paparazzi-style candid photo. (Nevermind that the candid photo was actually taken by CP+B and sent into the magazine; the point is, it ran right alongside all the magazine's other celebrity candids.) But even as CP+B has teased people with King sightings, the agency has been careful not to overuse the character in the overall BK® campaign. "If you put him in everything, he would quickly cease to be interesting," Bogusky says. (Herein lies an important lesson about maintaining momentum in Hoopla: Don't overplay your hand, even if it's a "royal" flush.)

Sometimes culture will help you generate momentum. Consider the Volkswagen GTI. Twenty years ago, when VW released this souped-up version of its popular Rabbit, the car spawned a cult following. But over the years, the GTI lost its way, especially with the hardcore GTI enthusiast.

CP+B saw the potential to convince these young, mostly male "dubbers" that they could believe in the spirit of the GTI again. They started by asking GTI fans to "make friends with your fast."

Weeks before the release of the GTI, a series of e-mails was sent to a few thousand select VW "hand-raisers," asking recipients to help VW with a scientific investigation dubbed "Project Fast." Each e-mail included a battery of questions about things like the shape, color, and size of "fast." VW chatrooms lit up with questions about the project.

The final Project Fast e-mail coincided with the launch of the GTI MK V. At last, GTI fans were introduced to their "fast"–a small, black totem with distinctively rabbit-like features. Meanwhile, television ads portrayed the fast as the GTI driver's scary alter ego, that part of him that puts the passion of driving above all else–his girl, the law, even his own common sense.

The VW community responded explosively. What was this "fast" thing? Where could they view the TV spots? And most of all, how could they get a fast of their own? Immediately, fasts started popping up on eBay, with some fetching as much as $800.

Bootlegged shirts soon followed. And window stickers and posters. One posting featured a GTI MK V for sale, custom-painted to resemble the little, black fast. Bloggers adopted the fast as their online icon. And some enthusiasts even launched their own fast-themed websites.

CP+B gave VW culture something fun to play with. And the culture took the ball and ran with it.

The agency maintains that without a constant flow of news, people tend to quickly compartmentalize–and forget–a brand and its message. "News *is* the pipeline," says Keller. "If there's no product news, then we have to make 'creative news' with content. That builds momentum." But how do you know what's newsworthy? "If you're about to spend advertising dollars on a campaign and you can't imagine that anybody is going to write about it or talk about it, you might want to rethink it," Bogusky says. "It means you probably missed injecting a truth or social tension into it. And if there isn't some aspect of news to your message, today's consumer has filters that will probably prevent the message from penetrating at all."

One of the ways CP+B injects news value into its communication is through topicality. "We find ways to tie into all kinds of stuff that is happening in the culture at the moment," says Keller. When the Atkins Diet was all the rage, CP+B invented the character Dr. Angus, who played off the movement on behalf of BURGER KING®. When the media was breathlessly hyping the "metrosexual" as a new gender-bending archetype, CP+B came up with a distinct twist on that by coining the term "jetrosexual" as a label for a new breed of traveler for Virgin Atlantic Airways. By taking a position– however tongue-in-cheek–on the issues of the day, the agency and its brands are able to stake out "thought-leadership" positions, says Keller. That creates news and keeps momentum going.

But as Bogusky points out, CP+B's objective is not just to react to what's going on in the culture. He believes it's possible for Hoopla to go further, actually serving as a catalyst for cultural change. Every time the zeitgeist is moving strongly in one direction, there's room for a daring communicator to come along and push things in a new and different direction. "Pop culture always wants to change," Bogusky says. But to make that change happen, you must be willing to go against the flow of current ideas and conventional wisdom. Call it the Hoopla law of momentum: *If you try to ride on everyone else's momentum, you'll never build up any of your own.*

These days, while trying to help brands like BURGER KING, Volkswagen, and Google maintain their momentum, CP+B faces a similar challenge with regard to its own operation: How does a red-hot agency stay that way? One of the ways is by applying the principles of Hoopla to its own brand. The agency continues to try to mutate, to reinvent itself. The next wave may bring cultural creations and entertainment done solely by the agency, without brand sponsorship. Bogusky and Porter believe that when it comes to creating the culture of tomorrow, the lines between ad agencies and entertainment producers will continue to blur and perhaps disappear altogether. Bogusky says the agency is also bracing and preparing to adapt to a coming age in which the consumer audience will be a full partner in the communications of brands. "This means that as a brand communicator," he says, "you'll have to be willing to give up control of the message"—a prospect that Bogusky finds both thrilling and scary.

As CP+B continues to mutate, it's also trying to preserve the aspects of the agency culture that have contributed to the successful production of Hoopla thus far. The agency is striving to remain informal and chaotic; Hoopla does not thrive in bureaucracies, and it's rarely created in formal meetings. But Bogusky does believe that if and when you have success at creating Hoopla, you should celebrate that success with a great deal of, well, hoopla. "To sustain a culture, you have to do a lot of cheesy stuff, like having parties, giving speeches, sending e-mails congratulating people on things," he says, "Every time something happens that reinforces the culture you're trying to create, you should celebrate it visually in front of everyone."

Still, as Bogusky's partner Porter notes, this doesn't mean you should revel in those successes for long. "Momentum is about looking forward, not backward," Porter says. "I think this agency is good at never looking back. We've never had a tenth-anniversary party or anything like that. Maybe when we're twenty, Alex and I will have a beer if we're both in town."

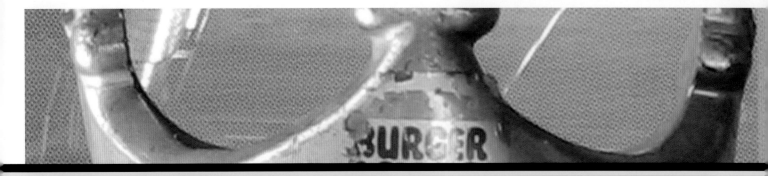

KING
NORMOUS

march 03, 2004 was a morning like any other morning.

Birds were chirping. Sprinklers were sprinkling. Lawnmowers were mowing. Everything seemed in order. But then, something happened. It seemed innocent enough at the time. A man woke up in bed next to another man. The second man stared at the first man for a moment and then offered him breakfast. The first man accepted it. He ate it. He enjoyed it. And afterward they both had a big laugh. Fairly routine stuff, at least on the surface.

But there were other factors in play. The first man woke up looking like he hadn't exactly been expecting the second man. The second guy looked as though he'd been staring at the first guy for God-knows-how-long. And finally, there was the matter of the second guy having a huge plastic King Head with a creepy, unchanging smile. To top it all off, the plastic-headed guy was a fast-food icon, and it was all shown on national TV. Repeatedly.

As the nation witnessed this event, reactions were all over the board. Some laughed. Some wept. Some gasped and assumed the fetal position. It was praised and condemned. People turned away from it and couldn't turn away from it, all at the same time. But no one could ignore it. Nor could anyone stop it.

Within weeks, the plastic-headed King would surprise others. One man awoke to find the King standing in his flower bed, staring through the window. Another man, alerted by his barking dog, spotted the King in the middle of his backyard. An instant later, the King was on his porch, face to face with him. A lumberjack in the Pacific Northwest, a steelworker on a skyscraper, a man riding a tandem bicycle in Spain, a college student doing his laundry in the wee hours of the morning, a guy at an ATM, and a young executive at a peep show all reported the same encounter. A royal with a polymer-based head and seemingly no understanding of personal space approaches, offers food, and makes them laugh uncontrollably.

As the public tried to get its head around these events, the King moved on to a different venue. The NFL. It soon became obvious that whatever the King lacked in 21st-century social protocol, he more than made up for in raw physical ability. He ran for touchdowns, intercepted passes, made diving catches, and completely baffled his opponents. And the fans went wild.

But just as the gridiron showcased the King's toughness, America was beginning to see his tender side, too.

Papparazzi pictures surfaced, showing him with model Brooke Burke—on the beach, riding horses, and shopping in Malibu. Questions abounded about where the relationship was headed. But the King—always the enigmatic gentleman—remained silent on the subject.

The King's next move is anyone's guess. He's unpredictable. He moves fast. He always seems to be two steps ahead of everyone else. The best strategy seems to be this: Just sit back and watch. When the King sets out in a new direction, rest assured, we'll all know about it. He attracts plenty of attention. And let's face it, with that enormous head of his, he's awfully hard to miss.

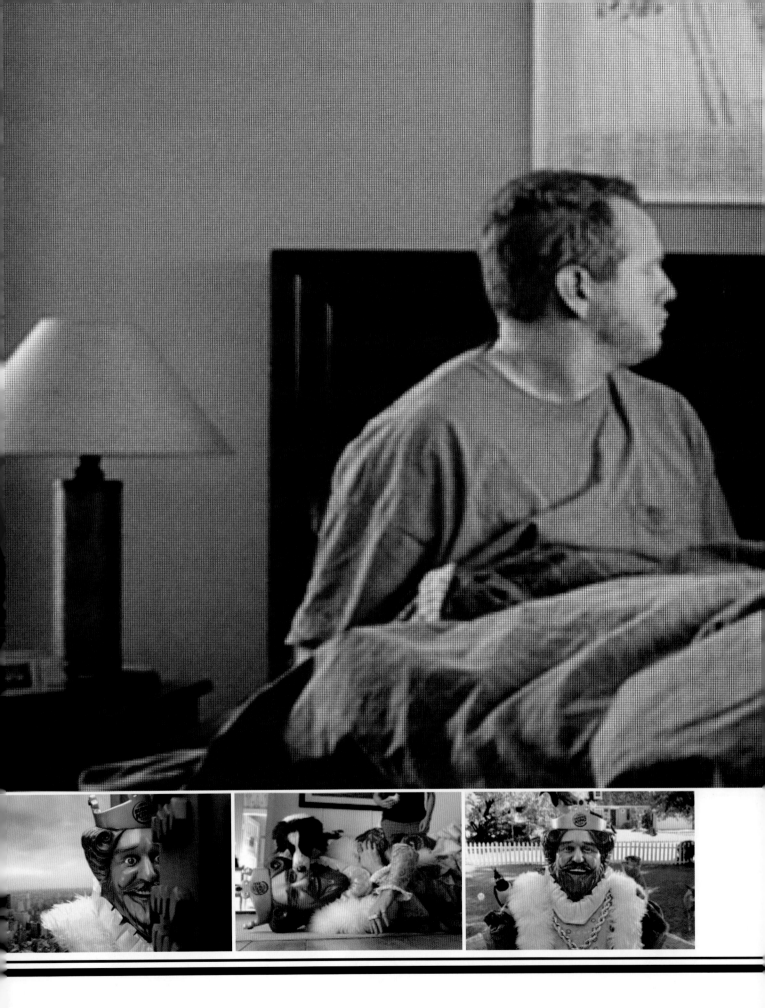

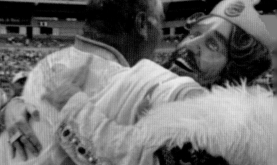

Having a billboard show up along some digital highway in a car-racing game is one thing. Having your company mascot play a supporting role in one of the most popular video games on Earth is another thing entirely.

| home | pay | register | sign in | services | site map | Start |

Buy | Sell | My eBay | Community | Help

ack to list of items   Listed in category: Toys & Hobbies > Fast Food, Cereal Premiur Food > Burger King

RGER KING PLASTIC HELIUM TANK TOPPER   Item number:

r of this item? **Sign in** for your status   **Watch this item** in My eBay | Ema

arger Picture

Starting bid: **US $12.50**

Place Bid >

Time left: **6 hours, 23 minutes**
7-day listing. Ends
May-1-04 9:00 EST

Apr-24-04 11:19:06 PDT

49 bids

Start time: Indiana

History:

Item location: United States, Canada, Europe

Description: Authentic 70's Burger King plastic bust used as heilum tank top.

Condition: Used
1970's Rare

Shipping, payment details and

...it was time. We had known it was coming ever since we took on the BK® account. Lots of BK® brand equities had been destroyed or diminished by generations of brand managers and agencies. But we knew from the beginning that no matter how logical it'd seemed when some long-gone brand manager had decided to put a bullet in the King's head, he would have to come back. The name of the place is BURGER KING®, after all.

Turned out the King spent his first 30 or so years going about his business. Changing and evolving the way icons do. Like Madonna. He had his reinvention, and his reinvention had reinventions. Most of them were long forgotten. But to us it all mattered. It's like fishing out the bits of DNA at a crime scene. We needed to get the clues as to who he was if we were to bring him back. The fishing was good, and as we pulled a big fiberglass head off the Web and into the agency, there was no "eureka" moment. Instead, it sat around the agency for months. Just smiling at me in my office. As if the head knew its big break was coming.

There are plenty of reasons the King was hard to forget–and kind of creepy. The biggest reason isn't his smile or even the way he would surprise people. The biggest reason is that we get freaked out when we see our culture as it actually is. The original King Head was a fiberglass shell designed to sit atop tanks of helium that would inflate balloons for kids birthday parties in the early 80s. We found it and bought if off eBay. I think it cost 40 bucks. You might remember it from when you were a kid at BURGER KING®. You might not. Or maybe you still have latent memories of it buried deep in your subconscious. But as a member of American society, you are certainly familiar with the idea that strange half-human creatures are used to sell burgers to kids. And you accept it as perfectly normal because you grew up with it. So all we did was change the audience. And did the same kind of advertising, but we did it to adults in adult situations–and suddenly it was outrageous. A year later we tried to buy a second fiberglass head off eBay, and people wound up bidding up to $1,500. The King was back...

Looking like a rock star, BROOKE BURKE takes in a Lakers game with the Burger King himself

KING ME

35 REASONS WHY SCHOOL SUCKS

MAD

IND ®

...HAVE IT **OUR** WAY!

BURGER KING

BARF BAG

#464 APRIL 2006 $3.99 CHEAP!

madmag.com

KING KONG • SPY VS. SPY
BONUS PULL-OUT POSTER

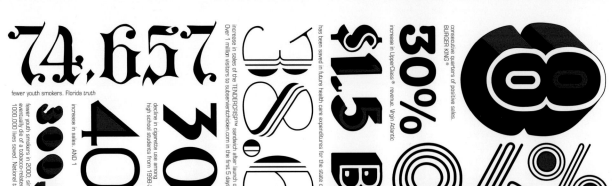

8%
consecutive quarters of positive sales. BURGER KING®

30% increase in UpperClass® revenue. Virgin Atlantic

$1.5 BILLION
has been saved in future health care expenditures for the state of Florida. Florida truth

38.6%
increase in sales of the TENDERCRISP™ sandwich after launch of campaign. Over 1 million visitors to subservientchicken.com in the first 5 days it launched. BURGER KING®

74,657
fewer youth smokers. Florida truth

increase in sales. AND 1

300,000 fewer youth smokers in 2000, since nearly 1/3 of youth smokers eventually die of a tobacco-related disease, this translates into 100,000 lives saved. National truth

400% increase in cigarette use among high school students from 1998-2001. Florida truth

30% years have passed since cigarette sales have hit an all-time low. National truth

55

4,575,325
total number of visitors to watchmechange.com from July-January; launched completely virally. GAP

26%
rise in comp sales of the premium TENDERCRISP™ chicken sandwich
80,000 people watched the fight online. 5 million voters for the winner. BURGER KING®

24,637 fewer premature deaths. Florida truth

62% increase in sales during 4 weeks of advertising versus previous 4 weeks. BURGER KING®

4 MILLION
Enormous sandwiches were sold at its launch. BURGER KING®

17%
lift in sales in first 4 weeks of breakfast advertising. BURGER KING®

5,000,000 voters for the Chicken Fight winner. BURGER KING®

15% above sales goals 2002-2004. MINI

60% greater likeability than McDonald's or Wendy's among ALL adults 18-34. BURGER KING®

23% above sales goal in 2002. MINI

47%
decline in cigarette use among middle school students from 1998-2001. Florida truth

73% increase in awareness of Andus after campaign launch. BURGER KING®

26% decrease in client hair loss

43%
increase in overall brand awareness. Virgin Atlantic

22% of the overall decline in youth smoking between 2000 and 2002 was attributable to truth. truth has continuously been voted one of the top six favorite TV campaigns by teenagers since its inception. National truth

#2
in basketball, challenging Nike as the thought leader in the category. AND 1

11,616 employee arrhythmias

5.4% average increase in UpperClass® fares for full fare tickets. Virgin Atlantic

319 MILLION media impressions were garnered by the King and his sandwich in press stories alone. BURGER KING®

80,000
people watched the Chicken Fight online. BURGER KING®

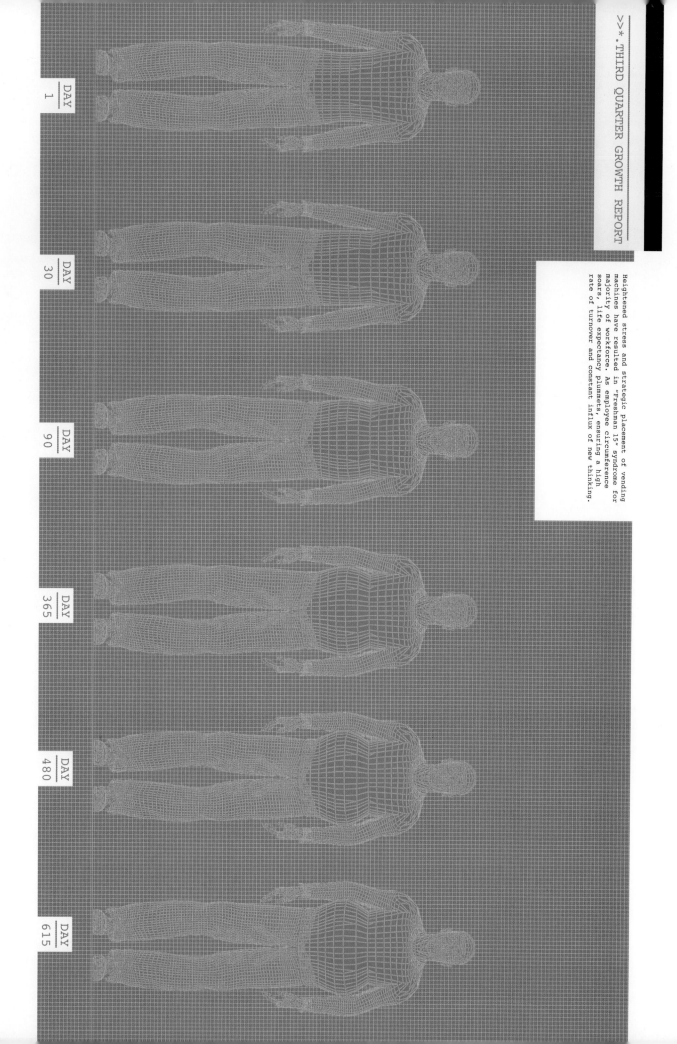

Heightened stress and strategic placement of vending machines have resulted in "Freshman 15" syndrome for majority of workforce. As employee circumference soars, life expectancy plummets, ensuring a high rate of turnover and constant influx of new thinking.

DAY 1

DAY 30

DAY 90

DAY 365

DAY 480

DAY 615

Employees run on a closely monitored mixture of caffeine, carbohydrates, and condiments, which gives them the energy to work long hours while cutting their lives short by an average of 10 years.

DAVID
SCHWARTZ
FOOD MONITOR

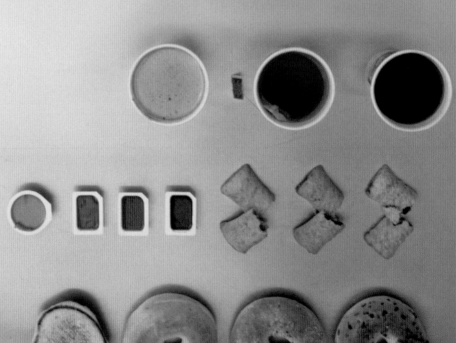

>>*.ON SITE OVERNIGHT
STAYS PER DEPARTMENT

Severely compromised nutritional practices
and erratic sleep patterns have allowed
workforce to meet and surpass weird idea
quotas for quarter.

*.IT

*.MEDIA

*.CREATIVE

*.ACCT. SERVICE

*.PRODUCTION

*.ACCOUNTING

"Postal"

Agency chairman Chuck Porter keeps a Ruger Mini-14 assault rifle behind his computer cabinet.

◯ Fake
◯ True